Turning Points

The Campaigns that Changed Canada
2004 and Before

Turning Points

The Campaigns that Changed Canada
2004 and Before

by

Ray Argyle

White Knight Publications
Toronto Canada

Published in 2004 by White Knight Publications,
a division of Bill Belfontaine Ltd.,
Suite 103, One Benvenuto Place, Toronto Ontario Canada M4V 2L1
T. 416-925-6458 F, 416-925-4165
e-mail whitekn@istar.ca

Ordering information
Hushion House
c/o Georgetown Terminal Warehouses
34 Armstrong Avenue, Georgetown ON, L7G 4R9
Tel: 866-485-5556   Fax: 866-485-6665
e-mail: orders@gtwcanada.com

National Library of Canada Cataloguing in Publication
Argyle, Ray
Turning points : the campaigns that changed Canada :
2004 and before / Ray Argyle.

ISBN 0-9734186-6-4
1. Political campaigns—Canada—History. 2. Elections—Canada—History.
3. Canada—Politics and government—1867-. I. Title.
JL193.A75 2004   324.971   C2004-903275-5

Cover and text design: Karen Petherick,
Intuitive Design International Ltd.
Font: Stemple Garamond
Editing: Bill Belfontaine
Printed and Bound in Canada

COVER PHOTOS:
J.A. Macdonald: A portrait of Sir John A. Macdonald, senior statesman, c. 1884. Oil painting by Thomas Horsburgh (active 1875-1885). Credit: www.canadianheritage.ca ID #23273, National Archives of Canada C-97288. **Wilfrid Laurier**: Sir Wilfrid Laurier in mid-career, 1907. Colour lithograph by John Wycliffe Lowes Forster (1850-1938). Credit: www.canadianheritage.ca ID #23277, National Archives of Canada C-104648. **W.L. Mackenzie King**: William Lyon Mackenzie King (1874-1950) was born in Berlin (Kitchener), Ontario, educated at Toronto, Chicago and Harvard, was federal member of parliament 1908-1911, Liberal leader in 1919 and Prime Minister in 1921. Credit: www.canadianheritage.ca ID #20876, National Archives of Canada C-27647. **Bill of Rights**: Prime Minister Diefenbaker displaying the Bill of Rights of 1958. Credit: "www.canadianheritage.ca ID #21012, National Archives of Canada PA-112659. **Pierre Trudeau**: Pierre Elliott Trudeau was Prime Minister of Canada April 20, 1968 to June 3, 1979, and March 3, 1980 to June 30, 1984. Credit: www.canadianheritage.ca ID #22223, National Archives of Canada PA-134512. **Brian Mulroney**: Brian Mulroney was Prime Minister of Canada from September 17, 1984 to June 13, 1993. Credit: www.canadianheritage.ca ID #23351. **Paul Martin**: Paul Martin after winning the 2004 Election on June 28. Credit: Liberal Party of Canada. **Flag**: Photodisc © 2004.

"Politics is still the greatest and most honourable adventure."
~ John Buchan, Lord Tweedsmuir,
Governor General of Canada 1935-1940

"The silent majority does not make a lot of noise; it is content to make history."
~ Pierre Elliott Trudeau, 1982

"History is fables agreed upon."
~ Voltaire, 1694-1778

CONTENTS

CONTENTS

PRELUDE

Turning points in a nation's history occur when cataclysmic events take place and choices are made that change a country's direction and its way of life. They are often etched in blood, such as the September 11, 2001 attack on the World Trade Center; the October 1917 declaration of the first Soviet in Russia; or the July 1789 fall of the Bastille in France. In Canadian history our turning points go back to the Battle of Queenston Heights in the War of 1812, the rebellions that shook Upper and Lower Canada in the years before Confederation, and the crushing of the Metis uprising on the western plains in the 1870s. These events were fundamental to the formation of Canada. Since then, it is our elections that have delivered up our major turning points, determining directions and fixing options that have shaped the soul and spirit of the nation. It is these, beginning with the federal election of 2004 that has set the compass points for Canada's voyage into the twenty-first century, that this book is about.

Canadian elections have turned on questions of war and peace, of national survival, of the construct and form of Confederation, and of how English and French – as well as people of other groups – are to live together in harmony. Quebec's tugging on the tether of Canadian nationhood, the challenge of the provinces for more autonomy from Ottawa, and our larger confusion over economic and cultural integration with the United States remain with us a century and a half after the first efforts to forge a nation from the northern half of the North American continent. Issues as fundamental as these run like a river through the Canadian political landscape. They are too important to go away, too difficult to readily resolve, and too complex to easily dismiss.

Newly emerging issues – the crisis of a global economic and religious counter reformation and Canada's place in that struggle, the defence of North America from terrorism, the protection of our communities from exotic diseases – are the stuff of future turning points. Each of these has the distinctive ring of the new century, depicting a world wrought by new science and threatened by new forces. Each will test the ability of Canadians to make sound judgments among the options open to us.

Canadian politicians have a compulsion to proclaim that every election is "crucial." When R. B. Bennett, whose ill-fated prime ministership was to flounder in the depression of the 1930s, told the tumultuous crowd at his first nomination meeting that "the destiny of a nation lies in your hands," he was coining an oratorical device since employed by most of his successors.[1] Whether spoken from a TV studio or from a hay wagon at a political picnic of an earlier age, the intent has been the same: to convince voters that opting for any other than the right choice will bring on a calamity. Paul Martin joined the parade by betraying his sense, at least, of being on a mission of transcending importance when he told his caucus that the 2004 election would be "the most important in our history."

Of the more than three hundred elections held in Canada since 1867, little more than a dozen can be said to have jarred the country out of its fixed political orbit and onto new paths, under new leadership bent on pursuing new economic and social policies. As a journalist and a political consultant, I have viewed a number of them in person, from both sides of the political-media divide. The campaigns that have most changed Canada are the ones that I have chosen to examine in this book.

Of the fifteen turning points, the federal election of June 28, 2004, sets the stage for our look at nine other federal votes held since Confederation. We examine two critically-important provincial elections and two decisive referendums – one of which added Newfoundland to Canada while in the other, we came very close to losing Quebec. Our time tunnel also takes us back to one year before Confederation and to the colonial election held in New Brunswick in 1866 where a combination of corruption, conspiracy and chicanery transformed British North America into the uncertain new Dominion of Canada.

The federal contests that shaped Canada range from John A. Macdonald's return from disgrace in 1878, when he embarked on his National Policy to build a tariff wall to protect the burgeoning industries of Central Canada, to the final demolition of that strategy by another Conservative prime minister, Brian Mulroney, whose re-election in 1988 opened the door to continental free trade. Other key federal turning points include the rise of Wilfrid Laurier as Canada's first French-speaking leader in the election of 1896, the creation of the "Unholy Alliance" of Conservatives and Quebec nationalists that defeated him on free trade in 1911, and Laurier's final repudiation in the bitter wartime election of 1917 – a campaign that followed the nation's coming of age through the blood-spilling of Vimy Ridge, and divided French and English voters into Canada's two solitudes. Mackenzie King used the election of 1926 to cement the supremacy of Parliament over Crown in the constitutional crisis that swirled around the powers of Governor General Lord Byng, later going on to usher in the modern welfare state in the campaign of 1945. The prairie populist, John Diefenbaker, changed Canadian politics in the election of 1957 with his repudiation of Conservative orthodoxy but ended as a glorious failure, the last Prime Minister of the old Canada. Pierre Elliott Trudeau, by his campaigns of 1968 and later, brought Canada full constitutional independence, as well as a Charter of Rights and Freedoms that has changed the established order of Canadian society.

The rise of the New West and its internal conflicts, as exemplified by the 1944 advent of the socialist government of the CCF's Tommy Douglas in Saskatchewan and the 1952 emergence of an anti-Ottawa free enterprise coalition under Social Credit's W.A.C. Bennett in British Columbia, also had permanent effects on the Canadian body politic. All of these campaigns share the three essential elements of which political legend is made: charismatic leadership, profoundly important issues and an unpredictable outcome, resulting in enduring change to the national landscape. We conclude with the 1995 Quebec Referendum on sovereignty and the consequences of that tumultuous vote on

Canada's domestic and foreign policy in the decade since then. The lesson of the Referendum – that Canada is not only worth saving but could be saved – has strengthened our ability to resist pressures that might have led to the virtual dissolution of Canada into a Fortress North America in the wake of the terrorist attacks of September 11, 2001 and the invasion of Iraq in 2003.

In remembering the great campaigns which served as crucibles of Canada's creation, we join politics to the evolution of society and technology and gain a better understanding of modern Canada. Just as we enter a different kind of world to see William Lyon Mackenzie King receive with a mixture of "joy and depression" the telegram from the Liberal organization in North Waterloo anointing him as its candidate for the 1911 election,[2] so we can observe another era passing from sight when the aging Louis St. Laurent insists in his fretful 1957 campaign that he is "more interested in seeing people than in talking to cameras."[3]

The events and people that have shaped these turning points are woven into the character of Canada. They offer a rich heritage for the new Canada coming into form in the twenty-first century.

Toronto, July 2004

CHAPTER ONE

The Federal Election of June 28, 2004

THE ISSUES

The worst corruption scandal in half a century shakes public confidence in the Liberal government, which had been expected to coast to a fourth majority under the leadership of Paul Martin. The election coincides with the healing of the decade-long fissure of the right wing and the creation of a new Conservative party under Stephen Harper, dedicated to smaller government and conservative social values. The position of some Conservative candidates on wedge issues such as abortion and gay rights and the Charter of Rights and Freedoms, troubles many voters and provides grounds for attack by the Liberals and the NDP. The election of a minority government is widely expected, a worrying prospect given the strong position of the Bloc Québécois.

THE PERSONALITIES

THE LIBERAL PARTY
Paul Martin, Prime Minister, MP for Lasalle-Emard, Quebec
Ralph Goodale, Minister of Finance, MP for Wascana, Sask.
Anne McLellan, Deputy Prime Minister,
MP for Edmonton Centre, Alberta

THE CONSERVATIVE PARTY
Stephen Harper, MP for Calgary Southwest, Leader of the Opposition
Peter McKay, former Progress Conservative leader,
MP for Central Nova, N.S

NEW DEMOCRATIC PARTY
Jack Layton, Leader and candidate, Toronto Danforth
Ed Broadbent, former leader and candidate, Ottawa Centre

BLOC QUEBECOIS
Gilles Duceppe, Leader, MP for Laurier, Quebec

THE RESULTS

SEATS VOTES (64,330 OF 64,538 POLLS)

	SEATS	VOTES
Liberal Party	135	4,955,050 (36.7%)
Conservative Party	99	3,996,835 (29.6%)
New Democratic Party	19	2,117,889 (15.7%)
Bloc Québécois	54	1,673,303 (12.4%)
Independent	1	47,661 (0.4%)
Other	–	707,690 (5.2%)

Prime Minister Paul Martin greeted cheering supporters on election night after winning a minority verdict in the 2004 election.

PAUL MARTIN AND THE QUEST FOR A NEW LIBERAL MAJORITY

The Federal Election of June 28, 2004

The warmth of early summer descended on Ottawa abruptly after the election, sending shoppers to the sidewalk cafes of the Byward market and emptying out government office buildings as civil servants took their annual vacations. In the Prime Minister's office at 80 Wellington Street, looking across to the Parliament Buildings, Paul Martin's staff prepared for his return from the campaign trail. Congratulatory phone calls from foreign leaders, briefing books on the costs of reducing medical waiting times, and the inevitable appeals for appointments – everything from the cabinet to the Senate, the Supreme Court and such agencies as the Immigration and Refugee Board – filled the Prime Minister's agenda. Paul Martin was back in Ottawa at the head of a minority government, having won the election of June 28, 2004, but having failed in his quest for a new Liberal majority. It was a quest on which he would set out again as soon as time and events provided him the opportunity.

The leader of the defeated Conservative party, Stephen Harper, returned to the capital on his campaign plane, mulling over messages complimenting him on the campaign and urging him to stay on to wage another fight, another time. As he had told his supporters on election night, "Until someone some day achieves a majority, the fight is not won or lost." The issues of prime concern to the country in this unsettled post-election stage span the realms of economics, national independence, and human rights and welfare: saving public health care, joining the U.S. in continental missile defence, meeting the obligations of the Kyoto accord, sanctioning same-sex marriage. Stir in further fall-out from the sponsorship scandal and the ever-present regional resentments of Quebec separatism and Western alienation, and it is clear that Canadians have entered a tumultuous new political era that will no longer be dominated by a single party, as in the decade just past.

In calling the election more than a year sooner than he was required to – but months later than he would have preferred – Paul Martin gambled on winning a fresh lease on life for his new team. One of the brightest new members of that team, Ujjal Dosanjh – a likely bet for a future cabinet post – awoke shortly before six o'clock on the morning of the election, dressed quickly and left his Southwest Marine Drive home in Vancouver to take his rottweiler Rasha ("always on a leash") on its morning walk. Running as a Liberal was a new experience for the former New Democratic premier of British Columbia, but his ritual of visiting the polls and delivering box lunches to party workers was something to which he was well accustomed. Four thousand kilometers to the east, with a three-hour start to the day, Dosanjh's leader was resting after his "red-eye" flight from Vancouver to Montreal. Paul Martin had campaigned from coast to coast on Sunday, stepping bare feet in both the Atlantic and Pacific oceans. He'd be voting in his Lasalle-Emard riding on the south side of Montreal later in the day.

Elsewhere in that city on June 28, Bloc Québécois chief Gilles Duceppe, the one-time union leader and convinced Maoist turned sovereignist, was confident that he would sweep Quebec with his sovereignist candidates who would work to advance the cause of separatism. In Toronto, Jack Layton, the leader of the NDP, voted for his wife Olivia Chow in her downtown riding before touring his polyglot Danforth district, a mix of upwardly mobile professional families, ethnic merchants of mainly Greek origin, and working class wage earners. He was optimistic that by the time the last votes were counted his party would find itself cast in the "central role" that he'd asked voters to give the NDP. Just over the Rocky Mountains from Vancouver, Stephen Harper, after running a tightly-controlled campaign targeting Liberal waste and mismanagement, had returned to Calgary only the day before. His grip on Calgary Southwest was so solid that he'd been able to spend almost every one of the thirty-six days of the campaign out across the country, urging voters to support the newly reconstituted party of the right, no longer torn apart between Western dissidents and eastern traditionalists.

It had been one hundred and ninety-nine days since that morning of Friday, December 12, 2003, when Paul Martin, a Canadian flag tucked under his arm, entered Rideau Hall in Ottawa where the Governor General, Adrienne Clarkson, was waiting to swear him in as Canada's 21st Prime Minister. The flag Martin carried had flown at half mast from the Parliament Building on the death of his father, Paul Martin Sr. in 1992. Thinking about that time, and about his father's career as an architect of Canada's social welfare system, he choked up with tears for a long moment as he addressed a news conference after the ceremony. Then he ticked off the three main goals of his new government: strengthening social foundations, fostering economic growth, and creating well-paying jobs. After a decade of an increasingly difficult relationship with his predecessor, and having just turned 65 years, Paul Martin was at last at the pinnacle of power. He had brought 22 new faces into his cabinet, replacing die-hard supporters of the former Prime Minister and shifting power out of the Liberal party's Quebec base. Ontario had been given 17 of the 39 Cabinet seats, and three hugely important posts had gone to Westerners. Ralph Goodale of Saskatchewan, a reliable workhorse who had done a commendable job for the departing Jean Chrétien in cleaning up some of the questionable practices involving advertising contracts issued through the Public Works department, would be the new finance minister. Anne McLellan, a feisty lawyer from Edmonton who had served in the Health and Justice portfolios, took the hugely important post of Minister of Public Safety (an unlikely Robespierre), as well as the more honourific position of deputy prime minister. Reg Alcock, recently diagnosed with diabetes after having brought his weight down from a morbidly obese 600 pounds, would become President of the Treasury Board, his first Cabinet posting.

Along with preparing a Speech from the Throne and a new budget, Martin and his team faced one other task that would preoccupy the new government in its early months. An early reading of the report of the Auditor General, Sheila Fraser, on the government's management of sponsorship funds – "I am appalled by what we've found" – left little doubt that a major scandal was in the making. The money had been meant to fly the Canadian flag in Quebec – via sponsorship of sports and cultural events – as part of the Chrétien government's strategy to fight separatism following the near loss of the 1995 referendum. Ms. Fraser's report had been given to the government in November, and by the time it became public on February 10, 2004, Martin might have wondered why he had not encouraged Chrétien to stay on until after the unleashing of the Auditor General's sudden maelstrom.[1]

Martin's advisors, who had spent a decade and a sum approaching ten million dollars in their campaign to dislodge Chrétien, were unanimous that there was only one route to go. They included Martin's campaign co-chair, the Earnscliffe Strategy Group lobbyist David Herle, and Herle's spouse and former Martin chief of staff Terrie O'Leary, along with Ottawa lawyer Richard Mahoney and principal secretary Francis Fox. All agreed Martin must cut himself clear of the Chrétien government and vow to get to the bottom of the scandal. By the weekend of the Auditor General's report, Martin was ready to go on the road. He awoke Saturday to the sorrowful news that his 94-year-old aunt, Lucille, had died in a nursing home in Pembroke, Ontario. After speaking on the phone with his father's two surviving sisters, Anita and Claire, Martin flew to St. John's, Newfoundland, where his staff had arranged for him to join the CBC's Rex Murphy in a national radio and TV broadcast of the weekly phone-in show, Cross-Country Checkup.

It was the start of the Prime Minister's month-long "mad as hell" tour into which he threw all his energy and emotions. "I'd like Canadians to have as much information as they can," Martin declared, somewhat contritely. With governing virtually at a halt, he travelled from coast to coast to condemn the political culture in which the scandal had been seeded. One of the first things he had done on becoming Prime Minister was to cancel the sponsorship program. Now, he promised to resign if he was found to have had any role in the scandal. He appointed Quebec Superior Court justice John Howard Gomery to conduct a public inquiry, and put the House of Commons public accounts committee, chaired by a member of the newly-united Conservative party, John Williams of St. Albert, Alberta, to work interviewing witnesses. Martin also ordered a controller appointed to every department and froze $435 million in government advertising about to be placed through Ottawa's "agency of record," Media IDA Vision.[2] He sent legislation to the House to protect whistle blowers in the public service, a bill that was still on the order paper when Parliament rose for the election. "No longer will the culture of Ottawa be one of entitlement," Martin promised in a speech in Quebec City. From the beginning, he declared flatly that there had been political direction in the misuse of sponsorship funds, pointing the finger at the former minister of public works, Alfonso Gagliano, and Chrétien's chief of staff, Jean Pelletier. Within days, Pelletier was gone from his job as chairman of Via Rail – skewered by his own intemperate remarks about a whistle-blowing employee, Olympic athlete Myriam Bedard – along with its president, Marc LaFrancois. Gagliano was out as ambassador to Denmark, while Canada Post head Andre Ouellet, an old Chrétien ally, was put on suspension. Soon, the inevitable lawsuits for wrongful dismissal were being filed in the courts.

Within 48 hours of the scandal having broken, polling by Ipsos-Reid showed Liberal support plummeting nine percentage points, from a commanding 48 per cent to a perilous 39 per cent, with the Conservatives still a distant 24 per cent and the NDP, at 18 per cent, registering twice the support it had enjoyed in the 2000 election. That's roughly where things would stand at the election call on May 23. It was especially dangerous territory when one considered that it took 40 per cent to form a majority government and every government of the past forty years – except Pierre Trudeau's in 1974 – had lost support during the election campaigns. In the weeks to come, many senior Liberals would argue that it was inept crisis management by the Martin team – the decision to attack the Chrétien administration being their greatest strategic mistake – that accounted for much of the Liberal reversal. Martin's repeated assertions that he knew nothing about the scandal – that Chrétien had kept him out of the loop on matters involving Quebec – seemed lame to the well over half of Canadians who thought that as Finance Minister, Martin either would, or should have known what was happening.

The Auditor General's original charges of "blatant misuse of public funds" had become something less in subsequent testimony by Ms. Fraser: "We have never stated that $100 million was missing or stolen," she wrote to the public accounts committee. By then, the RCMP had laid criminal charges against Chuck Guité, the head of the Communication Coordination and Services Branch (CCSB) of the Department of Public Works, and two Quebec advertising agency executives, Jean Brault of Groupaction Marketing and Paul Coffin of Coffin Communications. Their trials were put over until September, effectively removing their cases from public debate.

The CEO in the PMO – A Corporate Prime Minister

The House of Commons is the cockpit of Canadian politics, and Paul Martin, raised on a political diet since childhood, earned his seat on the front row of the government benches by winning his Montreal riding of Lasalle-Emard by increasingly comfortable margins in each of the four elections between 1988 and 2000. He also brought *the look* of belonging to this imposing chamber, with its 301 seats (increased to 308 after the election) carefully arranged to accommodate the members who face each other across the centre aisle. On this pre-election Spring day, the seats are filling slowly for the two o'clock opening. The Prime Minister, impressive in the reflected stature of his office and in his own bearing, enters from the government lobby on the west side of the chamber. He sits briefly with various backbenchers on his way to the front row desk he shares with his deputy, Anne McLellan. He takes his seat as members' statements are coming to an end and the

Question Period – the most theatrical hour of Parliament's day – is about to begin. Martin fends off the Opposition's questions without much difficulty, just as a corporate CEO would dismiss the nuisance of troublesome underlings.

It is in this parallel to the corporate world – a world in which Martin has been comfortable for most of his life – that the Prime Minister's approach and actions are most closely compared. Newly graduated from the University of Toronto law school, Martin saw his future in the business world, not politics. Hired by Maurice Strong to work at the Power Corp. of Canada, the powerful corporate giant run by Paul Desmarais and his sons, Martin was given the opportunity to take over Canada Steamship Lines when Desmarais decided to unload the company in 1981. Martin raised the purchase price, $180 million, from the Royal Bank and other sources – reserving a half-interest for himself – and went on to make CSL a global player in ocean freight. In August 2003, he passed his ownership to his sons. It did not prevent future embarrassment, especially when it became necessary to correct an official report that CSL had received $137,000 in government contracts. The actual sum was $161 million over eleven years.

In 1990, when John Turner resigned after being beaten twice by Brian Mulroney, Martin challenged Jean Chrétien for the Liberal leadership. He lost on the first ballot. Despite the tension between the two, Chrétien named Martin as finance critic and made him the minister after the Liberals were returned to power in 1993. For the next ten years, Martin's success in battling the deficit – a fight won largely through economic growth and by downloading costs to the provinces, especially in health – was the signal achievement of the Liberal government. The relationship between the two men grew more testy, especially when Chrétien learned that Martin supporters, which included many MPs, were meeting secretly to devise ways to pressure the Prime Minister to resign. Although only two of Canada's last seven Prime Ministers – Pierre Trudeau and Brian Mulroney – have been impervious to back-stabbing, undermining and general sabotage by their rivals,

Paul Martin's long campaign to dislodge Chrétien is unparalleled in Liberal party history. A final blow-up in 2002 led to Martin's dismissal from the cabinet. The Liberal leadership convention of November, 2003 completed the long and painful transition.

Governments of all stripes find their most effective advocates in the ranks of lobbyists and communications advisors – people whose political sympathies are with the party in power and who possess the creative skills to put a positive spin on a government's policies and help it win re-election. The Earnscliffe Strategy Group, the polling and lobbyist firm owned by a clutch of Martin advisors on whom the new Prime Minister relied heavily for strategic advice and comfort, benefited greatly from government contracts. The firm received its first contracts at the Ministry of Finance in the 1980s, aided by a few well-placed Tory connections. Its real success came after Martin became minister. Between 1993 and 2003, Earnscliffe garnered a reported six million dollars in government business. Among the most important jobs Earnscliffe was given was the planning of communications strategy for Martin's department. Earnscliffe's David Herle, the 2004 campaign co-chair, boasted to Don Newman of the CBC that the firm won 28 out of 30 competitive pitches, all on merit, a success ratio quite astonishing to those who watched such things. Herle, a native of Saskatchewan, was an early acolyte of Martin's. He had trained originally for the bar, had worked at Canada Steamship Lines, and was brought into Earnscliffe by founder Michael Robinson after the two had teamed up on Martin's 1990 leadership bid. Other Earnscliffe people around Martin include Scott Reid, who has become a key strategist in the PMO working on files ranging from the sponsorship scandal to aboriginal affairs, and Elly Alboim, the former CBC reporter, who had remained at Earnscliffe. Early in 2004, David Herle and two partners took out the communications wing of Earnscliffe, setting it up as Veraxis Research and Communications.

The eagerness of Martin's advisors to go for the election – Herle presented optimistic forecasts at every opportunity – was troubling to many Liberals. The government's mandate ran until

November, 2005, allowing time for a cooling of public anger. The distress of Quebec MPs who were most likely to suffer from the sponsorship scandal, intensified when Herle showed up at a caucus party to present an election outlook that ignored Quebec and for which there was no French translation. Steve Mahoney, the former Chrétien cabinet minister from Ontario who lost his nomination in a riding boundary change, called on Martin to "bury the hatchets and get rid of the thugs." John Manley, who succeeded Martin in finance and then dropped out of the leadership race when it became obvious he had no chance of winning, urged the Martin forces to "focus on the enemy rather than fighting among ourselves." The most outspoken of the disgruntled Liberals, former Chrétien aide Warren Kinsella, pronounced himself a "Liberal in exile" and wrote daily musings for his web site on the shortcomings of the Martin team. Party unity, in the face of the brutal treatment administered to Chrétien MPs such as Sheila Copps, Charles Cacchia, and Herb Dahliwall as well as Mahoney – all denied renomination by their Martin-controlled ridings – was by now tattered beyond repair. It was Sheila Copps' view that "if you are a separatist or a Conservative, you seem to be more welcome in the Liberal party than if you're a Liberal." Senator David Smith, a Chrétien appointee brought into the Martin camp as a senior advisor, tried to bring the two sides together but his efforts failed to overcome the antagonism between the two camps.

The Prime Minister's use of his power to appoint Liberal candidates deepened the growing division. He defended the appointments as a means of securing more women candidates, and a way of bringing in people who weren't in a position to compete for a nomination. Two of his appointments were especially divisive: Ruby Dhalla in Ontario's Brampton-Springdale, the first woman Sikh to stand for Parliament; and Bill Cunningham, the president of the B.C. Liberal association, in Burnaby-Douglas. Ms. Dhalla's appointment denied a former John Manley supporter the opportunity to contest the nomination. The message was not lost on the Liberal riding executive, who promptly resigned en masse, most later endorsing the NDP. The situation turned equally nasty in Burnaby-Douglas, where the entire executive of the association quit in protest after two Chinese-Canadian candidates who had signed up thousands of members were told to make way for the apple-cheeked Cunningham in a riding that had suddenly become winnable after the withdrawal of the disgraced NDP member, Svend Robinson. Liberal unity, nurtured on a mix of Chrétien populism and Martinite fiscal prudence and reinforced by the decade-long rupture on the right, was vanishing like the snow banks of a Canadian Spring. Perhaps because Martin realized that the soul of the party was at risk of being torn apart, he finally conceded: "We will run on our record for the last 10 years; we will run on Jean Chrétien's record." But he never really did so.

Reshaping the Right

The platform of the reunited Conservative party had been carefully structured to put voters' minds at ease; moderate and middle of the road, with no hints of redneck Reformism, it would give Stephen Harper the opportunity to reassure Canadians that they could safety entrust their votes to the new party. The campaign team had planned to release a carefully-balanced, middle-of-the-road platform once the election was called. It would put the party in the headlines, give candidates and their workers a lift, and build momentum. It didn't happen that way. On Friday afternoon, May 11 the CBC, working with a leaked copy of the still unfinished platform, broadcast its highlights. There is nothing worse than being upstaged on your own announcement, and the CBC report sent Harper's office into a panic. Two *National Post* reporters, Tim Naumetz and Sean Gordon, were given copies of the document, and their report dominated the front page the next day: "TORY PLAN WOULD CUT TAX BY 25%." Trying to recover the initiative, Harper followed up with a speech to the Frontier Centre for Public Policy in Winnipeg on May 17. There, he said the Conservatives would campaign on a fiscal platform of lower taxes rather than increased spending.

The platform had been responsive to the views of the former Progressive Conservative leader, Peter McKay, given in a paper on "Policy Advice to the Leader" that was presented to Harper shortly after the Conservative convention. While it retained some Canadian Alliance policies such as an elected Senate, abolition of the gun registry and new measures to get tougher on youth crime, it focused primarily on economics and tactfully avoided the wedge issues that excite social conservatives but offend everyone else. Middle income taxpayers would see their taxes drop from 22 to 16 per cent and a new lifetime retirement plan would allow tax-free gains on investments from after-tax income. The GST would be eliminated on gasoline over 85 cents a litre. Overall, the Liberals argued, Harper's promised tax cuts would cost $52 billion over five years, endangering social programs of all types. The stage was being sent for a classic fight over taxes vs public services, not necessarily the best fighting ground for the Conservative party.

Reunited only since late in 2003 and still in the early stages of merging rival riding associations, the Conservative party looked to the election as the opportunity to consolidate the disparate factions it had inherited from the PC and the Canadian Alliance parties and, with any luck, reduce the Liberals to a minority. If this could be achieved, it would set the stage for a Conservative victory in the next election and who knows, if the campaign went badly for Paul Martin, the Conservatives might even eke out a minority win in 2004. The merger itself had been highly controversial. Not all Progressive Conservatives opted to support the new party, and there was little prospect of it matching the 38 per cent of the vote that the Alliance and PCs had obtained in 2000. Let Stephen Harper be himself, Tory strategists advised; low key, unthreatening, non-controversial. Don't worry about his lack of visibility in the run-up to the election; the campaign would change all that. Keep the focus on the sponsorship scandal and other aspects of Liberal mismanagement, trusting to the adage that governments aren't elected, they're defeated. Still, it was evident that Harper would have a difficult time dodging ricocheting bullets fired by the Alliance. With the election call only days away, Harper called in journalists for a series of 15-minute interviews on May 13. One of them, Tonda MacCharles of the Toronto *Star*, confronted him with a news release from the party's foreign affairs critic, Stockwell Day, dated January 28, 2003, that called for the dispatch of Canadian troops to help disarm Sadaam Hussein. According to MacCharles, Harper became "visibly angry" and refused to look at the release. It didn't help that a few days earlier, Joe Clark, the former PC leader and staunch opponent of the PC-Alliance merger, had said that Harper would be dangerous for the country and that he felt more comfortable in supporting Paul Martin.

In many respects, Stephen Harper's background made him the quintessential earnest Canadian; raised in a middle-class Ontario family, a scholar at Richview High in suburban Toronto, he migrated to Alberta for a job in the oil industry, obtained a Masters degree in economics from the University of Alberta (picking up American-style political theories from right-wing faculty members), and worked as a political aide in Ottawa for the Progressive Conservative government of Brian Mulroney. At 45, he was the youngest of the party leaders. The biggest influence on Harper at university and since has been political scientist Tom Flanagan, his closest confidante and best personal friend, as well as being national director of the 2004 election campaign. It was Flanagan who recommended Harper to Reform party founder Preston Manning when Manning came looking for a bright young researcher. Flanagan likes to joke that he is possibly the only person to have ever lived in both Ottawa, Canada and Ottawa, Illinois, where he was born. He found receptive ground for his right-wing views at the University of Calgary, which he joined in 1968. In addition to authoring books advocating the assimilation of Canada's native population, Flanagan worked closely with Manning on the creation of the Reform party and served as its research director in 1991-92. He still disputes the argument that the party's conservative social views were out of touch with public opinion, but rather that they needed to be wrapped in a "coherent social philosophy" covering "the great issues of civil society." An architect of the "unite the right" movement that re-branded the Reform party as the Canadian Alliance, and a behind-the-scenes figure in the amalgamation of Alliance and the Progressive Conservatives, Flanagan would view the creation of the new Conservative party as the opportunity to embed social conservatism into a mainstream party.

Manning invited Harper to take part in the founding convention of the Reform party, where he gave an important speech at the age of 28. His only political setback was a losing bid against his PC mentor, Jim Hawkes, for a Commons seat in 1988. A self-admitted policy wonk, Harper did major work on the party's 1993 election platform, and won the Calgary West seat, arriving in Parliament along with 51 other Reformers from Alberta and B.C. Once in Ottawa, he worked hard to upgrade his high school French through the language training available to MPs. Harper's relationship with Manning – or with other Reformers, for that matter – was never easy. A dedicated neocon, Harper was strongly ideological at this stage of his life and he resented Manning's efforts to build the "big tent" that would turn Reform into a mainstream party. His crusty attitude also won him few friends in the Reform caucus. Harper dropped out of the 1997 election and took a job as president of the strongly right wing, Calgary-based National Citizens Coalition. He came back only following the resignation of Stockwell Day, whose disastrous spell as leader of the Canadian Alliance, formed out of Reform and a tiny right-wing rump of Progressive Conservatives, fell apart after the 2000 election.

As it turned out, Harper's timing was impeccable. The Progressive Conservatives, under a new leader, Peter McKay of Nova Scotia, were ready for a serious discussion of merger; forget Peter McKay's pledge to his own leadership rival, David Orchard, that the PC party would live on forever.

Harper demonstrated an unexpectedly high level of political skill in orchestrating the merger. He stayed in the background while using such veterans as Peter Lougheed and Mike Harris, former premiers of Alberta and Ontario, respectively, along with the new would-be Tory apparatchik, auto-parts heiress Belinda Stronach, to bring the quarrelsome factions together. Harper believed that by applying the principles of conservative pragmatism to the broader political stage, it would be possible to build a new right wing coalition within which marginalized social conservatives could find a home. He knew that the right-wing core of the Canadian electorate seldom exceeded 20 per cent at best, and that issue lines would have to be blurred to attract additional voters. When McKay declined to contest the new party leadership, Harper easily defeated Belinda Stronach and a former Ontario Tory health minister, Tony Clement. He became Conservative leader on March 20, 2004. He had only two months to prepare for the election call.

The New Democrats faced the most difficult challenge, but went into the election with an enlarged core of support; it reached as high as 20 per cent in some polls. The NDP struggled, as always, to reconcile its historic commitment to left-wing policies of nationalization, high taxes and large-scale public spending, with its need to capture a broader wedge of the middle-of-the-road vote concerned about taxes, jobs, waste in government, and secure neighbourhoods. Its leader, 54-year-old Jack Layton, came from a family that had been involved in politics for three generations. His grandfather, Robert, was a minister in what had been Canada's most right-wing regime, the Union Nationale government of Maurice Duplessis that ruled Quebec through much of the 1930s and 1940s. Jack's father, Robert, served in the cabinet of Brian Mulroney. Born in Hudson, Quebec, Layton grew up learning French on the streets of Montreal, but moved to Ontario, earned a Ph.D. in political science from York University, and taught at Ryerson University in Toronto. Layton served on the Toronto city council for many years and was involved in a variety of left-wing causes before becoming president of the Canadian Federation of Municipalities. He used that post to focus national attention on urban issues, and won the NDP leadership on the first ballot of a convention in January, 2003. He didn't allow his lack of a seat in the House of Commons to keep him out of the public eye; he haunted the foyer of Parliament and made himself quickly available to the media scrums that descended on MPs after each day's question period.

Rather than run in a traditional NDP constituency, Layton set his sights on defeating Dennis Mills, the inventive Liberal incumbent in Layton's home district of Toronto Danforth, turning the riding into the High Noon of the election. The mix was made still spicier when Layton's wife, the Hong Kong-born city councillor, Olivia Chow, decided to take on Liberal Tony Ianno in Toronto Spadina, re-fighting a battle she'd lost in 1997. Early on, Layton set out the NDP's price for supporting a minority government: a referendum on proportional representation and fixed election dates, and a commitment to the NDP's pledge to fund 25 per cent of provincial health care budgets.

If there was a question as to how important the NDP would be in the election, there was never any doubt about the critical status of the Bloc Québécois. In a near-death condition before the sponsorship scandal, its sudden return to dominance in Quebec added to the pressure on the Liberal party to hold its Ontario heartland; the Liberals were looking at huge losses in Quebec, belying Martin's admission at a campaign-style stop in Laval that "to accomplish everything I want to accomplish as prime minister, I need Quebec." The Bloc campaign was unveiled May 16 under the slogan *Un parti propre au Quebec*, a sly dig at both the Liberals and the sponsorship scandal. Bloc leader Gilles Duceppe outlined the issues the Bloc would work on in Ottawa. They included a child-tax credit, abolition of the fuel surtax, elimination of the GST on books, baby products and public education, tax deductions for public transit, and massive increases in provincial transfer payments and increased spending on social housing. With the Bloc ahead of the Liberals 48-28 in the polls, not much was being said about sovereignty. Duceppe had become the Bloc's first elected MP by winning a by-election in the Montreal working class riding of Laurier-Sainte Marie in 1990. Son of an immensely popular Quebec actor, a radical socialist in his youth (as a hospital worker he campaigned for the Maoist Marxist-Leninist party of Quebec), Duceppe had a difficult few years after becoming leader of the party. He had no hope of been able to dominate federal politics in Quebec as Lucien Bouchard had done when he was leader of the Bloc and head of the Official Opposition between 1993 and 1996. But now, with the Bloc re-emerging from obscurity, Duceppe never felt as comfortable in his own skin, as the French put it, as he did going into the campaign, the veteran among all the party leaders.

The Campaign and the Candidates

The woman who sat as Prime Minister for only a few months in 1993 – Kim Campbell – famously observed that an election is no time for a serious discussion of public policy. Her comment carried more truth that most politicians would care to admit. As the parties contemplated their election strategies, each faced some rock-hard realities. The Liberals, eyeing the difficult quest of gaining a fourth consecutive majority, were convinced they would win by presenting Paul Martin as the trustworthy, accomplished and experienced leader who could be counted on to manage the country's business and protect health care and other social programs, while rebuilding relationships with the United States. His qualities would be contrasted with the clearly right-wing views of Stephen Harper, who would be demonized as an assailant of Canada's social values and an advocate of American-style free market economics, jingoistic foreign adventuring, hard line justice and liassez-fair culture policies. The Liberals had one other tactic open to them in the pre-writ period and they used it well: government spending announcements made jointly by local MPs and cabinet ministers. They covered everything from new highways in Quebec to money for AIDS in Africa, and amounted, according to estimates by the CBC, to more than $923 million.[3]

On Sunday, May 20, Martin and his wife Sheila took mass at St. Joseph's Roman Catholic church in Ottawa and promptly at one o'clock turned up hand-in-hand at Rideau Hall, along with a phalanx of journalists and a clutch of tourists who had heard what was happening and wanted to be outside the Governor General's residence for the election call. After 37 minutes with Her Excellency, Adrienne Clarkson, the Prime Minister emerged to announce the date, and proclaim that the election would be about whether Canada would remain true to its social values, or abandon them in favour of lower taxes and a U.S.-style social system. "Do you want a Canada that builds on its historic strengths and values, such as medicare, generosity and an unflinching commitment to equality of opportunity? Or do you want a Canada that departs from much of its history – a Canada that rejects its valued tradition of collective responsibility? ... You can't have health care and social programs like Canada's with tax levels like the United States."

Martin was attempting to frame the ballot question – to use the new cliche of the media pack – as "What kind of Canada do you want?" He was presenting the election as a sort of referendum on the country's social fabric; the Liberals who would strengthen it, and the Conservatives who would destroy it by reducing taxes, allowing privatized health care and weakening the Charter of Rights by use of the notwithstanding clause to override controversial court decisions. To make the strategy work, Martin needed the implicit cooperation of his chief opponent, which he wasn't likely to get. The week before, Harper had prepared for this moment by announcing the Conservative party's commitment to a national pharmacare program. At a news conference in the green room of the National Press Building in Ottawa twenty minutes after Martin's election call, Harper got off what was arguably the best sound bite of the campaign: "In this country, you can be a Canadian without being a Liberal."

The polls were telling the Liberals that despite their reduced standing, there was strong support for Paul Martin as leader and for the Liberals as the party best able to govern the country. Martin spent the first week campaigning from Charlottetown to Victoria, and everywhere he went he focused on health care and his pledge to pump an additional $9 billion into the system. The numbers hardly mattered to most voters, who could neither track the costs nor measure how much good the new money would do, but it all created an impression that Martin's boast to reduce waiting times and fix healthcare "for a generation" at least had some big dollars behind it.

With mass rallies a thing of the past, the challenge for the leaders was to get their message out through the media. Martin's first Toronto appearance, at a banquet centre in suburban Markham, was like most of his appearances, a contrived happening staged to give the media a pseudo event to report. It attracted no members of the public and fewer than a thousand loyal Liberal workers who needed tickets to get in. For this occasion, like others, the big white and red Martin buses roared up to the banquet hall and disgorged media and party officials before Martin and his wife Sheila emerged to face a gauntlet of cheering party workers. Inside, flanked by 37 local candidates, the Prime Minister gave a pumped-up speech, finishing red-faced and bathed in sweat. Most of what Martin said had been read carefully from a script from his English speech writer, Scott Feschuk. At the back of the hall, aide Francis Fox worried about the stilted delivery and the constant buzz of conversation throughout the room. "When you have a script in front of you it becomes a crutch," he said. In twenty minutes, the campaign was back on the bus, roaring off down Highway 407 to pick up the Liberals' chartered plane for its flight to the West. The Prime Minister had been seen by few voters, had talked to none, and would depend on that night's TV and the next day's newspapers to deliver his message. In the first week of the campaign, according to McGill University's measurement of coverage in seven metropolitan newspapers, one-third of the stories about Martin had negative content. Only six per cent of the stories about Stephen Harper were rated negative.

Stephen Harper opened the Conservative campaign in Ontario, where the party would have to break through the political monoculture of the province where the Liberals won 101 of 103 seats in 2000. He went first to the St. Lawrence river town of Brockville where he attacked Liberal "mismanagement, waste and corruption," then moved on to Cornwall, centre of a large French-speaking community to pledge that "when I am prime minister, I will protect the rights and aspirations of francophones, here and everywhere." From there it was on to Montreal for a small but symbolic rally. Within 48 hours, he'd penetrated the two regions where the party was starting from a near zero base in seats. By the time he appeared later that week in St. John's, Newfoundland, Harper was following a tightly controlled agenda, leading reporters to complain that he was speaking to stacked halls, reading dull stump speeches, and allowing few photo opportunities. It didn't matter. Harper showed up in Vancouver at week's end where he went to the Airport Executive Hotel, a slightly seedy venue in suburban Richmond, for a noon-time rally. Flanked by MPs John Reynolds and Randy White plus 14 area candidates, his lanky 6 foot three inch frame comfortable at the podium (a developing paunch clearly visible through his open coat jacket), Harper was optimistic and upbeat as he spoke of his visit to Atlantic Canada. It was the region he'd once denigrated for its culture of defeat but now he boasted of support "for the new Conservative party" from all four Atlantic premiers. He referred to his visit to a military museum in Halifax to get off the line, "the Liberal government belongs in the museum of Canadian politics." On relations with the U.S., a Harper government would stand "shoulder to shoulder when we should, but eye to eye when we must." His best line, about leading "one united Conservative party ready to win in every part of Canada," drew a standing ovation.

The campaign began haltingly for the NDP, and Jack Layton's propensity for strong statements did the party little good. He was ridiculed for suggesting that Paul Martin was personally to blame for the deaths of homeless people in Toronto in the past winter. Then, on a visit to Sept-Isles, Quebec, he said an NDP government would repeal the Clarity Act and recognize a unilateral declaration of independence by Quebec after a referendum vote. Besides drawing a sharp letter of rebuke from Liberal MP Stéphane Dion, the architect of the Clarity Act, Layton's remarks enraged federalists, troubled his caucus and gained him little support in Quebec.

In the second week of the campaign, the polls were showing the inevitable decline in Liberal support. On June 5, Ipsos-Reid put the Liberals and Conservatives in a virtual tie, 32-31, and the NDP at 17 per cent. It meant the 13-point lead the Liberals held even after the Auditor General's disclosures had been cut to a single point. In Ontario, the Conservatives were said to be ahead of the Liberals, 35-32. In Quebec, the Bloc was 17 points ahead of the Liberals, 45-28. The shift was more sudden and dramatic than anyone had foreseen. It raised for the first time the possibility not merely of a minority government, but one that could be headed by Stephen Harper. "This is bad, bad, bad for the Liberals" said Darrell Bricker, president of Ipsos-Reid. "They've thrown everything but the kitchen sink at the Conservatives, and none of it seems to be working." In Quebec, Gilles Duceppe gloated at the prospect of a Harper minority dependent on Bloc support. The price would be concessions for Quebec; either way, the Bloc would win, if the concessions weren't forthcoming, that would simply prove federalism was unworkable. One Bloc MP, Yves Rocheleau of Trois-Riviéres, summed up the Bloc's hope for a Harper victory: It would finally show, he was sure, that "Canada is a madhouse. It's a country that cannot be administered, in my opinion."

How had the reversal come about so quickly? The Martin team had learned much about party in-fighting but little, apparently, about election campaigning. The Prime Minister appeared uninspiring and tired in his personal appearances and in his TV ads. But the most significant event in the campaign may not have been the rallies for the party leaders or the issuance of their platforms, but something that took place at the Ontario Parliament Building in Toronto on Tuesday, May 18, five days before the election call. That afternoon, the Ontario minister of finance, Greg Sorbara, rose in his seat to present the first budget of the recently-elected Liberal government of Dalton McGuinty. The new government was facing a $6 billion dollar deficit left by its tax-cutting Conservative predecessor, but during the campaign McGuinty had promised to balance the budget without raising taxes. Instead, Sorbara announced the imposition of a health care premium like that already in place in Alberta and British Columbia. It would cost taxpayers as much as $900 a year. It was not the only election promise on which the cash-strapped provincial Liberals had reneged. Angry Ontario voters took out their frustration on the first targets they could find – the federal Liberal candidates knocking on their doors. All this raised hackles in the Liberal camp when it was learned that David Herle's firm had run polling and focus groups for the budget exercise. The Ontario Liberals could have put the issue to a referendum under the Ontario Taxpayer Protection Act, asking to be relieved of their promise because of the huge deficit they'd inherited. It was dismissed without being seriously considered – a mistake later regretted – and Premier McGuinty gave Paul Martin a heads-up on the decision a few days before the budget. Martin's initial reaction was to sympathize with the plight of Ontario Liberals who had been left a sea of red ink. Faced with an unhappy public, he soon agreed that politicians need to keep their promises.

An aura of impending doom was now enveloping the Liberal campaign. Harper stepped up his tempo of attack, promising to inject $1.2 billion into the Canadian Forces for new equipment, then pledging to scrap the gun registry that had cost $2 billion to set up, and use the $100 million a year savings to strengthen policing. He ended the second week by releasing the complete Conservative platform at a rally in Toronto. The 44-page document, titled Demanding Better, set out $57 billion in tax cuts and new spending, all of which, Harper said, could be financed without going into deficit. He argued that because federal surpluses would be larger than Liberal forecasts, there would be room for new programs as well as tax cuts. Independent observers, including the left-leaning Centre for Policy Alternatives, responded that the Conservative platform, if enacted, would lead to a new round of federal deficits.

The Prime Minister returned to his home town of Windsor, Ontario for the formal release of the Liberal platform. It was no longer dressed up as the famous Red Book that had won three elections for Jean Chrétien. This time, the 60-page document was packaged in a white cover under the title, Moving Canada Forward. It set out $40 billion in new spending over five years, with its main planks calling for $5 billion in funding for day care and a sizable boost to the military. The day care pledge raised some eyebrows because the Liberals had pledged as early as 1993 to set up a plan modeled on Quebec's $7 a day child care program. It never happened, but this time, Martin insisted, it would because it would not be dependent on provincial participation. As a man of his word he would see that it came about.

Martin took time off from the campaign to attend the 60th anniversary observation of D-Day in France on June 6 and a meeting of the G-8 leaders in Atlanta, Georgia. While there, came news that one of his Ontario MPs, Carolyn Parrish, was calling the Liberal campaign a "comedy of errors." His only response was to refer to her as "smart politician," perhaps forgetting that at the height of the Iraq crisis Parrish had been heard to say she "hated those American bastards." Returning to Ottawa, Martin met with his campaign team and pondered the advice he was getting from a clutch of Trudeau-era operatives who had seen it all before, and knew pending disaster when they encountered it. Senator Jerry Grafstein, Martin Goldfarb, Dick O'Hagen and others were dispatching memos urging Martin to send voters a "message of hope" based on the strong economy and united country that Liberals had helped to build. There were a few promising signs. In Edmonton, a dozen prominent provincial Conservatives, including three former Alberta cabinet ministers, endorsed Anne McLellan for her strong voice on behalf of the province. None of it seemed to be of much help to the Liberals. In a conference call with MPs and candidates on June 10, David Herle admitted the party was in a downward spiral. "People are drifting to the Conservatives in an aimless fashion ... no one is paying attention. We are in a spiral right now that we have to address." It was the most brutal admission yet from the Martin team. A new series of attack ads would begin running on TV the next day. "We are expecting the ads to be effective, to shake up people," Herle added.[4]

The ads, created by the Red Leaf consortium, were the hardest-hitting of the campaign, criticizing Conservative policy while carefully avoiding personal attack. The first, read by a steady female voice, told viewers that "Stephen Harper would have sent our troops to Iraq. He'd spend billions on tanks and aircraft carriers, weaken our gun laws and scrap the Kyoto accord. He'd sacrifice Canadian-style health care for U.S.-style tax cuts. He won't protect a woman's right to choose. And he's prepared to work with the Bloc Québécois, Stephen Harper says when he's through with Canada we won't recognize it. And you know what? He's right. As the voice faded away, so did the red maple leaf in a fluttering Canadian flag. Harper, realizing he couldn't effectively debate the charges in the ads – sufficiently factual to at least be arguable – chose instead to charge the Liberals with a gutter attack. "When you throw mud, you lose ground. I will let the Liberals descend into the gutter and they will be punished accordingly." The June 14 issue of *Maclean's* was out with a smiling Stephen Harper on the cover, with a headline asking the question, "How do you like the sound of Prime Minister Harper?"

The debates of June 14 and 15 – French and English, back to back – took place at Ottawa's National Arts Centre on a set that had been dressed up to look like the foyer of Parliament Hill. They were to have been the defining moments of the campaign. They were not, although the French debate seemed more civilized that the donnybrook that played out the next night in English. The fact all four leaders were able to debate in French – from the native fluency of Gilles Duceppe to the passably acceptable French spoken by Harper – at least showed how far bilingualism has come. Next morning's *le Journal de Montréal*, Quebec's largest newspaper, filled its front page with a picture of a downcast Prime Minister headlined "Paul Martin Malmené" (Paul Martin Manhandled). Le Devoir put it aptly: "1er débat: avantage Duceppe." The English debate, for many of the three million viewers who watched it, fell well short of its lofty goal, drowned in a cacophony of shouts and insults. It may have been the style more than the substance of each leader that left the stronger impression: Martin, embattled, waving his arms as if to dismiss his critics, sometimes effective but more often stammering; Layton, a jay cock supremely confident in his own remarks, loudly interrupting the others when they spoke; Duceppe, effective and well briefed on the issues, but with no votes to win in the English debate; and Harper, cool, calm, and restrained, if not exactly Kennedyesque in his looks and mannerisms.

In the party's TV ads, the Conservative leader had been telling voters "My name is Stephen Harper." The debates offered him a chance to build on that introduction. The volleys fired at Harper by Martin and Layton were well aimed and effective, but at the end, he was still on his feet, responding directly and without equivocation. He pledged not to legislate against abortion and said he might use the notwithstanding clause against child pornography, regardless of how the courts might rule on freedom of expression. On healthcare, Harper conceded he didn't really care if private companies deliver services as long as they were paid through the public system. "I know this is a dangerous subject," Harper said. "My advisors say don't talk about it, but the fact is sometimes provinces have allowed in the past few years, they've brought in private services covered by public health insurance. Ordinary people can get them. Why do I care and why do we care as a federal government how they're managed?"

Within moments of the debate's end, an Internet survey of 2,107 pre-selected voters had 37 per cent picking Harper the winner, against 24 per cent for Martin and 18 per cent for Layton. The best headline the next day was in the *Vancouver Sun*: "The Debates are Over, the Campaign Begins." While the debates had captured the country's attention, few stayed with them for the full two hours. Gilles Duceppe, whose party put up no candidates outside Quebec, was allowed to take up one-quarter of the time of the English debate, but Jim Harris, the leader of the Green Party with candidates in all 308 ridings, was barred by the TV networks. Arguably, the debates could be better run, with more citizen participation, if they were turned over to a non-partisan organization such as the Canadian Clubs, to be held in different cities across the country, each devoted to a different issue, and opened up to all legitimate contenders.

Coming out of the debates the Conservative campaign seemed to be peaking, perhaps sooner than it should have. Harper had been able up to now to shrug off embarrassing remarks from errant candidates. Scott Reid, his bilingualism critic from Ontario, wanted to cut services to minority language groups. Rob Merrifield, the health critic from Alberta, thought it would be beneficial for women seeking abortions to receive counselling. Cheryll Gallant who had won the Renfrew North seat for the Alliance in 1993, told a pro-life rally in Ottawa that abortions were just as bad as the beheading of the American in Iraq by Muslim extremists. Other Conservatives condemned gay practices as unhealthy, forcing Harper to give reassurances that a Conservative government would legislate against neither homo-sexuality nor abortion – at least not in its first term. Candidates were told flat out to quit expressing personal opinions on these issues. While trying to live down these embarrassments, Harper himself was discussing the need to amend hate legislation protecting gays and lesbians, on the grounds it could deny religious groups their right to freedom of expression. Then, Harper committed what may have been his greatest tactical error of the campaign: publicly anticipating that he could win a majority. He went on to discuss the even more sensitive question of transition planning. Insiders were reporting that Tom Flanagan – emerging ever more certainly as the *eminence grise* of a Harper government – had brought in former Mulroney chief of staff Derek Burney and was in touch with high level civil servants to discuss a Harper transition. At this stage, the possibility of a Tory majority had the ring of plausibility if not certainty, but discussing it made Harper look over-confident. It also alerted voters worried about the Conservative party's stance on social issues that a Harper victory was now a realistic possibility.

More mishaps followed, squelching the lift Harper had gained from the debates. A petulant outburst from Alberta premier Ralph Klein about how he would announce changes to health care two days after the election, gave credence to the Liberal claim that Harper would allow privatized health care, a violation of the Canada Health Act. Klein soon caved in to the Prime Minister's demand for more disclosure; his health minister meekly announced that more money would be put into health care and no one need be concerned about other measures. The incident proved hugely damaging, spotlighting apparent Conservative willingness to tamper with medicare. This was followed by an inept news release from the Conservative war room attacking Paul Martin as soft on child pornography. Next came a flap over bilingualism on Air Canada, and finally, veteran Randy White's chilling denunciation of the Charter of Rights. He spoke of using the notwithstanding clause to override court decisions of which a Conservative government might not approve. Harper hurriedly pulled White off the platform of his final Vancouver rally, and refused to discuss the issue with the media. Skeletons though they might be, the old Alliance extremist positions were rattling out of the closet, throwing Harper off his message of a "moderate, mainstream" alternative at the very time he most needed to concentrate his fire on the Liberals. Somewhere in all of this, Harper found time to switch wardrobes, abandoning his less than flattering tan and brown jackets for dark suits and more stylish ties.

By now, a new Liberal attack ad was airing, built on themes picked up from focus groups. The Conservatives had run their own negative ads, notably one showing fifty dollar bills being thrown into a dumpster. The new Liberal ad would fan fears of a Harper government by questioning the soundness of Conservative financing. It shrewdly showed a picture of Brian Mulroney and asked "Can you increase expenditures, lower taxes and still balance the books? Prime Minister Brian Mulroney tried it. He left behind a deficit of $42-billion a year." It also linked Harper to Mike Harris, the former Tory premier of Ontario, whom it accused of leaving a $6-billion deficit after "nearly destroying" the province's social programs. Together, Martin's increased aggressiveness and the cumulative effect of the attack ads seemed to be staunching the Liberal bleeding. On June 22, Ipsos-Reid had the Liberals back on top, 34 per cent to 28, with the NDP stuck at 16 per cent. Three days later, the same pollster was reporting a virtual dead heat; 32-31 for the Liberals with the NDP at 17 per cent. This would put the parties back to where they were three weeks earlier. Another pollster, Ekos Research, reported similar numbers on June 26. Married to a seat projection, their numbers put the Liberals on track to form a minority with an eight-seat edge over the Conservatives, 117 to 109. The same day, Ipsos-Reid predicted the opposite result: a Tory minority government with 117 seats to 101 for the Liberals.

Martin was campaigning desperately in Quebec as the election drew near. He was there on Thursday, June 24, for *Fete Nationale* celebrating the day of St. Jean Baptiste, patron saint of French Canada, and he returned at the weekend. In many respects, Quebec represented Paul Martin's greatest frustration and his greatest challenge. He'd immersed himself in the business and political life of the province for three decades. Now, he faced losing even the support that had gone to Jean Chrétien. Martin had never been comfortable with Chrétien's militant anti-sovereignist attitude. He supported the Meech Lake agreement that would have recognized Quebec as a distinct society, and one of the first things he did as Liberal leader was to bring Jean Lapierre, a former Liberal turned Bloc MP, back to the fold as his Quebec lieutenant. Lapierre, who had left the Bloc to become a highly-paid radio show host, was supposed to be the magnet to bring Quebec's "soft nationalists" back to the Liberal camp. It wasn't happening. Lapierre embarrassed Martin on a number of occasions, notably when he called for quick prosecutions in the sponsorship scandal, and then when he mused about minority prospects at the beginning of the campaign. Midway in the campaign, Martin turned to Stéphane Dion, the architect of the Clarity Act and a former Chrétien confidant who had been dropped from the cabinet, to make the case against the Bloc.

The tightening of the race seemed to energize Martin, raising his optimism about the outcome. It made Harper more cautious.

His final Ontario swing before heading back to the West, was restricted to tightly-controlled rallies attended only by cheering supporters. Reporters travelling with him complained Harper was being kept in a bubble, accessible only for a few selected local interviews. Not all of them went off smoothly. On Toronto radio station MOJO, Harper was asked whether Adam and Eve was a myth and whether he accepted evolution. "It's certainly an allegory," he said of the Biblical story, adding that he does believe in the science of evolution. By the weekend before the vote, Harper was conducting rallies throughout the West, reminding voters of Liberal financial mismanagement. It had always been his strategy to wage an issueless campaign focusing on the sponsorship scandal, and he was anxious to get back to that. Martin continued to look for votes in Ontario and for ways to raise doubts about the Conservative party's commitment to social programs and the Charter of Rights. "A Conservative government would use the notwithstanding clause impulsively and would extend it to restrict fundamental rights of all Canadians," he said in Toronto, adding that the Liberal government had not used the clause once in 22 years. Layton was involved in a "Super Friday" tour of ten Ontario cities when he was handed the delicate compliment of a letter of support from the U.S. environmental activist and presidential candidate, Ralph Nader. Layton waved off the suggestion that Nader's help could be damaging. "That's ridiculous," he said. "I think he's a respected voice on behalf of ordinary people." Bloc leader Gilles Duceppe continued to revel in the possibility of holding the balance of power. "I'm telling all Quebeckers that they need honest representatives to defend the interests of Quebeckers with pride. That's the issue on the 28th. We're not about to decide the issue of sovereignty on the 28th. Those who say that will look stupid the day after."

As it had to, the campaign reached its merciful finale. On the final Sunday, the Prime Minister flew from Halifax to Vancouver, with stops in Quebec and Winnipeg, calling on "all progressives to come together" and promising to "govern for every region of Canada." He warned NDP supporters of the consequences of depriving the Liberals of the votes they would need to stop the Conservatives: "In a race as close as this, you may well help Stephen Harper become prime minister." On Sunday, Harper travelled from Edmonton to Calgary in a convoy of buses, promising power for the West: "We're going to change the system, we're going to make things better ... and we're going to bring this part of the country into power at Ottawa." The pollsters and pundits were still assaying the likelihood of a Harper minority government. The only small and perhaps prophetic indication that this might not be so was found in a little-noticed study of press coverage conducted by McGill University. It noted that "the primary Conservative issue, taxes, has largely been lost over the second half of the campaign. After the first week of substantive issues, attention turned away from the policies that parties stood for, and towards the issues that made other parties look bad."[5] It was telling Conservatives they may have lost control of the campaign.

A Night of Surprises and Shocks

Election night found the Prime Minister with his wife and three sons, surrounded by aides and friends, awaiting the returns in a suite at Montreal's Queen Elizabeth hotel. Martin spent little time in front of the TV, preferring to work quietly on the speech he would give later in the evening at the banquet hall in LaSalle where Liberals were already gathering. Stephen Harper, accompanied by his wife and children, was at the Hyatt hotel in Calgary, prepared to go to the Calgary Roundup Centre for a victory party celebrating the expected Conservative triumph. Gilles Duceppe and Jack Layton knew they couldn't form a government but they both eagerly anticipated the evening's results. Layton's NDP has rented a large hall in Toronto's Metro Convention Centre where he and his wife, Olivia Chow, would await the results of their own contests while tracking the national returns.

Because a court had struck down the law prohibiting the broadcast of returns before the closing of local polls, Canadians for the first time heard the results as the votes were counted. Atlantic Canada and its 32 seats had been expected to remain loyally Liberal, and the very first returns from Newfoundland shortly after 7 p.m. Eastern time set the pattern for the region. Within the hour, Liberal seats went from 19 to 22, leaving seven for the Conservatives and three for the NDP, a loss of one for each. A great swath of ridings – all the way from the St. Lawrence shores of eastern Quebec to the muskeg country of northern Alberta – began to report in at 9:30 p.m. The results came almost too quickly to be logged on the charts of the TV broadcasters, but they showed from the outset that the Bloc Québécois would live up to its billing in Quebec and that the Conservative party would be denied its hoped-for Ontario breakthrough. The first Quebec return, from a riding in the Gaspé that was on Atlantic time, produced an upset Bloc win when a well-regarded Liberal MP, Georges Farrah, was beaten by Bloc newcomer Raynald Blais. From there it was on to what Bloc leader Gilles Duceppe, handily re-elected in Laurier, would call "a beautiful victory … democracy in action," as he matched the number of seats Lucien Bouchard had won in taking the Bloc to Official Opposition status in 1993. With 54 of Quebec's 75 seats, Duceppe would lead a strong contingent into the new Parliament that could determine the fate of any minority government. The Bloc also succeeded in broadening its base beyond its traditional "pure laine" or French-Canadian bastion by electing two non-French MPs, Maka Kotto, the first African-Quebecker to win a seat, and Bernard Clearly, an aboriginal who was chief negotiator for the Innu-Montagnais-Atikamek Quebec council.

Pollsters and pundits had expected that Ontario, where the Liberals had won 101 of 103 seats in 2000 – since increased to 106 – might provide the springboard for the Conservative leap to minority government. The early returns soon demonstrated why that would not occur. Liberals were in the lead all over the province and less than an hour after the closing of the polls, the TV networks – led by Global and followed by the CBC and CTV – were declaring the election of a minority Liberal government. It was a stunningly unexpected outcome, and it had been driven by voters in Ontario, who allowed the Conservatives but 24 seats, the most meager of breakthroughs. Liberals held onto 75 ridings and the NDP seven. The results left Western Canadians wondering what they had to do to gain more clout in Ottawa; only 31 Conservatives had been elected east of the Manitoba-Ontario border. There was angry reaction, especially in Alberta. For some Conservative voters, winning 68 of the West's 92 seats simply turned back the clock to the early days of Reform. But it was Paul Martin's 14 victories in the West – the same as in 2000 – added to the three northern seats won by the Liberals, that delivered the new minority: 135 seats to 99 for the Conservatives, 19 NDP, 54 Bloc and one independent. A combination of the Liberals and NDP would still leave Paul Martin one seat short of a majority, but he would gladly settle for his "stable minority" – it had been far better than he or anyone else had expected at mid-campaign. The Liberals emerged from the night as the only party with MPs from every province, and with the lion's share of the seats in Montreal, Toronto and Vancouver. They captured almost 37 per cent of the vote, to less than 30 per cent for the Conservatives and under 16 per cent for the NDP. The Conservatives had fallen a full eight points short of the combined vote of PC and Alliance candidates in 2000.

Martin lost six cabinet ministers. The first to fall was Hélène Scherrer of Heritage Canada, the department tied most closely to the sponsorship scandal, who was beaten by the diminutive (5'2") Roger Clavet of the Bloc in the Quebec City riding of Louis-Hebert. He'd only recently moved from Winnipeg where he'd worked for Radio-Canada, the French TV wing of the CBC. He boasted that if he ever got to Ottawa, he'd been heard, if not seen. The losses of other senior ministers, including defence minister David Pratt, revenue minister Stan Keyes, and agriculture minister Bob Speller, came in Ontario. Two junior ministers, Gar Knutson (emerging markets) and Rey Pagtakhan (Western economic diversification) also fell, Pagtakhan the victim of redistribution that merged his riding with the Winnipeg North seat won by the NDP.

Prominent Liberal winners included Scott Brison, the former PC member for Kings-Hants in Nova Scotia who had left the party to become a parliamentary secretary to Paul Martin. He hailed his victory as a triumph for Canadian values. "People don't believe family values should be used as code words for bigotry and prejudice," the openly gay MP told TV viewers across the country. He also got in an appeal to voters in time zones where the polls hadn't yet closed, urging them to support Paul Martin. In New Brunswick, Liberal lobbyist Paul Zed, a member by marriage of the powerful Irving family that has dominated the economy of the Maritimes for years, picked up the seat formerly held by the retired Elsie Wayne, the maverick PC member. She'd been only one of two PCs to survive the Kim Campbell collapse of 1993.

Liberals lost 16 ridings in Quebec but managed to hold the seats of such high profile Quebec MPs as health minister Pierre Pettigrew and the former Chrétien cabinet minister, Stéphane Dion who had come to Paul Martin's rescue in the dying stages of the campaign. Dion racked up a better than 20,000 vote margin over his BQ challenger. The Prime Minister was easily returned in LaSalle-Emard. The minister of justice, Irwin Cottler, won Pierre Trudeau's old riding of Mount Royal – probably the safest Liberal seat in Canada – by 25,000 votes. Even Jean Lapierre, Martin's Quebec lieutenant who'd been a disappointment in the campaign, held leafy Outremont, the mid-town Montreal enclave of academics and professionals by a 3,000 vote margin. Liberals clung tightly to their Toronto heartland, holding 21 of the city's 22 seats. Hockey star Ken Dryden easily held the safest of them, York Centre. The West, however, failed to produce the results Martin had most wanted. Star Liberal recruit Glen Murray, the former mayor of Winnipeg, lost to Conservative newcomer Steven Fletcher, a wheelchair-bound quadriplegic in Charleswood-St. James by 826 votes. The House of Commons rules barring "strangers" from the floor of the Commons will have to be changed to permit Fletcher's medical aides to be with him. Treasury Board head Reg Alcock had a comfortable win in neighbouring Winnipeg South. In Saskatchewan, finance minister Ralph Goodale was the only Liberal to survive the Conservative tide. Both Alberta Liberals, Anne McLellan in Edmonton Centre and David Kilgour in Edmonton-Beaumont, held their seats. British Columbia – led by Vancouver and Victoria – contributed eight seats to the Liberal victory, including two of the four members of Paul Martin's "dream team" – former premier Ujjal Dosanjh in Vancouver South and businessman David Emerson in Vancouver Kingsway. Dosanjh skipped supper, gathered his workers at his side in their tiny campaign headquarters on Fraser Street, then adjourned to an empty store two blocks away for an impromptu victory party when it became clear he would win the riding. "The place is so tiny, we're celebrating on the streets," bubbled campaign manager Veronica Cheng. In the North, the Liberals won the Yukon, Western Arctic and Nunavut. The Liberals returned to Ottawa with 37 fewer members, but they came from every province of Canada. Their vote had increased in each of the four Western provinces and Liberals could still claim they constituted a "national government," even though their representation in Quebec and on the prairies was woefully weak.

Former Progressive Conservative leader Peter McKay had little difficulty retaining Central Nova and the two other Nova Scotia PC hold-overs also kept their seats. For McKay, this was going to be "a long night. Clearly there is a sense of disappointment in Atlantic Canada." Despite running many well qualified candidates in Quebec, not a single Conservative was elected there. In Ontario Belinda Stronach, the glamorous auto parts heiress, narrowly won Newmarket-Aurora but fellow leadership candidate Tony Clement, the former Ontario minister of health, lost to Liberal Coleen Beaumier in Brampton West. It was the fourth political defeat for Clement in two years; he'd lost a run at the Ontario PC leadership, been defeated in the 2003 Ontario provincial election; and fell to Stephen Harper in the Conservative leadership race. "I can take a hint," he quipped, surveying the debris of his latest defeat. Walter Robinson, the former head of the Canadian Taxpayers Federation – and stand-in for Paul Martin in Stephen Harper's debate rehearsals – lost a close fight in Ottawa-Orleans. Scott Reid and Cheryll Gallant were re-elected in their eastern Ontario ridings. The 22 newly-elected Conservatives included the former PC federal president, Peter Van Loan, and Mike Chong, co-founder of the history think tank, the Dominion Institute. Among the defeated Ontario Tories were several with close ties to evangelical organizations, underscoring Ontario's reluctance to support the party's social conservative wing.

Only the prairie heartland did its job for Stephen Harper: it gave him seven of 14 seats in Manitoba, all but one of 14 in Saskatchewan and 26 of 28 in Alberta, including his own seat of Calgary Southwest. Only in British Columbia did the tide recede; Liberal and NDP strength in Vancouver and Victoria held the Conservatives to 22 of B.C.'s 36 seats. Two Conservatives, Germant Grewal in Newton-North Delta and his wife Nina Grewal in Fleetwood-Port Kells – both Surrey area ridings with large Indo-Canadian populations – became the only husband-wife team ever elected to Parliament. In Surrey North, former Alliance MP turned Conservative, Chuck Cadman, running now as an independent, defeated the official Conservative candidate who'd beaten him for the nomination. Cadman was fighting another battle at the same time: he had recently been diagnosed with cancer. Among high profile former Alliance members in the Conservative caucus, Randy White, Rob Merrithew and Myron Thompson held their seats despite the controversies that swirled around them during the campaign. Stockwell Day, the former Alliance leader who stayed out of the limelight during the campaign, held his Okanagan-Coquihalla seat in B.C. by a comfortable 13,000 votes. John Reynolds, the Conservative House leader, was re-elected in West Vancouver-Sunshine Coast after trailing much of the evening, his winning margin reduced from more than 11,000 votes in 2000 to less than 1,700.

The NDP hailed its biggest victories in Ontario, where the current and former leaders of the party, Jack Layton in Toronto Danforth and Ed Broadbent in Ottawa Centre, defeated high profile Liberals. The fight between Layton and longtime Liberal MP Dennis Mills was one of the most closely-watched in the election. Layton's status as a leader plus the determined efforts of NDP workers reinforced by volunteers from other ridings, gained him a 2,400-vote margin. Broadbent fought a street by street contest against Martin advisor Richard Mahoney, winning by 6,000 votes. Layton's wife, city councillor Olivia Chow, failed for the second time to dislodge Liberal Tony Ianno in Toronto Spadina, losing even the Chinatown polls. In Hamilton Centre, NDP veteran Dave Christopherson was the victor over the revenue minister, Stan Keyes. Former NDP leader Alexa McDonough was re-elected in Halifax. Bill Siksay of the NDP held the Burnaby-Douglas seat of his former boss, Svend Robinson, crushing the hopes of B.C. Liberal president Bill Cunningham.

When Stephen Harper spoke to his supporters at the Calgary Roundup Centre, it was to a silent and disappointed crowd. He struggled for the words to rally them for another day: "Until someone some day achieves a majority, the fight is not won or lost." Then he added, some thought ominously, that the struggle will go on until "the voice of the West will some day be heard and accepted in the corridors of power." Jack Layton, subdued at the fact the NDP had failed to come close to its seat target despite a near-doubling in the popular vote, declared that "Parliament is about to get a new dose of energy." The NDP members would go to Ottawa to help build "a greener country, a fairer country, a more caring society." The last words for the night were left to Paul Martin, humbled but feeling nonetheless vindicated in having submitted his new government to the will of the people. "The message was unmistakable. Canadians expected and expect more from us. And as a party and as a government, we must do better. And we will. I pledge that to you tonight." Newspapers across the country the next day carried almost identical headlines: LIBERAL MINORITY (*Vancouver Sun, London Free Press, the National Post*). The *Edmonton Journal* varied it to MARTIN MINORITY. "Ontario Rescues Martin," declared the *Globe and Mail*. "Paul

Martin Minoritaire à Cause du Bloc," announced *le Journal de Montréal*. The *Winnipeg Sun* printed what many Westerners thought: "Scare tactics work as Liberals win minority."

The Aftermath

The period between election day and the return of Parliament gave Canadians time to reflect on the fact they had been through a suspenseful and at times savage campaign. For the first time in a decade, voters had been challenged to make a meaningful choice between clear options on the right and left. They had witnessed an election of ironies: a Liberal Prime Minister who ran against the legacy of his own party as much as against the Opposition, criticized not for the failure but for the *success* of his policies, facing his main opposition from a newly reconstituted Conservative party that was unable to control the worrisome views of some of its most prominent adherents. The outcome was determined not so much by the merits of the winning party, but by the demerits of the loser. Voters usually vote to throw out a government; this time they voted to throw out the Opposition, abandoning any mid-campaign thoughts they may have had of giving them the government. They also voted overwhelmingly to protect the principles that Pierre Trudeau infused into the bedrock of Canadian public life: bilingualism, the Charter of Rights, and the Canada Health Act. Every attack that was made on these principles – Scott Reid's dismissal of bilingualism, Randy White's rant against the Charter of Rights, and Alberta Premier Ralph Klein's threats to shake up medicare – alienated voters who might otherwise have supported the Conservative party. Stephen Harper knew what was happening, but he was powerless to prevent "the incoming attacks that I've had to sustain from my own troops."[6]

It was not a campaign that cheered the Liberal party, saved as it was only by a late splurge of negative advertising. The ads were more successful than the Conservative negative ads because they had a stronger factual basis, even if they exaggerated the facts. It was a fact that Stephen Harper had been anxious to line up Canada with the U.S. in the war on Iraq, that previous Conservatives governments at Ottawa and in the provinces had run up huge deficits by cutting taxes while allowing spending to rise, and that large numbers of former Alliance MPs in the Conservative ranks were strongly opposed to abortion and gay rights. While Harper had disclaimed any intention of legislating against either free choice or homosexuality in a Conservative government's first term, his tentativeness raised the prospect they might do so some time in the future.

Those around Stephen Harper came out of the election convinced the party had done very well, even if it hadn't been able to fulfill the expectations built up early in the campaign. To Michael Coates, president of PR firm Hill and Knowlton and a Harper strategist, bringing the Alliance and the PCs together, electing a new leader, and waging a strong campaign all within six months was an "incredible achievement." The "turning point of the campaign actually came last December, when the two parties merged," he thought. "That's what allowed this election to be as exciting as it was." Coates accepts that the election demonstrated there are "some issues in urban Canada today that are just beyond any discussion" and that the Conservative party will have to find a way to remove abortion and homosexuality from its agenda. He points to the fact that the most telling Liberal ads were precipitated by the comments of Conservative MPs, and "underscored people's concerns that we weren't ready."

Support for the Liberals, however, came from a wider pool of voters. The Liberals drew a critical mass of votes from the segment of the electorate that obtains significant benefits through entitlements of various kinds. In addition to public sector workers whose jobs might be put in jeopardy by serious cost-cutting, these include pensioners, professions in fields receiving public support such as culture and science and research, corporate executives and shareholders of companies that obtain government grants and loans, farmers receiving crop subsidies, and recipients of Employment Insurance and social assistance; all of whom benefit from the status quo and would perceive a more conservative approach to government as a threat to their well-being. The experience of Ontario voters with the socially disruptive consequences of the Mike Harris "Common Sense Revolution" served to reinforce these reservations. Some of these voters would have normally supported the NDP but switched to the Liberals in the late change in voter behaviour that was not detected in pre-election polls. This also explains in part why the Conservative party lost twenty per cent of the combined PC-Alliance vote of 2000. This analysis demonstrates how difficult it is for an opposition party to overcome the deeply-rooted dependency of voters who have received benefits from income redistribution and are content to support the government of the day, as long as it does not behave so egregiously (i.e., become involved in scandals and blatant misspending) as to lose all claim to legitimacy. Add to these numbers those members of interest groups concerned about socially conservative policies (including gays, feminists, and free choice advocates) and the result is a very large and significant voting bloc impervious to any appeal of the Conservative party.

The Prime Minister, for his part, overreacted to the sponsorship scandal and was never able to focus on the achievements of the government of which he was minister of finance, or explain the practical steps he'd take to turn his grandiose campaign rhetoric into reality. The Liberal party constitution requires a leadership review within two years after a general election, giving Paul Martin 24 months at most to soothe defeated candidates, rebuild connections with the left-leaning Trudeau-Chrétien wing of the party, and carry forward the Liberal legislative program on health, child care, and international cooperation. Failure to accomplish these missions would brand Paul Martin as a Prime Minister of mediocrity and leave him at the mercy of dissident Liberals in the leadership review vote.

Martin's cabinet choices reflected the dilemma he faced in mixing old faces and new and selecting ministers who could protect the government's minority in the House. He gave the all-important House leader's job to Hamilton's Tony Valeri (he of the

Sheila Copps war) and brought the staunch federalist, Stéphane Dion, back to the cabinet to sit alongside the ex-separatist, Jean Lapierre. He added newcomers such as Ujjal Dosanjh, David Emerson, Ken Dryden and the ex-Tory Scott Brison, while leaving stalwarts such as Ralph Goodale, Anne McLellan and Reg Alcock in their old positions. It was meant to be a cabinet of performance as well as protection.

In the end, the election results were a win-win for Gilles Duceppe, a win-loss for Paul Martin and Stephen Harper, and a loss-loss for Jack Layton. Duceppe won by matching the high water mark of 54 seats won by Lucien Bouchard, and by demonstrating his maturity and grasp of the issues. Martin won the election but lost his majority; Harper won by electing the strongest Opposition since 1980 but lost by failing to capture the minority government the polls said he'd won at mid-campaign. Layton lost by falling one seat short of being able to provide the Liberals with a majority, and by winning only one-third the number of seats captured by the NDP in 1988, in its best election, despite a doubling of its vote. The high optimism that drove Jack Layton at the outset of the campaign dribbled away into resigned acceptance that the "central role" the NDP had sought would be a marginal one, at best, in the new Parliament. Despite the NDP having been squeezed in an election day showdown between Liberals and Tories, his well-financed campaign should have produced better results. The Green party, which took nearly six hundred thousand votes and gained access to future public funding, would now have the capacity to mount a serious challenge in the next election. And the 13.5 million Canadians who bothered to vote – only 60.2 per cent of those eligible, a record low turn-out – were left wondering how their new House of minorities would manage Canada's role in a world troubled by global terrorism and the descent of a growing list of failed states into chaos and disorder.

The polling companies, who failed to detect the last-minute swing to the Liberals and were far off in their attempts to translate polling numbers into seats, were perhaps the biggest losers of the election. Their excuse was that because the publication of new polls is banned on election day, their media sponsors wouldn't pay for polling in the last few days of the campaign. They argued that it was the last-minute shift of voters away from the Conservatives – estimated at six per cent by Compass Research – that ensured the survival of the Martin Liberals. Michael Coates agreed, remembering the twenty Ontario ridings that Conservative polling showed the party should have won, but didn't. Donna Dasko of Environics Research could not remember "a campaign that had that kind of movement in the last couple of days."[7] The media, while providing the most intensive coverage ever given a Canadian election, were unable to overcome their obsession with the election as a horse race. All major outlets except the CBC fed on the poll reports as a substitute for serious policy examination.

With the possibility of the Martin minority stretching out to two and possibly three years, attention has switched from election strategies to parliamentary tactics, where the shrewdness of the House leaders, the impartiality of the Speaker, and the ability of the Opposition to influence the agenda will determine Parliament's effectiveness. The 38th Parliament will be measured against the achievements of the Pearson minorities of the 1960s, years that delivered the Canada Pension Plan, the maple leaf flag, medicare, old age supplements, bilingualism, and colour-blind immigration. They changed Canada fundamentally, a prospect unlikely to be repeated in the first decade of the 21st century. The 2004 election will stand as a turning point of deep significance for the way in which it restored competitive democracy to Canada and ended a decade of one-party rule. It tested anew our ability to build trust and restore confidence across a vast geography of attitudes, experiences and aspirations. It linked us yet again to the beginnings of Confederation, to the campaigns that were waged when the country was raw and sparsely settled, before the arrival of multiculturalism, the advent of the global economy, and the making of the New Canada with its myriad of races, cultures and languages. We can find it all there in our past, if only we take the time to look for it.

CHAPTER TWO

The New Brunswick Election of 1866

THE ISSUES

After the scheme to unite the British colonies of North America into a new nation, Canada, runs into stiff opposition, politicians in Ottawa conspire with British colonial authorities to force the resignation of New Brunswick's anti-Confederate Premier, Albert Smith, and hold a new election. The outcome, bringing to power a government committed to joining Canada, ensures that Confederation will prevail against Atlantic region resentment of the power and influence of Upper Canada.

THE PERSONALITIES

THE CROWN
Sir Arthur Hamilton Gordon, Governor of New Brunswick;
Sir Edward Cardwell, Secretary of State for Colonial Affairs,
Her Majesty's Government, London

THE CONFEDERATION PARTY
Samuel Leonard Tilley, Premier, 1861-1865;
Peter Mitchell, Premier, 1866

THE CONSTITUTIONAL PARTY
Albert J. Smith, Premier, 1865-66;
Timothy W. Anglin, MLA, 1865-66

PROVINCE OF CANADA
John A. Macdonald, Attorney General;
Alexander T. Galt, Minister of Finance

THE RESULTS

	SEATS	VOTES
Confederation Party	33	55,665 (62%)
Constitutionalist Party	8	33,767 (38%)

Illustration: Chris Penna, 2004.

*Rowdy gatherings, like that depicted at the polling place in Tracadie,
New Brunswick, were common in early Canadian politics.*

THE CONFEDERATION CONSPIRACY

The New Brunswick Election of 1866

The men who crowded into the little schoolhouse at Tracadie, an Acadian settlement in New Brunswick's north shore county of Gloucester, eyed the Sheriff sullenly as he stood guarding the ballot box. The officer, comforted by the presence of no less a personage than the new Premier of the colony, the Hon. Peter Mitchell, was sure he could stare down this rabble. For their part, it was with a mixture of surprise and suspicion that these loggers, farmers and fishermen, mostly French-speaking and Catholic, had seen the arrival of the Premier and his party in this austere fishing port on the Gulf of St. Lawrence.[1] Their distrust was heightened by a realization that the elections going on throughout New Brunswick – and today it was the turn of Gloucester to choose its two members for the Legislature – would decide whether they would become Canadians, owing loyalty not just to their own province but to the new Confederation that the leading politicians of the day were planning for the colonies of British North America.

On this May morning in 1866, anti-Confederation feeling ran high in New Brunswick. While the campaign had gone well for the Confederation Party (fuelled, it was said, by $40,000 in Canadian money), the idea of Union had few supporters in the poor Acadian outports of the colony. Those who clustered around the Tracadie schoolhouse this morning knew that Premier Mitchell, a well-to-do lumberman and shipbuilder from around the Bay of Miramichi, was working in the interests of the famous Samuel Leonard Tilley, and that the two of them would take New Brunswick into Canada if they had their way.

On the porch of the schoolhouse, arguments over the treatment Acadians could expect from Confederation flared up and died as quickly as they started, sputtering out in the misty morning air. It was known that Premier Mitchell was challenging many of the men as they came to vote, demanding proof they were property owners. By law, before any Catholic could vote, each man had to swear the detested oath of loyalty to Queen Victoria and her Protestant heirs. That done, Mitchell was making sure that as many who could be cajoled or bought, were marking their ballots for the Confederation candidate, Dr. Gordon. There was one among Mitchell's canvassers, a John Sutton, who raised the special ire of the crowd; he was making insulting remarks about the local priest that these villagers – still faithful to their church even though the Bishop had urged Catholics to vote for Confederation – simply couldn't tolerate.

Suddenly, "a large Frenchman" (as the Saint John newspapers would report), picked up a stone and lunged at Sutton, knocking him to the ground. Premier Mitchell, hearing the commotion, rushed from the school. Reaching into his coat, he drew a revolver and pointed it at the crowd, giving Sutton time to escape to the safety of the house where they'd spent the night. For 20 minutes the angry crowd surrounded the Premier, some men waving fence posts they'd wrenched from the ground, before permitting him to retreat to the safety of the polling place.

The Making of the New Dominion

So went the voting in New Brunswick from May 25 to June 12 of this fateful year, in the election that was to determine the future of the grand scheme to federate the colonies of British North America into the new Dominion of Canada. This new Canada, its designers hoped, would be able to resist the "Manifest Destiny" of the United States, that brawling democracy which was flexing its muscles after a horrendous civil war, already enviously eyeing the natural wealth of the vast stretch of continent that had not yet come under its flag. The issues that played out at Tracadie that day would be neither resolved nor forgotten in shaping the Canadian future, although few realized it then, or fully appreciate it today. Differing only in time and context, Canadian politics at the opening of the 21st century revolves still around fundamental choices that were present at the birth of the country and have challenged every generation of voters: the attractions of regionalism vs. a broader Canadian nationalism, whether in a disaffected Maritimes, an alienated Quebec or a disenchanted West; the challenge of maintaining independence from the U.S. vs accepting an escalating integration, economically, culturally and technologically, with the American giant; and the country's struggle to find a balance between elitism vs populism, between the cultural and economic dictates of powerful business, church and social establishments, and the populist views of many Canadians about how they wish to live their lives and how they are to be governed.

In the New Brunswick election of 1866, however, voters were offered a clear choice, and the outcome, whatever it might be, would mark a turning point for the colonies of British North America. It also was one in which the result could not be left to mere chance, because on it would rest the fate of Confederation. For the new nation to become a reality, the vote had to be won by the Confederation party of Leonard Tilley and Peter Mitchell. The previous premier, Albert Smith, a man opposed to Confederation, unmindful of the blandishments of the Canadians and unheeding of the directives of the Imperial Cabinet in London, must be denied a return to power. Only in this way, could there be a clear and convincing demonstration of the colony's willingness to embrace the new union.

The job was made the more difficult by the fact that only 15 months earlier, New Brunswickers had thrown Tilley and his nominally Liberal administration out of office, repudiating him massively at the polls after he had returned from the Quebec Conference on Confederation to announce his support for the scheme. As if Tilley's defeat was not enough to make the prospects of union bleak, there was at least as much resistance in the other Atlantic colonies.

Newfoundland, after having grudgingly permitted two delegates to go to Quebec, while warning them they were being given no authority to commit the old colony, had drifted out of the picture, not to return for more than 80 years. Prince Edward Island, beset with a virtual revolt of tenant farmers over the control of its million best acres by absentee landlords in England, had more pressing problems at home. Nova Scotia, the wealthiest and most influential of the Atlantic colonies, had seen its embarrassed premier, Dr. Charles Tupper, bow to the onslaughts of Joseph Howe and concede, in a resolution to the Legislative Assembly, that union had become "impracticable." This left only the Province of Canada, lurching along as an improbable Siamese twin born of the racial antagonisms of Upper and Lower Canada, firmly committed to the concept of Confederation. How could a new nation be forged out of such quarrelsome brats, already displaying all the signs of divergent personality that would in future lead to the regional fractiousness that generations of Canadians would have to accept as a normal part of political life?

New Brunswick would be the key. Because only New Brunswick could provide a physical link between the Canadas and Nova Scotia, this forested and sparsely-settled province was to become the cockpit of Confederation in the critical years of 1865 and 1866. Frantic messages would pass by telegraph and sea mail between Fredericton, Ottawa and London, out of which would emerge an elaborate conspiracy to clear the way for the union – even at the cost of bringing down a government by unconstitutional means, and installing its successor in office on the strength of votes bought by hard cash drawn secretly from public funds of the Province of Canada. It would mark the first great turning point in the unfolding political saga of the new nation.

When the delegates to the Quebec Conference had gathered in October, 1864, settling in at the St. Louis hotel amid an unseasonable snowstorm (many dragging their wives and daughters in their wake), they were dead-set on two things. The meeting would be conducted in absolute secrecy, with no details of the agreement on Confederation – if one could be reached – to be made public until after the Terms of Union had been presented to each colonial Governor and to the British cabinet. There would be no purpose served by submitting Confederation to the electors for their approval; the sanction of a popularly-elected Legislature would give each government the authority needed to proceed with the grand design.[2]

The Commitment of Samuel Leonard Tilley

As Premier and head of the New Brunswick delegation to Quebec, Leonard Tilley had no quarrel with the strategy to bring on Confederation. He was already an ardent advocate, seeing it as preferable to the more limited Maritime union he had earlier promoted. Tilley faced a particular difficulty of timing: his current term of office was soon to expire. Dare he push through Confederation at the tail-end of his mandate, just before having to face the voters in another election?

It was not the first time Tilley had faced a difficult political decision. He was 46 in 1864, and had 14 years of public life behind him. His first nomination to the Legislature came at a meeting in 1850 he hadn't bothered to attend. Tilley headed the polls in Saint John that year and was elected to the Opposition, but resigned in disgust over members indiscriminately switching sides, a common occurrence in the murky world of New Brunswick politics. Re-elected in 1854, he became Provincial Secretary and was responsible for a short-lived attempt at prohibition that brought down the government in 1856. (Tilley's prohibitionist sentiments were sincere; he'd taken a vow of abstinence at 19 and he was a loyal supporter of the Temperance Society, and a member of the Church of England.)

The new government lasted just long enough to restore the privileges of the 200 taverns in Saint John (a town of 40,000) and Tilley found himself back in office the next year. After winning re-election in 1861, Tilley quickly took up the cause of Maritime union, a scheme to unite the three colonies on the Atlantic. As Premier, he was an organizer of the 1864 Charlottetown conference that became the genesis for Confederation when a self-invited Canadian delegation turned up to argue for a greater union; that of all the colonies of British North America.

Tilley was the great-grandson of a Loyalist who had abandoned his farm near Brooklyn, New York, to join the exodus of 13,500 compatriots to the New Brunswick frontier after the American Revolution. He spent a carefree childhood in Gagetown, and with eight years of schooling went to Saint John where at 13 he became a pharmacy clerk.

The pharmacies of the era dispensed pain relievers and potions to reduce fever, but the foundations of modern pharmacology had scarcely been laid. The apothecaries of the day did their heaviest business in patent medicines, hair oils, soaps and spices. Among the fastest sellers were Hostetter's Stomach Bitters, Judson's Mountain Herb Pills (to "cleanse and purify the blood") and Sarsaparilla Compound ("the great spring medicine and blood purifier").[3]

Tilley's years in the drug trade – he set up his own partnership in 1838 and sold out, prosperous, in 1855 – saw him marry Julia Ann Hanford, who died in 1862 after having delivered two sons and five daughters. (He would remarry in 1867 and father two more sons).

Tilley was short in stature, handsome, with a high forehead from which he combed his hair straight back. Beardless, but with sideburns growing full on his face, Tilley's appearance was memorable for his prominent nose and sturdy chin. One biographer described him as a precise speaker with "that magnetism which enabled him to retain the attention and to awaken the sympathy of his audience."[4]

If Tilley thought the delegates to the Quebec conference would keep their mouths shut long enough for him to coast back to power without dealing with the Confederation issue, he was mistaken. The terms of Union were soon spelled out in local newspapers, and Tilley was forced to arrange a round of public meetings to explain their benefits. The resulting outcry from local merchants, financiers and railway promoters, fearful of their tight domain being invaded by Canadians, quickly descended about his head. On November 11, 1864, Tilley wrote of his difficulties to Alexander Galt, the Canadian Minister of Finance and sponsor of the Grand Trunk Railway who had joined the government in 1858 on condition that it pursue a policy of Confederation. He told Galt that he had found in New Brunswick "a strong current rising against Federation."[5]

Tilley was beset by questions for which there were no firm answers. What would Confederation cost? Would it increase taxes? Would it stimulate business? Would it facilitate trade and ensure the safety of New Brunswick and the Empire?[6] New Brunswick's rapacious gang of railway promoters was especially alarmed, fearful of being outmanoeuvred by their Canadian rivals. The proposed North American and European Railway, to run from Portland, Maine, through Saint John to Halifax, was especially vulnerable to the rival Intercolonial project, which had the support of Canada and London and would link Quebec with Halifax, bypassing Saint John in the process. As well, the large Irish Catholic and Acadian populations of New Brunswick feared the prospect of Protestant domination, especially by rapidly-growing Upper Canada.

The opposition to Confederation grew by the day. One riotous public meeting after another forced Tilley to pledge there would be no action on Union until after a new election. That decision earned him the wrath of John A. Macdonald, the ardent Confederation advocate who was Attorney General of Canada. Macdonald knew a political blunder when he saw one; he was all for pushing the Quebec resolution through the present House. Turning Confederation into an election issue in New Brunswick was not only risky, but would raise demands in other colonies for similar appeals to the people.

The lawyer from Kingston was not the only mentor Tilley had to please. Forever looking over his shoulder was the enigmatic Governor of New Brunswick, Sir Arthur Hamilton Gordon. The son of Britain's Prime Minister during the Crimean War, Gordon busied himself about every facet of commercial and political life in the colony. The Governor had expressed to his superior, Sir Edward Cardwell, the British Colonial Secretary, his "warm interest" in Maritime union. Perhaps Gordon saw himself as Governor of a greater colony of Acadia. He was blunt in his opposition to Confederation, claiming it provided for a weak central government and could "inflict a lasting injury" on British North America.[7] But his opposition melted away after Sir Edward, the scion of a wealthy Liverpool merchant family and holder of a directorship in an English railway, rejected his letter of resignation. From this point on, Gordon strove to be Cardwell's willing agent, throwing all his influence behind the Quebec resolution.

In January, 1865, Tilley decided to risk a quick election, but soon began to sense a political disaster in the making. On January 30, he wrote Gordon that "we have many prejudices to overcome ... our chance of success would have been increased by adhering to our original design."[8] Tilley's political instincts were to prove sounder than Gordon's. While the Governor was reporting to London that Tilley's forces would sweep the colony except for Saint John and the counties of Westmorland and York, Tilley found himself waging a losing campaign in the voting conducted throughout February and March.

Tilley campaigned under the disadvantage of being unable to come out in favour of a definite route for the Intercolonial Railway; a north shore line would have enraged the southern counties, and vice versa. It pained him to bear the ridicule of his opponents:

Mr. Tilley, will you stop your puffing and blowing
And tell us which way the railway is going?[9]

But the most devastating criticism to befall Tilley was that Confederation would mean higher taxes for New Brunswickers: "that every cow, every horse, and every sheep which they owned would be taxed, and that even their poultry would not escape the grasp of the Canadian tax-gatherers."[10] Tilley, running in the two-member seat of Saint John, bore the brunt of the cry that the eighty cents per head annual subsidy proposed for each province represented a sell-out for New Brunswick. One of his opponents, ship-owner A.R. Wetmore, made effective use of an imaginary dialogue between himself and his small son, having the boy ask: "Father, what country do we live in?" to which Wetmore would reply, "My dear son you have no country, for Mr. Tilley has sold us all to the Canadians for eighty cents a head."[11]

As election results came in, it was quickly evident that Tilley's government was headed for a resounding defeat. Opponents of Confederation, both Liberals and Conservatives, were joining forces to fight the scheme. They elected such worthy candidates as Timothy Warren Anglin, Irish-born editor of the Saint John *Morning Freeman*; Robert W. Wilmot, prominent Conservative who had come out of retirement from his calf and swine farm; Joseph Coram, the leading Orangeman; and George L. Hatheway, Chief Commissioner of the Board of Works and former Tilley supporter. Finally, there was the leather-lunged Albert J. Smith, the "Lion of Westmorland," and Tilley's one-time Attorney General who had broken with him three years earlier in another of the interminable arguments over the Intercolonial railway.

The election of 1865 ended in the most devastating defeat that any New Brunswick government would experience for the next 125 years. Every government supporter in the old House, except for Surveyor-General John McMillan, was beaten, including Tilley. Anti-Confederation candidates filled 35 of the 41 seats. It fell to Governor Gordon to write to London on March 6 that Confederation had met "with a most decided rejection in New Brunswick."[12]

The Smith Interregnum

Leonard Tilley and his cabinet resigned on March 27, leaving Gordon no choice but to call in the Opposition. Albert Smith became Premier and president of the executive council, moving quickly to impress on London the fact that public opinion in New Brunswick opposed Confederation. In a dispatch to Gordon that was meant for the Colonial Secretary, Smith and Robert Wilmot took pains to contradict the report of the *London Times* that the plans for Confederation were "progressing favourably. We would request your Excellency at once to inform the Secretary of State for the Colonies how entirely this scheme has been rejected by the people of this province, and that we have strong reason to believe ... that Canada is the only province in British North America favourable to the scheme."[13]

The new Premier and the Governor had feuded for years. Smith, who came from a poverty-stricken Loyalist background, had talked his way into one of the province's leading law firms, and later found himself a place in politics as a Reformer. Suspicious of British aristocracy, he had publicly accused Gordon of "excessive interference in local affairs and, even worse, embezzlement of provincial funds."[14]

Given this enmity, and the constant entreaties Gordon was receiving from London, it was not surprising that the Governor became a willing conspirator with Tilley in bringing down Smith. His letters to Sir Edward spoke of his many meetings with Tilley at which the former Premier would tell of plans to use rallies of the Temperance Union to whip up public opinion against the government, clearing the way for the Governor to dissolve the Legislature. It was no secret in New Brunswick that Gordon was violating the first precept of responsible government by plotting with the Opposition.

The debates that took place in the new Assembly made clear the attitude of most members on Confederation: one argued that under union, New Brunswick "would be confined to making laws to prevent cows from running on the commons, providing that sheep wear bells, and to issuing tavern licenses."[15]

The first blow against Premier Smith's government was struck that fall, when the pro-Confederation candidate, Charles Fisher, won a by-election in York brought on by the elevation of Attorney General John C. Allen to the bench. There is no doubt Fisher was financed with Canadian money. He had been through the political mill and he knew John A. Macdonald well enough to write him that the by-election could be won for eight to ten thousand dollars, but that he didn't have that kind of cash. After the voting, Fisher would remind Macdonald that "we look to you to help us out of this scrape, for if every dollar is not paid it will kill us at the general election. Do not allow us to want now or we are all gone together." Tilley had also appealed to Macdonald, asking "is there any chance of the friends in Canada providing half the expenditure, not to exceed five thousand dollars for their share?" He was sure York could be won "if we can go into the field with a fair share of the needful." Macdonald passed the note on to Finance Minister Galt, writing on the back of it: "My dear Galt, read this. What about the monies? J. A. MacD."[16]

Other blows were soon to fall on a beleaguered Albert Smith. The tempestuous Timothy Anglin of the *Freeman* split over Smith's inability to find money to build the North American and European Railway from Saint John to the Maine border. No sooner had he quit his seat, than Robert Wilmot, the old Conservative, walked out when his cousin was passed over for a judgeship. A.R. Wetmore, the man who had teased Tilley for "selling us all to the Canadians," then announced his break with the anti-Confederates.

This chain of misfortune culminated in yet another setback; the failure of Smith's mission to Washington to renew the expiring reciprocity agreement between the United States and British North America. For years, New Brunswick had thrived on the export of timber and fish to the U.S. and Britain. Smith had hoped the prospect of continued free trade with the New England states would overcome any inclination to gamble on Confederation.

The conspiracy to dislodge Smith from power now gathered force. Sir Edward issued fresh reminders from London that the Imperial cabinet earnestly desired Confederation. Tilley knew he could count on his friends in Canada "for the needful," and Gordon sat up in his sparse rooms at Government House to work out his strategy for his *coup de main* that would force Smith either to accept Confederation or resign. Gordon decided, he confided to Sir Edward, to come out in his speech from the Throne and "express a hope ... that a union will speedily be accomplished." Smith would either have to go along, in which case "all difficulty is at an end," or dissolution would be ordered.[17]

The New Brunswick Legislature opened its 1866 session on March 8, a raw late winter day. Fredericton summoned up as much formality as the little colonial capital could muster. The MLAs had been streaming in from across the province for days, making the six-hour trip by steamer up river from Saint John, and by stage from the outlying counties. The little capital's muddy main street took on a busy new air as hotels and eating houses prepared for their most profitable season.

Governor Gordon, clad in his bemedalled uniform with gold lace and wearing the peaked hat of his office, felt he could hear the barriers to Confederation going down as he read the Speech from the Throne – a speech he had written himself. It was "the strong and deliberate opinion of Her Majesty's government that it is an object much to be desired that all the B.N.A. colonies should agree to unite in one government." It was out in the open: London wanted Confederation; no loyal New Brunswicker would go against the wishes of Queen and Empire.

But the Assembly's debate dragged on for a month while Gordon, knowing that he could always fall back on the support of the Legislative Council in the colony's Upper House, grew frustrated with the delaying tactics of the government. He then decided on a new strategem; instead of waiting to receive the addresses in answer to the Throne Speech from both Houses simultaneously, as was usually the case, he would call in the Council first. And he would have a reply ready for them, a reply he would prepare entirely on his own, without consulting his ministers.

The execution had to be deft. The Governor summoned the Legislative Council for three o'clock on the afternoon of Saturday, April 7. Gordon sent off a note to the Premier's office at noon, when he knew Smith would be taking his mid-day meal at the Barker House. Returning to the Legislature about two-thirty, Smith read the message and rushed to Government House. There he found the Legislative Council assembled, with an address supporting Confederation. Angry at the Council, Smith was even more furious with Gordon for having prepared a reply rejoicing at the Council's message as one "which cannot but tend to hasten the accomplishment of Confederation."

In the argument that followed, the Governor suggested that Smith resign, and on the following Tuesday, April 10, Smith and his cabinet did just that. The reason, as he laid out in his letter of resignation, was that Gordon had acted "without consulting your constitutional advisors and in direct opposition to their views, thereby violating the constitution, and ignoring the principles of responsible government."

Smith made a blistering personal attack on Gordon in a speech to the Assembly later in the week. Thus it became a full-blown constitutional crisis, but one that Gordon was sure he could ride out. He wanted Leonard Tilley back in the Premier's office, but because Tilley didn't have a seat, Gordon summoned Robert Wilmot and Peter Mitchell to form a new government. Mitchell became Premier, with Tilley going in as Provincial Secretary, and on May 9 the Legislature was dissolved and a general election ordered. The decision to go again to the people was reached against the advice of John A. Macdonald. Realizing that another rejection in New Brunswick would make Confederation impossible, Macdonald had wired Tilley to urge him to avoid such a risky course. But the die was cast: it was either win the election, or see the smash-up of the scheme for Confederation.

The Campaign and the Candidates

The New Brunswick election of 1866 pitted the determined weight of British colonial authority, supported by the most powerful elements of the political and business establishment of British North America, against a parochial provincial movement that had few allies in its cause. Leonard Tilley, who had spent the past year speaking and moving about New Brunswick to build support for Confederation, decided that his appeal to the people would be on the general principle of Confederation; as to the details, they could be worked out later. The fact that the Quebec Conference had already set out specific Terms of Union would he played down; Tilley was not about to be caught having to defend the complicated "balance sheet" of Canadian tariffs vs. local revenues. The Confederation party also would characterize the constitutional issue swirling around Governor Gordon as little more than a personal squabble between he and Albert Smith. The only alternative to Confederation, according to Tilley, would be annexation by the U.S. and destruction of the British connection. The Ottawa *Times*, virtually a personal organ of John A. Macdonald, summed up the strategy neatly:

> The election in New Brunswick, as the Ministry is not pledged to any particular scheme of Union, will turn on the general principle of Confederation, and not upon the details of any proposed Union ... the opponents of Union ... will now be unable to put their objections in any tangible shape ...

Smith's supporters organized themselves into the Constitutionalist Party. It was their intention not to allow the voters to forget that responsible government had been subverted in New Brunswick. Their best campaign issue, they felt, was the heavier tax burden they were sure would fall on the province. The leading anti-Confederate organ, Timothy Anglin's *Morning Freeman*, devoted endless columns arguing that the provincial subsidy promised by the Terms of Union would fall short by $480,000 (an enormous sum) in meeting New Brunswick's current level of spending. The loss to the province would have to be made up by new taxes that would further impoverish the colony.

Political arguments aside, Tilley knew that it would be money, and plenty of it, that would win New Brunswick for Confederation. The conspiracy between Fredericton and London to bring down Smith's regime had achieved its goal, now the second part of the Confederation conspiracy, involving the supply of campaign funds by the Government of Canada, would come into play.

Throughout April, the appeals went into Ottawa. First Tilley wrote to Macdonald: "We must have the arrangement carried out and without delay that we talked of when I met you at Quebec. Telegraph me in cypher saying what we can rely on."[18] He followed this with an even blunter message: "Assistance must be had of a substantial character," suggesting $40,000 to $50,000 would do the job. A third letter left no doubt of Tilley's need:

> "I think we can, with good management and with means, carry a majority in the province ... to be frank with you the election in this province can be made certain if the means are used. It will remain for the friends in Canada to say how the arrangements are to be made. It must be done with great caution and in such a way as not to awaken suspicion."[19]

Tilley went on to suggest a method of laundering the campaign funds: he would send "a responsible man, such as Mr. Wright ... one of our wealthiest merchants" to Portland, Maine to pick up the cash from a Canadian emissary. And who might that be? None other than C. J. Brydges, General Manager of the Grand Trunk Railway, who had been privileged to sit in on the Quebec Conference although he was not a delegate. Furnished with cash from the Province of Canada's Secret Service Fund, Brydges became the most important courier of Canadian money in the Confederation conspiracy.[20]

A correspondent of the Halifax *Recorder*, reporting from Saint John, wrote that "both parties seemed confident of success at the polls." But he included in his account a perceptive interview with "a very shrewd man who calls himself a Unionist, and a Tilleyite," who posed the question, "Is it reasonable to suppose that Canada will allow us to be beaten in this struggle? If there are objections to secret service money, how long would it take George Brown with a hat in Toronto, and Galt with another hat in Montreal to collect enough to pay the expenses of this election here? Half a forenoon."

The Confederation party circulated "flaming posters" announcing "A Grand Rally" in Saint John on May 14 to kick off its campaign in New Brunswick's largest city. The rally was neither less nor more riotous than most political gatherings of the time, half civic duty and half drunken entertainment. R. D.

Wilmot met with cheers and hisses as he denounced the Smith regime as a "one-man government" while A.R. Wetmore "stood like a statue" as epithets were flung, calling those who hissed him "jackasses." But the crowd of 500 which filled the dance hall of the Mechanic's Institute, wanted only Leonard Tilley. He waited for the calls to become louder and more boisterous, then rushed to the platform, "spoke very loud and thumped the table very hard."

The Constitutionalists also held a large rally in Saint John. It passed resolutions expressing confidence in Albert Smith, opposing Confederation, and supporting responsible government. But Smith seemed not to have his heart in the campaign. He stuck close to his own Westmorland county, where his crowds were small and often hostile, and the main burden of the campaign fell on Anglin who ranged across the province while neglecting his own candidacy in Saint John County.

Nomination day in Northumberland found Anglin sharing a platform with Premier Mitchell at Newcastle. Anglin spoke for nearly three hours, then went on the next night to Chatham where he belaboured a crowd at the Masonic hall for four and a half hours, not finishing up until one o'clock in the morning. A few days later Anglin went to Richibucto, the largest town in Kent County. Unable to get permission for a meeting in the Court House, he dragged a table from the dining room of the Kent Hotel and set it up in the street to address an afternoon crowd. The Confederate candidate from Restigouche County, L.P.W. des Brisay, was on the scene and suggested they take turns speaking, "hour about." But Anglin rejected the offer, saying his throat wouldn't last for an hour, with the result that des Brisay heckled him from the sidelines until dark, when the meeting ended with a volley of eggs descending on Anglin. At least one found its target.

The afternoon of Thursday, May 10, was cool and damp. Rain clouds glowered over the Bay of Fundy as they did throughout much of this unseasonably cool and wet month. But that did not stop several thousand citizens from giving a cheering send-off to the Saint John Volunteer Battalion as it paraded at the wharf, to the martial airs of a 1ocal band, before filing aboard a ferry to be taken out to the sloop Simoon, sailing for the Maine frontier. These shop clerks, farmers and fishermen had answered the call of the colours when word came that the much-feared invasion of New Brunswick by the Fenians was about to commence.

It was this threatened invasion that gave the supporters of Confederation their final, clinching argument for union. The Fenians, a deluded band of Irish emigrants who became a powerful para-military force in the United States after the Civil War, were committed to the crack-pot scheme of invading British North America and holding it as a base to launch a freedom army that would sail against the British rulers of Ireland.[21]

Under their chief, Doram Killian, secure in the comparative safety of New York, the Fenians had dispatched an armed force of 400 to 500 men in April to the Maine border. The seizure by the U.S. authorities of the Fenian schooner Ocean Spray off Eastport, Maine, from which 117 cases of arms and ammunition were taken, was clear proof of the Fenians' hostile intentions. The Fenians had intended to seize the undefended island of Campobello; two days earlier a small force had raided the customs house on Indian Island and carried off a Union Jack. On April 7, the very day that Leonard Tilley was forming his pro-Confederation government, the Campobello attack was forestalled by the arrival of the 81-gun H.M.S. Duncan, carrying 700 British regulars, and a U.S. vessel, the Winooski. As the alarm spread through New Brunswick and units of the York County Militia, the Charlotte County Militia and the New Brunswick Artillery Regiment hastened to the border, even more ominous word was en route from Upper Canada. A Fenian army was gathering in upstate New York, and on May 31 – the timing could not have been more critical for its impact on public opinion in New Brunswick – the Fenians crossed the Niagara river for their 24-hour occupation of Fort Erie. Anti-Confederate candidates, their reputations blackened as annexationists and pro-Fenian, protested bitterly that the Fenian proclamations which began showing up in New Brunswick were the products of a "dirty tricks" squad working for Tilley.

The elections in New Brunswick's 14 counties and the City of Saint John were carefully scheduled to give the Confederation party its best possible start. Politically backward in many respects, New Brunswick was the only province with the secret ballot; in the rest of British North America it was considered the manly, British thing to declare one's support openly. It was also the best method of ensuring that the "loose fish" who were bought outside the polls would stay bought inside. But in New Brunswick, the existence of the secret ballot didn't eliminate the custom of money changing hands at the polling booth.

Northumberland County was the first to vote May 25 – the day after the traditional exhortations to loyalty that accompanied celebration of Queen Victoria's birthday – and all four Confederation candidates were swept in with large majorities. Carleton County, voting the next day, had only Union supporters to choose from and re-elected its two members from the last Assembly. Albert County went for Confederation by electing two Tilley supporters on May 29. Voting ended for the month on May 30 in Restigouche, Sunbury and Gloucester. Des Brisay, who had heckled Anglin at Richibucto, won in Restigouche along with his running mate, John McMillen, who had been the sole Tilleyite to survive the 1865 disaster. Sunbury returned two Confederation supporters and it was only in Gloucester, where Premier Mitchell had gotten himself in trouble in the famous gun-waving incident at Tracadie that the Constitutionalists stemmed the tide, electing two members. Mitchell himself, as a member of the appointive Upper House, the Legislative Council, was not a candidate.

Attention then shifted to York, which included the capital, Fredericton, and a stiff contest for the County's four seats was expected on June 1. This was where Charles Fisher had renewed the chance for Confederation with his by-election victory of the previous November. The question now was whether he could repeat his win in the general election. In the last week of the campaign, the Constitutionalist party was shocked when Hon. George L. Hatheway, an architect of Smith's victory in 1865, withdrew along with a second anti-Confederate candidate, a Dr.

Brown. Hatheway pleaded ill health: he took an advertisement in the Fredericton *Head Quarters* to explain that "in the tremendous effort made here on Nomination Day, not only by the opposing candidates, but by their great champion, S. L. Tilley, to break me down, I was unwittingly compelled to address the audience for five hours, the result of which has completely destroyed my voice and impaired my health." Fisher was returned along with his three Confederation party running-mates, by a vote of more than two to one.

The counties continued to fall like dominoes for the Confederation party; two seats in Queen's on June 5; two in Victoria and four in Saint John County the next day, including R.D. Wilmot, with Timothy Anglin being among the beaten anti-Confederates. Leonard Tilley and A.R. Wetmore were elected in Saint John City on June 7. The momentum for Confederation was slowed only in Westmorland where Albert J. Smith and three supporters were elected on June 5, and in Kent, where the Constitutionalists swept both seats on June 7. The voting ended on June 12 in Kings and in Charlotte, a Maine border county where, as could be expected, the Confedertion party won three and four seats, respectively. The final tally: 33 Confederation Party candidates elected, eight for the Constitutionalists. The *Morning Telegraph* calculated that the Confederation party had gained 55,665 votes, to 33,767 for the Constitutionalists.

The new Legislature with Mitchell in the Premier's chair met on June 21 (the day after Militia forces on the Maine border had been demobilized), and the House quickly approved the appointment of delegates to negotiate Confederation "upon such terms as will secure the just rights and interests of New Brunswick, accompanied with provision for the immediate con-struction of the Intercolonial Railway ..." One final effort by Albert J. Smith to amend the Terms of Union met with defeat: his demand for a constitutional court to mediate federal-provincial differences, and equal representation in the Senate for each province, fell on deaf ears.

The Aftermath

How fair had the election been, and would its outcome stand? How had the Confederates succeeded in achieving such a turnover in public opinion in just over a year? The unfairness of the vote went beyond the usual degree of vote buying and fraudulent counting present in elections of that era, in that a large section of the population – French-speaking Catholic voters – was effectively disenfranchised. The ballot was printed in English, and voting was of course restricted to males over 21, who had to be either property-owners or willing to pay a poll tax. If they were Catholic, they had to swear an oath of allegiance to the Crown and worse, specifically to the "Protestant heirs" of the reigning monarch.[22]

The campaign pitted the establishment of the colony, acting on a clear agenda, against what amounted to a disorganized group of independent candidates, united only in their opposition to Confederation, offering only negative views to their supporters. The Constitutionalists were virtually without funds, while backers of Confederation has access to money raised from the taxes of the Canadians. Under the circumstances, it is surprising the outcome was not more clear-cut.

With New Brunswick's role in Confederation assured, Tilley and five others of the government sailed to London to help prepare the British North America Act that the Imperial cabinet would put through Parliament. They needn't have rushed; John A. Macdonald and the Canadians didn't get there until November, and the discussions in the chilly drawing room assigned them at the Westminster Palace hotel went on all winter. Macdonald found time to take a new wife after meeting, by accident, the sister of his secretary. They wed at St. George's church on February 16, four days after the BNA Act had gone through the House of Lords. The new Act would survive as British legislation until Canada's Parliament would finally reclaim it, renaming it the Constitution Act, incorporating Pierre Elliot Trudeau's Charter of Rights and Freedoms, in 1982.

Tilley's biggest contribution to the sessions in London was

his choice of a term for Canada's form of government. Macdonald's suggestion, the "Kingdom of Canada," horrified the British Prime Minister, the Earl of Derby, who feared it would provoke Washington. Tilley, drawing on his familiarity with the Bible, suggested "Dominion" from Psalm 72: "dominion ... from sea to sea."[23]

With the BNA Act proclaimed and Confederation in force as of July 1, 1867, the summer and fall saw the politicians of the new Dominion preoccupied by electioneering. The four provinces, Ontario, Quebec, New Brunswick, and Nova Scotia were electing their new Legislatures at the same time as the federal voting for the new Parliament. Party lines were still highly fluid in 1867. Macdonald had built his Liberal Conservative coalition out of a variety of pro-Confederation forces: the English-speaking Conservatives and the French-speaking Bleus of Quebec; most of the Reformers and Conservatives of Ontario; and the pro-Confederation elements of both Liberals and Conservatives in New Brunswick and Nova Scotia.

Arrayed against this solid bloc were the remnants of the Clear Grits in Ontario, now organized into the Reform Association, along with the anti-clerical and anti-Confederate Parti Rouge of French Quebec and a smattering of English-speaking Quebec Liberals, plus the remaining intractable opponents of union in the Maritimes.

The Dominion election was conducted under the pre-Confederation election laws of each province. Except in New Brunswick, there was still no secret ballot and only Nova Scotia required that voting be held in all ridings on the same day. In all other provinces, Macdonald's Liberal Conservatives were able to run off their strongest candidates first, "picking the soft spots first and working cautiously into the hard ones." The government took advantage of the fact that Ontario and Quebec allowed 48 hours for voting. Macdonald's canvassers didn't hesitate to use a combination of threats and rewards to bring out enough supporters on the second day to overcome many of the leads built up by Opposition candidates on the first day. One of many victims was

George Brown, the *Toronto Globe* publisher, and Reformer. Emerging from the first day's balloting with an 11-vote lead, he saw his majority trickle away as Conservative money and whisky was splashed about the polls the next day, bringing a 96-vote victory for the government.

By the time Maritimers went to the polls, 87 government supporters had been elected in Ontario and Quebec, to only 17 for the Opposition. Eight of New Brunswick's 15 MPs emerged as Macdonald supporters, including Leonard Tilley in Saint John, whom Macdonald chose as his Minister of Customs. Tilley would go on to serve as Macdonald's Minister of Finance in 1872 and again from 1878 to 1885, would be knighted, and would twice hold the post of Lieutenant Governor of New Brunswick. His arch-rival, Albert Smith, was elected as a Liberal in 1867 and he, too, would serve in a Dominion cabinet, as Minister of Marine and Fisheries for Alexander Mackenzie from 1873 to 1878. Smith would turn down the Lieutenant Governorship of the province but he too would accept a knighthood, in 1878 – the first native New Brunswicker so honoured.

John A. Macdonald met with rejection only in Nova Scotia in 1867 where the fires of anti-unionism still burned strongly, then and for many years later. Of 19 new MPs, only Dr. Charles Tupper was successful as a Macdonald supporter. Crusading newspaper publisher Joseph Howe deserved most of the credit for organizing opposition to Confederation. He won his own federal seat in Hants, enabling him to continue his battle for the "better terms" which would be partially granted Nova Scotia two years later. In 1869, Howe found it convenient to cross the floor, support Macdonald, and take a cabinet position.

The appeal of a greater nation, which by now had come into being and deserved a chance of success, had made John A. Macdonald's victory inevitable. He was soon assured of a comfortable majority – 108 seats to 72 for the Opposition – and for most Canadians in that fall of 1867, it was time to get on with the harvest and with winter preparations, and leave politics to the politicians.

The struggle for Confederation was a contest between rival visions, fought between uneven forces. Canada came into being not as a result of a people uniting in a common cause to fulfil a national aspiration, but as a consequence of an imposed decision, designed in London and executed in Ottawa, Montreal and Fredericton, to consolidate British North America into a new entity that would be more resistant to American expansionism and more amenable to colonial control. The process had begun on the Plains of Abraham as a test of military strength between British and French in 1759. It culminated in a political show of force in the polling places of New Brunswick in 1866, clearing the last obstacle to uniting British North America. That Canada would become one nation from sea to sea had become a geopolitical inevitability; how it was going to come about was of lesser importance. The first turning point had been met. Now Canada must face the tests that would measure the ability of its peoples and its institutions to make Confederation work.

CHAPTER THREE

The Federal Election of September 17, 1878

THE ISSUES

Fighting to regain power after the Pacific Scandal, Sir John A. Macdonald and his Liberal-Conservative party pledge a "National Policy" of high tariffs that will protect Canada's emerging manufacturing industries from American competition. Promising to finish the Canadian Pacific railway to British Columbia, the Tories attack Liberal Prime Minister Alexander Mackenzie's handling of the recession. In Quebec, Roman Catholic church intrusion into party politics is an issue. By regaining power, Macdonald sets the course for Canada's national development behind a tariff wall favouring eastern industry over western agriculture.

THE PERSONALITIES

LIBERAL-CONSERVATIVE PARTY (TORIES)

John A. Macdonald, Prime Minister, 1867-73;
Leader of the Opposition, 1873-78
Hector Louis Langevin, Leader of Quebec Federal Conservatives;
Cabinet Minister in Macdonald Government,
Samuel L. Tilley, Former Premier Of New Brunswick;
Cabinet Minister in Macdonald Government,
Charles Tupper, Former Premier Of Nova Scotia;
Cabinet Minister in Macdonald Government

THE LIBERAL PARTY (CLEAR GRITS AND REFORMERS)

Sir Alexander Mackenzie, Prime Minister, 1873-78
Edward Blake, Former Premier of Ontario; President of the Privy Council
Richard Cartwright, Minister of Finance
Wilfrid Laurier, Minister of Inland Revenue

THE RESULTS

	SEATS	VOTES
Liberal-Conservative Party	142	280,224 (52.5%)
Liberal Party	64	247,043 (46.3%)
Others		6,674 (1.2%)

Sir John A. Macdonald addresses rally at Toronto's Victoria Park in his campaign for "National Policy" of protective tariffs.

HIGH TARIFFS, HIGH PROFITS:
JOHN A. MACDONALD
ON THE PATH OF DESTINY

The Federal Election of 1878

Even by the standards of the great political rallies that had taken over the picnic grounds of Ontario for the past two years, it was an impressive affair. The date was August 27, 1878 and the East York Liberal-Conservative Association was sponsoring one of the largest picnics of the election campaign. It was billed as a "Grand Conservative Demonstration" and everyone from Toronto and the countryside for miles around was invited to hear Sir John A. Macdonald and "other leading Men of the Party." The place was Victoria Park, a privately owned "place of recreation for summer purposes" which reached upward from the shore of Lake Ontario some seven miles east of Yonge Street. A large arch had been erected at the park's entrance to support two signs proclaiming the twin themes of the rally, "Welcome to our Chieftain" and "Protect our Industries." The seven thousand or so who had come by train and excursion boat had packed lunches and brought blankets to spread on the grass while they listened to the speeches that would go on long into the hot and humid afternoon.

Political picnics were a new and highly successful tactic to reach the growing ranks of Canadian voters. They were an invention of the Liberal-Conservative party, the name by which the Conservatives would be known well into the 20th century. It reflected the "Grand Coalition" by which John A. Macdonald had put together the framework of Confederation in the 1860s. His first great outdoor rally took place at Uxbridge, Ontario on Dominion Day, July 1, 1876. Such meetings had since become a powerful tool in helping Macdonald overcome the public disgrace into which he'd fallen after revelations of election corruption in 1872. Macdonald's campaign that year had been fuelled by large sums of money from Sir Hugh Allen and the consortium to which he was planning to hand over rights to build the Pacific railway to British Columbia. The resignation of Macdonald and his government in 1873 was the inevitable outcome of this first great Canadian political scandal. In the six short years leading up to that fateful demise, Macdonald had brought all of British North America except Newfoundland into Canada's orbit – Manitoba and the North West Territories in 1870, British Columbia in 1871, and Prince Edward Island in 1873.

A spectacle of colour and variety greeted Macdonald as he strode into the Park, escorted by Conservative dignitaries. Businessmen and lawyers from the city, clad in formal suits and silk top hats brushed elbows with stout farmers, labourers and others of the lesser classes, all equally enthusiastic at the prospect of exchanging a word or two with "the old Chieftain." Macdonald headed straight for the pavilion reserved for ladies, where women in bright taffeta gowns and cotton frocks waited nervously to be formally presented. He shook hands with several hundred of them, offering each a wisecrack or a compliment. In many cases, there was a brief renewal of acquaintance with those he had met since moving his law practice from Kingston to Toronto and taking up residence in the comfortable home he had built for himself, his wife Agnes, and their invalid daughter Mary on St. George Street. At 63, Macdonald remained a tall and impressive figure, his somewhat homely features rendered less craggy by age, his hair still thick and dark. After nearly five years in Opposition, it was as the unrelenting antagonist of the weak Liberal government of Alexander Mackenzie that Macdonald came today to Victoria Park, determined to avenge the humiliation of his resignation and his party's defeat in the election of 1874.

He began his speech jocularly enough, twitting Mackenzie's fractious Liberal administration, preparing the men in the audience for the appeal he would make for the restoration of Conservative power. "I am perhaps rather fond of the sound of my own voice," he allowed, "and I have been wandering – like the Wandering Jew – from one part of Ontario to the other, speaking in this province as well as the Eastern Townships of Quebec." He set the audience to laughing by telling them "what the old fox-hunter said, 'This year, I have the best lot of dogs that ever I had in my pack.' And they will worry the Grit rat, if you only give them a fair field and no favour ... they will follow the Grit rat, they shall catch the Grit rat, and we will send his skin to Paris to make gloves of. I have been, as you know, all my life a Conservative, yet I have been a liberal man ... The Grits, you know, are not Reformers; they are hybrids, a cross between a Democrat and an Annexationist."

Macdonald's attack on the Liberals as annexationists was the most devastating indictment that could be made of a political opponent in post-Confederation Canada. He was determined to portray the government as an uneasy collection of free traders, continentalists and radical Reformers who, if left to their devices, would soon permit the new nation to be swallowed up by the United States. The only antidote to the deadly poison of annexation, Macdonald would argue in this election of 1878, was the Conservative party's new National Policy. It would get on with the building of Canada, pushing the Pacific railway to the coast and filling the land with settlers. And key to it all, the National Policy would use a strategy of higher tariffs to protect Canada's infant manufacturing industries from U.S. competition and assure the government of the revenue it would need for its ambitious expansion plans.

"I greatly mistake the signs of the times if the people have not come to the conclusion that if we cannot get reciprocity of trade we must have reciprocity of tariff," Macdonald declared. The Liberal-Conservatives were the party of Canadians, independent, proud and determined not to be hewers of wood and drawers of water to the United States.[1] It was almost a new John A. Macdonald who campaigned on the picnic grounds of Ontario in 1878. Gone – for now, at least – were the drunken binges that had sullied his first term when he had sought relief from the tensions and stresses of office in the bottles of brandy he would take with him to bed for days at a time. Nor was there any sign of the indecisiveness and temerity, the stalling and the playing for time that had earned him the title "Old Tomorrow." The crowd at Victoria Park responded lustily to Macdonald's good humour, his self-assurance and his grand design for the next stage in the building of Canada. His reception here and his unerring reading of the political portents on the campaign trail would lead Macdonald to declare, a few days before the voting, "If we do well, we shall have a majority of sixty; if badly, thirty."[2]

Reaching for the West

The election of September 17, 1878 came just more than a decade after the launching of Confederation but already Canada was beginning to think and act as a nation following its own path to destiny. The four million Canadians – most of them native-born, immigration having slowed to a trickle – by now occupied the best farmland in Ontario and Quebec. Growing numbers were anxious to break out of the narrow strictures of the mean towns and the hard life of the raw new country. The vast Northwest, a land of shimmering vision beyond the Great Lakes was beginning to exert its magnetic pull. The deep depression that had begun in 1873 following collapse of the Reconstruction boom in the post-Civil War United States and the end of the Franco-Prussian war in Europe, caused the impoverishment of many farmers and stunted the growth of industry. The fiercely anti-Catholic Orange Order held sway in Ontario, making more difficult the reconciliation of the French and English wings of the two political parties. In Quebec, Roman Catholic Church strictures against "Catholic Liberalism" were bringing on a showdown between priests and politicians.

Almost from the day of Confederation, the focus of Canada had been moving west. Macdonald had hardly taken up his office in the newly-completed Parliament Buildings in Ottawa when he began negotiations for the purchase (at a cost of £300,000), of Rupert's Land, the old Hudson's Bay Company territory stretching toward the Rocky Mountains. No sooner had the deal been completed and an official party dispatched to the Red River valley, than the few thousand French-speaking Metis in that part of the plains rose in resistance to the Canadian take-over. The Metis were the offspring of early French trappers and plains Indians, ably but erratically led by the Quebec seminary-trained Louis Riel. In Quebec, the struggle was seen as a valiant effort to establish a French-speaking domain in the West to counter-balance the power of Ontario. In Ontario, Riel's execution of Protestant troublemaker Thomas Scott inflamed Orange and Protestant opinion. Macdonald gave in to Riel's provisional government by granting the region provincial status. With the creation of Manitoba in 1870 – along with the provision that publicly-financed Catholic separate schools be established – the new Dominion had emerged from its first political crisis. It was done on terms that would reverberate in rebellion and schism for decades to come.

All of this was not much more than an inconvenience to Macdonald as he pressed ahead toward his major goal: the building of a railway to the Pacific. In negotiations with British Columbia for the colony's entry into Confederation in 1871, he had committed Canada to starting the line within two years and finishing it within ten. The Reformist or Clear Grit Opposition, led in Parliament by the Sarnia, Ontario, stonemason, Alexander Mackenzie, quickly condemned the government bill to give $30 million and 50 million acres to the company that would build the railway. Mackenzie urged a go-slow policy and advocated as a less costly alternative, a marine transport system based on the rivers of the North West. As the 1872 election approached, Macdonald considered changing the name of his Liberal-Conservatives to the Constitutional Union party, but found a more pressing matter taking up his time: the need for funds to finance the difficult campaigns his followers faced in Ontario and Quebec. The Manitoba troubles had cost Macdonald support in both provinces and he recognized – as would all future Prime Ministers – that his only hope of governing lay in building a broad consensus among English and French, and among farmers, labourers and the rising new mercantile class.

Macdonald's opportunity to confound his Reform opposition and extend his support to the growing ranks of working men in Ontario came early in 1872 when the Typographical Union struck George Brown's Toronto *Globe.* The union was demanding a 10-hour day with no reduction in pay. Brown, still the senior Reform politician in the land, denounced the strikers and in an allegation that would become almost a standard tactic for generations of Canadian employers, branded their leaders as "foreign agitators." He had 13 strikers arrested for criminal conspiracy in restraint of trade, a charge then quite valid under common law. Macdonald, gleefully following the precedent established by the Gladstone Liberal government in England, pushed through Parliament Canada's first piece of labour legislation, the Trades Union Act, exempting unions from the provisions of common law.

Macdonald was toying even before the 1872 campaign with the idea of a National Policy based on a tariff protection for Canadian manufacturers. He wrote to a confidant: "Mackenzie, Brown & Co. are thoroughly committed to free trade. Now you are, I know, a hot free trader, as am I; but I quite agree … that our game is to coquet with the protectionists. The word 'protection' itself must be taboo, but we can ring the changes on National Policy, paying the U.S. in their own coin, etc."[3]

As it turned out, Macdonald was able to save the National Policy for a campaign in which he would need it more – the 1878 election. In the 1872 voting that ran from July to September of that year the Liberal-Conservatives were returned to power with 104 seats to 96 for the Opposition, despite losses in Ontario and Quebec. Macdonald would be caught out only months later for his indiscretions in having taken campaign funds from the Canadian Pacific interests. On April 2, 1873, Lucius Seth Huntington, the Liberal member from Shefford, Quebec, rose in the House of Commons to assert that the Canada Pacific Railway Company was in reality controlled by American interests and that its president, Sir Hugh Allen, had advanced large sums of money, often in American funds, to Macdonald and his ministers in return for a contract to build the line. Later revelations would produce what has probably become Canada's most famous exchange of telegrams – the desperate plea of August 26, 1872, from Macdonald to Allen's lawyer, "I must have another ten thousand; will be the last time of calling; do not fail me; answer today," and the reply of a few hours later from J. J. C. Abbott, "Draw on me for another ten thousand." These were immense sums for the day, and represented a depth of corruption that has hardly been equalled since. Macdonald – himself penurious, his law practice neglected – stoutly denied that three hundred and fifty thousand dollars in campaign handouts had sealed a conspiracy to grant the railway contract. Nevertheless, it was the desertion of many of his parliamentary followers that forced his resignation as leader of the government. The infamous "Pacific Scandal" was now part of Canadian legend.

The responsibility of government now fell to Alexander Mackenzie, whose loosely knit Liberals or Reformers had only recently agreed to recognize a single leader. At that he was a second choice. The Liberal caucus accepted Mackenzie only because they could not lure the former Reform premier of Ontario, Edward Blake, to Ottawa. Mackenzie, inaugurating his campaign for the late winter election of 1874, drew a direct bead on the Pacific Scandal by committing himself to "conduct public affairs upon principles of which honest men can approve." He also promised to clean up the election laws by introducing the secret ballot, along with simultaneous voting in all ridings. More to the point, he would also negotiate relaxation of the "impossible terms of union" with British Columbia and save Canada $60 to $80 million by substituting "the enormous stretches of magnificent water communication" between central Ontario and the Rockies for 1,300 miles of railway.

Mackenzie's program and his assault on corruption was welcomed by the voters everywhere but in British Columbia. Canadian men cast ballots throughout January and February of 1874, sending 138 Liberals to the enlarged 206-seat House of Commons, while electing only 67 Conservatives. John A.

Macdonald retained his seat in Kingston by a mere 38 votes. In Manitoba, Louis Riel – despite the confusion of an alleged amnesty that was never officially proclaimed – was elected in absentia as the MP for Provencher.

Alexander Mackenzie proved to be one of Canada's most highly principled but least effective Prime Ministers. He spent more time micro-managing his own Department of Public Works, which had responsibility for railway construction, than attending to the affairs of First Minister. Cast from the same Scottish heritage as Macdonald – as were most leading politicians and businessmen of the era in Canada – Mackenzie lacked the charisma and the vision of Macdonald. The cabinet he assembled reflected the divisions, jealousies and antagonisms that ran rampant through the ranks of Ontario Reformers, Quebec English-speaking Liberals and French-speaking *rouges.*

But the Mackenzie government was not entirely without accomplishment. The Supreme Court of Canada was established notwithstanding the painful (and as it turned out, erroneous) cries of Macdonald's Tories that the new body would deprive England's Privy Council of the last word on Canadian legal matters. Mackenzie pushed through his new Election Act replacing the old method of open oral voting with the secret ballot, and extending the franchise to all men over 21. Future federal elections – beginning in 1878 – would be held on a single day.

The 1874 election brought an infusion of new MPs, one of the most promising being the young lawyer from Drummond-Arthabaska in Quebec, Wilfrid Laurier. He had given up his provincial seat for a future at the federal level. Laurier's emergence was fraught with all the religious tensions of the era. His celebrated address to the Young Men's Liberal Association at Quebec City on June 26, 1877 brought him national prominence and went far toward convincing moderate elements in the Church that one could be a good Catholic and a Liberal, too. Laurier's speech warned that "the rights of each man end precisely at the point where they encroach upon the rights of others." If the Catholic clergy continued to force their flock by "intimidation" and "terror" to vote a certain way, "sooner or later, here as elsewhere, the pressure will culminate in explosion, violence and ruin." Laurier soon found himself invited into Mackenzie's cabinet as Minister of Inland Revenue but in the by-election to which every new minister was required to submit himself, conservative ultramontanist interests in the Church worked successfully for his defeat. A vacancy was quickly arranged in Quebec East and this time, a more watchful *rouge* machine saw to it that Laurier won.

The Liberal party's difficulties in Quebec were only a symptom of the trials that Mackenzie had to confront. With the Liberals both unwilling and unable to let a contract for the Pacific railway, Canada for a time was in danger of losing British Columbia. Construction went slowly, the work held back by the trickle of money available from tariff revenues, the government's major source of funds. The tariff, set at 15 per cent by John A. Macdonald, had been raised to 17.5 per cent by the Mackenzie government. The country nervously awaited the budget of February 25, 1876, when Finance Minister Richard Cartwright would reveal whether he would raise tariffs still further – forcing up the cost of imports – as the only way of filling depleted government coffers. In the end, faced with rebellion from Maritime supporters, he opted to hold the line. "Every increase in taxation," he told the House bluntly, was "a positive evil in itself." Higher tariffs were as always, anathema to Liberals. In one of its first acts in office, Mackenzie's government had tried desperately to renew the old reciprocity agreement with the United States, dispatching George Brown to Washington as a special British plenipotentiary charged with finding a way of overcoming the high tariffs hindering exports to the American market. His mission failed, the U.S. Senate adjourning without even discussing a proffered treaty.

With the Cartwright budget, the long-awaited opening had come for Macdonald. On March 10, 1876, in moving the Opposition's amendment to the budget, John A. at last argued openly for protection for Canadian industries. The government, he said, should order a "readjustment of the tariff," a move that would "afford fitting protection to the struggling manufacturers and industries, as well as the agriculture products of the country." Macdonald was now ready to "ring the changes on National Policy." It was to the picnic grounds of Ontario for the next two summers that the Old Chieftain went to prepare the way for the election of 1878. He was convinced he now had an issue that would obliterate memories of the Pacific Scandal.

When the House rose in May, Prime Minister Mackenzie wrote to his brother Charles that he'd finally been delivered from the worst session he was ever in.

The Campaign and the Candidates

The 1878 campaign was the first in which the state of the economy would be a major issue for voters and the candidates. The depression was spreading, creating unrest throughout the country. With a population of just over four million, Canada was losing more people to the States than it was gaining from Great Britain. There had been disturbances in Belleville, Ontario, followed by a riot in Quebec City. Striking labourers attacked a mob of strike-breakers and one man was killed when the government brought in 800 troops to restore order. With social assistance limited to that of church charities or occasional hand-outs by mean-spirited town councils, the unemployed, the ill and the aged were dependent on the meagre resources of themselves or their families. Many sent their young children into cold and ill-lit textile mills for 10 to 12 hours a day. Labourers were paid fifty cents a day and the more skilled, such as cotton carders in the textile mills, got only a dollar a day; butchers $1.25 and carpenters $1.50. It was some consolation that the 10-hour day, six days a week, was slowly replacing the 12-hour day. Female domestic servants got $6 to $9 a month and board. Farm workers, whose hours knew no limit, did well to earn $15 a month and food and lodging.[4] More attractive jobs could be found in the cities, and out of a work force of one and a quarter million, some 184,000 men had left the farms to take up manufacturing jobs. Sawmills and lumber yards were the biggest employers, followed by iron and steel foundries, clothing and shoe factories, leather tanneries, flour mills and food processing plants, and carriage works turning out everything from buggies to rolling stock for the new railways. They were the very industries that might benefit the most from higher tariffs.

Alexander Mackenzie's campaign faltered before it began, with the cabinet divided over whether the election should be held promptly in June, or put off until the fall. Liberal governments in the provinces wanted delay, as did the influential Edward Blake, the former Ontario premier and Reform MP who'd quit Ottawa because of ill health. Mackenzie, complaining of chest pains and loss of sleep, had planned to launch his campaign in Lindsay, Ontario, on May 28. He decided to hold the rally even though the election had not been called and brought his chief lieutenants, Cartwright and Laurier, with him. The crowd warmed more to Laurier's stirring call for national unity than it did to Mackenzie's defence of his government's tariff policy; he defended it as one that raises sufficient funds for the government but does not (as would Macdonald's) compel people "to pay a large taxation for the purpose of filling the pockets of some of our fellow citizens."[5] Moreover, "It was impossible for a nation to supply the entire home market by a protective tariff and to compete successfully in foreign markets." In Toronto the next day Mackenzie spoke at a carefully-staged "workingman's demonstration" where he put himself up as the friend of labour. He spoke of working long hours as a stonemason and declared that under a Liberal government "the humblest son of the humblest working man may find his way to the position that I now occupy." Mackenzie described Macdonald's proposal to apply the tariff to imported breadstuffs as the equivalent of taxing the bread that workers eat, the coal they burn, and the oil they consume. From Toronto, he went on to Sarnia and his home riding of Lambton, returning two weeks later to Ottawa.

The respite was brief. Mackenzie and his wife Jane planned a small party at their home in Ottawa on June 17, in celebration of their silver wedding anniversary. It turned sour, however, when a crowd of well-wishers showed up with gifts. Their generosity embarrassed the strait-laced Mackenzie, and he ordered Jane to re-wrap all the gifts and return them. He was glad, a few days later, to get out of the capital, first for a swing through Quebec and later a tour of the Maritimes. Still, he procrastinated at calling the election and it was not until August 17 that Mackenzie had the Governor General dissolve the House and issue a writ for voting to be held on September 17.

Neither party put out an official platform, but the snatches of speeches of Mackenzie and Macdonald reported by the press laid out clearly different approaches to the issues of the day. Macdonald grew more confident as he polished his picnic oratory, proclaiming at his campaign's biggest rally on August 27:

"There has risen in this country a Canadian party which declares that we must have Canada for the Canadians, which says that which is sauce for the goose is sauce for the gander, and which holds that if the Americans charge us twenty, or twenty-five, or thirty-five per cent on what we raise or produce there was no reason why we should not charge the same, if we pleased. I do not at all mean to say that we should copy the American tariff, because I believe it is very unscientific in many respects, but we have to follow in the direction of the American tariff, and if we do, we are going to have reciprocity of trade with the United States.

"The time has come, gentlemen, when the people of this Dominion have to declare whether Canada is for the Canadians, or whether it is to be a pasture for cows to be sent to England. It is for the electors to say whether every appliance of civilization shall be manufactured within her bounds for our own use, or whether we shall remain hewers of wood and drawers of water for the United States."[6]

The full account in the *Mail* was something of an exception in political reporting of the time; most coverage of political events consisted of descriptions long on colour and commentary but short on facts. The *Globe* especially, under the editorship of the elder statesman of the Reform and Liberal parties, George Brown, was given to printing lavish praise of Mackenzie ("the Premier") and Reformers. On September 6, in a front page article headlined Enthusiastic Ovation to the Premier, the *Globe* reported from Paisley, Ontario:

> "The Premier today added another to the list of ovations which he has received in the course of his progress through the Dominion. As was frequently remarked by the inhabitants of Paisley, that progressive little town had never before had so many people on its streets as assembled today in honour of Mr. Mackenzie."

The report added that Conservative candidate Alex Sproat had attempted to hijack the Liberal meeting by bringing in a crowd of supporters and forcing his way onto the platform. The *Globe* mainly paraphrased what Mackenzie said in his two-hour speech, asserting he had shown that protection was "utterly indefensible." A typical report on September 10 gave few direct quotes from Mackenzie's speech in Alvinston, Ontario, but assured readers that he had "clearly showed the hollowness of their (Tory) arguments, and that no high protective tariff would enrich all." A better insight into issues affecting the campaign was offered by a September 6 report from Hamilton, where four thousand people attended a Liberal rally at a newly-opened amphitheatre. A Liberal member of the provincial legislature, J.M. Williams, lamely tried to exonerate the government for the depression: "While no party regretted such depression more than himself and the political body to which he has the honour to belong, he has during his twenty years' business career in Canada experienced far harder times than now." His words must have been little consolation to those without jobs.

The Conservative Toronto *Telegram* carried quite impartial accounts of John A. Macdonald's speeches, but in the style of the day confined itself to paraphrasing his remarks. Under a headline The Coming Conflict, the paper reported on September 5: "On the matter of free trade, John A. Macdonald told a meeting at Albert Hall that everything else being equal, free trade might have its attractions, but to talk of a young people like us entering into free trade with people like those of the United States was simply to talk nonsense. Retail trade was said to be the worst that has been experienced for the last 20 years." As most newspaper readers shared the publisher's political views, the press of the era had little impact on most voters. Canadian newspapers were, however, trying to assert their independence from monied groups who backed them for political reasons. The president of the Canadian Press Association told his annual meeting that most newspapers had "got from under the control of the politicians; a paper very rarely depends for its support on any individual or party."

Across the country, the fever of the campaign depended on the heat of regional issues, a characteristic that was to become an enduring feature of Canadian politics. Prince Edward Island was voting in only its second federal election, with six seats at stake. Its former Premier, James Pope, campaigned in Queens County on his success in having won better terms for the island for its entrance to Confederation. As a Conservative, he supported the National Policy but painted it as a strategy that would force the U.S. into a free trade agreement. In New Brunswick, Leonard Tilley was again at the helm of Conservative forces after a turn as Lieutenant Governor. He warned Macdonald that higher tariffs to benefit Nova Scotia coal miners or Ontario flour millers were not popular in his province's 16 ridings. His old rivals, Albert J. Smith and Timothy Anglin, were standing again for the Liberals. In Nova Scotia another father of Confederation, Charles Tupper, was comfortably predicting a sweep for the Conservatives of most of that province's 21 seats.

The Roman Catholic hierarchy in Quebec, bitterly opposed to Catholic Liberalism, accused Wilfrid Laurier and other Liberals of promoting the principles of the French revolution. In turn, Archbishop Taschereau was accused of practicing "a reign of terror." The leading Conservative strategist, J. Israel Tarte, wisely switched off his party's attack on the *rouge* Liberals for spouting anticlericalism, to focus instead on the economic distress so widespread throughout Quebec. The campaign brought out huge audiences for the traditional all-candidate meetings, the *assemblées contradictoire*, and there was fierce competition in all sections of the province. Only four of 65 seats were filled by acclamation, compared to 29 in the 1874 election.

The commitment to build a Pacific railway remained the biggest issue in the West, although Manitoba was troubled by continuing friction between whites and Metis. Despite Mackenzie's lack of enthusiasm for the railway, he was closing the gap between Lake Superior and Winnipeg and had almost completed the Winnipeg-Pembina stretch that would link up with the American railroads. He had chosen a route through the Rocky Mountains via the Yellowhead Pass and surveying for the line was underway between Kamloops and Yale. The railway's speedy completion, far more than debate over tariffs, preoccupied those who would vote in the ten Western Canadian seats – four in Manitoba and six in British Columbia.

A majority of Ontario's 88 ridings – holding not far from half of the 206 seats in the House of Commons – would be needed to win the election. John A. Macdonald was renominated in Kingston and Alexander Mackenzie again carried the Liberal flag in Lambton. They were both Ontario Scots, but as dissimilar in personality and attitude as could be found between two men of similar background. Mackenzie, a frugal, family-centered, workaholic (although that term would never be heard in his lifetime) thought the voters would reward his honesty and diligence, if not his grand accomplishments. Macdonald was a totally different kind of man. Hard-drinking, high-spirited, he cared little for detail but very much for grand vision; his was of a united Canada from coast to coast, interconnected by rail, self-sufficient in all that mattered, and whatever might come, a loyal subject of the Crown. He had thought the Liberals could win if they called a June election; now he was convinced that his summer of picnic campaigning would carry him back to office. Still, he told his confidantes, "An election is like a horse race, you can tell more about it the next day."

A week before the election most of Canada basked in late summer weather. As southern Ontario residents went to bed on Tuesday night, September 10, it began to rain heavily and did not let up for four days. No one knew it at the time, but Ontario was being battered by Storm 5 of the 1878 hurricane season. It brought electioneering as well as most travel and business to a halt. The hurricane had made landfall at the Florida Keys, but rather than skirting the east coast it headed directly north, the eye crossing Lake Ontario just east of Toronto. HEAVEN'S OUTPOURING the *Telegram* headlined, while a *Globe* account of THE GREAT RAIN STORM recorded that forty thousand people turned out to view the demolished bridges, downed trees and damaged houses along the Don river. "Policemen stationed there had considerable difficulty in keeping the crowd back." Toronto's many ravines filled to overflowing, carrying off the garbage routinely left in the streets and swilling out the outhouses in people's backyards.

On election day, the storm now forgotten, party workers were out in force with liquor and money to entice supporters to the polls. The practice was so endemic in Canadian politics and both parties were so accustomed to such tactics that the misbehaviour of one side was likely to cancel out the sins of the other. More than half a million ballots would be marked in this first federal election to be held on a single day across Canada. Alexander Mackenzie had returned by train to Ottawa the previous afternoon, and he awaited the results that evening with his wife and a few aides. As telegrams from the ridings came in, the early results looked positive for the Liberals. Mackenzie carried 11 New Brunswick seats, including those of Albert Smith in Westmoreland and Timothy Anglin in Gloucester. As expected, Tilley won in Saint John, but by only nine votes, one of four Conservatives elected. In Prince Edward Island the picture was different, five of six seats going Conservative. The victors included James Pope, the former Premier, in Queen's County. Charles Tupper did almost as well for the Conservatives in Nova Scotia, winning his own riding of Cumberland along with 13 other seats. Two cabinet ministers went down, Alfred Jones, militia, in Halifax; and Thomas Coffin, receiver general, a poor third in Shelburne after the winning Tory and an unknown independent. The Maritime tally was 24 Conservatives, 19 Liberals, close enough for Mackenzie to yet draw even and perhaps even pull ahead.

The depth of the disaster that Mackenzie and the Liberals would suffer in 1878 became clear as the Quebec ridings reported. The Conservative strategy to draw out a protest vote against hard times worked almost flawlessly. Conservatives candidates won 57 of the province's 65 seats. The Tory tide was not strong enough to elect all the leading Conservatives, however; Hector Langevin, Macdonald's Quebec lieutenant, lost in Rimouski and J.J.C. Abbott, the railway lawyer and a future prime minister, was beaten in Argenteuil. A thousand supporters of Abbot's Liberal opponent, Dr. Thomas Christie, marched through the streets of Lachute, enjoyed a bonfire and the music of the Silver Cornet band imported from Montreal, and then set off fireworks to celebrate their victory.

The news was no better in Ontario. Richard Cartwright, who as minister of finance had stoutly resisted higher tariffs, became the third Liberal cabinet minister to be defeated when he lost Lennox riding by 59 votes, 1,299 to 1,358. Edward Blake, the former minister of justice, took a nomination in Bruce South and then went off to England for three months. Conservative lawyer Alexander Shaw defeated him by 75 votes, 2,673 to 2,598. Mackenzie won comfortably in Lambton, beating a J.A. Mackenzie by 146 votes, 2,707 to 2,561. Liberal pangs of defeat were only partly assuaged by the startling news from Kingston that John A. Macdonald had been rejected by his own voters; he drew just 847 votes to 991 for Alexander Gunn, a wholesale grocer standing for the Liberals. Ontario would send 62 Conservatives and just 26 Liberals to the new House of Commons. Added to the three out of four Manitoba seats the Conservatives would win, plus all six in British Columbia, Macdonald would return in triumph to Ottawa at the head of a phalanx of 142 government supporters, facing down 64 Liberals. It was almost the reverse of the 1874 outcome; Macdonald had won more than 53 per cent of the popular vote and a two to one margin in the House with a 68-seat majority. A few defections would take place but the Macdonald landslide would stand. "All gone," Mackenzie wrote to his friend James Young. "What a splendid lot of men ... There are hardly enough left to form a skeletal battalion."[7]

The Aftermath

Protection had carried the day and John A. Macdonald was to be given another chance to move Canada forward on what he saw as its path of destiny. The outcome of the 1878 election had by no means been certain; the likelihood of a discredited former prime minister regaining power would not have seemed great at the outset of the campaign. By capitalizing on the dissatisfaction over economic conditions and offering the appealing prospect of protective tariffs, Macdonald was able to win back enough former supporters to carry the day. Fewer than one in twenty voters switched from the party they'd supported in 1874, but it was sufficient to create a comfortable Conservative majority. The election had been hard-fought and both Liberal and Conservative newspapers expressed surprise at the outcome.

"Contrary to the anticipations of most persons, the verdict of the electors at the ballot boxes yesterday was unfavourable to Mr. Mackenzie's Administration," George Brown wrote in the *Globe*. "The Opposition has carried a majority of seats in the House of Commons – and the new Parliament will take its tone from this constitutional declaration of the people's will ... The issue on which the electoral contest mainly turned was the promise of Sir John A. Macdonald and his supporters, if elected, to enforce a system of thorough protection for home manufactures by the imposition of increased duties; and to retaliate upon the United States by the imposition against them of the same prohibitory Customs duties they now levy. That a policy so short-sighted and injurious should have been endorsed by the Canadian people is a regret." The *Telegram* agreed that the outcome was unexpected: "The result of the general election has been a great surprise – we may say a startling surprise, for even the most sanguine of Conservatives could not have expected so decided a triumph. Many Conservatives, indeed, would not have been surprised if the Mackenzie Administration had succeeded on squeezing in again by a bare majority. The result, however, shows that the feeling in favour of such a readjustment of the tariff as will give Canadian industry fair play was stronger and more general than anybody supposed – for, of course, this was the main plank upon which the Conservative party sailed into power."

Sir John A. Macdonald took the oath of office on October 17, 1878 and set about creating a new cabinet. Leonard Tilley took on finance and the responsibility for the higher tariffs promised by the National Policy. In his first budget, Tilley swept away the old Liberal tariff structure with new import duties ranging from 20 to 40 per cent. This would serve two purposes: to increase government revenue – essential in the era before income or sales taxes – and to provide protection for Canada's nascent industrial machine. The assault on American imports was wide-ranging. Farm implements from the U.S. were hit with 25 per cent duty, bringing immediate joy to the Massey and Harris families in Toronto, as well as their employees.

The extent to which Macdonald believed in tariff protection as an economic necessity for a young and developing country, or whether he saw the National Policy simply as a winning political strategy, has never been satisfactorily established. In either case, the "NP" became the third of the chief planks on which Macdonald consolidated his political base. It differed from the other two – westward expansion and an all-Canadian railway route – by providing Canada with an economic strategy that would endure without major change for almost a century. Introduction of the new tariffs coincided with a return to prosperity and the "departure of the dark days of deficits." Conservatives attributed higher government revenues and better business conditions to "the timely adoption of a wise and well-considered National Policy."[8]

Having been beaten soundly on issues as well as personality, Mackenzie hung on as Leader of the Opposition until the spring of 1880. He resigned, unsure of his health and uncertain of his future, to turn over the leadership to Edward Blake, the favourite of the Liberal caucus who had returned to the House via a by-election. Blake recognized the political liability of the traditional Reform-Liberal stance on free trade. In the session of 1882, he began to call for lower tariffs to reduce the cost of living. In preparation for the general election that year Macdonald used the need for redistribution of seats in Parliament as the opportunity to inflict "the Great Gerrymander" on his opponents. While enlarging the House to 211 seats he managed to inject Conservative-voting districts into many Liberal constituencies. It was helpful in retaining his hold on power in the 1882 election. Macdonald went back with 139 seats, only three fewer than he'd won four years earlier. The Liberals suffered their worst-ever showing in Quebec, electing only 13 members. Macdonald was by now truly the "Old Chieftain" and his followers paid tribute to him with huge banquets in Toronto and Montreal, one to honour his forty years in politics and the other to mark his 70th birthday.

The 1878 election marked a crucial turning point in Canada's political and economic development. By embracing the National Policy, the country committed to building its own manufacturing industries rather than relying on the United States for factory-made goods. Nor would it try to compete with American producers, whose larger market would finance the new technology and better training needed for a new era of mass production. Canada's determination to go it alone would be tested time and again in its future, but the 1878 election set the country firmly if stubbornly on its own irreversible path of destiny.

CHAPTER FOUR

The Federal Election of June 23, 1896

THE ISSUES

Antagonisms of race, religion and language threaten Canada's peaceful growth, especially in the West, as the country ponders its direction into the 20th century. Divisions between French-speaking Roman Catholics and the majority British Protestant population – notably over the Manitoba Schools Question – mar national unity. The performance of the Conservative government under four Prime Ministers in five years following the death of Sir John A. Macdonald plays a major role in the election. The victory of Wilfrid Laurier as Canada's first French-speaking Prime Minister eases English-French divisions, sets the stage for an era of Liberal party paramountcy, and opens the West for rapid settlement.

THE PERSONALITIES

CONSERVATIVE PARTY

Sir Charles Tupper, Prime Minister and last Father of Confederation
Dalton McCarthy, MP and Protestant activist
George E. Foster, MP, Minister of Finance
Sir Hector Langevin, MP, ousted for corruption

LIBERAL PARTY

Wilfrid Laurier, MP, Arthabaska, Leader of the Opposition
J. Israel Tarte, MP, Montmorency (former Conservative)
Honoré Mercier, Premier of Quebec, dismissed for corruption
Sir Oliver Mowat, Premier of Ontario
Thomas Greenway, Premier of Manitoba

THE RESULTS

	SEATS	VOTES
Liberal Party	118	405,185 (45.1%)
Conservative Party	88	414,838 (46.1%)
Others	7	79,023 (8.8%)

Wilfrid Laurier campaigning in Berlin (Kitchener), Ontario, for the election that made him Canada's first French-speaking Prime Minister.

WILFRID LAURIER
AND THE CANADIAN CENTURY

The Federal Election of 1896

The skilled workmen who built the Massey Music Hall, the grand edifice that brought culture to the people of Toronto, considered it one of their greatest achievements. The masons, carpenters, and painters who had worried over every detail of architect Sidney Badgley's fine new building would come back often to gaze on their work, if not to actually attend the fancy concerts and lectures that were filling its more than three thousand seats night after night. Tonight, just two years after industrialist Hart Massey had opened his "gift to aid in the development of the arts," a performance of a different sort was taking place. The federal election was only a few days away, and Sir Charles Tupper, the Premier – as Canada's government leaders were then known – was here for one of the last big rallies in the Conservative government's campaign to win a fifth successive term.

The crowd began to gather early, skirmishing for places in line just after five o'clock of this mild June Friday, filling St. Enoch's Square, the open space that the hall looked out on at the corner of Shuter and Victoria streets. Organizers had distributed hundreds of tickets to Tory employers and known party supporters, intending to restrict admission to those who would give Sir Charles a warm welcome. The police were here to help screen out doubtful cases, but it soon became impossible to tell friend from foe, so many were reaching out to demand tickets. By half past six, with the hall filling rapidly, more workmen began to pour in from nearby factories. A hundred came from Kemp Manufacturing, and as many from the rival Cobban Manufacturing, up the street. A hundred and fifty men from Thompson's Silverplate factory wore tin badges attesting to their place of work. Most elbowed their way in without tickets. For many it was a chance for an evening of entertainment as much as to hear the Premier and consider his message before voting on Tuesday. They sang lustily from the song sheets given them, all the while peering around the hall where Union Jacks hung at both sides of the stage. A large framed painting of a maple leaf had been erected above the rows of platform seats that were now being filled by important guests. Banners had been hung, emblazoned with Tory slogans: Canada for the Canadians; A British Subject I Was Born, a British Subject I Will Die. One banner, pointing up the success of the government's National Policy on tariffs, posed the question: How Many Bicycles Would Have Been Manufactured in Canada Under Free Trade?

Tupper faced a hostile audience from the moment he stepped on the platform. For two and a half hours, he endured jeers, groans, and catcalls, giving as good as he received. It was the rowdiest of the 42 rallies – from Winnipeg to Cape Breton – that he would address in the last three weeks of the campaign. "You are the most ruffianly set of cowards I ever looked at," Tupper finally told his hecklers. "You ought to be hounded out of Toronto to prevent its being disgraced by your presence." The next day, the Toronto *Telegram* called it "the most disorderly meeting ever held in the city." The rabidly Liberal *Globe* headlined its report: "TUPPER COMES – He Sees Also, But Does Not Conquer."

It was the eve of the twentieth century, near the end of a decade that would come to be known as the Gay Nineties, the prelude to a great new century that would mark the young country of Canada for future greatness. At Massey Hall this night, Tupper would confront all the issues that were making this election such a tumultuous one. He knew that his government's resistance to Manitoba's abolition of its separate school system for Catholics and French speakers was eating away at the British Protestant support that had been a bedrock of Sir John A. Macdonald's Liberal-Conservative coalition. While Tupper's stance on the "Manitoba Schools Question" was earning him the reluctant endorsement of Catholic prelates, he understood very well that the rank and file of Quebeckers was inclined toward supporting the Liberal chieftain, Wilfrid Laurier. They were drawn to Laurier by race and religion as much as by politics and would be voting Liberal in hopes of putting a French-Canadian in power at Ottawa.

Sir Charles Tupper was the last Father of Confederation to fill the office of Prime Minister. He faced the task, nearly thirty years after the union of British North America, of convincing a new generation of Canadians that Macdonald's coalition, having built the Canada they knew of railways, factories and prospering farms, still had the best men to manage the affairs of the country. The Conservative government had been floundering since Sir John A's death in 1891, and Tupper was the fourth Prime Minister of the country in as many years. His political career went back to his doctoring days in pre-Confederation Nova Scotia where he rose to be Premier, won a seat in the new Canadian Parliament in 1867, and sat in Macdonald's cabinets until becoming High Commissioner to Britain in 1880. Tupper was now 76 but his face, with its frame of wavy hair and its penetrating eyes, still showed much of the devilish handsomeness that had captivated his many female friends. He would almost certainly have become Prime Minister sooner were it not for his dreadful reputation as an incorrigible womanizer and adulterer. Lady Aberdeen, wife of the Governor General Lord Aberdeen, would have none of him.[1]

Standing in Tupper's way was a politician of a younger generation, Wilfrid Laurier, reared in a devout French Catholic family but educated in English at McGill University, an *avocat*, an editorialist, and a *rouge* who had been condemned by the Roman Catholic hierarchy as a revolutionary, a blasphemer and a hypocrite. Fifty-five years old – a much younger man from an entirely different milieu than Tupper – Laurier possessed a vision of a different kind of Canada. In his nine years as leader of the Liberal party, he had extolled the ideal of a bi-racial Canada with English and French living in harmony, independent of Britain but committed to British values of justice, law and order. Laurier pictured the country as moving through "an era of transition" from the early days of Confederation to full nationhood, a loyal member of the Empire but with its destiny in the new world, not the old. He put himself among those who recognized that Canada faced "abuses to be reformed, new horizons to be opened up, and new forces to be developed."

The last spike in the Canadian Pacific railway had been driven in far off Craigallachie, B.C., in 1885, fulfilling John A. Macdonald's promise of a transcontinental rail link between east and west. Macdonald was truly building a nation, founded on the English-French entente that he had crafted in creating Canada in 1867. Completion of the railway followed Macdonald's comfortable re-election in 1882, when he won his biggest majority ever in Quebec, 51 of 65 seats. Within months, the Canadian Pacific would be used to carry Northwest Mounted Police and militia to the western plains. There, Canadian troops would put down Louis Riel's abortive North West rebellion, sowing the seeds of Conservative disintegration along the banks of the South Saskatchewan river. The Metis leader's short-lived provisional government lasted just long enough to justify a charge of treason. Riel was hanged in Regina, his appeal for clemency denied by Macdonald and his cabinet. The decision inflamed Catholic Quebec. Mass rallies in Montreal demanded revenge, which came in the next provincial election when voters turned out a Conservative regime in favour of a new nationalist party headed by ex-Liberal Honoré Mercier. Generations would pass before most Quebeckers would feel completely comfortable voting for the Conservative party. In 1887, campaigning against the mercurial Liberal leader Edward Blake, Macdonald managed to hold on to 33 seats in Quebec, enough to give him a third consecutive majority, 126-89. Blake soon resigned, to be succeeded by the young Wilfrid Laurier. Macdonald would have yet one more election in him – 1891 – when in his "last hurrah" he would face the rising new star of the Liberal party from Quebec.

The Fateful Mix: Religion, School and Language

The religious and racial divisions of post-Confederation Canada deepened in the last years of Macdonald's life. The accord between English and French, Protestant and Catholic, survived as long as there was little economic rivalry or social contact between the groups. As industry developed and social mobility increased, religious prejudices overlapped into the political and economic arenas. No one was more adept at fuelling Protestant resentments than Dalton McCarthy, a prominent Conservative driven by an obsessive fear of Catholics and the French. McCarthy, born in northern Ireland of a staunch Protestant family, came to Canada as an 11-year-old, his family settling near Barrie, Ontario. McCarthy became a lawyer, was elected to the House of Commons in 1876, and sat continuously for North Simcoe until his death in 1898. He whetted his anti-Catholicism on the Jesuits Estates Act, a Quebec government bill that compensated church institutions for the loss of property taken over after the British conquest of New France. He and his followers demanded that Macdonald's government disallow the legislation, but it never did.

Supporting McCarthy and his allies were such groups as the Equal Rights League, the Protestant Protective Association in Ontario, and the Loyal Orange Order throughout English Canada. They would be satisfied by nothing less than suppression of the French language in Canada and abolition of Roman Catholic separate schools in the North West Territories, an area still under federal jurisdiction, and in Manitoba. Like McCarthy, the Orange Order drew its inspiration from Irish Protestantism. It was founded there in 1795 to commemorate the victory of England's William II, known as William of Orange, over the Catholics at the Battle of the Boyne in 1690. King Billy's victory was faithfully marked by lusty Orange parades in every Ontario town on July 15 each year, well into the 20th century. Its strident anti-Catholic and pro-British propaganda led often to social disturbances that sometimes turned into riots.

McCarthy had a strong following in still sparsely-settled Manitoba and the Liberal government of Thomas Greenway was pleased to oblige he and his followers on the schools question; it faced its own pressures from a largely English-speaking electorate and had been fending off the embarrassments of a series of scandals. At a meeting that McCarthy was addressing in Portage la Prairie in 1889, the Attorney General of the Province, Joseph Martin, rose to announce brusquely that henceforth French would no longer be used in the schools and that Catholic schools would be cut off from public funds. True to Martin's word, the Manitoba Legislature in 1890 abolished the official use of French in the government and the courts and merged Catholic separate and Protestant public schools into a single non-denominational system. The actions violated the Manitoba Act of 1870 under which the new province had promised unqualified protection to the French-speaking and Catholic minorities and their schools. The terms of Confederation empowered the Dominion government to override provincial legislation. The denial of con-stitutionally-guaranteed rights to any minority arguably called for federal intervention. Thus began what would become known as the Manitoba Schools Question. It would drag out for seven years and would confront four Conservative prime ministers, none of whom would be able to bring about a solution, with the most intractable puzzle in Canadian political history. The issue was barely mentioned, however, in the 1891 election; both sides were content to wait for the courts to adjudicate the legality of Manitoba's action.

Laurier's first election was a disappointment for the Liberals. Running against a tired but entrenched government, Laurier committed a serious strategic error. Instead of attacking the weaknesses of the administration he put a radical policy of his own to the voters: complete free trade with the United States, or in the language of the era, "unrestricted reciprocity (U.R.)." Macdonald seized on the issue with glee. Ironically, he had tried and failed to win reciprocity in trade with Washington just a year earlier. The Conservative poster summed it up neatly: The Old Flag, The Old Policy, The Old Leader. Anything different was treasonous and annexationist. UR was just a smokescreen to lead Canada into complete commercial union and eventual annexation by the United States. Macdonald made it clear in his election manifesto: "As for myself, my course is clear. A British subject I was born – a British subject I will die." On March 5, 1891, he carried over fifty-six per cent of the vote, winning 121 seats against 94 for the Liberals. Laurier's appeal in Quebec, however, cost Macdonald his majority there; 37 Liberals were elected to just 28 Conservatives. Three months after the election, Macdonald would be dead of a stroke in his sleep.

It took a combination of fresh corruption scandals, unimaginative leadership, and interminable squabbling over the Manitoba Schools Question to create the opening to bring Wilfrid Laurier to power. After Macdonald's death the Conservative caucus turned first to the aging Sir John J.C. Abbott, Montreal lawyer and Senator who lasted but a year as Prime Minister, claiming it was the worst experience of his life. His successor, the Nova Scotian John Thompson, had to overcome the prejudice of his conversion to Catholicism (a "pervert" some called him), and might well have navigated the shoals of the schools issue had he lived longer. He died after two years in office, collapsing while having lunch at Windsor Castle with Queen Victoria and her cabinet.

In December 1894, it became the turn of another Senator, newspaper owner Mackenzie Bowell from Belleville, Ontario, to try to patch together a solution. Bowell was an unlikely choice for the task. As the former Grand Master of the Orange Order in Canada, he was torn between devotion to his fiercely Protestant religious principles that permitted little tolerance for Catholic institutions, and his dread that failure to reverse Manitoba's actions would further imperil his government's already tremulous support in Quebec. Within a month of his taking office, the Judicial Committee of the Privy Council in London made its final ruling on the schools issue: the Dominion government had all the legal power it needed to pass remedial legislation restoring minority rights in Manitoba. The government no longer had room to maneuver, it was either remediate, or abandon its constitutional obligations. One last appeal would be made to Manitoba: restore the separate schools or face a legislative *diktat*. Letters went back and forth between Ottawa and Winnipeg, each causing more dissension in Bowell's cabinet; resignations flew as English ministers quit because the demands were too intrusive, French ministers quit because Bowell wasn't firm enough in his orders to Manitoba. With another session of Parliament frittered away without a resolution, Bowell promised in July that if no agreement could be reached with Manitoba, a remedial bill would be introduced in Parliament not later than January 2, 1896.

Among the cast of characters involved in plotting Liberal strategy over the Manitoba Schools Question, none was closer to Laurier's heart than Joseph-Israel Tarte, the brilliant, caustic and often impulsive former Conservative who had turned his back on Macdonald to become one of the Liberal leader's chief advisors in Quebec. "They are in the den of lions," laughed Tarte, observing the near-impossible situation in which the government had gotten itself. In the tradition of many Quebec politicians in this era, Tarte owned newspapers in Montreal and Quebec City and used them to advance his interests. Once an ultramontane, an adherent of an especially authoritarian strain of Catholicism, he had strongly supported the role of the Roman Catholic church in public life. After breaking with Macdonald and being elected as an independent in 1891, Tarte had brought a delightful package of evidence to Parliament about corruption in high levels of the government. It concerned dealings between Thomas McGreevy, an MP and building contractor, and Hector Langevin, Macdonald's chief lieutenant in Quebec and the minister of public works. Tarte's disclosures led to a Parliamentary inquiry. McGreevy went to jail and Langevin, who might have become Prime Minister, was forced to resign. It wasn't the only scandal of the time. In 1892, a large part of a railway subsidy meant for construction of a new line in Quebec was found to have been diverted to the provincial Liberal party. The lieutenant governor of the day had no choice but to dismiss the premier, Honoré Mercier, resulting in a Conservative landslide in the election that followed.

Tarte, as a good Catholic, felt strongly about separate school rights in Manitoba. He urged Laurier to support remedial legislation. At the opposite pole, John Willison, the influential Liberal editor of the Toronto *Globe*, harped on the need to respect provincial rights. Coercion against Manitoba, he warned Laurier in letter after letter, would lead to a backlash in the rest of the country and threaten the very existence of Confederation. Willison's pragmatic advice finally convinced Laurier. He realized that whatever chance he had of carrying English Canada would evaporate if he supported remediation. He had no choice; better to lose Catholic support than to lose the country.

With Manitoba flatly resisting Ottawa's entreaties to reconsider, Bowell took the government into the fifth year of its mandate with the schools issue still unsettled. Sir Charles Tupper has been brought back to Ottawa late in 1895, ostensibly for consultations but actually to be ready backstage for a coup that would dump the ineffectual Bowell. There was soon another round of cabinet resignations, while Tupper found himself back in the House after winning a by-election in Nova Scotia. The very day of Tupper's return, February 11, Bowell had the long-promised "Remedial Act of Manitoba," Bill 28, given first reading. It ordered the province to set up a Board of Education for separate schools, and to exempt Roman Catholic parents from public school taxes. The furor was all but unbearable. In Manitoba, Premier Greenway called the bill "monstrous." Dalton McCarthy and his Protestant rights' groups were outraged, while Roman Catholic clerics demanded swift passage. Father Lacombe, the pioneering priest of the western prairies, wrote to Laurier that if the Conservative government fell over remediation, "the episcopacy, like one man, united to the clergy, will rise to support those who may have fallen to defend us."[2]

The remedial bill put Laurier and his Liberals in a difficult position. The whole problem had been caused by a provincial Liberal government in the first place, and the federal Liberals at this time were strongly committed to supporting provincial rights; it was the Conservatives who were the centralists of the day. Laurier also knew that as a Catholic, he would risk losing what support he had of the English Protestant population by endorsing remediation. For five years, Laurier had skillfully avoided taking a firm position. He held to his view that the solution to the crisis would be found in accommodation rather than coercion. Recalling Aesop's fable of the blustering wind and the warm sun, he asked an Ontario audience which of them had been able to make the traveller take off his coat? "The government have blown and raged and threatened, but the more they have threatened and raged and blown the more that man Greenway has stuck to his coat. If it were in my power, I would try the sunny way."[3]

Admirers from that day forward would praise Laurier for his "sunny ways." When he rose in Parliament on March 3 to speak on the Remedial Act, he cleverly executed the one tactic that could save him from condemnation by either side: delay. "Never," Laurier told the House, "did I feel so strong in the consciousness of right, as I do now, at this anxious moment; when, in the name of the constitution so outrageously misinterpreted by the government, in the name of peace and harmony in this land; when in the name of the minority which this bill seeks or pretends to help, in the name of this young nation on which so many hopes are centered, I rise to ask this Parliament not to proceed any further with this bill." He concluded by calling for a six-month "hoist" – a position also favoured by Dalton McCarthy – realizing full well that would mean the death of the bill, as Parliament's five-year mandate would soon expire. Laurier's amendment, as he knew it would be, was defeated when it came to a vote at 6 a.m. on March 20, after an all-night debate: 115 for the government, 91 for the Liberal motion. Seven Liberal Catholics broke ranks to support Bowell; 18 anti-remedial Conservatives voted with the opposition. Later that day, Bill 28 cleared second reading, 112 to 94. The Justice committee began clause by clause examination on April 6, but a Liberal filibuster ensured that the bill would go no further. On April 24, two days before Parliament's five-year mandate was to come to an end, Bowell gave up. The House was prorogued and an election was called for June 23. Only on May 1 did Tupper become Prime Minister in fact as well as in form.

Trains, Ships and Mounted Police

In the run-up to the 1896 election, the scope of government was still remote from the average citizen. The Canadian government's main concerns were building and operating the railways, canals, and public buildings that made up the country's infrastructure. So close were ties with the railways that the Toronto *Globe* referred to the Canadian Pacific as the "Tory government on wheels." The Sault Ste. Marie canal had just been completed and the St. Lawrence River canals that allowed ship passage above Montreal had been deepened to 14 feet. It all meant Canada was "nearing the end of extraordinary expenditures for heavy public works," the minister of finance, George Foster of New Brunswick, told the House in his 1894 budget speech. He asked parliament to spend just thirty eight million dollars, hardly more than seven dollars for each of the country's five million people, but even this would mean a two million dollar deficit. Throne speeches, rather than setting out ambitious plans for the future, ran to no more than a few paragraphs. The Throne speech that year noted the necessity to "observe the greatest possible economy" in government spending due to reductions in revenues caused by the depression "which has prevailed throughout the world for the past few years." One hundred and fifty thousand dollars would be saved by cutting the ranks of the Northwest Mounted Police from 900 to 700 men. Later, MPs such as Frank Oliver, newspaper owner and Liberal from Edmonton, would complain that too much was being spent educating Indians in government residential schools.

Along with religion, it was tariffs, always tariffs, that dominated the political debates of the last decades of the nineteenth century. Foster's budgets set out the details of customs tariffs and excise taxes in excruciating detail, every jot of revenue being totaled whether it be from the import of molasses, alcohol, biscuits, jams or metals. He explained it this way: "There are only three possible principles on which our tariff can be modelled: free trade, under which you have no customs imposts at all; a revenue tariff which selects a list of articles with a view to the quickest, easiest and best method of raising the amount which is necessary; and the protective tariff, by which you select a certain list of articles and place upon them certain rates with a view to raising a certain amount of money ... (whilst you) stimulate the development of the country, help make its industrial life broad and diversified ... to manufacture in the country as much as possible of what the people have to consume."[4] It was the third option that Canada has chosen under the National Policy of Macdonald and his successors.

With all the talk about tariffs, social issues such as health services or the conditions of workers or children earned scant attention on the hustings. The labour movement was agitating for laws on working conditions, universal education and civil rights, but it hadn't yet begun to put up candidates or organize voters. The Toronto District Labour Council sketched the early outlines of a welfare state with a long and prophetic list of demands that included public ownership of public utilities, an eight-hour day, abolition of child labour under sixteen, and abolition of the Senate. The Council also sought "equal pay, civil and political rights for men and women; abolition of laws discriminating against women; national insurance of working people against accidents, lack of employment and want in old age." None of these issues, however, would be spoken of in the 1896 campaign.

Canadians on the cusp of the twentieth century were accustomed to sickness and disease, with practically every family losing children or parents prematurely from such ills as typhoid, diphtheria, and tuberculosis. In Toronto, the newly appointed Medical Health officer, Dr. Hastings, targeted the water and milk supply for cleanup, as well as the barns and stables that housed thousands of horses. The electric streetcar and occasional motor vehicles built by local wagon makers such as Dixon's Carriage Works were slowly replacing horse-drawn carriages, reducing the manure deposited on the city's streets. The best streets were paved with cobblestone, or cedar blocks, and the city's 180,000 residents trod wooden sidewalks. Lamplighters made regular rounds, lighting gas-fueled street lamps each evening and extinguishing them in the morning. Bicycles were rapidly becoming the most popular form of transportation, aided by Dr. Dunlop's new invention, the pneumatic tire. On the Sunday before the election, thousands rode out College Street to High Park to enjoy an afternoon of picnics.

The Campaign and the Candidates

Both parties had known for months that an election was imminent, and Sir Charles Tupper plunged into the campaign from the moment of his swearing in as Prime Minister. He was on his way the next day to Montreal where he spent the rest of the week before swinging out West to Winnipeg, with rallies en route at North Bay, Fort William and Port Arthur (now Thunder Bay). Tupper held a strategy session with candidates in Winnipeg, going over the consequences of the Schools Act. To put things in a better light in Manitoba, he recruited star candidate Hugh John Macdonald, son of the late Prime Minister, to be his new Minister of the Interior. Hugh John would run in Winnipeg against the Liberal attorney general Joseph Martin, on the secret under-standing that he could resign right after the election. In Quebec, Tupper struggled in the absence of a powerful and committed lieutenant. Georges E. Cartier, Macdonald's partner in Confederation was long dead; J-A Tarte's defection was now only a memory; Hector Langevin was forgotten; and now J-A Chapleau, a former premier and Macdonald cabinet member, refused to run because of the failure to pass the remedial bill. Tupper found a weak replacement in the current premier, Louis Taillion. With his party in Quebec in disarray, Tupper knew that Conservative prospects would rest more heavily on the influence of the Catholic Church than on any provincial politician. Throughout English Canada, Tupper would have to put up with defections by Dalton McCarthy and a gaggle of Protestant opponents of remediation. All told, there would be seventy inde-pendents in the race, mostly anti-remedial, including nine supporters of McCarthy, 26 disgruntled Liberals under the banner of the farm-based Patrons of Industry, and five from the anti-Catholic Protestant Protective Association. For the first time, a serious third party presence was being felt in a Canadian election campaign. One couldn't be sure which side would suffer more: Conservatives were losing supporters disdainful of the government's efforts to bring Manitoba to account, while many Liberals were disgruntled with a leader who might bring back separate schools.

The Conservative campaign would be both negative and duplicitous; in Quebec Wilfrid Laurier would be painted as a traitor to his race and religion; in Ontario and the rest of English Canada as an untrustworthy and disloyal Frenchman, sure to hand over the reins of power and privilege to his Catholic friends and ultimately likely to deliver the country to the Yankees. English and French Canada were still largely unilingual and isolated from each other; what was uttered in Quebec in French was unlikely to be repeated elsewhere in English or vice versa. Tupper was determined to wage an aggressive campaign, and this he did, from his first campaign meeting in Winnipeg, Sir John A's son at his side, to his last big rally, in Toronto. When Tupper arrived at Brydon's Skating Rink in Winnipeg that Friday evening of May 8, there were a number of women in the overflow audience, a noteworthy enough twist to a political meeting of that era to cause comments in the local newspapers. Appealing to those who "have turned their backs upon me," Tupper tackled the schools question head on. He spoke as a father of Confederation, and recalled his days with Macdonald, Cartier and the others who accepted separate schools as a condition of bringing Upper and Lower Canada together. The issue in the election, he declared, "is not a question of separate schools, but simply whether the constitution is to be respected." Protestants were given the same rights in Quebec, Tupper added. None of his arguments, however, seemed to win over the crowd. Manitoba had been first settled, it was true, by French and Irish Catholics but the burgeoning population of the young province was becoming more heavily English. Tupper had been speaking for only a few minutes, the Winnipeg *Tribune* reported, when "it became evident to all that the anti-remedialists were in possession of the meeting." Nor did Tupper get much help from the son of John A. Hugh John supported the rights of the Catholic minority, but added: "I want to see Protestant and Catholic children educated together. That would do much to remove the ignorance that lies at the root of bigotry."

This was a line not greatly different from that taken by Wilfrid Laurier. The Liberal leader of the Opposition had learned a lot since his loss in 1891. He knew that rather than put forward a firm Liberal alternative to the Remedial Act, it would be far wiser to concentrate on how four Conservative Prime Ministers had left the issue unresolved; once in power, Laurier would find a way to reach an accommodation that all sides could live with. Laurier also understood very well that he needed to reach out to all Canadians as someone they could trust. His English was impeccable, he was an ardent admirer of British institutions including the monarchy, and he was fully committed to Canada's increased autonomy and independence within the Empire. It was this message that Laurier had carried to voters in Western Canada just two years before, and which he honed in further speeches across Ontario in the fall of 1895. He and his wife Zoë, accompanied by a phalanx of English-speaking Liberals, had introduced themselves to the West via a campaign-style train trip that took them through northern Ontario and to all the new cities beyond the Lakes. Liberal organizers, capitalizing on public curiosity, delivered full houses everywhere Laurier went; six thousand at the Brydon rink in Winnipeg; smaller but equally enthusiastic audiences in Brandon and Regina; another five thousand, or a third of the population, at the Market Building in Victoria; rapturous crowds in Vancouver, Edmonton and Calgary, towns then of only a few thousand people. Everywhere in the West he went, his message was the same: "The one aim that I have is to unite all the races on this continent into a Canadian nation, to develop this confederation upon the lines that once impelled Sir John Macdonald and George Brown to cease a life-long struggle and unite for the common good." And he prophesied: "The day will not be far distant when these fertile plains shall be teeming with population – with millions of population, happy, contented and progressive."[5]

Having enjoyed such success in his Western tour in 1894, Laurier had no intention of spending campaign time there in 1896. Nor was Ontario likely to offer many friendly platforms for the Liberal leader; he would spend no more than 10 days of the two-month campaign there. He would concentrate on Quebec. If he could pick off most of its 65 seats, he'd be well on his way to a Liberal majority.

If Tupper faced skeptical audiences as he opened his campaign, Laurier was surrounded with cheering crowds at his opening rally in Montreal the day after Parliament was dissolved. It all began with a torch light parade to Sohmer Park and a crowd said to number twelve thousand, with stops on the way at Champ de Mars (scene of the Riel riots back in 1885) and Place Viger. The entire Liberal delegation from Quebec was with him, and Laurier was speaking to his own people, promising them a future better than anything they'd known before. It also bore signs of Israël Tarte's work, the careful organization, the adequate funding from various sources, and an array of new candidates like Henri Bourassa, the grandson of the revered Louis Papineau, *le Patriot*. The English were well represented, too: the presence of English-Canadian Liberals like R.R. Dobell, president of the Quebec Board of Trade, and Sydney Fisher from Brome, gave solid evidence of Laurier's broad support.

All that was very well in Quebec, but how was Laurier to carry Ontario? On May 5, came the triumphal announcement: The long-time Premier of Ontario, Sir Oliver Mowat, would join a Laurier government. It is to be a Laurier-Mowat ticket, Liberal newspapers headlined. Mowat would not be standing as a candidate, but he had agreed to accept appointment to the Senate in the event of a Liberal victory, and to join the cabinet, perhaps as minister of justice. It was a popular choice not only in Ontario. Mowat's name also meant a lot in Quebec; the Ontario premier was well regarded for his tolerant treatment of Catholics and his respect for their rights to separate schools. When Mowat came to Montreal to join Laurier on the platform at Cochrane's Auditorium, the crowd's reception was "absolutely without limit," the *Globe* reported. The Ontario premier apologized for not being able to speak French, but this was hardly expected, and it didn't seem to matter. The rally also gave Laurier the opportunity, which he would take at every meeting in his home province, to contrast the unity of the Liberal party with the dissension in Conservative ranks. While Quebec Conservatives were shouting for remedial legislation, every Conservative in Ontario was opposed to it, he was telling his audiences. He would "secure justice for the minority without estranging the majority."

Both parties had set out their platforms in formal statements. Voters learned about them in long newspaper articles. The Liberal platform came from the 1893 Liberal convention in Ottawa, the first national gathering by either party. The idea had come from John Willison, and it pushed Liberal branches in every province into setting up riding associations where there had been none, and reorganizing and expanding existing ones. Two thousand delegates showed up. It gave Laurier the chance to attack the National Policy as "a fraud, a failure, and dangerous" to the future of the country. The platform that came out of the meeting charged the Conservatives with using the tariff system "as a corrupting agency wherewith to keep themselves in office." The Liberals pledged to seek a reciprocity agreement with the United States, run a pure administration, practice "the strictest economy" in administering the government, and ensure that free public lands in the West "go to actual settlers only, not to speculators." There was also a call for Senate reform, vague though it was: amend the constitution to bring the Senate "into harmony with the principles of popular government." The Liberal-Conservative party, as it was still formally known, devoted its platform to reciting the achievements of past governments: a great railway and canal system, development of processing and manufacturing, and a future that would see Canada grow rich on transshipping goods from Asia and Australia to Britain and Europe via its railways and a new fast steamship service across the Atlantic.

Laurier presented himself as the almost perfect candidate, beautifully-spoken, handsome, free of the taint of scandal or suspicion, and "more English than the English" in his admiration of British institutions. Tupper, simply because he'd been in public life so long, attracted the inevitable criticisms that come to a veteran office-holder. But Tupper also had some personal mannerisms that worked against him. He was taunted constantly for his incessant use of "I" in his speeches, as if he was personally responsible for everything accomplished in Canada the past thirty years. He also was the butt of cruel remarks about his personal life. Dalton McCarthy, denying that Tupper was ashamed of having been his political godfather, said that he, McCarthy, would be ashamed "to be numbered among the numerous progeny who claimed Sir Charles as father." He added coyly that there were other facts about Tupper he would not raise in the presence of ladies.[6]

Laurier expected attacks from the church and they were not long in coming. On Sunday, May 16, a *mandemant* was read in all of Quebec's churches, signed by every bishop in the province. It didn't specifically tell parishioners to vote Conservative; rather, they should support only those candidates who could solemnly affirm their commitment to vote in Parliament to restore separate school rights. Only Laurier and seven other Liberal candidates refused to give such a pledge.

In many parts of Canada, arguments over the tariff outranked the schools question. Young Robert Borden, running in Halifax, decried the time spent by Parliament on the schools issue as "out of all proportion to its importance." The Halifax *Morning Herald* declared that "the great issue must, of course, be that same great issue which has divided the two political parties in Canada for twenty years or more, namely the trade issue." Trade and the National Policy also helped Tupper throughout Ontario. His meetings there brought out local manufacturers and their workers to shout support for the tariffs that helped keep their factories running. The N.P. is the Life of the Town, declared a banner hung at Tupper's meeting in Berlin, Ontario (now Kitchener). At his Ottawa rally, in a hall festooned with signs declaring Canada for the Canadians, No Annexation, Tupper said he'd found great changes since he'd last lived in Ottawa. "Those who remember the dark days from 1873 to 1878 during which the Liberal party administered the public affairs of this country will bear witness with pride to the marvelous contrast which Ottawa presents today to its appearance in 1878." In British Columbia, Conservatives felt they had a winner in former Premier Richard McBride, who ran in New Westminster. However, voters seemed more concerned about flooding of the Fraser river than arguments about schools in Manitoba. McBride's opponent, Aulay Morrison, was against Native fish traps in the river and "coolie labour coming in to compete with white men." In Victoria, the weekly *Province* listed the election issues, in order, as "the trade question of the country, the Manitoba school question, purity of administration." It added, "Conservatives have at their head of affairs men whose political reputations have been ... seriously aspersed, while the Liberals are led by a man against whom the veriest breath of suspicion has never been raised."

Thursday, June 23 was a lovely Summer day across most of Canada. Both parties were equally confident of victory. There were the usual ballot box tiffs and scuffles between scrutineers, and at many polls police had to be called to eject would-be voters claiming to be someone other than whom they were. Laurier spent the day with his workers in Quebec City where he was standing again in Quebec East. Tupper waited out the results in Ottawa.

It stayed light late that longest night in Quebec, one of the most northerly capitals in the world. The Liberal newspaper *L'Electeur* had set up an illuminated board on the Dufferin Terrace in Quebec City, and would be projecting the results there. The Aberdeens were in Quebec, too; the next day was St. Jean Baptiste day and the Governor General and his lady had come for it and for the celebrations that were to take place on Dominion Day, July 1. The results came fairly quickly, as often by telephone as by wire. Tupper was an early winner in Cape Breton, as was Borden in Halifax. The Conservatives held onto half the seats in Nova Scotia and won a majority in New Brunswick and Prince Edward Island, leading 22-17 overall. In Quebec, however, the tide turned; despite Conservative tradition and the best efforts of the episcopy, *les Canadiens* and their English neighbours filled 49 of Quebec's 65 seats with Liberals. Tarte won in Beauharnois, Bourassa in LaBelle, and Laurier easily carried Quebec East, 2,175 votes to 1,706. Ontario's 92 seats could still make the difference, but the two parties ended the evening with an equal split, 43 seats each. The other six Ontario seats had gone astray: three to Dalton McCarthy and two candidates of the McCarthyite League, two to Patrons of Industry candidates, and one to an independent.

With only 17 seats left to be filled in the West, Laurier already had 109, the Conservatives only 69. The fact that Tupper would hold onto four of Manitoba's seven seats including Hugh John Macdonald's Winnipeg riding, against three Liberals and one McCarthyite hardly mattered. In the Northwest Territories, Liberals won four of six seats, including Frank Oliver's in Edmonton. Richard McBride was not among the two Conservatives elected in B.C.'s six ridings. The final count of 118 Liberals, 88 Conservatives and seven others gave the Liberals a solid majority in the new Parliament. The results clouded the fact, however, that Tupper's candidates actually outpolled Laurier's in the popular vote by a full percentage point, 46.1 to 45.1 per cent. The count was Conservative 414,838, Liberal 405,185, and independents and others 79,023. Had the nearly eighty thousand votes cast for third party candidates, McCarthyites, Patrons and Protestant Protectionists split the non-Liberal vote, or had Laurier been equally damaged? There was no way of knowing.

Newspaper headlines the next day reflected the partisanship of their owners. The Vancouver *World* headlined its report "Hurrah for the Liberals!" Its Toronto correspondent wrote that "the downtown streets contained thousands and thousands of people last night who anxiously awaited results." The *Globe* headline read simply, "Laurier, Mowat and Victory." The government-supporting Ottawa *Citizen* gave over its front page to news of conflicts in Venezuela and Greece, but found space on page two for a two-column headline, "GOVERNMENT DEFEATED," over a list of riding results. By Thursday, the *Citizen* had assessed the situation and concluded that Laurier's victory was due to "the desire of French Canadians to have a Premier of their own race. It was Quebec that won the day for Laurier."

The Aftermath

On July 2 the Aberdeens returned to Government House and called in Tupper, who grudgingly agreed to resign, but not for another week. In the meantime, he wanted a number of appointments made, this being his last opportunity to reward friends and faithful. Lord Aberdeen refused; the election had been held, Tupper had lost, and that was it. Laurier was living once again at the Russell hotel in Ottawa. On Saturday morning, July 11, he took a carriage to Rideau Hall and there was sworn in as Canada's seventh, and first *Canadien*, Prime Minister. He had decided on most of his cabinet. He reached outside the ranks of his elected MPs for his key appointments. Three premiers would be joining Laurier's Ministry; Mowat would serve as minister of justice, William S. Fielding would leave Nova Scotia to take over finance, and Andrew G. Blair would come up from New Brunswick to look after railways and canals. He matched those key nominations by picking Clifford Sifton, the Manitoba attorney general, to join the cabinet as minister of the interior. Tarte got Public Works, and from Ontario, Richard Cartwright took on trade and commerce and William Mulock was put in charge of the post office.

The 1896 election was a turning point that brought to an end the post-Confederation era in Canadian politics. The coalition that Sir John A. Macdonald had forged to create Confederation and build Canada into a nation had been shattered. The Liberal-Conservative party's demise came about significantly because of its inability to bring Western Canada into the marriage of convenience that had bound together the disparate parts of the old Province of Canada; tolerance for each other's language and religion, supported by legislated guarantees for minority rights. Confederation was never at risk in the 1896 election – the leadership of both parties took principled stands for tolerance and understanding – but clearly there had to be a re-shaping of Confederation's form. The West was for pioneers, a country in which an influx of English-speaking newcomers, mainly from Ontario, had submerged the original French Catholic settlers and Metis. They saw little reason to replicate on the western plains the society that existed in Quebec or even, for that matter, in Ontario. After Laurier's election, as the West began to fill up with immigrants from all parts of Europe, there was dwindling support for the idea of Canada as a partnership of only the two founding races. It was a concept the West would never willingly embrace.

The accommodation that Wilfrid Laurier reached with Manitoba did not restore separate schools. Instead, it provided for religious instruction outside regular class hours and allowed teaching in French or any other language when requested by the parents of ten or more children. That provision became increasingly controversial as schools bowed to pressure to teach in the language of new arrivals, speaking many tongues. Within a decade, as the immigration campaign launched by Clifford Sifton brought Canada more than a million new settlers, schools in three hundred Manitoba districts were conducting bilingual classes in more than a dozen languages. What had begun as a compromise between English and French was threatening to Balkanize the new Manitoba society. Finally, in 1915 a new Liberal provincial government acted to make English the sole language of instruction.

The election of Laurier's Liberal government came at a time of general worldwide economic recovery. Grain prices rose rapidly and as Sifton's immigration campaign brought "men in sheepskin coats" to "the last, best West," the new settlers who were filling up the plains were soon able to replace their sod huts with substantial homes and out buildings. For Laurier, it was the beginning of a record-setting 15 continuous years as Prime Minister. He ruled over his cabinet sternly, successfully resisting both Imperial demands for subservience to Empire policy, and pressures in Quebec for a more independent Canadian position. In 1899, Laurier lost the support of nationalists such as Henri Bourassa over his decision to fund a Canadian contingent to fight alongside the British in the South Africa war. None of this affected his success in the elections of 1900 and then 1904, when he won his greatest majority, 138 to 75 Conservatives, with fifty-two percent of the popular vote. Even the new Conservative leader, Robert Borden, went down to defeat.

For most Canadians, the first decade of the 20th century was one of rising expectations fulfilled. Wilfrid Laurier and his "sunny ways" accomplished what great leaders always strive for: to encourage their people to feel good about themselves and their country. Laurier went far beyond this; his greatest legacy for Canadians was his conviction that the twentieth century would belong to Canada; after all, he had promised nothing less.[7] A century later, in comparison with most nations, it can be said that the twentieth century has been a journey of success for Canada. Britain lost its Empire, a vast stretch of Europe and Asia fell for a long time under brutal totalitarianism, most of Africa and Asia still struggle against poverty, while the United States has become a country of economic and cultural division, facing a world of often bitter hatred. The Canadian century began as it has ended, with Canada a country still in search of itself.

CHAPTER FIVE

The Federal Election
of September 21, 1911

THE ISSUES

When Wilfrid Laurier reaches agreement with the United States for reciprocal free trade, the pact invokes ridicule and resentment in English Canada. In French Canada, emotions are focused on the building of a Canadian Navy and the fear of conscription in a future overseas war. Defeat of the Liberal government puts a halt to closer trade ties with the United States and brings to power a Conservative administration anxious to support the British Empire in the growing struggle with Germany.

THE PERSONALITIES

THE LIBERAL PARTY
Sir Wilfrid Laurier, Prime Minister, 1896-1911
William S. Fielding, Minister of Finance
William Lyon Mackenzie King, Minister of Labour
Rodolphe Lemieux, Minister of Marine

THE CONSERVATIVE PARTY
Robert Laird Borden, Leader of the Opposition, 1901-1911
Frank Cochrane, Minister of Lands and Mines, Ontario
John S. Willison, Editor, Toronto News

THE NATIONALIST MOVEMENT:
Henri Bourassa, Editor and Publisher, Le Devoir;
Frederick Monk, MP, Jacques Cartier

ANTI-RECIPROCITY LIBERALS:
Zebulon Lash, Chief Counsel, Canadian Northern Railway
Clifford Sifton, Minister of the Interior, 1896-1905
Sir Edmund Walker, President, Canadian Bank Of Commerce
William T. White, General Manager, National Trust Company

THE RESULTS

	SEATS	VOTES
Conservative Party	134	666,074 (50.9%)
Liberal Party	87	623,554 (47.7%)
Other	–	17,900 (1.4%)

Conservative leader Robert Borden campaigns
at a rally for the 1911 election.

FREE TRADE I:
THE REVOLT AGAINST RECIPROCITY

The Federal Election of 1911

By early afternoon the dusty parade grounds in front of the Armouries in St. Hyacinthe, a mostly French-speaking manufacturing and market town fifty miles east of Montreal, were crammed with thirty thousand people who had come to support their favourites at this traditional Quebec meeting of election candidates – the *assemblée contradictoire* that pits political rivals against each other on a single platform. The Armoury grounds, usually the scene of proper militia reviews and other official functions, offers on this sweltering Sunday, the 13th of August, a scene of excitement and confusion beyond that of any political rally ever held in Canada.

The tumultuous meeting marked the opening of the 1911 federal election campaign, which by election day would divide Canada into bitterly opposing camps over the issue of reciprocal free trade with the United States. Fierce debate has been stirred by the intention of Prime Minister Sir Wilfrid Laurier's Liberal government to enter into a reciprocity agreement with the United States calling on both countries to abolish tariffs on the natural products of farms, fisheries and forests, while reducing duties on a long list of manufactured goods. Legislation had already cleared the U.S. Congress, and only the re-election of the Laurier government, with the promise of speedy passage of a reciprocity act through the Canadian Parliament, was needed to usher in a new economic era.

But little would be heard of reciprocity in St. Hyacinthe today. Another controversy, Laurier's scheme for a Canadian Naval Service of five cruisers and six destroyers, had set aflame the hustings of Quebec. The Liberal chieftain was being forced to wage a two-front war, against Conservatives across Canada and their new-found allies the Nationalists of French Canada, in his bid for a fifth successive term of office. Thirteen special trains, as packed as streetcars in rush hour brought Liberal and Nationalist partisans from Montreal, Three Rivers, Sherbrooke and other towns. In St. Hyacinthe, the streets leading to the Armouries were lined with open model cars, especially the popular new Model T Ford, as well as horse-drawn buggies and wagons. As the grounds filled up with sweating men in wool suits – the temperature would be officially recorded at 81° but it was much hotter in the sun – police roamed the crowd, arresting pickpockets and drunks. The voices from the platform, sometimes aided by a megaphone, carried to barely a quarter of the crowd so that most had to rely on snatches of conversation relayed from those in front if they were to share in the choice insults being hurled into the summer air.

Laurier was not present today. His Minister of Marine, Rodolphe Lemieux, was the first to speak for the Liberals. Mixing his French oration with the argot of the streets and the political invective of the times, Lemieux took dead aim at the Nationalists' beloved leader, Henri Bourassa. He called Bourassa a fool, a liar, and a lunatic leading a following of sheep he was unable to care for. As a crescendo of boos swept the crowd, men began to push against the speakers' stand. Suddenly, the platform railing gave way, dumping a dozen people to the ground. No sooner had order been restored than the crowd surged against the platform again, smashing the section holding newspapermen at their worktable. The reporters fell, bruised and bleeding, their table broken in half.

For four hours the affair went on. When Bourassa finally got to speak, the crowd "cheered themselves hoarse and waved little flags and tricolours." Bourassa insisted that the real reason for reciprocity was to distract Quebec's attention from the *"marine de guerre"* that Laurier planned for Canada. "I do not say the law provides for conscription, but I do object to participation in Imperial wars in which Canada has no interest or concern. I admire Mr. Laurier as a private citizen, but it is our duty to punish him for the betrayal in his public capacity of our most sacred rights and liberties." A more stark warning came from Bourassa's cohort, Armand Lavergne, a young man who, if common gossip could be believed, was the illegitimate son of the great Laurier. If so, this fact did not soften Lavergne' s indictment: "The day will come when the country will judge its traitors and renegades."[1]

The Making of the 'Unholy Alliance'

The rally at St. Hyacinthe, although not matched for disorder and insult, set the pattern for the 1911 election. It pitted Laurier against a combination of inspired Conservatives and defecting Liberals in English Canada, while forcing him to fight a rearguard action to prevent his once-solid bloc of support in French Canada from slipping into the arms of an 'unholy alliance' of Tories and Quebec Nationalists. For Conservative leader Robert Laird Borden, the election was his third – and unless successful, probably his last – chance to unseat Laurier, whose years in office coincided with Canada's greatest period of expansion and prosperity. Borden's hold on his party had become tenuous as a result of his inability to mount a sustained attack on Laurier's Canadian Naval Service. After initially supporting the government's plan to create a Canadian Navy rather than give money to Britain so it could build more dreadnoughts, Borden had reversed himself on the insistence of powerful Imperialist interests in the Conservative party who were still following the will-o'-the-wisp of an Imperial Federation in which Canada would have equal say – and equal responsibility – in shaping and defending the British Empire.

Prime Minister Laurier was clearly the dominant political personality of the day. His charm and culture had captivated Canadians from all walks of life and all parts of the country. Quebec took pride in at last having a French-Canadian at the helm of government. English Canada accepted his ardent support of British institutions as evidence that they could trust their destiny to his hands. The decade had seen the creation of the provinces of Saskatchewan and Alberta in 1905; the construction of two new railways, the Grand Trunk Pacific and the Canadian National; and the beginning of Canadian management of the country's foreign relations. The Boundary Waters Treaty of 1909 empowered

Canada to deal equally with the U.S. on power and navigation questions along the whole of the border. That same year came formation of a Department of External Affairs.

Against this tide of development, Robert Borden struggled to strengthen the haphazard organization of the Conservative party and to find policy options that would appeal over the "sunny ways" of Wilfrid Laurier. Borden was never really happy in public life; the long separations from his wife Laura depressed him, and his concern about his health led to bouts of hypochondria in which he was convinced that his physical frailties made him unequal to the demands of office. Born in Grand Pré, Nova Scotia in 1854, Borden taught at the private school he had attended, Acacia Villa, before tutoring for a term at the similarly genteel Glenwood Institute in New Jersey. That was enough to convince him he would find more opportunity in another vocation. Returning to Halifax, Borden arranged the four years of articling that at the time substituted for a university course in law. He passed first in his group in the final examinations and was admitted to the bar of Nova Scotia in August, 1878. He became a junior partner in a local firm in 1882. Although nominally a Liberal, Borden began to build the connections that would lead in 1896 to an invitation from Sir Charles Tupper to stand for Parliament as a Conservative in Halifax. He managed to hold the seat for the Tories in the voting that saw Laurier come to power. After the 1900 election, Borden was chosen by Tupper to take up the leadership of the Opposition.

Throughout Borden's years in opposition, he was constantly advancing policies that alarmed Conservative business supporters. He advocated government ownership of all public resources, arguing that natural resources, public utilities and the new railway franchise were "the property of the State, and they must be administered and exploited for the public benefit." For the 1908 election, Borden proposed "the most advanced and progressive policy ever put forward in Federal affairs," including elimination of corruption, an elected Senate, transfer of public lands from federal to provincial control in Alberta and Saskatchewan, government-owned telephones and telegraph, and free rural mail delivery.

Borden struggled to maintain an uneasy partnership with Quebec's Tories, most of whom were in the hands of his Quebec lieutenant, Frederick Monk. While the Imperialist wing of the party was undercutting Borden's support for a Canadian Navy, Monk demanded a plebiscite on naval policy. The split drove Monk into the arms of Henri Bourassa, the Quebec Nationalist who was denouncing both Laurier's Naval Service Act and Borden's new policy of an emergency financial contribution to England.

The basis for the Conservative-Nationalist alliance in Quebec in the 1911 election was laid in November, 1910, when Monk and Bourassa campaigned jointly in support of an anti-Liberal candidate, Arthur Gilbert, in a by-election in Drummond-Arthabaska. Monk shared the platform with Bourassa at a rally where Bourassa charged that establishment of a Canadian Navy would inevitably lead to conscription. Gilbert, a farmer, beat the Liberal candidate by 200 votes.

Henri Bourassa would be considered by many the spiritual father of Quebec independence, although there was little in his career to justify such dubious recognition. A grandson of the rebel Louis Joseph Papineau, he sat as a Liberal at Ottawa from 1896 to 1907, and fought Laurier over participation in the South African war. He entered the Quebec legislature in opposition to the provincial Liberal government in 1908, and in 1910 founded *Le Devoir* as a voice of religious conservatism and nationalist reform. Bourassa stood for Canadian independence, not Quebec separatism. He had tried, in a speech to the Canadian Club of Toronto in 1907, to explain his perceptions of Canada at a time when the Anglo-Canadian establishment still viewed the country as little more than a North American extension of the British realm. The Nationalist movement, Bourassa said, "is based on the only principles by which a true Canadian patriotism can be developed, a thing I venture to say is not now in existence ... The main object of the movement is to develop the national forces of Canada. Canada must remain a federation of Provinces and races.

Unless there is room enough for the whole, there is not room for any. It is too late to make history over again."[2]

In Pursuit of the Liberal Dream

Free trade with the United States – or at least, freer trade – had beckoned since Confederation as the Holy Grail of Canadian Liberalism. There had been reciprocity between British North America and the United States from 1854 to 1866; the ending of that pact helped bring the provinces into Confederation in their search for new markets to replace those lost in the American republic. In 1873, the Liberal government of Alexander Mackenzie had George Brown appointed British plenipotentiary to negotiate a new treaty but the U.S. Senate adjourned without ever voting on it. Half-hearted attempts since then had met with renewed failures. In his first test as Liberal leader, Laurier had lost the 1891 election on "Unrestricted Reciprocity." Two years later the party's "Ottawa Platform" was still declaring that "a fair and liberal reciprocity treaty would develop the great natural resources of Canada, would enormously increase the trade and commerce between the, two countries, would tend to encourage friendly relations between the two peoples. "

In point of fact, however, Laurier was heir to the National Policy of Sir John A. Macdonald. Since 1879, it had provided a tariff wall behind which Canadian manufacturing was cushioned from the competition of aggressive American trusts. Canadian farmers had benefited since the 1890s from an upward trend in world agricultural prices. Massive immigration in the first decade of the new century brought a fresh surge of economic growth, as one and a half million Europeans and Americans immigrated to Canada, settling mostly in the West. All these factors tempered much of the earlier demand for tariff reform. Until now, Laurier had put his faith in a "revenue tariff" that would be just high enough to produce the revenues his government needed; the fact that this meant adequate protection for manufacturing earned the Liberal party wide support in the business community.

Laurier had been thinking of retirement since 1907, and of passing the Liberal leadership to his Minister of Finance, William Stevens Fielding, the former premier of Nova Scotia. He sent Fielding to France to negotiate (under British auspices) a new trade treaty with the country that was then Canada's third trading partner. The agreement with Paris neither interfered with the Imperial preference that Canada had granted Britain in 1897, nor in the opinion of the Canadians, compromised Canada's trade relations with the United States. But when the Americans realized that Canadian exports, especially agricultural implements, would be admitted to France at a lower rate of duty than U.S. goods, Washington threatened to impose a 25 per cent surtax on all imports from Canada.

Following the personal intervention of President William Howard Taft, Fielding found himself in Washington in March, 1910 with George P. Graham, the Minister of Railways and MP for Brockville, Ontario. They managed to get the U.S. surtax threat lifted by agreeing to reductions in Canadian tariffs on 13 categories of American goods. This success led the Americans to press their case further; Secretary of State P.C. Knox wrote to Fielding to propose "consideration of a readjustment of our trade relations upon broader and more liberal lines ..." By this time, Fielding realized he was into the biggest gamble of his political career. With Laurier' s support, the long-sought Liberal dream of reciprocity with the United States might now be realized. A political coup of this magnitude would surely catapult him into the Prime Minister's office when Laurier retired. Fielding had sat 14 years in the Nova Scotia legislature – for all but two of them as premier – before coming to Ottawa as Laurier's Minister of Finance in 1896. His regret that he had never been able to amass personal wealth during his editorship of the Halifax *Morning Chronicle,* or his subsequent political career, was eased when his admirers raised a $110,000 trust fund. The interest would assure him security no matter what the future might hold.

Fielding returned to Ottawa in late September wearing a patch over his left eye, the result of facial paralysis caused, it was thought, by either a cerebral hemorrhage or by being badly chilled on a boat trip in Nova Scotia. The ailment made him irritable and affected his speech, but when President Taft proposed that talks on a reciprocity agreement should begin no later than the U.S. mid-term elections in November, Fielding was agreeable. While officials carried on the discussions at Ottawa, Fielding went south in search of relief from his facial agony, taking electrical treatments and massages. The cold December weather in Virginia hastened his return to Ottawa before Christmas.

By now, it was clear that reciprocity was being seriously considered in Ottawa and Washington. A delegation of the Canadian Council of Agriculture arrived in Ottawa shortly before Christmas to put its weight behind reciprocity. On January 14, 1911, fifty men representing the Canadian Manufacturers' Association met with Laurier and several ministers to express their opposition. Fielding, with Customs Minister William Patterson, was now back in Washington, putting the finishing touches to what the Toronto *Globe* described on January 23 as "an agreement which marks an epoch in the commercial relations of Canada with the United States." The day before, the *Globe* reported, the State Department had announced that "the negotiators have reached an understanding which, when certain formalities are completed, will be made public at Washington and Ottawa. It is thought this may be done next Thursday (the 26th)."

The House of Commons met Thursday afternoon as frigid air coiled about Ottawa and winter snow lay heavily on the grounds in front of the Parliament Buildings. Inside, there was an air of hushed expectancy. The galleries were filled with wives and friends of the members, along with a sprinkling of civil servants and diplomats who knew that a historic occasion was at hand. The government and Opposition benches were virtually all filled, and Laurier lounged casually at his desk next to Fielding's as the House went through its opening routines. Finally Fielding rose from behind a stack of papers and reports to tell of the government's plan for the new trade agreement. It was a speech that would drone on for most of the afternoon.

When Fielding finally got to the list of goods that would be reciprocally admitted free of duty by both countries, the members strained to catch every word, aware that nothing that had transpired in Ottawa for many years would so capture the attention of voters. An astonishing list if was: Live farm animals; hay, wheat, corn, and other grains; eggs, honey and fish of all kinds; timber, lumber and many wood products; asbestos, brass, and rolled and galvanized iron; cream separators, typesetting machines; all together, some $95 million worth of goods would pass across the border free of tariffs, opening up to Canada's eight million people the market of 92 million that the United States then represented. Tariffs would remain on most manufactured goods.

The House was silent as Fielding sketched out the dimensions of the reciprocity agreement, but the excitement in the air was tangible. As Fielding sat down, "triumph was written on the faces of the Liberals and dismay on the visages of the Opposition."[3]

The desk-pounding and hurrahs rolled across the aisles as "the Liberals cheered and cheered again." The next morning, the *Globe* was on the streets with a screaming front page headline:

SWEEPING TRADE AGREEMENT WITH UNITED STATES, DETAILED TERMS ANNOUNCED BY MINISTER OF FINANCE

William S. Fielding had "made history," the *Globe's* correspondent reported by presenting to Parliament "a fiscal program ... which blazes a new trail for the greater commercial expansion of the Dominion." Robert Borden, largely alienated from the business community as a result of Laurier' s skill in pre-empting the loyalty of the leading financiers and industrialists of the day, had little forewarning of the storm of protest that the government's proposals would soon set off in the boardrooms of Toronto and Montreal. He met his caucus in a hurriedly-called session the next morning. "There was the deepest dejection in our party, and many of our members were confident that the

Government's proposals would appeal to the country and give it another term of office." It was a dispirited group of Ontario and Quebec Conservative MPs who set out by train that night to spend the weekend in their constituencies. In fact, the first stirrings of the anti-reciprocity movement were already taking place. The prominent Toronto financier, J.W. Flavelle, had composed a letter to the Toronto *Star* within hours of Fielding's speech. Published on Friday, it warned that reciprocity would kill interprovincial trade and would wreck Canada's economy. The president of the Toronto Board of Trade, R.S. Gourlay, was quoted in Friday's papers that he would "dread the influence" of the U.S. under reciprocity, even though it might bring "increased financial prosperity." Conservative and Liberal MPs alike were told over the weekend that reciprocity in natural products could only lead to the eventual elimination of tariffs on manufactured goods.

The Plot of the Toronto Eighteen

Parliament was scheduled to resume debate on Fielding's reciprocity motion on February 9. This left a bare two weeks for opponents of the program – especially influential businessmen in Toronto and Montreal – to lay the groundwork for a revolt against reciprocity that would stiffen the opposition of Borden's Conservative party, and force an exasperated Laurier to gamble on winning a fresh mandate in an early election. Food industry brokers and wholesalers were in the vanguard of the emerging anti-reciprocity movement. The list of groups attacking the agreement included the Montreal Produce Merchants Association, the Dominion Millers Association, the Winnipeg Grain Exchange and the Toronto Live Stock Exchange. George L. Cairns, president of the Montreal Board of Trade, called reciprocity "suicidal to the trade interests and Imperial aspirations of Canada."

The potentially most devasting opposition, however, was surfacing from the ranks of Wilfrid Laurier's own Liberal party. Among the letters that went to him in the week after the tabling of Fielding's resolution, was one from six Liberal MPs appealing for a delay in debate until after the U.S. Congress had reached its decision. Those signing this letter included the former Minister of the Interior, Clifford Sifton, along with Lloyd Harris, J.R. Stratton, W.O. Seally, and D.A. Gordon. More would be heard from them.

Laurier's only response to such appeals was to hold inflexibly to his position; those opposed to the agreement just didn't understand its benefits. When Zebulon A. Lash, the Toronto lawyer who was chief counsel to the Canadian Northern Railway and the Canadian Bank of Commerce, wrote that despite his past Liberal loyalty he found himself in agreement with the Conservative opposition, Laurier seemed to barely take notice: "Your views and mine are so far apart that I scarcely hope it will be possible to reconcile them. It may be my own fault, and I suppose it is, but I still persist in believing reciprocity in natural products cannot injure vested interests and cannot be a bar to our natural development."[4]

It did not take long for the Conservatives to learn of the incipient Liberal revolt. A leading Tory strategist, Albert E. Kemp of Toronto, wrote to Robert Borden that the "best thinking people in the community," especially those who were in business "in a large way, could be expected to oppose reciprocity." Even "some of the strongest Liberals in this city would be willing to take almost any legitimate steps" to stop the agreement. He added mysteriously: "I anticipate that there will be demonstrations of some character or other shortly."

It didn't take long for the city's corporate community to give birth to the "Toronto Eighteen," a group of influential business-men, mostly active Liberals, who controlled much of Canada's commerce through interlocking directorships. They publicly issued a manifesto attacking reciprocity, while privately pledging to commit their influence and money to the Conservative party in the struggle to preserve the markets of Canada as a protected domain for Canadian enterpreneurs.

The chief protagonist of the Toronto Eighteen was Sir Edmund Walker, whose Bank of Commerce was the leading creditor of Mackenzie and Mann, the railway promoters whose Canadian Northern was the latest and perhaps most audacious of the railway schemes that had dominated the making of public policy since the building of the Canadian Pacific. For Walker and other backers of Canadian railways, the threat of reciprocity was clear; a major re-direction of trade along north-south routes could leave the country's east-west railway network rusting and unused, the prospect of profits gone, its promoters unable to pay their bank loans. Similar fear haunted Sir William Van Horne, the former president of the CPR. He took a leading hand in the formation of an Anti-Reciprocity League in Montreal. He declared he was "out to bust the damned thing." Walker had little difficulty bringing other Toronto bankers into the fold: G.T. Somers, president of the Sterling Bank and the Ontario Securities Co.; W.K. George, vice-president of the Sterling Bank; W. Francis, a director of the Standard Bank; and W.D. Matthews, vice-president of the Dominion Bank. They were joined by Henry S. Strathy, retired counsellor of the Canadian Banker's Association.

R.S. Gourlay, the Board of Trade president, was an importer and manufacturer of pianos, while Zebulon Lash, in addition to his legal role, was a director of companies as diverse as the National Trust Co. and the Rio de Janeiro Tramway, Light and Power Co. Mortgage interests were represented by John L. Blaikie, president of the Canada Land and National Investment Co., and Sir William M. Clark, a former lieutenant governor of Ontario and president of the Toronto Mortgage Co. Insurance company investors included L. Goldman, managing director of the North American Life Insurance Co., and George A. Somerville, managing director of the Manufacturers' Life Insurance Co.

Also prominent among the Toronto Eighteen was John C. Eaton, president of the T. Eaton Co. and owner at the time of many factories in Ontario. The food industry had Hugh Blain, founder of the grocery wholesale firm of Ely, Blain & Co., and R.J. Christie, president of Christie, Brown & Co. who was said to have turned against the Liberals when the government allowed

English biscuits into Canada. Rounding out the group were James D. Allen, past president of the Toronto Board of Trade; E.R. Wood, vice-president of the Central Canada Loan and Savings Co., and William Thomas White, the young and forceful vice-president and general manager of the National Trust Co., who would have such a bright future as a political ally of Robert Borden.[5]

The manifesto issued by the Toronto Eighteen was cleverly worded to shift the reciprocity debate from economics to patriotism. It argued that reciprocity would weaken the ties that bind Canada to the Empire and make it more difficult to avoid political union with the United States. Therefore, everyone who placed the interests of Canada first should declare their opposition "openly and fearlessly," just as they, "who have hitherto supported the Liberal party," were doing.

Hovering in the background of the Toronto Eighteen was the imposing figure of Clifford Sifton, the Liberal gad-fly who had been mercilessly assailed by the Tories when he was Laurier's Minister of the Interior, but who was now to become the chief architect of the revolt against reciprocity. Sifton had once supported free trade but now believed the time had passed when Canada could prosper on a mainly agrarian economy; its thin manufacturing establishment would be unable to compete with U.S. industry without a tariff barrier. There would be no longer any motivation for American financiers to invest in Canada. The one discussion he had with Laurier on the subject was curt and to the point. He wouldn't go so far as to join the Conservative party, but neither would he stand for re-election. This would leave him free to counsel the Conservatives in the election campaign, whenever it came.

After an enthusiastic rally at Massey Hall March 9, it was decided to launch the Canadian National League to fight Laurier and reciprocity. During a long lunch at the York Club, "Zeb" Lash agreed to be chairman, with Bill White as treasurer. An intinerant English newspaperman and propagandist for the Canadian Northern, Arthur Hawkes, was hired as secretary. Lash personally paid the $24,600 of expenses run up by the League. The cost would have been higher, but even more clouded in secrecy, the Canadian Manufacturer's Association formed the Canadian Home Market Association, which paid for and fed propaganda to the National League for dispersal to some three hundred daily and weekly papers.

A Toronto-Montreal axis of opposition to reciprocity came into being when Sifton and Lash met in Montreal with Sir Hugh Graham, owner of the Montreal *Star*. At this meeting, "the country was more or less definitely marked out for propaganda purposes." One of the key elements in the campaign was Arthur Hawkes' own paper, the *British News of Canada*, which kept up an incessant barrage of anti-American propaganda. Hawkes made speeches, churned out articles for other papers and wrote pamphlets. The most widely-read was his "Appeal to the British-Born," in which he painted reciprocity as a betrayal of everything a loyal British subject should stand for.

The campaign of Sifton, the Toronto Eighteen, and the others now took on feverish proportions; it was in fact the first politically-oriented public relations campaign to be mounted in Canada, and it lacked neither zeal, money or manpower. Breakaway Liberals began giving interviews to newspapers across the country, warning that reciprocity would end in a take-over of Canada by the United States. It was not long before Canadian public opinion began to respond. The editor of the Montreal magazine, *Canadian Century*, wrote to Finance Minister Fielding that he had "interviewed every farmer in North Monaghan Township, County of Peterborough, Ontario, except nine who were absent from home. Eighty-five per cent signed a strong dec-laration against reciprocity and advocating higher protection for both farm products and manufactured goods. This district fairly represents the sentiments of farmers near manufacturing towns ... no distinction was made between Liberals and Conservatives." In another poll, the *Toronto News*, a Conservative organ, reported on April 28 that it had surveyed people in 99 Ontario towns, with 18,060 saying they were against the government's plan, and only 4,867 in support.

Laurier's letters reflected his confidence that his government would survive. In answer to Edward Brown of Winnipeg, he conceded that "reciprocity will be bitterly attacked in some quarters." To Judson F. Clarke, a Vancouver forestry engineer who complained that the tariff on food "has been a means of maintaining excessive prices," Laurier replied: "I believe you have correctly gauged the situation. There is froth and nothing else on the part of the Opposition ..." To F. S. Spence, a Toronto city controller, Laurier sang the same tune: "... as far as I can see the treaty will be popular everywhere and will be supported by the large majority of the Canadian people." Laurier's chief Liberal organizer in Ontario, Ottawa lawyer Alexander Smith, wrote to report that many people "have really no notion" of what reciprocity was all about. He urged that the agreement be published with a "short introductory letter ... in a couple of hundred papers." Laurier's reply was a one sentence "very sincere thanks."

With the anti-government campaign gaining momentum, Clifford Sifton stood in the House of Commons on the last day of February and delivered a condemnation of reciprocity that was described as "the loveliest music the Conservatives had heard for many moons." The government had no mandate to go into reciprocity because nothing had been said of the issue in the last three elections. It was not true that everyone in Canada had been in favour of it for the past forty years. Then his criticism turned savage: "I do not believe that in the recent history of Canada anything has happened which has given to the thinking people of Canada so painful and so sudden a shock as the sudden realization that four or five gentlemen who, by reason of their ability, their years of service and their high position in their party, can suddenly, of their own notion, without discussion, without debate, without the knowledge of the country, commit the country to a radical change of fiscal policy. That is not, I am bound to say, the doctrine of constitutional government as I was taught it in the Liberal party."

Laurier's reply a few days later soared far beyond the mere details of the reciprocity agreement; his speech had the sweep of history about it, but it was by now irrelevant to Sifton and his defecting Liberals. They had met secretly in Sifton's office on March 1 with Robert Borden and John S. Willison, the editor of the *Toronto News*. There they gained the Conservative leader's acceptance of a strategy that would give Toronto Liberals a virtual veto on cabinet appointments in return for their support in the coming election. They stipulated that a Borden cabinet should include "reasonable representation therein of the views of those Liberals who may unite with Conservatives against the policy of reciprocity." Any future Borden government was asked to "resist American encroachments and American blandishments and be vigilant under all circumstances to preserve and strengthen the Canadian nationality and the connection with the Mother Country." Finally, a Borden government, while giving proper representation to Quebec, "should not be subservient to Roman Catholic influences in public policy or in the administration of patronage."[6]

Borden was agreeable to all these propositions; he even went so far as to offer to resign if it seemed another leader could better accomplish the common aim of defeating Laurier and reciprocity. When word of the meeting leaked out, a rump group in the Conservative caucus called for Borden to step aside. He offered to do so, suggesting that Richard McBride, the premier of British Columbia, might better lead the party. But the cabal soon dissolved of its own inconsequence, and after 65 Conservative MPs signed a petition urging him to stay on, Borden for the first time since the fiasco of the Naval debate found his leadership unchallenged.

Closure had not yet been adopted as a parliamentary device to choke off debate, and Borden was determined to prevent the reciprocity resolution from coming to a vote. On May 9, in return for a supply vote that would pay government expenses to September, Laurier ordered a two-month adjournment of the House. He would use the time to attend the Coronation of George V and to take part in an Imperial Conference in London. Borden, knowing that an election could not be put off beyond the fall, set out on a whistle-stop tour of the prairies.

Because the Opposition was arguing that Canada would be unable to resist ultimate absorption by the United States in an environment of reciprocity, the attitudes of American politicians became critical in the pre-election months of 1911. They couldn't have been more insensitive to Canadian fears. After the U.S. Congress gathered for a special session in April to consider the agreement, President Taft famously remarked that "Canada is at the parting of the ways." Worse, the Speaker of the House of Representatives, Champ Clark, blurted out that he hoped to see the day "when the American flag will float over every square foot of the British North American possessions, clear to the North Pole." It was all fodder for the Conservative attack, further evidence that reciprocity could bring only "continentalism," "annexation" and the destruction of Canada as a British nation. The U.S. House moved swiftly to pass the reciprocity agreement April 21, although debate in the Senate lasted until July 22.

The Coronation and the Imperial Conference over, Prime Minister Laurier set sail from Southampton July 1, to find the crisis at home even more critical than when he had left. Parliament resumed on July 18 and after a further ten days of fruitless debate, Laurier called his cabinet together Saturday morning, July 29, for the fateful decision. There no longer seemed any prospect of getting the agreement through the House. Barely more than three years into his latest term, Laurier decided to ask the Governor General, Lord Earl Grey, for dissolution. He went that afternoon to Government House, and on his return to the Parliament Buildings called in reporters, telling them Finance Minister Fielding had an announcement to make. It fell to Fielding to advise the country that the eleventh Parliament had been dissolved, with the election writ issued for September 21. The fatal mistake had been made; the lesson of Laurier's first campaign in 1891, that reciprocity was a hard sell to Canadians, seemed to have been forgotten.

The Campaign and the Candidates

Wilfrid Laurier went into the 1911 election approaching 70 years of age, but still vigorous and determined to vindicate himself at the polls. "Follow my white plume," he had told a meeting of young Quebeckers in July, "and you will find it always in the forefront of honour." But his private doubts belied his public confidence. "The important thing at this moment is to put up the boldest front everywhere,"[7] he wrote his MP from North Essex, Ontario, A.H. Clarke. But even Laurier could not realize that he was setting out on what would be almost a one-man campaign. He had allowed the Liberal party's organization to wither during his years in office. Laurier found himself personally appointing returning officers, arguing with disgruntled party officials in the ridings, and trying to encourage reluctant incumbents like Clarke to stand for re-election. Clarke finally agreed to run again "on condition, that I may retire after the election or say one session." F.W. Wilson, owner of the Port Hope *Guide*, wrote to Laurier on July 31 that there was "absolutely no enthusiasm" for the election in his riding because "we are that unfortunate constituency that was disowned and denounced by our leader." Wilson was referring to a speech in which Laurier, recalling the loss of the seat in 1908, had said, "They may be forgiven perhaps in the next world but certainly not in this world." Wilson's complaint was "absolutely unjust and unfair," Laurier declared, adding lamely that he had meant to point his finger at the voters of Port Hope, not the district's Liberals.

In Ontario, where the Liberals had won just 36 of 86 seats in 1908, the "bold front" that the party must put up was in the hands of George Graham, the Minister of Railways and Canals. As the campaign was about to begin, Graham was shattered by the death of his son and withdrew to his Brockville home for three weeks of mourning. Organizing tasks fell briefly on the shoulders of the party's nondescript provincial leader, J.F. Mackay. Graham got little help from other cabinet ministers; William Lyon Mackenzie King, the Minister of Labour, peppered him constantly with letters seeking advice and approval for his own campaign plans and speeches. Fielding, realizing that as Minister of Finance he would be held responsible for the reciprocity agreement, thought it "most important to have an abundant supply of literature." The party needed a pamphlet showing that reciprocity had been the policy of all parties "from the beginning of Confederation and even before." He also felt "a few carefully prepared cartoons may play an effective part in the campaign."[8]

The Conservative party, sensing its first Dominion victory in 20 years, was well prepared for the campaign. In Ontario, Conservative organizers were able to assess Tory prospects in every single riding weeks before the election was called; one calculated that 36 of the 50 Conservative seats were "absolutely sure" and that the Tories would be able to pick off 22 of the Liberal ridings. These 22 seats, even if all were won, would not quite produce a Conservative majority, however, and it was to Quebec, where Henri Bourassa and Frederick Monk were busy undercutting Laurier's traditional support, that the Tories must look to finish the job. Bourassa was determined that his Nationalists would field no candidates under the party's banner, but would instead "support any Liberal or Conservative candidate, whether he is in favour of reciprocity or not, who will pledge himself to oppose any policy of direct or indirect participation in the ways of the Empire outside of Canada."

The solution that Monk struck on was to set up a new organization under the name of the "Autonomist party." The Autonomist campaign was launched at Three Rivers on August 6. Monk ran in his old riding of Jacques Cartier, and his strategy was made clear in a manifesto unveiled that day. "Reciprocity is not so important," Monk said, "the dominant question for us is the establishment of a Canadian navy." There were other issues equally important to Quebec: the "full recognition of the rights of the minority, the need for a better system of immigration, and reform of the banking system so as to 'give better protection to the deposits and savings of the people.'"

On Monday, August 14, the day after the *assemblée contradictoire* at St. Hyacinthe, both Laurier and Borden left Ottawa by train for their first campaign swings through Ontario. Laurier had issued his election manifesto on July 29, the day of dissolution. It was both a defense of reciprocity and a promise of a quick opening up of American markets to Canadian farmers if the Liberals were re-elected. The Conservatives had for eight months willfully obstructed efforts to get the reciprocity agreement through Parliament and further debate would mean more "wasted time, and perhaps, in the end, the loss for this season to the Canadian producer of the free American market." The government had therefore decided to "remit the issue to the people," and let the voters decide "whether they are still in favour of reciprocity in natural products, and whether they will or will not have the American market for the promising crop soon to be garnered in Canada."

The weather turned cool and damp that week in Ontario, and rain fell on Laurier's train Tuesday morning as it travelled from Toronto to Simcoe, where he would open his campaign with an afternoon rally in Lynwood Park. The Liberals of Western Ontario were determined to give Laurier a warm welcome and several thousand came in by train, car and buggy for the rally. Laurier had lunch on board the train with the Liberal candidate for Norfolk, W.A. Charlton, and afterwards made his way to Lynwood Park in a motorcade that included mounted men and bands. The speaker's platform, set in a natural amphitheatre, was covered in bunting and draped with Union Jacks, set off by red, white and blue roses and gladiolas. A voice from the crowd, "Can't stand it any longer – let's have three cheers for Laurier," brought the massed assembly to its feet. It was several minutes before Laurier could begin his speech.

Laurier's Simcoe speech was to set the tone for his campaign. "Reciprocity will not only be a powerful factor in the material prosperity of our country, but it is an advance toward that higher civilization which recent events have shown to be within the range of practical politics," Laurier said. He spoke from only a few notes: 'Reciprocity has become law in the United States and we can have it tomorrow if the Canadian people will approve it. Will you have it or not?" The cheering response of the farmers and their wives in this audience showed that the Liberal leader had begun his campaign in promising territory, even if the seat was held by a Conservative.

It was part of the political ritual of the era for party leaders to be welcomed at each town by a delegation of supporters at the railway station, and this was how Robert Borden was greeted when his train reached London. Borden was to make his first campaign address there on Wednesday night and newspapers were already on the streets with his "Manifesto to the People of Canada." In it, he appealed for an election verdict that "will be for unity and not for the disintegration of Canada, for the strengthening and not the loosening of the ties which bind this Dominion to the British empire."[9]

A band led his procession to the Grand Opera House. There, 2,000 Conservatives heard him warn that "unrestricted continental free trade is the goal" of Liberal reciprocity from which "Canada would be as capable of withdrawing, without consent, from this agreement as the fly from the spider's web." Nor did Borden neglect the Naval issue, one sure to touch a nerve in this predominantly pro-British City: "The government propose, at great expense, to construct a so-called Navy which will be absolutely useless as a fighting force." He'd later call it a "tin-pot Navy."

Laurier doubled back to Quebec after his rally at Simcoe, but Borden stayed in Ontario, reaching Toronto for a rally at Massey Hall on August 23. The Toronto Eighteen were assembled on the platform to welcome him along with Mayor G.R. Geary and George E. Foster, the Conservative MP for Toronto North, the party's strongest front-bencher from Ontario. Borden lost no time in praising his new-found allies to the 4,000 applauding Tories: "They are entitled to just recognition as men who have stood shoulder to shoulder with us in this fight to prevent a national disaster, as men who have cast aside strong party ties for the sake and in the cause of a United Canada and a United Empire."

Borden wound up his strenuous Ontario tour by visiting the strongly Conservative eastern ridings, where he spoke at

Peterborough, Hastings, Warkworth – where 800 stood in the rain to hear him – Campbellford, Napanee, Smith's Falls and Brockville. Here, he spoke in a voice "perceptibly weak and hardly audible." The Union Jack hung over the rostrum and miniature flags were handed out at the door. At Napanee, he criticized Laurier for being soft on Imperial loyalty, accusing the Prime Minister of taking the stand that Canada can be neutral when the rest of the Empire is at war. "So long as Canada is part of the British Empire," Borden said, "this country cannot be at peace when the rest of the Empire is at war. Our ships would be subject to attack on the high seas; our coasts would be subject to raid and invasion. The Prime Minister declares that Canada may be neutral when Britain is attacked. He must then equally maintain that Britain may be neutral when Canada is attacked. Such a conception involves the dismemberment of the Empire."

In line with the strategy agreed on with Monk and the Nationalists, Borden spent little time in Quebec. He could not speak French, and his one Montreal appearance was notable for the absence of both Monk and Bourassa. Borden's election train whistle-stopped through the English-speaking Eastern Townships, entering New Brunswick early in September. He shared rostrums at St. Andrews and St. Stephens with Sir William Van Horne, who was holidaying at CPR resorts there, and then went on to two meetings at Saint John, where crowds gathered in the streets to cheer him.

In Washington, a jingoistic American president Theodore Roosevelt who had boasted he would "walk softly and carry a big stick," had made a strong impression on Canadians. The Conservatives, exploiting fears of American domination, came up with such slogans as "No truck or trade with the Yankees" and "One Fleet, One Flag, One Throne." The Liberal slogan, "Laurier and Larger Markets," was hardly inspiring and it left the field clear to the Conservatives to take advantage of the growing animosity toward the United States. The Conservative candidate in Saint John, Dr. J.W. Daniel, aptly summed up the Canadian view of American power when he noted that the Spanish-American War had left Cuba practically a dependency of the U.S., and that Canada had now become "the football of American politics."

Robert Borden spent the final week of the 1911 campaign in Nova Scotia, after a hurried visit to Prince Edward Island where he held out the promise of a survey to determine whether a tunnel to the mainland would be feasible; "If the tunnel is reasonably feasible, it should be built." Back in his home province Borden picked his way through the Cape Breton ridings. The welcoming banner at Sydney Mines read "Canada for the Canadians – the British Empire our Safeguard." He received a rousing welcome from six thousand supporters at Halifax on September 12. There, Borden had former Prime Minister Sir Charles Tupper with him on the platform.

Wilfrid Laurier had gone directly from Simcoe to Three Rivers, Quebec, where on August 17, ten thousand Liberal loyalists braved a drenching rainstorm to hear him defend the need for a Canadian Navy. Canada had become a nation of eight million, he said, soon to become 15 million, "and it is an unfortunate necessity that as nations grow, they must take steps for self-defence." He admitted the Navy would cost "a good deal of money," but that the sum would amount to only three per cent of government revenues. The next day in Quebec City, a staggeringly large crowd, estimated by even opposition papers as close to 30,000 gathered in Place Jacques Cartier for Laurier's biggest rally of the campaign. On the platform with the Prime Minister at most of his meetings in Quebec were the strong men of his party: Dr. Béland, the postmaster-general; Rodolphe Lemieux, the minister of marine; and Sir Lomer Gouin, the premier of the province. Most of the meetings were in French, but an exception was Laurier's rally at Farnham, where he switched from the navy issue to reciprocity, attacking the Conservative qualms of annexation as an insult to Canadian manhood. "The cry of annexation is simply rant and nonsense," he said. But not all Laurier's speeches were on these issues. He liked to use scriptural references in an amusing way, and at St. Julienne, Laurier told his supporters that "the Liberal government is like the Kingdom of

Heaven, 'ask and you will receive.' When St. Donat asks for a railway extension from Rawdon, I say 'Ask and you will receive.'" He also lightened his appeals with ridicule. At St. Eustache, he said of the Bourassa-Borden-Monk alliance, "What a salad!" Mr. Monk was the oil, Mr. Bourassa the vinegar, and Mr. Borden had to eat the dose. Laurier arrived in Saint John, New Brunswick, a week before Borden, to find a torch-lit procession to lead him to the local arena where a crowd of seven thousand had gathered. Laurier made one of his most stirring addresses in this old Loyalist city:

> I appeal to you who know me and the work of my Administration to uphold me and my Government against the unholy alliance of the Tories of Quebec and the Tories of Ontario. I am branded in Quebec as a traitor to the French, and in Ontario as a traitor to the English. In Quebec I am branded as a Jingo and in Ontario as a Separatist. In Quebec I am attacked as an Imperialist and in Ontario as an anti-Imperialist. I am neither. I am a Canadian. Canada has been the inspiration of my life. I have had before me as a pillar of fire by night and a pillar of cloud by day a policy of true Canadianism, of moderation and of conciliation. I have followed it consistently since the day of our triumph in 1896, and I now appeal with confidence to the whole Canadian people to uphold me in this policy of sound Canadianism which makes for the greatness of our country and of the Empire.

Back to Ontario went the Laurier campaign train. The tour was strenuous, and Laurier was tiring. At Cobourg, his personal secretary, E.J. Lemaire, got off a wire to a party worker in Ottawa, Dr. R. Chevrier, who had asked if the Prime Minister could address a meeting there. Lemaire agreed, but cautioned: "On account of severe strain put upon him the chief cannot promise address of more than 30 minutes." Hoping for a respite when he got back to Montreal at the weekend, Laurier had Lemaire send a letter to Foster Brown, a Montreal bookseller, asking that copies of Longfellow's Poems and Robinson Crusoe be sent to the Windsor Hotel so that the Prime Minister "will find them on his arrival there Sunday morning."[10]

There was other correspondence to be handled. Dr. Margaret McAlpine of Toronto, secretary of the Canadian Suffrage Association, had written to ask when the Liberal party would support giving the vote to women. "The women of Canada are as deeply stirred by the issues before the country as are their husbands, brothers, fathers and sons yet they are not permitted to accord their votes and to take their share of responsibility in the shaping of the destiny of their own country which a large proportion of foreign men are, by a short term of residence in Canada, qualified to do." The reply Laurier dictated was worded carefully to avoid the issue: "Under the existing system in Canada we have no Dominion franchise … the electoral vote is exercised under franchise granted to each provincial legislature."[11]

After Sunday's rest in Montreal, Laurier plunged back into the campaign in Quebec where the Nationalists were again his main target. At Joliette, he said rejection of reciprocity would be a crime against civilization. In a side visit to Ottawa, he declared he was "sick and tired of this annexation talk." Two days before the election, Laurier addressed three meetings in Montreal attended, it was estimated, by seventy thousand people. Leaving the Ontario Avenue rink that evening, Laurier's car was surrounded by a jeering crowd of youths who hissed and booed the Prime Minister.

Elections are not won by party leaders alone, and this was especially true in the era before leaders could easily reach voters through the media. There were 221 seats to be filled in Canada's 12th Parliament, and each was fought for town by town and poll by poll. Money flowed into the Conservative campaign coffers in an abundant stream; there would be no shortage of cash for Tory poll workers whose generous distribution of liquor and "tips" could fatten the vote for many candidates. The Liberals, cut off by the Canadian Pacific Railway and reduced to accepting small contributions wherever they could find them, left many candidates to raise their own funds.

One Liberal who had difficulty with free trade was the young William Lyon Mackenzie King. King had spent eight years as deputy minister of Labour and privately opposed reciprocity "on the ground of political expediency, and so stated my position strongly in the Cabinet."[12] But he defended the agreement on the hustings, risking his perilous grip on his own riding, with its many manufacturing plants, to speak for Liberal candidates in 17 constituencies.

King had no Illusions as to the difficult campaign he faced. Robert Borden had prevailed on Adam Beck, the founder of Ontario Hydro, to find a candidate. They settled on W.G. Weichel, the popular mayor of Waterloo. Weichel was of German descent and King, fearful of losing the support of the many German voters in the riding, took the risky step of accusing the Conservatives of wanting to "finance England to build warships to fight Germany." The Conservative press jumped gleefully on the apparent words of disloyalty falling from the lips of a minister of the Crown. It was a further embarrassment for a government already under siege for its willingness to risk annexation by the United States.

The Conservative machine worked flawlessly in Ontario. No Conservative organizer was more relentless than Dr. J. D. Reid, responsible for the eastern Ontario ridings. Seeking a candidate for Glengarry, he urged Duncan McMartin, a prospect who did not live in the riding, to become a landowner there. "Buy a farm – put some good thoroughbred stock on it," he advised him.[13] The eager McMartin did so and soon found himself with the Tory nomination.

The cabinet minister at the epicentre of the reciprocity issue, Finance Minister Fielding, was re-nominated in his Nova Scotia riding of Shelburne and Queens on August 16. Two days later, the Conservatives sent a prominent Halifax broker, F.B. McCurdy, into the riding as the party's candidate. Fielding had still not entirely recovered from his illness of the previous winter. When he began showing up on platforms sounding hoarse and looking tired, his health became an issue. "Mr. Fielding has the appearance of a broken down old man," the Conservative Bridgewater *Bulletin* declared. Fielding drew the cream of the provincial Liberal cabinet into his campaign and shared platforms with Laurier when the Prime Minister came to Nova Scotia, as well as with the province's other federal minister, Sir Frederick Borden.

In South Cape Breton, organizers sent out pamphlets offering "Pointers for Liberals." Election workers were admonished to "see every elector in your section individually and talk to him, see one or two today if possible. Keep at it. Get a list of the voters in your section who are away. When a meeting is advertised for your district, see that everyone knows. Bring the Tories along and crowd the hall. How many did you contact today? How many did you give literature to today? We are going to win if you do your share. Keep in constant touch with new and doubtful voters." The Liberal candidate, W.F. Carroll, handed out cards headed I STAND FOR, showing that he stood for "10,000,000 more buyers for our fresh fish. Cheaper meats, cheaper fruits, cheaper canned goods. More coal markets. More industries to use our steel products."

Throughout the West, where Laurier had hoped for a solid endorsement of reciprocity except possibly in British Columbia, the Conservative machine was picking up momentum. In Manitoba, Premier Roblin put his attorney-general, Robert Rogers, and virtually the entire civil service, at Borden's disposal. Roblin went on the stump himself, declaring that a vote for Laurier was a vote to put Manitoba into shackles. Surprisingly, Sifton's *Manitoba Free Press* remained loyal to the Liberal cause. Its famous editor, John Wesley Dafoe, would permit no interference from the paper's owner in his fiercely pro-Laurier stance. Liberal hopes here were highest for J.F. Greenway, son of the former premier, who was standing in Lisgar against a Conservative newcomer, W.H. Sharpe. One other big contest in Manitoba was in Portage la Prairie, where Arthur Meighen was defending the Conservative seat he had won in 1908.

In Saskatchewan, the Liberal machine had held a stranglehold on both federal and provincial politics since 1905. In Alberta, the chief Conservative hope was to elect R. B. Bennett, who had resigned his provincial seat to stand in Calgary. Bennett had the effusive support of the Calgary *Herald*, which greeted his nomination August 28 with the front page headline, "Conservative Candidate Flays Reciprocity in a Magnificent Deliverance." Five thousand people had crowded into Sherman's Rink for what the *Herald* said was the largest political meeting in Calgary's history. "I oppose reciprocity because it has been bought at too great a price," Bennett declared. "It is reciprocity bought for the mills of Minneapolis, for the packing houses of Chicago and the industries south of the 49th parallel."

In British Columbia, the Conservatives under Premier Richard McBride mounted what even the Liberals recognized as a nearly invincible organization. The "people's Dick" was at the peak of his power and popularity, and McBride campaigned tirelessly across the province, in lumber towns, mining camps, and crowded Vancouver wards. His message was simple, and everywhere the same: defeat the Frenchman Laurier, reject reciprocity, keep Canada British. B.C.'s cabinet representative, William Templeman, the Minister of Revenue, was severely attacked in Victoria for allowing so many Orientals into the province.

With the exception of such traditional Liberal newspapers as the Toronto *Globe*, Toronto *Star* and Winnipeg *Free Press*, most of the country's leading papers swung strongly behind Borden. The press still adhered loyally to party lines, although the 1909 convention of the Canadian Press Association had been told that editors should try to "direct the public mind towards the betterment of the condition of the people rather than towards the exaltation of a party or an individual." The propaganda machine set up to fight the Liberals and reciprocity remained carefully sheltered behind Zeb Lash's Canadian National League, which by the end of the campaign had fired off some ten million copies of pamphlets and newspaper articles. One of its most effective methods was to place anti-reciprocity articles in the "readyprint" services of various agencies supplying country weeklies. Between 700 and 800 weeklies delivered to their readers a steady diet of anti-reciprocity propaganda. Many of these pieces were written by Professor Stephen Leacock of McGill University.

Laurier made little or no attempt to influence the press himself. When the New York *World* asked for a statement on the reciprocity agreement Laurier responded by wire: I REGRET THAT I NEVER GIVE INTERVIEWS TO NEWSPAPERS.[14] He apparently never answered a letter from E.F. Slack, manager of The Canadian Press, who offered at the outset of the campaign to "place the news distributing facilities of The Canadian Press at your disposal." Slack asked that advance copies of important "speeches, addresses or reports" be delivered to him at the Montreal *Gazette* three days ahead of time, so that they could be sent by mail to the newspapers served by CP. This would save "a large amount in telegraph tolls." Newspaper advertisements were all but unknown as a political tool, and one of the few which appeared was an unsigned attack on reciprocity, bought at a cost of $280, in the September 18 issue of the Toronto *Globe.* It argued that the U.S. would not have approved of reciprocity unless it was sure of getting the best of the bargain. As to the ability of the Canadian negotiators, "It is as if you sent a 'darkey' to bargain for a watermelon. He wants the watermelon so badly he would pay almost anything for it." A second ad appeared in the same issue, apparently inserted by the *Globe*, in support of reciprocity.

In the last days of the campaign, the newspapers were filled with Robert Borden's final appeal, a "message to the people of Canada" issued from Halifax which reminded voters that "the momentous choice which you make is for all time:"

> We must decide whether the spirit of Canadianism or of Continentalism shall prevail on the northern half of this continent ...With Canada's youthful vitality, her rapidly-increasing population, her marvelous material resources, her spirit of hopefulness and energy, she can place herself within a comparatively brief period in the

highest position within this mighty Empire. To all who are proud of her past, to all who hope for her future … I beg them to cast a soberly considered and serious vote for the preservation of our heritage, for the maintenance of our commercial and political freedom, for the permanence of Canada as an autonomous nation within the British Empire.

Every possible appeal was made to British loyalties. Rudyard Kipling, who had an immense following in Canada, was induced by Hugh Graham of the Montreal *Star* to author a lyrical message to Canadians that was published in newspapers across the country. The Halifax *Herald* on September 11 devoted its entire front page to Kipling's statement, under the headline, "It is Her Own Soul That Canada Risks Today." Kipling wrote: "Once that soul is pawned for any consideration, Canada must inevitably conform to the commercial, legal, financial, social and ethical standards which will be imposed upon her by the sheer admitted weight of the United States … I see nothing for Canada in reciprocity except a little ready money she does not need, and a very long repentance." Kipling's message could not have had anything less than a profound effect on many Canadians.

The night before the election, Laurier checked into the Chateau Frontenac in Quebec City. There was no need for any last-minute campaigning, as he had won Quebec East by acclamation following the withdrawal of the Conservative candidate, René Leduc. This had occurred in somewhat bizarre circumstances. In a statement addressed to Laurier September 17, Leduc claimed "One of your most important chiefs in Quebec East extorted from me, whilst I was under the influence of liquor, my resignation as candidate against you." Laurier offered to resign and stand in a by-election if the charge could be proven. The case later went to court, where Leduc's complaint was held groundless.

The last day of summer, Thursday, September 21, dawned warm and clear across most of Canada. The polls were open from 9 a.m. to 5 p.m. and by the end of the day, 1,307,528 Canadian males – 70.2 per cent of the eligible electorate – had voted. In Winnipeg, a Liberal election worker was arrested on complaints that he had padded the voter's list with phony names. In Edmonton, W.A. Griesbach, the Conservative candidate against Frank Oliver, the Minister of the Interior, warned that false ballot boxes were being put about by the Liberals in some parts of the riding. In Montreal, gangs of party workers, both Liberal and Conservative, roamed the polling stations, voting in the names of persons now resting in the city's cemeteries.

Robert Borden and his closest supporters, including the last Conservative Prime Minister, Sir Charles Tupper, stood by in Halifax as the results were telegraphed from constituencies across the Maritimes. Prince Edward Island split its four seats, two each for the Liberals and Conservatives. New Brunswick, where Borden had looked for better things, went Liberal by a margin of eight seats to five. But the sign that a more favourable trend might be developing came in Borden's own Nova Scotia where the architect of reciprocity, William Fielding, went down to defeat along with Frederick Borden. This brought the Conservatives an even split of Nova Scotia's 18 seats – Borden winning easily in Halifax and gave them 16 of 35 Maritime ridings.

In Quebec, the Nationalist-Conservative alliance was cutting deeply into Liberal support, just as Laurier had feared. Sitting quietly in his ill-lit and uncomfortable Quebec committee rooms, Laurier saw the defeat of his third cabinet minister as Sydney A. Fisher lost the mainly English-speaking riding of Brome. A total of 27 Conservatives or Autonomistes – it was impossible to distinguish them apart – were elected. A Liberal newcomer, L.J. Gauthier, held St. Hyacinthe, scene of the massive *assemblée contradictoire* which had launched the campaign, while an impressive young government supporter, Ernest Lapointe, managed to get elected in Kamouraska. The final accounting of Quebec's 65 seats would show a Conservative net gain of 16, leaving Laurier with but 38 members in his own province. Among the Conservative winners was Frederick Monk, the architect of the alliance with Henri Bourassa. The Conservative surge, which began as a trickle in the Maritimes and ran as a river in flood through the English-speaking townships and back country French ridings of Quebec, next turned to a tidal wave as it swept over the cities and towns of Ontario.

Religion, language, patriotism and economics were all on the side of the Conservatives. In Ontario, Tory candidates took a remarkable 56.2 per cent of the popular vote, and with it, 73 of 86 constituencies; 23 more than they had been able to win in 1908. The list of Liberals defeated in Ontario seemed unending; it included three more cabinet ministers, Labour Minister Mackenzie King in Waterloo North; Railway Minister George P. Graham in Brockville; and Customs Minister William Patterson in Brant. The only cabinet minister to be returned in Ontario was Secretary of State Charles Murphy, whose supporters in Russell had given him little chance for a victory.

The Conservative list of Ontario winners was as long as the Liberal list of losers. It included front-bencher George Foster in Toronto North; Borden advisor Albert E. Kemp in Toronto East; and eastern Ontario organizer Dr. J.D. Reid in Grenville. Another Tory winner was Col. Sam Hughes, whose Orange connections helped him to a landslide in Victoria County. Less successful was Reid's hand-picked candidate in Glengarry; Duncan McMartin' s purchase of a farm there was not enough to convince voters to elect him.

In Ontario and Quebec, the Conservatives carried 100 seats to 51 for the Liberals. When added to the earlier returns from the Maritimes, the Conservative lead stood at 116 seats to 70, assuring Robert Borden a majority in the new Parliament. Even if the Liberals could sweep all 39 seats in Western Canada, a political impossibility, the new Conservative majority would not be endangered. As it was, the Conservative party took eight of Manitoba's ten seats, re-electing Arthur Meighen in Portage la Prairie, and defeating Liberal J.F. Greenway, son of the former premier of the province, in Lisgar. Only Saskatchewan and Alberta held faithful to "Laurier and Larger Markets." The Liberal machine in Saskatchewan retained all but one of ten seats, and in Alberta, Liberals won six of seven ridings, with R.B. Bennett in Calgary the only Conservative winner. In British Columbia, Conservative candidates gained a record 58.8 per cent of the popular vote, sweeping all seven seats.

With the Western returns included, the final result would be 134 Conservatives and 87 Liberals. It was an almost total reversal of the 1908 election. But the popular vote across the country was close; 666,074 for the Conservatives, 623,554 for the Liberals, a difference of 42,520 votes. An average of fewer than 200 votes per riding had enabled the Conservatives to bring the 15-year regime of Wilfrid Laurier to an end.

Long before the ballots in Western Canada had been counted, and even before the results were complete in Quebec and Ontario, Laurier knew he had been beaten. Leaving his committee rooms, he went to St. Peter's Market in Quebec, where a crowd had gathered to hear the results. Laurier betrayed little of the disappointment that he felt, saying only that he had fought with truth and honour, and that he remained convinced of the cause for which he stood.

It was a different scene in Halifax, where there was pandemonium at Robert Borden's headquarters in the recently-vacated premises of the Union Bank. Older Conservatives thought it was like 1878 all over again, when the Tories had come back from oblivion on a wave of support for the National Policy of John A. Macdonald. Borden and his running-mate in the two-member Halifax riding, A.B. Crosby, spent the early part of the evening closeted in the bank's former board room with Charles Tupper and other close supporters. At word of the growing Conservative triumph, the crowd in the street below grew to several thousand. Borden, confident now of victory, went onto a balcony to thank his cheering supporters. The celebration was only slightly tarnished by the fact that Crosby had not been re-elected.

Across Canada, crowds gathered in front of newspaper offices after the polls closed. One hundred and fifty thousand people jammed the dozen city blocks between Queen and Front Streets, and Church and York Streets, in downtown Toronto.

Conservatives went to the *News* and the *Telegram*, Liberals to the *Globe* and the *Star*, to hear the results shouted through megaphones as they were posted in the windows. The *Globe* boasted of its arrangements with the Burroughs Company for messengers to rush results from each poll in the city's five ridings to the company's office on Bay Street, where the returns were quickly totaled on adding machines and phoned over a direct line to the newspaper. By ten o'clock, processions of jubilant Tories marched on the offices of the *Star* and the *Globe*, hissing, booing and singing to the music of accompanying bands. A brick sailed through the window of the newspaper office, but by midnight, the excitement had worn itself out and Tory Toronto slept the sleep of the good. A telegram was delivered to Laurier's suite at the Chateau Frontenac the next day, from one A.A. Desrocher of Montreal. It read ORANGE IGNORANCE AND CATHOLIC FANATACISM DEFEATED YOU.[15]

The Aftermath

For two weeks after the election, Robert Borden struggled to fend off demands from all sections of the party and all parts of the country for appointments to his cabinet. Laurier formally resigned on October 6 and Borden presented his list of ministers to Governor General Earl Grey the next day. The roster began with George E. Foster, who had wanted to be Minister of Finance, but had to settle for Trade and Commerce in order to make way for William White, the bright young anti-reciprocity Liberal. This meant the two most important economic posts in the government would belong to Toronto. Most of the other prominent names from the Conservative campaign were on the list: Col. Sam Hughes in Militia and Defence; J.D. Reid (after first being subjected to a lecture for past disloyalty), in Customs; Albert E. Kemp as minister without portfolio; and two former ministers in Tory provincial governments, Robert Rogers from Manitoba as Minister of the Interior and Frank Cochrane from Ontario as Minister of Railways and Canals.

The former Premier of New Brunswick, John Hazen, came in as Minister of Marine. Frederick Monk was there, too, as Minister of Public Works but his *Autonomist* allies in Quebec would have little influence in Ottawa; Borden's triumph was so great that he had no need to rely on the 16 extra seats they had helped him win in that province. From the Senate, Borden called on James A. Lougheed as Alberta's representative in the cabinet. Within two years another westerner, Arthur Meighen of Manitoba, would find himself in the cabinet as Solicitor-General.

In the 1911 election, voting patterns based on education, occupation, income, religion, and ethnic background were twisted sufficiently by the heat of the reciprocity and naval issues to change the outcome. Canadians in 1911, as they still do today, made their choices on three factors; party loyalty, leadership, and the local candidate. With 45 per cent of Canadians now living in urban centres, factory workers had become a significant voting bloc. Pressured by employers, many broke away from class traditions that would have encouraged them to vote Liberal, to support Borden.

Canadian living standards had risen over the previous decade and the revolt against reciprocity counted heavily on the fear of losing these gains. Real wages, spurred by the rise of skilled trades, advanced 43 per cent. Manufacturing output soared 126.5 per cent, while the labour force increased by 35 per cent. But the improvements in living conditions were not equally shared; while a nouveau riche class contributed to a thousand-fold increase in imports of jewelry and perfume, the number of families living in one room grew by 74 per cent, and house rents soared by 60 to 70 per cent.[16]

The 1911 election ensured that Canadian manufacturers would continue to benefit from high tariffs. Combined with other federal policies benefiting the industries of Ontario and Quebec, they would feed a growing alienation among western Canadians. The higher unit costs of Canadian manufacturers, their lower productivity and lack of specialization resulting from manufacturing for a small market, left Canada with a living standard that would never match that of the United States. Conventional wisdom painted this as the price Canadians willingly paid for national independence. This independence became increasingly fragile by mid-century with the take-over of more Canadian companies by American multi-nationals, eager to operate branch plants behind Canada's tariff walls. The defeat of reciprocity thus made the branch plant economy a model for much of Canada's future. By the time late in the century when a Conservative government took up the cause of free trade, some two-thirds of Canadian manufacturing had passed into American hands.

If reciprocity had been accepted in 1911, Canadians would have been tested earlier in the competitiveness of a continental economy. Canadians also would have had the opportunity to build viable industries, assemble the financial resources and create the business philosophy needed to thrust outward to international markets. Mackenzie King flirted briefly with a scheme for "real reciprocity" before rejecting a draft treaty on free trade in 1948. The Auto Pact of 1965 brought managed trade if not free trade to one important sector of the economy. Echoes of the grand design returned in the 1978 report of Donald Macdonald's royal commission on Canada's economic prospects. Macdonald, a former Liberal minister of finance, urged a "leap of faith" by Canada to embrace free trade. It took Brian Mulroney in 1988 to grandly disregard his own party's nationalistic heritage and plunge ahead, first with the U.S.-Canada Free Trade Agreement (FTA) and later the expanded North American Free Trade Agreement (NAFTA). But none of this could be foreseen. The success of the revolt against reciprocity and the passions it aroused made the 1911 election a turning point. Free trade had been wiped from the Canadian political slate, not to return for three-quarters of a century.

CHAPTER SIX

The Federal Election of December 17, 1917

THE ISSUES

The election revolves around the government's handling of Canada's role in World War I, especially the formation by Prime Minister Sir Robert Borden of a Unionist coalition of Conservatives and pro-conscription Liberals to enforce the drafting of men for the Canadian Expeditionary Force. Wartime profiteering, the disenfranchisement of recent immigrants from now enemy countries, and the poor leadership of generals at the front, are also election issues. By abandoning Liberal leader Sir Wilfrid Laurier, pro-conscription Liberals reduce their party to a French Canadian bloc isolated within Quebec. The Unionist victory leaves the Conservative party with an anti-French legacy it will never fully overcome.

THE PERSONALITIES

UNIONIST (LIBERAL-CONSERVATIVE) PARTY

Sir Robert Borden, Prime Minister and Minister of External Affairs
Arthur Meighen, Minister of the Interior
Sir Thomas White, Minister of Finance
Newton W. Rowell, former Ontario Liberal leader; President of Privy Council
Arthur Sifton, former Liberal Premier of Alberta; Minister of Customs
Thomas A. Crerar, President of United Grain Growers;
Minister of Agriculture

LAURIER LIBERALS

Sir Wilfrid Laurier, Leader of the Opposition
Mackenzie King, former Minister of Labour
Henri Bourassa, Quebec Nationalist leader

THE RESULTS

	SEATS	VOTES
Unionist	153	1,074,701 (57.0%)
Laurier Liberals	82	751,493 (39.9%)
Other	–	59,135 (3.1%)

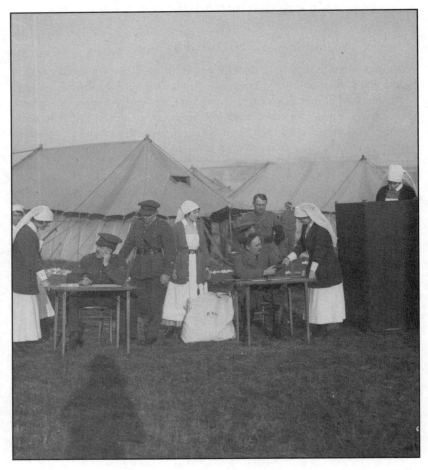

Canadian Army nurses cast their ballots at a 1917 election poll in France.

BLOOD AND THE BALLOT:
DEMOCRACY ON HOLD

The Federal Election of 1917

The Imperial Limited, the pride of the Canadian Pacific Railway, paused in Fort William on this snowy December night, its crew taking on fresh coal and water for the final dash along the north shore of Lake Superior before heading into the spruce forests of northern Ontario and down past the farm settlements of the Ottawa valley. Through the windows of its finest coach, the Matapedia, the tall figure of the elderly statesman could be seen leaning on the back of a velvet-upholstered coach chair, shuffling a batch of telegrams just handed him. Each conveyed the same remorseless message of defeat almost everywhere but in Quebec. The Unionist coalition was holding a narrow lead, and the votes from the West were yet to be counted. Exhausted from 10 days of frantic campaigning across Western Canada, Sir Wilfrid Laurier on this election night had hopes that the warm reception he'd received there would yet bring him the seats he'd need for victory. More than anything, he yearned just to be home, to forget the recriminations of this most bitter of elections, to be again with his wife Zoë in the familiar surroundings of Arthabaska. At 76, with forty years of public service behind him, his flowing white hair, stylish dress and upright bearing still cast an image of courtly elegance matched by no other public figure of the day.

The train had steamed out of Vancouver Friday night, battling first torrential rains and then snowdrifts as it crossed the mountains and plains of Western Canada. Sir Wilfrid and three of his closest confidants, Walter Mitchell and J.F.B. Casgrain from Quebec and Hartley Dewart, the Toronto lawyer, were winding up their biggest tour of the campaign. Enthusiastic crowds had given the old Liberal leader "a cyclone of applause" despite his refusal to support conscription to reinforce the Canadian troops fighting valiantly for the Empire in Europe. His conviction had torn apart his Liberal party, sending dissidents into the arms of Sir

Robert Borden and allowing the Conservative Prime Minister to appeal to the country at the head of a wartime Unionist government. By evening, when the train stopped at the tiny way station of Kaministiqua, 24 miles west of Fort William, its brakeman was one of the first to hear the telegraphed results. He bellowed out, "Laurier's beat," causing Unionist supporters on board to break into cheers.[1]

The ballots that voters cast this wintry day were, figuratively, soaked in the blood of the nearly sixty thousand Canadians who would die in the mud-filled trenches of France and Belgium in this bloodiest of all wars. The loss was enormous for a country of Canada's eight million, far greater than would be experienced in World War II, and a decisive factor in the social and economic malaise into which the country soon would fall. The war was draining Canada of much of its best young blood. Of those who would come back, many would suffer the consequences of shell shock, or what a future generation would call "post-traumatic stress disorder." They would be in no condition mentally or physically to confront the challenge of building a new postwar life.

Since assuming office after winning the 1911 election, Prime Minister Borden had come to realize how difficult it was to put into practice many of the progressive policies he had advocated. He was able to do nothing about making the Senate elective, nationalizing natural resources, or providing government-owned telegraphs and telephones. Nor was he able, in the face of determined Liberal opposition in the Senate, to put through an emergency naval aid bill in 1912 that would have sent thirty-eight million dollars to Britain, to be spent on new warships. Borden was more successful in convincing the United States that Tory anti-American election rhetoric did not represent the attitude of his government; his administration sought nothing but the best in U.S.-Canadian relations. He also moved to shore up the fledgling Department of External Affairs established by Laurier in 1909. Borden took on the portfolio himself, picking his way carefully through the thickets of Imperial diplomacy, intent on having

Canada speak with its own voice on the world stage. At home, Borden's election victory had been so great that he was able to govern without having to rely on the support of his French Canadian Nationalist allies. Convenient though this was, it left the government – and the country – fatally vulnerable when a great national crisis would require a unity of purpose from both of Canada's founding races.

Britain's declaration of war against Germany and Austria-Hungary on August 3, 1914 meant Canada also was at war. The cabinet prepared draconian steps to mobilize the country, setting out powers under a new War Measures Act to impose censorship, curb dissent, and give the government a free hand to put the country on a war footing. The Governor General cabled the King that "Canada stands united from the Pacific to the Atlantic in her determination to uphold the honour and traditions of our Empire." In both English and French Canada, there was an outpouring of enthusiasm and loyalty toward the British Empire. Even in Montreal, streets were filled with cheering crowds at patriotic demonstrations. French-language newspapers ran headlines supporting the war. "There are no longer French Canadians and English Canadians," declared Montreal's *La Presse* on August 5, 1914. "Only one race now exists, united by the closest bonds in a common cause." Few were more passionate that Wilfrid Laurier, who saw the war as a great opportunity for his countrymen to demonstrate their loyalty to the crown. In Quebec, Liberal and Nationalist MPs spoke in support of the war, as did prominent French Canadian businessmen. Even Laurier's arch-critic, Henri Bourassa, filled the pages of his *Le Devoir* with pro-war writings, calling on Canada to "contribute in the measure of her strength." It seemed as if Canada would be united in a common cause to give backing to both Britain and France. It was not to be; the two solitudes of English and French would soon again diverge, the offsprings of different language, history, culture and religion.

The initial euphoria over the war lasted barely through that first winter. September's volunteers imagined they'd be home for Christmas. When it didn't turn out that way the ardour to take up arms cooled considerably in both English and French Canada. The Ontario government's enforcement of Regulation 17, its new law restricting French-language school instruction to the first two grades, inflamed public opinion in Quebec. Once again English Canada was doing its best to subvert French expression. First it had been Manitoba with its abolition of bilingual schools, then the new provinces of the Nortwest Territories that attacked Catholic education; now Canada's most populous English-speaking domain was set to crush the development of a French nationality outside Quebec. Ontario's French school commissioners were fined, children went on strike, school boards defied the government and grants to bilingual schools were cancelled as the province's separate school system descended into chaos. Six hundred thousand people signed a petition asking redress, but nothing came of it. Laurier's effort to have Parliament appeal to Ontario to allow French instruction failed to win the support of even his own party outside Quebec. Quebec newspapers ran articles on the mistreatment of francophone Ontarians, reinforcing the view that Canada outside of Quebec was an unfriendly place for the French language and culture. Why should Quebec's boys go overseas to fight for the Empire when the English abused their cousins here at home? People in Quebec felt no attachment to Britain and little to France; the loyalty of New France had been lost long ago when the revolutionaries of 1793 stormed the Bastille and overthrew the *ancienne regime*. As discontent rose in Quebec, Parliament returned to its fractious ways. Expecting an election in 1915, Laurier and the Liberals hounded the government over wartime scandals and profiteering. There was no shortage of issues to debate, especially those "sweet deals" cooked up by government supporters to exploit oppor- tunities in the new armaments industry that Canada was building to supply the weapons, uniforms, and equipment needed by a rapidly-growing military.

Canada sent its first division of thirty thousand volunteers to Britain a bare three months after the outbreak of war. These first members of the Canadian Expeditionary Force were mostly

British-born, a fact that disguised the reluctance of many Canadians, English as well as French, to rush to enlist. By war's end, some six hundred and fifty thousand men, including one hundred thousand conscripts, would serve in uniform. Only thirty thousand, or fewer than five per cent, would be French-speaking Quebeckers, at a time when Quebec accounted for thirty per cent of Canada's population. A new French-Canadian regiment, the Royal 22nd Rifles, performed nobly and sons of Quebec were to be found in other regiments, but it soon became evident that the CEF was to be overwhelmingly English. Government blundering didn't help. An English-speaking Protestant clergyman was appointed chief recruiting officer in Quebec. At the big Valcartier base outside Montreal, units of French-Canadian volunteers were split up and scattered among English regiments. The anti-Catholic prejudice of Borden's minister of militia, Col. Sam Hughes, an Orangeman, was blamed for a number of quite competent French officers being relegated to minor posts. If that weren't enough, Hughes became embroiled in a controversy over his favoured weapon, the Ross rifle that he'd ordered for the Canadian Corps. It had a disturbing habit of jamming in action and had to be withdrawn. Borden eventually had to dismiss Hughes from cabinet for interfering with the chain of command. Oblivious to all this, when the Prime Minister came to Montreal, it was to address a delegation of Orangemen at the Ritz Carleton hotel. Recruiting in Quebec slowed to a trickle, despite Laurier's call to his countrymen to fulfill "the supreme honour of bearing arms in this holy cause." The threat of conscription, the Liberal leader thought, "is as groundless today as it was in 1911."

As the war deepened, both political parties realized that a wartime election would be both difficult and divisive. The government hesitated to call by-elections for the twenty vacant House seats, so fearful was it of defeat. Since 1915, the Conservatives had lost five provincial elections in a row. Reluctantly, Laurier agreed to a request from Borden to extend the life of Parliament, but only by another year; there would have to be an election sometime in 1917. Debates in the House of Commons continued to focus on the drab routine of daily domestic affairs. So it was that on the night of Thursday, February 3, 1916, MPs were debating the future of the fisheries industry when the Conservative member for Middlesex East in Ontario, Frank Glass, burst into the House of Commons chamber to shout, "The building is all on fire. Get out as quickly as you can." The ornate Italian Gothic stone works making up Canada's first Parliament Building had been opened in 1866, its construction a daring accomplishment by the old Province of Canada a year before Confederation. By dawn, only that section housing the library of Parliament still stood, the rest having collapsed in rubble. The fire had started in the pine paneled reading room and spread quickly, forcing MPs to escape by climbing out of washroom windows or down back stairs. Prime Minister Borden was in his office in the West Wing and had to find his way through "a great volume of thick, black smoke through which darted long tongues of flame."[2] Wilfrid Laurier had been at a concert in the Russell Theatre when he was notified of the fire. Returning to Parliament Hill, he found his own office destroyed, including all his papers for the years 1912-15. By the time the fire burned out, seven people were dead, including the Liberal MP for Yarmouth, Nova Scotia, Bowman Law, and two young secretaries with whom Laurier and his wife had dined just the night before. A subdued and reflective body of MPs, many of them still in shock, met in emergency session the next afternoon in the auditorium of the Victoria Memorial Museum. The Senate met in (perhaps appropriately) the museum's Hall of Invertebrate Fossils.

As casualties at the front mounted and the pace of volunteers slowed, desperate measures were needed to keep the Canadian Corps at strength in France. Canadian troops were bloodied early in 1915, with over six thousand being killed in the first battle of Ypres in Belgium – their heroics immortalized in Canadian medic John McCrae's poem, "In Flanders Field." The battle of the Somme alone, fought in September 1916 cost twenty-four thousand Canadian casualties. In April 1917 the Easter Monday conquest by Canadians of Vimy Ridge added another ten thousand to the toll of killed and wounded. For a time the government hoped its new system of registering able-bodied men for National Service would turn up additional recruits. The cabinet minister in charge of the scheme, Calgary's R.B. Bennett, was able to report more than a million and a half men had returned their registration cards. Of those, nearly five hundred thousand were considered military prospects. That was twice the number of volunteers who enlisted during the month. The entry of the United States into the war on April 6 raised morale but did nothing to ease the pressure to get more Canadians to Europe.

Prime Minister Borden had sailed in secrecy and a snowstorm for Britain in February. After attending an Imperial War Conference and touring the front lines and hospitals in France, he returned to Canada convinced there would have to be conscription if the Canadian Corps was to remain an effective fighting force. On May 14 – a mere four days after his return from London – Borden told the House of Commons that the government was preparing a bill to require "compulsory military enlistment on a selective basis." Canada would have to conscript at least fifty thousand – and possibly a hundred thousand – men to join the three hundred and sixty thousand that by this time "have left the shores of Canada." He'd been there with them, Borden reminded the House, and "Only those who have seen them at the front can realize how much they do love this dear land of Canada."

Birth of the Unionist Government

The PM understood the war was far from over and that his government would have to either secure an accord with Laurier and the Liberal party, or face the people. If he could arrange for conscription to be enacted by a coalition government, the country might be saved from a wrenching English-French split. It would also, conveniently, help preserve a future for the Conservative party in Quebec. The first alarm that conscription would cause a furor in French Canada came from Borden's Nationalist allies, who knew to a man that Quebec voters would never accept forced recruitment. Henri Bourassa was the most inflammatory of the lot; his warning that conscription would turn Quebeckers into "a revolutionary people" seemed excessive even for him. None of this deterred Borden from appealing directly to Laurier. For twenty weeks throughout much of 1917 – from May 25 to October 12 – Borden struggled to put together a coalition Liberal-Conservative government that would have Laurier as a member. The discussions began with a series of remarkable personal letters that went back and forth – "Dear Sir Wilfrid Laurier," "My Dear Sir Robert" – and included four face-to-face meetings, the first at the Prime Minister's home at Sandy Hill. Borden proposed a coalition cabinet composed equally of Conservatives and Liberals plus himself as Prime Minister. When Laurier took the offer back to his cohorts, he found them divided. The young Mackenzie King thought there should be conscription of workers and capital as well as men – a conscription election could "annihilate" the Liberal party. Four days later, his decision made, Laurier told Borden that he could accept conscription only on condition that a referendum or an election be held first. Amazingly, Borden agreed. He said he would proceed with his Military Service Act, but it would not be implemented until a coalition government was elected. Playing for time, Laurier stalled again. Finally, on June 6, he gave his last word. Laurier would not join a coalition or support conscription; that would mean abandoning Quebec to the extreme Nationalists, a betrayal of everything that had always been dear to him. But if conscription became the law of the land, he would urge all Canadians to obey it.

New measures to strengthen Canada's war capability were taken throughout the year. An income tax was introduced as a "temporary" wartime measure, along with prohibition of alcohol. The government's Military Service Act spelled out the conditions of conscription; all men from 20 to 45 would be covered but there would be exemptions for those in vital industries or who were needed on the farms. Still, Laurier could not be turned. He told Parliament: "We are face to face with a cleavage which, unless it is checked, may rend and tear this Canada of ours to the very roots." In the vote, Laurier lost 22 of his caucus; they included stalwarts like his ex-finance minister, W.S. Fielding, and his close friend Frank Carvell of New Brunswick, "Fighting Frank."

Conscription was approved, 102-44. Only five French-Canadians supported the bill. Shortly after, Parliament voted to give itself another year's extension. But by now, it was clear the Opposition was in disarray, unable to effectively oppose the government, and fearful of causing an election. Borden had no such qualms. Disregarding the vote for extension, he had decided on an election after all, but not "until the ground has been carefully and completely prepared." He confided to his diary, "Our first duty is to win, at any cost the coming election in order that we may continue to do our part in winning the war and that Canada be not disgraced."[3] Borden's strategy was now clear: to bring over enough Liberals without Laurier to enable him to go to the people at the head of a Unionist government, dedicated to finishing the war with Canada's valour intact.

There would be one last attempt to co-opt Laurier. Borden had the Governor General, the Duke of Devonshire, summon a secret conference of some of Canada's most powerful men. There was Lord Shaughnessey of the CPR, Lomer Gouin, the Premier of Quebec, Clifford Sifton, the Winnipeg newspaper publisher who had broken with Laurier over free trade in 1911 and was now an ardent conscriptionist, George Foster, Borden's minister of trade and commerce, along with Wilfrid Laurier and Borden himself. It was to no avail; despite Borden's offer to suspend conscription while another call went out for recruits, Laurier again rebuffed the invitation. Perhaps he felt emboldened by Sifton's failure to mount a coup against him. More than a thousand Western Liberals had just met in Winnipeg, called together by Sifton's brother Arthur, the premier of Alberta, ostensibly to discuss wartime policy but actually to pressure Laurier into either accepting conscription or resigning. It didn't work. "Convention over," Laurier's loyal supporter Frank Oliver of Edmonton wired him that morning. "You were endorsed by almost unanimous standing vote."

The Borden cabinet's plan for a "winning election" now took a more ominous turn. Two additional emergency bills were about to be presented to Parliament. Together, they would represent the greatest assault ever mounted on individual democratic rights in Canada, and would effectively put democracy on hold for the duration of the war. Both blatantly partisan but each cloaked in "win the war" patriotism, they were calculated to fix the outcome of the election by giving the vote to those who would be most likely to support the government, and taking it away from those most likely to vote against it. The first, the Military Voters Act, extended the vote to all men and women who were serving in the Canadian forces, regardless of how long they'd been resident in Canada. Besides giving votes to women for the first time as well to immigrants who had joined up without being British subjects, the bill also conveniently arranged that overseas votes would be cast by party rather than by candidate. Soldiers were to direct to which riding their ballot should be sent, an invitation to ballot box-stuffing for any government candidate short a few votes at home. The second, the Wartime Elections Act designed by Borden's Secretary of State, Arthur Meighen, made a direct assault on the citizenship rights of immigrants who had arrived from enemy countries in the last fifteen years. These included Germans, Austrians, Czechs, Slovaks, Poles, Ruthenians, and Galicians, as well as other former inhabitants of parts of Russia since incorporated into Germany. Anyone of these nationalities who had not been naturalized before 1902 was to be deprived of the right to vote, unless they had male relatives serving overseas in the Canadian or British armed forces. They would also, incidentally, be exempt from conscription. It was no coincidence that those who lost their vote had mostly settled in the West under Laurier and Sifton's great immigration campaign of the first decade of the century, and were natural supporters of the Liberal party. In addition, the Act gave the vote to all women with relatives in the forces. By extending voting rights to these women, and withholding it from others, thousands of additional votes were assured for Union candidates. If these measures weren't enough to ensure a government victory, a reorganization of the federal ridings that had recently taken place would surely do the trick. Through careful gerrymandering, riding boundaries in Ontario, New Brunswick and Nova Scotia were redrawn to the detriment of Liberals. In the West, twenty-two seats were added to reflect population growth, further tipping the balance of power away from Quebec. Borden knew that he would have a fight on his hands to disenfranchise qualified immigrants who were also British subjects. The bill faced "vehement opposition and violent controversy," Borden noted in his diary. The debate set off "fierce and protracted resistance," and the government had to resort to closure on September 8. Borden defended the legislation with the argument that it would be unrealistic to conscript recent arrivals from enemy countries and expect them to fight against their homeland and their families. If they were to be exempted from conscription, they should not be entrusted with a vote.

With both bills finally approved and his emissaries at work on cajoling dissident Liberals to abandon Laurier, Borden went fishing in the Laurentians in late September. Borden recognized that for many in Laurier's caucus, "the idea of breaking with his leadership seemed almost inconceivable." But by early October, even the most faithful had to choose between supporting a coalition, or having to answer to their electorate of mostly avid conscriptionists. Like dominos, Liberal followers began to fall. Among the first to go were provincial Liberal leaders in New Brunswick, Ontario, Manitoba, Saskatchewan and Alberta. The Ontario provincial leader, Newton Wesley Rowell, progenitor of a family that would have great influence in Canada for decades to come, was insistent for conscription.[4] In the West the Sifton brothers, joined by Manitoba's Liberal Premier Tobias Norris and James A. Calder, a minister in Saskatchewan's Liberal government, trumpeted the need for a solid front against Quebec. A delegation had confronted Laurier in his office, suggesting he resign. Resistance of the last Liberals hold-outs crumbled after October 11 when Rowell, accompanied by Arthur Sifton, Calder, and Thomas A. Crerar, a promising young farm leader from Manitoba, made a midnight walk from the Chateau Laurier, the new hotel named in honour of the Liberal leader, to the Parliament Building. There, they told a waiting Borden that most Liberal MPs from outside Quebec were prepared to support a Union government; in fact thirty-eight of Laurier's forty-nine non-Quebec members would abandon him. The next day, a cabinet of twelve Conservatives and nine Liberals was presented to Parliament. They included Arthur Sifton, Calder and Crerar from the West; Rowell, Hugh Guthrie and General S. C. Mewburn from Ontario; and Frank Carvell from New Brunswick, A.K. MacLean from Nova Scotia, and C.C. Ballantyne, a Montreal businessman. The Conservative powerhouses were still there: Arthur Meighen as Minister of the Interior, George Foster in Trade and Commerce, Thomas White in Finance, and J.D. Reid in railways. Borden's token Quebec representatives were also rewarded; Pierre E. Blondin as postmaster-general and Joseph P.A. Sevigny at Inland Revenue. Neither figures of consequence, they would not long survive the bitter trench warfare of Quebec politics.

The Campaign and the Candidates

"This election is a matter of life and death and every ballot is a bullet."
— *John W. Dafoe, Winnipeg Free Press, November 22, 1917*

On October 31, the Governor General granted Borden's request for dissolution of Parliament, and a federal vote – Canada's first in six years – was called for December 17. The prospect was for "a murderous winter election" Sir Wilfrid Laurier wrote, resignedly, to one of his few remaining English Canadian supporters. Defections left him with but the skeleton of a party across the country; there was no loyal Liberal available to run in Ottawa and so Laurier, in accordance with the election laws of the day, allowed his name to be put forward there as well as in his home riding of Quebec East. Two days after the election call, four hundred Ontario Liberals met in Hamilton to endorse their newly-minted

Unionist cabinet members. "Our country first," read the banner over the podium as the crowd cheered the introduction of General Mewburn as the new Minister of the Militia, Frank Carvell ("Hero of a Hundred Fights"), the new Postmaster-General, and Newton Rowell, now president of the Privy Council. General Mewburn boasted it was his first political speech: "I am not supporting either Borden or Laurier. What we want today is action and we are going to have it." He thought the way the war effort had been handled was "deplorable" and that even a hundred thousand conscripts might not be sufficient in view of the one hundred and twenty-five thousand casualties the Canadians had already suffered.[5]

Across the country, the task of choosing a single candidate from Conservatives and pro-conscription Liberals did not always go easily. The nod generally went to the incumbent as long as a Liberal MP was prepared to join the Unionist camp. In cases where he wasn't, such as Frank Oliver in Edmonton, the government nominated an opponent, in this case lawyer Bill Griesbach, scion of a pioneering Alberta family. Only in the Mackenzie riding of Saskatchewan were the two parties unable to agree on a single pro-conscription candidate. It didn't matter; no Laurier Liberal came forward to oppose the two Unionists on the ballot.

The Prime Minister unveiled the government's election platform in two installments. On October 19, Borden promised "vigorous prosecution of the war ... immediate enforcement of the Military Service act, and the most thorough cooperation with the governments of the United Kingdom and of the other Dominions in all matters relating to the war." A second and longer version was released in Ottawa on November 12 on the eve of Borden's first campaign swing through the Maritimes. While Canada had performed gloriously in enlisting four hundred thousand volunteers and sending three hundred and fifty thousand of them overseas, conscription now was needed. But there would be no chance selection as originally intended; instead, there would be "intelligent selection" in order that there be no "prejudicial interference with agriculture or industry." Borden was promising exemptions for farm and factory workers and, in fact, up to fifty per cent of those originally conscripted in Ontario filed for exemptions. The Unionist government, Borden's platform declared, was determined "to sink differences and overcome prejudices." It was time to bury party differences, "no party wall divides the wounded in the hospitals." It also was time to abolish patronage in government appointments by filling public offices "by merit and not by favouritism." To meet wartime needs, the government would ensure "adequate taxation" of war profits and "increased taxation of income." And after the war, returning soldiers would be re-educated, the maimed and broken protected, the widow and orphan helped and cherished. "Those who are saving democracy shall not find democracy a house of privilege, or a school of poverty and hardship."[6]

In Halifax, Borden was met by a cheering crowd of four thousand at the Market hall. He'd chosen to seek re-election in the rural riding of Kings, leaving the two Halifax seats to be filled by acclamation; again no Laurier Liberal had come forward. Borden spent most of his speech attacking Laurier's call to hold a referendum before putting conscription into effect. Such a vote would delay the sending of reinforcements and "would be hailed with great joy by the German high command," Borden said. "The spirit of our men would be broken and their ranks more and more depleted."[7]

Borden counted on a strong showing in the Maritimes and was sure he could sweep Ontario and the West. Having toured the West earlier in the war, he decided to concentrate on the eastern half of the country, while generally ignoring Quebec. The few government rallies there were disasters; police had to be called out to quell riotous anti-conscriptionists who fiercely shouted down government supporters. For the first time in years, Quebec's Nationalists were fully in support of the Liberals. Returning to Ontario from his first swing through the Maritimes, Borden embraced every Unionist Liberal with whom he could share a platform. He ran into trouble only in the former city of Berlin, a centre of largely German population that had recently changed its name to honour the British commander in France, Lord Kitchener. Borden's rally there on November 24 was so rowdy he was forced to cancel his speech, retreating from the platform in a hail of insults and derision. When news got out, the city's manufacturers were inundated with cancelled orders. "The Kitchener incident was much more effective than any speech I could have delivered," Borden confessed in his diary.

Then it was back to the east coast again, where the three Maritime premiers favoured conscription, although none would actually campaign for the Unionist cause. After receiving a warm reception in Charlottetown, Borden crossed over to the mainland on December 6 and boarded a train for Pictou, Nova Scotia. Then came news of a dreadful accident. It was the disaster that would become known as the Halifax Explosion, unequalled in Canadian history, and the largest man-made eruption until Hiroshima. The French munitions ship Mont Blanc carrying three thousand tons of TNT, had collided that morning with a Belgian relief vessel, wiping out a large portion of the city. Cancelling his Pictou rally, Borden rushed to his home city where he found its fifty thousand people in shock – two thousand dead, eleven thousand injured, twenty thousand homeless. Borden ordered a half million dollars in federal aid and stayed to tour hospitals, visit victims in their homes, and set in motion the official inquiry into the accident.

The intensity of Unionist campaigning seemed to strengthen Laurier's determination to make a fight of the election, no matter how low his campaign funds or how great his loss of supporters. He'd put the finishing touches to his platform within days of the election call. The unveiling took place at his first rally in his home riding of Quebec East on November 9. The large crowd awaiting Laurier at the railway station included hundreds of women who viewed him as the saviour of their sons. At the rally that night at the Martineau Skating Rink, French Canada closed ranks around their undisputed leader. Henri Bourassa was there, "accepting Laurier as the lesser devil," along with the likes of Lomer Gouin, the Premier, and Ernest Lapointe, Laurier's first lieutenant.

Calling up his best salvos from his election platform, Laurier tried to move the election off conscription and onto economic issues. He attacked the Tory failure to curb the cost of living and criticized the government for raising import duties. "I would not hesitate to commandeer all food factories," he declared, promising "to put a stop to profiteering on war supplies." On conscription, he thought it "was bound more to hinder than to help the war," and pledged, if elected, to suspend the draft pending the outcome of a referendum. He suggested wealth should be conscripted as well as men, and promised to "seek out the ablest of the country," regardless of party, to form a cabinet "whose first object will be to find the men, money and resources necessary to ensure the fullest measure of support to our heroic soldiers." Laurier also zeroed in on the Wartime Elections act, a foul bill that deprived honest citizens of the right to vote, "a blot upon every instinct of justice, honesty and fair play."

The day after the awful news from Halifax, Laurier boarded the Matapedia, the private railway car put at his disposal by CPR president Edward Beatty for his desperate tour of Western Canada. The leading newspapers declined to send reporters; the Toronto *World*, the *Globe* and the *News* all saw it as a pointless exercise for Laurier to scour the prairies and the mountains for votes that weren't there. Laurier thought otherwise, and the warmth of the welcoming delegation at Winnipeg's Fort Garry hotel helped offset the minus -20 degree weather outside. Yet there was disturbing news, too; General Mewburn was promising the government would exempt farmers' sons in Ontario, confirming that it was not only in Quebec that young men did not wish to go to war. A telegram came advising of the death of the former PM, Mackenzie Bowell, who had retired in 1896. That night, five thousand filled the streets outside the Industrial Hall, with another six thousand jammed inside. Little heckling was heard, giving Laurier and his party hope that his arguments were winning over the undecideds.

In Regina, Laurier addressed meetings in three churches, with hundreds inside and more hundreds outside. The next night, his train was hours late in reaching Calgary, not arriving until almost midnight for the first of four rallies where around six thousand people had waited patiently through the tedium of choir singing and minor speeches. Laurier was the "same accomplished platform figure," wrote the reporter for the Calgary *Herald*, with "the same graceful features which go so far towards charming an audience."[8] But it was also clear that they must be "seeing and hearing for the last time a man whose name was once one to conjure with, but whose reputation as a great political leader still gained for him a reception overwhelmingly enthusiastic from every one of the big audiences which he addressed." Laurier's warmest reception, however, was ahead of him in Vancouver. "Seldom has Vancouver witnessed such a tremendous personal triumph," the Vancouver *World* reporter wrote of the five meetings Laurier addressed there. A "deep-throated roar of male voices breaking into cheer after cheer greeted him as he appeared on the stage ... the political warrior par excellence, the fighting party leader appealing confidently to his supporters to follow him into the fray." The warmth of Laurier's reception in the West reminded him of his first visit to this part of Canada in 1894; that tour had set the stage for his election victory two years later. Might the enthusiasm of his crowds this time not auger a similar result the following week?

At every stop, Laurier took pains to answer the charges of disloyalty flung at him by Unionist supporters, especially in the newspapers. Except in Quebec, the press was universally against him, led by former friends such as John Willison of the Toronto *Globe* and John W. Dafoe, the editor of the Winnipeg *Free Press*. Willison headed up the Unionist publicity committee and his tactics of merciless criticism set the tone for the government's campaign. In one tract, it was asserted that "Laurier, Bourassa and Quebec ... are in favour of deserting our men, breaking our pledge ... and trailing Canada's honour in the mud of world opinion." One of the most vicious pieces was a poster asking, "Who Would the Kaiser Vote For?" The *Globe* ran cartoons depicting Laurier and his supporters hiding behind the German defence position in

France, the Hindenburg Line. To the Toronto *News*, the Liberal leader had become "a demagogue, a charlatan and a mountebank." The thunderings of Dafoe, perhaps the most influential editor of the day, were even more frenetic. Declaring every ballot to be cast on election day a bullet to be fired at the enemy, he asked: "Shall your bullet pierce the obscene heart that, emerging from the lairs of ancient Hundum, is trampling the nations of the world beneath its swinish feet? Or shall it find lodgment in the heart of Canada? Shall Quebec, which will neither fight nor pay, rule? No! You must vote the way your sons shoot." There was more: "This contest is not an election but a destiny. Beyond all reasonable doubt it is a conflict for the soul of the nation."[9] In Calgary, the *Herald* drew the line between the government and the Opposition: The former consisted of "Liberal and Conservative party men who have sunk party in order to more effectively prosecute the war," the latter "Slackers and shirkers in Quebec, and all other parts of the Dominion, who want to get back at the government which is forcing them to do their duty as four hundred thousand other Canadians have done theirs voluntarily."

The few prominent Liberals who remained loyal to Laurier included Mackenzie King, fighting a lonely battle in York constituency north of Toronto. His Conservative opponent John A. Macdonald Armstrong had been MP since 1911 and knew every family in the area, having grown up in the district. At some meetings, King faced bus-loads of returned soldiers, brought in from hospitals for no other purpose than to disrupt his speeches. But he held his ground, often winning begrudging applause from tormentors. Campaigning from the King George hotel in Newmarket, King put out his own platform statement which he called The Two Policies. He saw Borden's conscription policy as a grave threat to national unity: "It is a question of how Canada shall be united in the face of a terrible foe menacing the liberties of mankind."

As the polls opened on election day, Unionist scrutineers were vigilant in challenging suspected enemy aliens who might turn up to vote. In most cases, the work of purging the voters' list had already been done. A north Winnipeg poll where many Austro-Germans lived saw its numbers reduced from two hundred and forty-one to only twenty. The turn-out was reported to be heavy throughout the country, and reports of incidents were rare. While Sir Wilfrid Laurier contemplated the outcome from his railway car rolling east from the Manitoba border, Sir Robert Borden and his wife went to the temporary Senate offices in the Victoria Museum in Ottawa to receive the results. Relying on both telephone and telegraph, Borden found "The returns came in quickly … the result was beyond our anticipation." In actual fact, the evening started poorly for the government. With only the civilian vote being counted election night, Laurier and the Liberals were leading in all four Prince Edward Island seats, nine of sixteen in Nova Scotia, as well as in the four predominately Acadian seats in New Brunswick. In Nova Scotia, Borden carried Kings easily, 3,941 votes to 2,524 for Liberal James Sealy. There was worry in the Senate offices that the score for the Maritimes, seventeen Laurier Liberals and fourteen Unionists, would be multiplied as the Quebec results became known. There, as expected, it was no contest: Laurier's candidates carried all but three of the province's sixty-five seats. Both French Canadian Unionist cabinet ministers, P.E. Blondin and Joseph Sévingy, were defeated. Only Charles C. Ballantyne, the Liberal-Unionist minister without portfolio, held his seat, the Montreal riding of Saint Laurent-Saint Georges. Laurier won handily in Quebec East, defeating one Ferdinand Drouin, 6,957 to 562.

For all that Quebec stood solidly behind Laurier, it would be in Ontario and the West that the election would be decided. From the closing of the polls in Ontario's cities, the tide built for conscription and the Union government. By the end of the counting, seventy-four Unionists would be declared winners in Ontario, to only eight Laurier Liberals. Mackenzie King suffered the embarrassment of a trouncing in Newmarket, more than a thousand votes behind his Conservative opponent. Newton Rowell had an easy time in Durham, winning by nearly five thousand votes. The margins of the finance minister, Sir Thomas

White in Leeds, and the trade minister, Sir George Foster in Toronto North, were even more impressive. White virtually doubled his opponent's vote and Foster won with over twenty-one thousand votes compared to fewer than three thousand for the Laurier Liberal, Alfred James Young.

On hearing the results from the West the morning after the election Laurier is said to have remarked, "They cheered for me, but they didn't vote for me." Only one Liberal was elected among Manitoba's fifteen ridings, which was better than Saskatchewan where Unionists swept all sixteen seats. Alberta voted for the Union government in eleven out of twelve seats. British Columbia gave all its thirteen seats to the government, as did Yukon voters their single riding. Thomas Crerar, the new minister of agriculture, led the victory parade in the Manitoba riding of Marquette, while Arthur Meighen won easily in Portage la Prairie, 4,611 votes to 1,152. Laurier's man, Frank Oliver was beaten in Edmonton West while the former Premier of the province, Arthur Sifton, won Medicine Hat. The magnitude of Laurier's Western disaster became apparent with the election of fifty-five Unionists to only two Liberals. When counting stopped across the country for the night, one hundred and forty one Unionists had been elected, a solid majority, to ninety-six Laurier Liberals. The addition of the soldier vote would add another dozen ridings to the government ranks, including seven that would switch to Unionist in the Maritimes. The final standing would be one hundred and fifty-three Unionists, eighty-two Laurier Liberals. The turn-out had been the heaviest yet for a Canadian federal election, a full seventy-eight per cent of eligible voters, for a total vote of nearly a million and a half. Over four hundred thousand soldiers, and one hundred and eighty-five thousand women, had bolstered the Unionist totals. Ninety-two per cent of the armed forces vote went to the government, compared to fifty-two per cent of the civilian vote. The results gave Borden a clear mandate to press forward with conscription; his margin of victory over Laurier, fifty-seven per cent to just under forty per cent would never be equaled by a Canadian leader in the twentieth century.

The next day, Canadian newspapers unleashed a barrage of jingoistic headlines hailing the outcome. "Vancouver Rings Out its Message to Berlin," headlined the Vancouver *World*, adding the results were a "Night-mare for the Kaiser." Under the caption "Saved" the Winnipeg *Free Press* declared that Canada had been saved "from treason to the holiest cause for which men ever fought and died." A picture of Laurier was captioned, "Swept Aside by Patriotic Canada." The Toronto *Mail and Empire* wrote: "Whatever else may be remembered against Sir Wilfrid Laurier, the country cannot forgive him for this war time election. He was in a position to force one on the country and without compunction he did it."

The Aftermath

After the election, Borden issued a statement congratulating voters for having "splendidly fulfilled their duty." … "No severer trial of the courage, self-sacrifice and endurance of a democracy was ever made." Canada had indeed come through a great trial. Unionists would probably have won without the denial of voting rights, the manipulation of the soldier vote, and the selective extension of the vote to some women. Unquestionably, however, these tactics, combined with the War Measures Act and the outlawing of strikes, effectively suspended democratic rule in Canada. The 1917 election was fought over conscription, but the underlying issue was the even more divisive question of the role of French Canada in Confederation and the future of francophones outside Quebec. In a perceptive analysis written twenty years after the election, American academic Elizabeth Armstrong concluded that the vote plunged Canada into "the greatest crisis in her history" and threatened to wreck Confederation "on the jagged rocks of nationalism."[10] It did all of this, and more. Coming in the wake of the rejection by Ontario and the West of bilingual education, the 1917 election earned its ranking as a turning point by effectively destroying any prospect of a meaningful French-English partnership in the provinces beyond Quebec, with the possible exception of New Brunswick. It ended the Confederation dream of a bi-national French and English Canada and reduced Quebec to the status of a province like the others. For the first time, the election brought to the surface the possibility of Quebec's separation, an issue that nearly a century later still has not been totally resolved. Early in 1918, the Quebec provincial assembly debated for the first time a resolution on separation. It was worded vaguely, but the message was clear: "the province of Quebec would be disposed to accept the breaking of the Confederation Pact if in the other provinces it is believed that she is an obstacle to the union, progress and development of Canada." Its author, J. N. Francoeur, withdrew the motion only after an impassioned speech by the premier, Sir Lomer Gouin, defending the progress that had been achieved under Confederation. The idea of separation, the French speakers in the debate declared, was clearly a response to the humiliations and insults that had been visited on French Canadians by the English in other provinces. There was no support for separatism in Quebec at the time; the province's newspapers universally derided the idea (while conceding the motion provided a platform to talk about the wrongs done to Quebec) and church authorities made it clear they were against secession. But the seed of separatism had been planted, even if it would lie unnourished in barren soil for decades to come.

Enforcement of conscription sparked disturbances throughout Quebec, with the most serious outbreak taking place in Quebec City over Easter weekend, 1918. It started on Good Friday with the arrest by the Dominion police of a suspected draft evader who, when taken to his house, was able to produce a certificate of exemption. As rumours spread throughout the neighbourhood, a crowd of several thousand descended on the police station and burned it to the ground. The next night a mob attacked the offices of the Military Service Registry. It too was burned, along with all its records. Sporadic rioting went on all day Easter Sunday. A thousand troops arrived from Toronto, later to be reinforced by another three thousand from the West. Mounted cavalry charged the mob with drawn swords as snipers fired at the troops from rooftops and doorways. By the end of the rioting the next day, four civilians were dead and several soldiers wounded. A cabinet order-in-council permitted the holding of prisoners without bail. A coroner's jury would later blame federal police for the incident.

The Prime Minister was on board a ship headed for Britain when a purser brought him the news early on the morning of November 11, 1918, that an armistice would be declared at eleven o'clock. Borden stayed in Europe until May, 1919 – an absence from Ottawa of six months – during which he won for Canada the right to be a separate signatory to the Versailles Treaty, and become an autonomous member of the League of Nations. He returned to a Canada where he would no longer have Sir Wilfrid Laurier as an adversary. The old man had died of a stroke on February 17, 1919, while dressing for church. Fifty thousand people lined the route of his funeral cortege in Ottawa, further evidence of the sentiment in which Canadians held this revered figure of a passing era.

CHAPTER SEVEN

The Federal Election of September 18, 1926

THE ISSUES

The refusal of the Governor General, Lord Byng, to grant Mackenzie King's request for an election when he faces defeat in Parliament – Byng instead invites Conservative leader Arthur Meighen to form a government – becomes the central issue of the election when Meighen's government falls four days after taking office. The incident will become known as the "King-Byng affair," testing Canada's parliamentary tradition in which no Governor General has ever refused to heed the advice of the Prime Minister. A customs scandal involving officials of King's government is also an important issue.

THE PERSONALITIES

THE CROWN
Governor General Lord Julian Byng
(Commander of Canadian forces at Vimy Ridge)

CONSERVATIVE PARTY
Arthur Meighen, MP for Portage la Prairie, Man., Prime Minister
Harry H. Stevens, MP, Vancouver, Chair of House of Commons Customs
Committee investigating allegations of Liberal wrong-doing

LIBERAL PARTY
Mackenzie King, MP for Prince Albert, Sask.,
Leader of the Official Opposition

THE PROGRESSIVE PARTY
Robert Forke, leader and MP for Brandon, Man.

THE RESULTS

	SEATS	VOTES
Liberal Party*	128	1,500,302 (46.1%)
Conservative Party	91	1,474,283 (45.3%)
Progressive Party**	20	171,516 (5.3%)
Other	6	110,407 (3.0%)

*Includes 11 Liberal-Progressives, one Liberal-Labour and two Liberal-Labour-Progressives. **Includes 11 United Farmer of Alberta.

Sir Arthur Meighen, seen here signing autographs in formal garb,
gloried in his upper class status but lost the 1926 election while
defending the Governor General and Canada's British connection.

KING, CROWN AND COUNTRY:
CRISIS OR CON JOB?

The Federal Election of 1926

Conservative party workers moved in and out of the crowd gathered around the entrance of the British Columbia Legislative Building, an edifice that had stood guard since 1897 over Victoria's Inner Harbour. They were urging everyone to ignore the summer rain that was beginning to fall and to wait out the arrival of the Prime Minister, Arthur Meighen. A policeman told the waiting crowd, erroneously, that the rally had been moved to the nearby Empress hotel, causing confusion and much scurrying about before the official party finally assembled at the building's main door, just as the sun broke out. The B.C. premier, John Oliver, a Liberal, was there to extend a courtesy welcome, calculating his remarks carefully to ensure they did not go beyond the platitudes appropriate to the occasion. When Meighen finally got to speak, he began by roundly condemning Mackenzie King for his attacks on the Governor General, Lord Byng, who had refused King the election that might have rescued the Liberals from the morass of scandal that was drowning their minority government. It was clear these two men did not like each other – King had lately called Meighen an autocrat and a dictator for moving into the Prime Minister's office – and Meighen's tone reflected the sharp animosity the two held for each other. "The most contemptible charlatan ever to darken the annals of Canadian politics," Meighen had said of King.[1] Their mutual loathing stretched back over the many years both had been prominent figures in the public life of Canada.

British Columbia was turning out to be one of the most important battlegrounds of the 1926 election. Meighen had been touring the province by train and boat and Mackenzie King was due to follow him into Victoria in a few days. In a province relatively free of the virus of agricultural rebellion that had infected the prairies, Meighen hoped the natural conservative bent of its first-generation English settlers would earn him more seats to add to those he'd won just eleven months before, when the Conservatives emerged from the 1925 election as the largest party in Parliament. If Meighen could just hang on to last year's winnings, and bring in a few more recalcitrant ridings on the prairies to add to those he was sure of in Ontario and the Maritime provinces, he and the country would be finished with King, once and for all. British Columbians had their own particular set of worries on this mid-August day, just over halfway through the decade that was becoming known as "the Roaring Twenties." Forest fires were raging in the East Kootenay threatening visitors to the new national park near Banff, and drought throughout the interior was blamed for numerous other fires. There was always time to have a little fun, though, and in Kelowna a delegation of businessmen from the Vancouver Board of Trade were let in on a secret: the legendary sea serpent of Okanagan lake was about to be given the name of Ogopogo.

To Meighen's mind, the serpent he had to do battle with was Mackenzie King, who had refused to step aside despite the fact the Conservatives had been beaten him soundly in the election of October 29, 1925. Since then, King had used every intrigue and tactic his mind could devise to hang onto office, begging the support of the Progressive faction in Parliament and the backing of assorted independents, labourites and farmer representatives to keep his minority regime alive. King made it work for awhile, but was finally backed into a corner when the Governor General refused his request to dissolve parliament and allow a new election. Knowing that the scandal raging in his Customs department would lead to his defeat in the House, the rebuke left King no choice but to strike a pre-emptive blow by resigning. Lord Byng promptly called on Arthur Meighen to form a ministry and to take his chances with Parliament. After four days in office the House voted the Meighen government down. The election King had wanted was about to take place but with Meighen, not King, campaigning across the country as the Prime Minister of an incumbent government. It was all part of the most convoluted and confusing episode in Canadian political history, a contrived constitutional crisis that caused Canadians to question the future of our relationship with Britain and the British monarchy.

The two-party system which formed the basis of Canadian politics was coming apart in the nineteen twenties, weakened by tensions arising from the wartime conscription crisis that led to the Liberal-Conservative Unionist government, and the rise of labour and farm radicalism that demanded change in the country's social and economic order. The great victory achieved by the Conservative-led Unionists in the election of 1917 barely carried the government of Sir Robert Borden through the last year of the war. The split between English and French had widened immeasurably, with the Liberal party reduced to a painful minority of Quebec seats. As the soldiers began to return from Europe they heard stories of malpractice and profiteering in war industries at home. Farmers struggled to cope with declining markets while workers scrounged for jobs in the now-idle war plants and their families bore the pain of rising costs of food, rent and clothing. The National Policy of the Conservative party that used high tariffs to keep out low-cost competition was working, but the benefits were going to a declining number of factory owners and manufacturing workers.

Protest and the Mood for Change

The end of the war brought a new generation of politicians to the fore – men in their forties whose careers had been shaped by the war and by the Western expansion that added two new provinces to Canada, with the country's population nudging the nine million mark. It also brought votes to all women, a permanent tax on incomes, and unprecedented protest and a deep-seated demand for change in the way Canada's affairs were being managed. Prime Minister Robert Borden, struggling with ill health, resigned in July 1920 and the Conservative caucus deliberated with care before choosing the forty-six-year-old Arthur Meighen, the Minister of the Interior and the architect of much of Borden's wartime legislation, as its new leader and Prime Minister. In an attempt to retain the legitimacy of the Unionist cause the government would present itself as the National Liberal-Conservative party, but few doubted it was anything more than the old Tory wartime conscriptionist machine, anti-French and anti-labour, if in somewhat different clothing. Meighen brought a lot of baggage to the job. He'd shepherded Borden's conscription act through Parliament, master-minded the war time elections act that deprived thousands of the right to vote, and took an active part in putting down the Winnipeg Strike of 1919. For all the man's admitted brilliance – Meighen was arguably without peer intellectually and possessed of the greatest oratorical power of any MP of his day – it would have been difficult for the Conservative party to have chosen a less acceptable leader. Hated in Quebec, Meighen's austere manner and icy reserve – a product of shyness as much as anything – gave him a chilling public persona. Born the son of an Ontario farmer in 1874, Meighen tried to make himself a Westerner by moving to Winnipeg where he articled with a local law firm before taking over a near-bankrupt law practice in the Manitoba town of Portage la Prairie. He surprised himself and the Conservative party by winning the seat in the 1908 election, and was re-elected in 1911 and 1917.

The Liberals had also reorganized themselves. Their new leader – elected at the party's first-ever leadership convention in 1919 – was Mackenzie King, the former Ontario MP who by standing steadfast with Wilfrid Laurier had spared himself the recriminations that beset other Liberals who had joined the Unionist government. Like Meighen – both were the same age – King had come to Parliament in 1908, but had lost his seat in the 1911 reciprocity election and had gone down to defeat in 1917 as a Laurier Liberal. Since then, King had been out of politics – and out of the country – working for the Rockefeller interests in the United States as an advisor on labour and social issues. He'd published a book on industrial theory, *Industry and Humanity*, and building on his experience as a deputy minister of labour and later as an MP and minister of the same department, had developed deep-seated if somewhat vague ideas on the need for the state to intervene in the marketplace to achieve a more equitable distribution of wealth. King had Quebec on his side and it was the French Canadian delegates to the convention that enabled him to defeat Laurier's old minister of finance, W. S. Fielding who had made the mistake of supporting the Unionist cause in 1917. "The more I think of that whole event the more the hand of God seems in it all," King confided to his diary, the daily journal he would keep for all of his adult years and to which he entrusted his most intimate thoughts.[2] The Liberals who supported King were confident they had found someone who would be able to keep harmony among the party's factions. Little did they realize they had chosen such a master of political compromise and caution in the grandson of William Lyon Mackenzie, who led the Upper Canada Rebellion against the entrenched Family Compact that dominated colonial affairs in pre-Confederation Canada.

King's re-engineering of the Liberal party failed to blunt the farm-based radicalism that swept Ontario and the prairies following the war. The nascent postwar agricultural protest movement brought victory to farm candidates in a string of federal by-elections and resulted in the election of a farmers' government in Ontario in 1919. In December 1920, the two-party system that had carried Canada since Confederation came to an end with the birth of the National Progressive party, led by Borden's former minister of agriculture, Thomas A. Crerar. A Liberal, the founder of the United Grain Growers and a towering figure in Manitoba farm circles, Crerar had walked out of the government to protest its refusal to lower tariffs at war's end. Around him gathered a mixed breed of western protesters, arch-conservative free traders and social reformers, united in their opposition to high tariffs, high freight rates and big business. The Progressives had little in the way of practical legislation to offer the voters, but their clamor for change resonated in the homes of farmers and workers alike. When Meighen went to the people on December 6, 1921 after just sixteen months in office, his results were disastrous. His government had accomplished little and the country had just come through the worst recession it had ever suffered. The Conservative slogan, "Canada Needs Meighen," failed to convince voters that economic salvation could only come by keeping tariffs high. The Tories ended up as the third party in parliament, holding just fifty seats from but three provinces, New Brunswick, Ontario and British Columbia. Mackenzie King's Liberals formed Canada's first minority government with one hundred and sixteen seats. The surprise of the election was the success of the Progressives, who gained sixty-four seats. Five other seats went to labour and independent Liberals. Meighen himself was beaten in Portage la Prairie by a Progressive, keeping him out of the House until he could get elected in a by-election in Ontario. King's first four years in government were generally undistinguished, notable just for one budget which featured a round of tariff reductions. King did manage to keep Canada out of fresh European entanglements, drawing the ire of anglophiles like Meighen by refusing to send troops to support Britain in its Chanak dispute with Turkey. Meighen's response was that Canada should be "ready, aye ready" to answer the call of the Empire when Britain beckoned. Only one short of a majority, King managed to keep control over the House with the help of the impractical visionaries at the helm of the Progressives. Torn between their desire for reform and an idealistic view of a parliament unsullied by party influence, the Progressives refused to take on the role of the Official Opposition, leaving that task to the Conservatives. A frustrated Crerar soon resigned as leader.[3]

Having tip-toed through four years of catering to the powerful Progressive wing in Parliament, King saw the 1925 election as the opportunity to restore Liberal hegemony and bring those "Liberals in a hurry" back into the fold. He had a solid bloc of Quebec seats to build on and was sure he could find his needed majority among the dozen new seats that had been created when the House was enlarged to two hundred and thirty-five. King's recent discovery of spiritualism and the belief that he was able to commune with the spirits of his departed mother and his dog, Pat

– facts never known publicly during his life – encouraged him to think that a higher force was directing his life. Things looked good for King when he prepared for the election of October 29, 1925. The Progressive party was continuing to splinter, with a radical Ginger Group including such supporters as J.S. Woodsworth of Winnipeg, a future leader of the socialist CCF, striking off on its own. The remaining Progressive members, led by Crerar's successor Robert Forke of Brandon, Manitoba, acted more like a collection of independents than a unified party. It was true the Conservatives had seen some revival of their fortunes and a Tory provincial government was now in power in Toronto. Quebec remained the the Tories' greatest stumbling block with the party locked out of all but a few English-speaking ridings.

King should have won a comfortable majority but he did not. Quebec, of course, remained loyal and King's French-Canadian lieutenant, Ernest Lapointe, delivered all but six of its sixty-five ridings. Everywhere else there was disaster, with the collapsing Progressive party vote going mainly to the Conservatives. In Ontario, where the Liberals and Progressives had arranged to keep out of each other's way in all but eight seats, a Tory landslide gave Meighen sixty-eight seats, to eleven Liberals and two Progressives. The Conservatives swept the Maritimes and the West, except for Saskatchewan where the Liberal machine of Premier Charles Dunning won fifteen of twenty-one ridings. When it was all over, Meighen had regained his old seat in Portage la Prairie and the Conservatives were the largest party in the House, exactly reversing the numbers of the 1921 election, one hundred and sixteen Conservatives to ninety-nine Liberals. The Progressive party had fallen to just twenty-four members. Six other assorted independents and labourites were elected. King had lost his own seat in Kitchener, Ontario. By logic and tradition he might have vacated office immediately, but the very next day newspaper headlines were hinting he would not be giving up so easily. KING DENIES RUMOR OF INTENDED RESIGNATION, the Toronto *Star* bannered. "When all the results are in," King told reporters, "I intend to discuss the situation with the Governor General and I shall then make a statement on my intentions." Foreshadowing the constitutional crisis that was already building, the *Star* went on to quote Joseph Pope, the recognized authority, that it is customary for a ministry to resign if it is defeated by a decisive majority. But when the result is inconclusive, Pope added, a government is justified in holding office until it learns its fate from a vote of the House of Commons. That was exactly what King set out to do. He first met with the Governor General, Lord Byng, to discuss the options before him. Over tea at Rideau Hall, Byng made his preference clear; the "dignified" course for King would be to resign and let Meighen govern. To the Governor General, whose close ties with Canada were forged in the trenches of France as commander of the Canadian Corps that captured Vimy Ridge, it seemed a simple matter of fair play, not much different in principle to the game of hockey where his wife had put up a trophy (one still awarded to this day) for the most sportsmanlike player in the National Hockey League. King mulled over that advice for a few days, and decided not to take it. On November 4, Byng issued a press release stating he had been pleased to accept King's advice that Parliament should be recalled to determine "the very important question raised by the numerical position of the respective political parties." King had won the first round.

To Meighen, King's action was contemptible; the Conservatives not only had more seats but had outpolled the Liberals, forty-six and one-half per cent, to a mere thirty per cent. Then came what seemed like an act of providence; the death of the Liberal member for Bagot, Quebec opened up a by-election, giving the Conservatives another opportunity to gain a French-speaking riding. It might have happened, too, except that Meighen destroyed what little credibility he had in Quebec by suggesting that in any future war he would impose conscription if necessary, but would not implement it without an election first. It was an impossible position, and earned Meighen ridicule on all sides. The Tories lost Bagot, and King, running in the safe Saskatchewan seat of Prince Albert, got back into the House in February, 1926 by defeating a little-known Conservative opponent, John Diefenbaker. The second round also went to King.

All through the fateful spring of 1926 King's minority government, held up by the shifting but usually faithful support of the remaining Progressives, United Farmer MPs and assorted independents, counted its future in days and sometimes hours. King won the crucial support of the two Labour members, Woodsworth and A.A. Heaps, by promising legislation to set up old age pensions and unemployment insurance. They had directed the same request to Meighen but he refused to give his support to either issue. There were various want of confidence motions, all of which the Liberals survived, but nothing so threatening as the disclosure by the Conservative member from Vancouver, H.H. Stevens, that racketeers had gained control of the federal Customs office in Montreal and were moving goods into the country without payment of customs tariffs. In fact, the head of the office had been tried for bribery, acquitted and then dismissed, and a new minister, George Boivin, had been put in charge of the department. In the face of Stevens' demand for a public inquiry, King agreed to let him head up a parliamentary committee to investigate the situation. It would consist of four Liberals, four Tories and one Progressive.

Predictably, Conservative members voted for censure of Boivin, the Liberals against. It was left to the lone Progressive, Alberta farmer D.M. Kennedy, to tip the balance. King thought a lot about how to bring Kennedy around before deciding to ask a friendly journalist to intervene on his behalf. His inspiration for this, King was sure, came from his mother. Kennedy sided with the Liberals but it was to be only a temporary respite. Meighen gave a rousing speech on the scandal on his fifty-second birthday, Tuesday, June 16. When the Liberal caucus came together the next day the talk was about the inevitable election, each member weighing his chances of being returned to Ottawa. King told his MPs that if the Liberals were defeated in the House, the Governor General would be unlikely to grant dissolution, but would instead call on Arthur Meighen to form a government. What was worse,

King added, Liberal party coffers were empty while the Conservatives would be generously bankrolled by the country's manufacturing interests. That evening, King huddled again with key members of the Progressive party, desperate to retain their support against the next Tory want of confidence motion. "They all professed the desire not to see the government defeated," King wrote in his diary. The battle of motions raged all through the following week. Stevens presented his committee's report on Tuesday, June 22, moving an amendment to condemn Boivin's behaviour as "utterly unjustifiable." Were it to pass, the government would fall. The next day J.S. Woodsworth, choking on his distress over Liberal corruption but unable to bring himself to support the Tories, moved a sub-amendment calling for a royal commission of inquiry. Debate raged until one o'clock that night. The next afternoon, "tired, weary and exhausted," King spoke for two hours followed by Meighen, who stayed on his feet for three hours. The Woodsworth and Stevens motions were both to be voted on at Friday's sitting and crowds swarmed the Parliament Building, lining up for the few seats available in the public gallery. First came Woodsworth's pro-government motion; it lost by two votes. The Conservatives cheered and celebrated, sure of an ultimate victory on the Stevens motion. After a night of procedural arguments, the House adjourned at ten minutes to five on Saturday morning, leaving the crucial vote to be taken on Monday. "When the House adjourned there was great cheering, as tho the event were a very significant one," King wrote. "The press followed me to my room. I gave them no information."

The weekend gave Mackenzie King time to consider his next steps. It was now obvious he would lose the vote on Monday. If that happened, he would have no option but to recommend to the Governor General that Meighen be given a chance to form a government. With the customs scandal the cause of King's downfall, Meighen would have a wonderful issue to campaign on and would likely win whenever an election was called. By the time King met with his cabinet he was sure he had the answer: he would go to Lord Byng stressing that dissolution of Parliament was a necessity "owing to the equality of the parties in the House and the impossibility of anyone being able to control the situation." King would point out that "it was the constitutional duty of the Governor General to give a dissolution on the advice of the Prime Minister." That weekend, King travelled twice to Rideau Hall for tension-filled meetings with Lord Byng. The Governor General was insistent that he could grant no dissolution, nor would he consider King's request to refer the matter to the British government for an opinion on whether he was obliged to follow his Prime Minister's advice. At a third meeting on Monday just an hour before Parliament was due to sit, King handed the Governor General his letter of resignation. In it, he hinted broadly at his election strategy: "... there will be raised, I fear, by the refusal on Your Excellency's part to accept the advice tendered a grave constitutional question without precedent in the history of Great Britain for a century, and in the history of Canada since Confederation." King then returned to Parliament and told a shocked Commons that there was no business to conduct, that he had resigned, and that he was moving adjournment of the House. As silence engulfed the chamber, Meighen rose to speak. King cut him off, observing that an adjournment motion was not debatable, and that it was impossible for the House to carry on because no government existed. Even in defeat, King had won again.

Meighen went to Government House at noon on Tuesday, June 29, to accept Lord Byng's invitation to form a government. "My contention," Lord Byng had written to King, "is that Mr. Meighen has not been given a chance of trying to govern, or saying that he cannot do so, and that all reasonable expedients should be tried before resorting to another Election." Meighen's ministry would have the shortest parliamentary life of any in Canadian history, lasting just four days before a pre-dawn vote in the House on Friday, July 2, would force him to go back to the Governor General and ask for dissolution and a new election. The issue on which Meighen's government would be tested was an arcane one, and Mackenzie King found a way of cleverly manipulating it to his advantage. Under the rules of Parliament at the time, an MP who succeeded to a cabinet position was required to resign and stand in a by-election. Meighen knew that if he applied this rule to each of his cabinet, he would stand little chance of surviving even the most routine of House votes. He planned to get around this by appointing six acting ministers who would draw no salaries; he alone would have to resign. Mackenzie King challenged that approach during debate on a motion for supply – money to be provided for government operations. Drawing from each acting minister the admission that he was administering his department without having taken an oath of office, King declared the government to be legally non-existent. "I say there is not a single member of this administration sitting in his seat tonight who is entitled to ask the House to vote him a single dollar." As a result, King argued, "we have reached a condition in this country that threatens constitutional liberty, freedom and right in all parts of the world." Moreover, it was not just Meighen, but the Governor General, who was at fault. Here King was treading on treacherous ground, for loyalty to the British connection was still a bedrock of political life in Canada. Nevertheless he pressed on. Byng's action in refusing his (King's) advice, King alleged, "reduces this Dominion of Canada from the status of a self-governing Dominion to the status of a Crown Colony." The House was in an uproar and the country held its breath as the House debated the Liberal motion to condemn the government for a cabinet which had either been illegally appointed or appointed legally but did not hold office and thus could not govern. The motion passed by just one vote, ninety-six to ninety-five, and Meighen's government was finished. A Liberal member has been credited with breaking a tie by voting when he had been "paired" with an absent Progressive, in a time-honoured tradition by which MPs would match an absence on the other side. Other versions give the honour to the lone woman MP, Progressive party supporter Agnes Macphail, who voted for the Opposition motion. It would earn her a unanimous nomination for re-election from her United Farmer constituency association when it met back in Grey Southwest that weekend.

The next morning, July 3, Governor General Byng granted Meighen's request for dissolution. The fifteenth Parliament was no more, and a new election would soon be set for September 18, 1926. The stress over the fall of Meighen's government exhausted King and Saturday night he slept around the clock. He awoke refreshed, alert as always for signs that his beloved mother was reaching to him from the beyond. When "a beautiful bird came & perched on the side of the bird-bath looking toward me and drinking of the water," King thought instantly of the time his dying mother had spoken of herself as a bird. It was surely a sign of her presence. He was also thinking how the voters would react to his challenge to the Governor General. He was sure the "people are with me ... French Canadians, the Irish who love home rule, the Scotch who are for constitutional government, the foreign elements who do not like interference by Kings, Labour that wishes democratic institutions to prevail." That left "only the English Tories" and "whether the mffrs. (manufacturers) will stand and help Meighen is one & only danger."

The Campaign and the Candidates

Arriving back on Parliament Hill with his writ of dissolution in hand, the new Prime Minister set out to organize the campaign that he was convinced would restore him to rightful office. Returning officers and enumerators had to be appointed, giving the Conservatives an opportunity to gain mastery over the election machinery. An election cabinet had to be selected, corporation donations needed to be solicited, and candidates were still to be chosen in many ridings. Plans were already drawn up for advertising and party literature. Meighen was Prime Minister by virtue of the fact the King government had chosen to resign rather than face defeat over the Customs scandal. Meighen's view was that he was entitled to the office because of the popular vote he'd gained and the plurality of seats he'd won. Up to now he'd not been given a fair chance to govern. He knew King would campaign on the constitutional issue in what was already being called the "King Byng affair." He was convinced the public would see through this craven attempt by King to hold on to power after having been rejected by both the country and by parliament. By July 14, Meighen had put together a caretaker cabinet although it was one in which Quebecers were notably absent; an oversight that was partially corrected a week later.

Both Meighen and King had to find the best ways of making their respective cases to the electorate. Meighen felt strongly that the best vote-getter for the Conservatives was still their commitment to a protective tariff. This had been Tory policy for fifty years, going back to Sir John A. Macdonald's declaration of protectionism as a National Policy for Canada. Because Meighen was convinced the Liberals were soft on the tariff, he would drum away at the advantages protection gave Canadian manufacturers and their workers. He knew the tariff was unpopular among Western farmers but he believed in the principle and would sell it as an adopted Westerner. As far as Meighen was concerned, there was no constitutional issue to be debated in the campaign; the election would be about Liberal corruption and King's greed for power. The scandal in the Customs department was still fresh in voters' minds and far more important, Meighen thought. That and the tariff would be his main points of attack.

Mackenzie King had quite a different view of his election strategy. He was quite prepared to defend how he had handled the Customs scandal – putting in a new minister and letting the police deal with any lawbreaking – but his focus would be on Canadian rights and privileges in relation to Britain and the Crown. King had to be careful not to be thought anti-British; his criticism would be solely of the Governor General's behavior, not of the system that sent Lord Byng to Ottawa as the king's representative. King also would stress his commitment to bringing back his pension bill that would provide twenty dollars a month to the needy over seventy, an issue close to the hearts of the nearly four hundred thousand voters who had backed the Progressives in 1925. He saw Ontario as the main battleground of the election and thought he had a good chance of picking up enough Conservative seats there to gain a majority.

Prime Minister Meighen opened his campaign on July 20 before a sweat-drenched crowd of four thousand at the Ottawa Auditorium. Meighen went on about the need for keeping protective tariffs in place, but was at his most indignant in attacking King over the customs scandal. "The government made itself the ally of fraudulent traders of other countries to enable them to dispose of their wares to the people of Canada," he asserted. There had been an army of stolen automobiles, prison-made goods, and "tons upon tons of stuff, laden in all probability with disease-carrying germs to the merchant's counters and to the people's homes in order that a few violators of the law might make themselves rich." There is no constitutional issue to be decided by the voters, Meighen declared. The Governor General has acted properly and the British tradition of responsible government has been fully upheld.

Three days later King was in the same building to launch his crusade to win back power. He was picked up at home – Laurier House, the residence that the old chieftain's widow had willed to the Liberal party – and driven to the Auditorium where a pipe band marched him to the platform. King's Quebec lieutenant, Ernest Lapointe, spoke first in French appealing to the thousand or so Quebeckers, mostly from Hull, who had crossed the river for the rally. King didn't get to speak until almost ten o'clock but he went on until midnight, encouraged by the fact his speech was being carried by radio across the country and to the United States. "I feel we have a great issue," he wrote later that night. It was "the settling once and for all of our right to complete self-government & the making of Canada a nation. Full national status will date from the completion of this campaign." From Ottawa, King travelled by train around Ontario making his constitutional case and reminding voters of his springtime budget in which he lowered income taxes and cut tariffs on automobiles. The Progressives were no longer a force in Ontario politics – in only four ridings were there three-way races – and King would only have to bring Conservative swing voters around if he was to improve on the meagre showing Liberals had made in 1925. As to Quebec, King gave barely a thought. Conservative prospects there were near zero and King's lieutenant Ernest Lapointe, had things well under control. Henri Bourassa had returned to the fray with his nomination as an independent in Labelle. He was likely to be elected but that would represent hardly a dent in the Liberal fortress Quebec. On his swing through Quebec King wrote, "I felt much touched by the throngs of people & their apparent friendliness & even affection. The French Canadians are a delightful people – so courteous, chivalrous and not afraid to be demonstrative."

Western Canada figured importantly in Meighen's campaign planning. Regarding himself as a Westerner, he was convinced he could balance off the unpopularity of his tariff policy against King's arrogance and power lust. Prairie farmers were more concerned about the harvest than the election, and at the height of the campaign the annual trek of farm workers to bring in the harvest had attracted twenty thousand men from eastern Canada. Another thirty thousand would be needed, pitchforks in hand, to fill out the threshing crews that would bring in a bumper wheat crop. At Deloraine, Manitoba, Meighen told a meeting on August 10 that "we will give every industry in Canada a chance – a moderate tariff protective of all products, agricultural and everything else." Meighen considered it only a slight setback that in Portage la Prairie the Progressive candidate from last year's election had withdrawn in favour of the Liberal, lawyer Ewan A. McPherson.

In sticking to his hard line on protection – unpopular among farmers who saw tariffs as a big factor in the high cost of farm implements – Meighen demonstrated how oblivious he was to the key regional issues affecting the West. His threat to abolish the Crow's Nest Pass agreement which guaranteed farmers low rates on grain shipments to west coast ports, severely handicapped Tory candidates on the prairies. His opposition to public support for the building of the Hudson Bay Railway – a line that would cut freight costs on grain shipments to Europe – further eroded rural support. Meighen followed the dictates of his conscience on all these issues, believing protectionism was a bedrock of Canada's nationhood, that farmers should pay the true cost of shipping their produce, and that government no longer had any business in financing railway construction. Reflecting the ethics of an earlier time, he also thought it simply morally wrong to offer unearned pensions to the old and the poor.

After campaign stops across the prairies, Meighen began his tour of B.C. by taking the Grand Trunk Railway to the northern port of Prince Rupert. Along the way, he made brief speeches from the steps of his rail car or from platforms hurridly set up at each station. Touring Vancouver island, Meighen was having trouble sleeping and had a makeshift bed put aboard the day coach. At Royston, in the heart of Vancouver island's dairy country, he promised to amend Canada's trade treaty with Australia so as to curb the import of low-cost butter. When he got to Vancouver, it was raining for a rally at the Horse Show building in Hastings Park. There he promised to bring in old age pensions after all, predicting "There will be a Conservative government with a definite working majority, or a further period of group government with continued instability and all the consequences that will follow." At Fernie, B.C., Meighen attacked King's handling of the customs scandal, charging that King knew what was going on for over a year before word leaked out. "It was driven into him and his ministers by a delegation of businessmen, but not one of them would move." Instead, Meighen said, books had been destroyed and malefactors had manipulated records and then skipped the country. Meighen also spoke of the collapse of the Home bank, but offered little comfort to the thousands of depositors who had lost their savings when the Toronto-based bank went under in 1923. "Parliament could not be convinced by any government, Liberal or Conservative, to pay everybody, rich and poor alike." The City of Fernie had lost the eight hundred thousand dollars it had with the bank when it failed.

Mackenzie King was also determined to make a good showing in B.C., and his schedule took him there the same week as Meighen. At Victoria a thousand people, including Premier Oliver, met his boat as it docked in the Inner Harbour. A band waited to lead a parade through the city, where he went from reception to reception. "Mr. King," Oliver said, "is still the prime minister of this Dominion, as he will be in fact after September eighteenth." That evening King told a rally of two thousand, "I stand for the British connection through and through. I make this statement because of attempts to mislead the people of this country. It should not be necessary to ask any Canadian to proclaim his loyalty – it should be assumed. No party in Canada wants annexation or advocates annexation." In Vancouver he also spoke to large and enthusiastic crowds, attacking the Tories for having derailed his old age pension bill.

Meighen made several forays into Quebec, trying desperately to revive Conservative fortunes there. He hoped to rebuild the party's French wing with the help of E. L. Patenaude, a veteran Quebec Conservative who had broken with Borden over conscription. Patenaude had the backing of the powerful Lord Atholston, publisher of the Montreal *Star* and came into Meighen's cabinet only on condition that he would run his own campaign in Quebec, independent of the national Tories. Meighen's Quebec meetings often turned emotional and at Lac Megantic, it took the intervention of a parish priest to quiet hecklers and gain the Prime Minister a hearing. Speaking partly in French, Meighen urged that future leaders be able to speak both official languages. As for conscription, "We never wanted war. We took the course we did because we thought we could in honour take no other course. No one shares more earnestly than I in the ardent desire that this Dominion has seen the last of war."[4]

Wherever he went, Meighen always returned to the tariff. At a rousing meeting in Toronto's Massey Hall, bedecked with Union Jacks and campaign signs, Meighen stressed that without a protective tariff Canada would have no chance for an industrial life. The alternative, a Mackenzie King government, would be one dependent on a group of men elected from three provinces in the West, "all fighting for a downward revision of the tariff until the goal of free trade is reached." Majority government itself was an issue for some. Eric W. Beatty, the president of the Canadian Pacific Railway, spoke for many business people when he said in an interview that "it is imperative some party go back to Ottawa able to carry on the affairs of government ... the moment has arrived for a decided forward government." He didn't care which party won, as long as it had a majority.

Only on Sundays did the campaigning cease. Across Canada, the Lord's Day Act held sway, preventing all forms of commerce and entertainment everywhere but in some cities of Quebec. In Niagara Falls, citizens were scandalized by Sunday evening dances at the Prince of Wales Restaurant, where one could buy a bottle of beer and a sandwich for fifty cents. They took their complaint to the attorney-general in Toronto where it fell on eager ears. The Sunday dancing would have to stop, the province's leading officer of the law told the press. "If it doesn't, I'm going to take steps to prevent it." The tight control on Sunday activity was all part of the churchly domination that most Canadians accepted without question at the time. Another was the prominent role of the Orange Order, which on July 12 sent a four-mile long parade of ten thousand marching Irish Protestant men through the streets of Toronto – and countless other towns – in their annual com-memoration of the Battle of the Boyne and the triumph of King William over his Catholic rivals. This year's march made the streets "rhythmic with the martial tread of marching men," the *Globe* recorded.

Election coverage in the newspapers was becoming fairer and better balanced. Most newspapers were moving their opinions to the editorial page, leaving the news columns relatively free to report the actions of the parties and their leaders. A lot of attention was given to the campaign of Canada's only woman MP, Agnes Macphail. It was generally agreed there was little likelihood of other women joining her at Ottawa anytime soon, but the question of females as politicians was at least being discussed. The Toronto *Globe* interviewed a dozen women and concluded there was "not even the faintest ray of hope" that a female could be elected in any of the city's ridings. "Toronto is still a man's town and federal campaigns a man's business." Liberals and Conservatives "share alike the same hopeless point of view."

King's last big rally was in Ottawa on the Saturday before the election, in the building where he had launched the Liberal campaign two months before. Eight thousand were present for his campaign wind-up, which included an attack on Meighen for spending a million dollars a day on Governor General's warrants after the House had refused to vote supply. King spent the last day of the campaign in the Ottawa valley. He attended a luncheon and a street parade at Pembroke, then went on to Eganville and Renfrew where he had "a splendid audience." King closed out the day in Arnprior with a rally at a movie theatre. He took a train back to Ottawa and spent the night peacefully in his Pullman coach, hardly aware that the coach bringing Prime Minister Meighen back from Montreal had also returned that evening, both being shunted onto the same siding. King slept until ten-thirty and on leaving the train thanked the black porters who had served him; "I like these darkies very much." He went directly from the station to his home poll on Charlotte street where he voted. Meighen voted at Poll 122 on Lisgar street.

Across the country, Canadians enjoyed a mild fall day. The skies were clear from Cape Breton to Windsor, Ont., while light rain fell throughout most of the West. Federal government workers were given the afternoon off. In Nova Scotia, five hundred uniformed Boy Scouts were recruited to pick up the results from polling booths and "rush to a nearby telephone" where the vote would be communicated to each returning office. Back at Laurier House, King rested in bed for much of the afternoon but by seven-thirty was in his office at the House of Commons, awaiting news of the returns. Meighen also returned to Parliament Hill to hear the results. As the first returns came in from the Maritimes King thought "it was apparent Tory majorities were being greatly reduced." In fact, the Liberals lost one of the three seats they'd held in Nova Scotia, picked up one seat in Prince Edward Island and added three seats in the Acadian region of

New Brunswick. The Quebec results were more encouraging for King. The Liberals actually picked up a seat to increase their total to sixty, notwithstanding Henri's Bourassa's success as an independent. He swamped his Conservative opponent by a margin of better than seven to one. Other Conservatives also fared poorly. All three of Meighen's Quebec cabinet appointees, including Patenaude, were defeated.

Returns from Ontario showed the Conservatives holding most of their seats, but with the Liberals scoring sizeable gains. Fifty-three Conservatives were elected, down from sixty-eight a year earlier. By the end of the evening twenty-six Liberals had been elected, an increase from eleven in 1925. The Progressives just managed to hang onto two ridings. It was largely a case of Liberal voters who had strayed the year before coming home to the fold. In Grey Southeast, Agnes McPhail coasted to an easy win as a United Farmer candidate unopposed by the Liberals. The Conservative winners included a future short-term leader of the party, Dr. R. J. Manion in Fort William. "By ten o'clock I knew I was Prime Minister again if not still Prime Minister," King wrote later. The news got even better for King from the West; not a single Meighen candidate was elected in Manitoba and the Conservative leader himself lost in Portage la Prairie. The defeat was especially painful to Meighen; he had been beaten by a friend and former law partner, the Liberal Ewen McPherson who won by almost a two-to-one margin. The Progressives held onto only four Manitoba seats, but they included the present and past party leaders, Robert Forke in Brandon and Thomas A. Crerar in Marquette. The Liberal success was spectacular, going to eleven seats from just one the year before.

With the support of rural voters, Liberals held all their seats in Saskatchewan – eighteen of twenty-one, the remaining three going to the Progressives. King was returned comfortably in Prince Albert, with more than eighty-nine hundred votes compared to just forty-eight hundred for the young Conservative candidate, John George Diefenbaker. Only the Alberta returns disappointed King; the United Farmers took eleven of the sixteen seats. Three Liberals were elected, two in Edmonton, and one riding went for a Labour candidate. Only R. B. Bennett, in Calgary, the heir apparent to the defeated Meighen, was successful for the Conservatives. In British Columbia, the results were more encouraging for Meighen, but it was too late. H. H. Stevens, the architect of King's Customs embarrassments carried Vancouver Centre easily, and Conservatives gained two Vancouver seats from the Liberals. The much-respected Dr. Simon Fraser Tolmie held Victoria for Meighen. When the counting was done the Conservatives had twelve of fourteen B. C. seats, against one Liberal and one independent.

"About 2 a.m." King wrote later that day, "it seemed we were on the verge of a majority over all, without counting Liberal Progressives, who are really Liberal, or Labour, or Progressives other than U.F.A. many of whom are also real Liberals. Altogether we have a majority of about forty to fifty against the Tories with these groups." In the end, the Liberals would have one hundred and twenty-eight seats, a majority of five not counting the twenty Progressive and U.F.A. members and six independents who were likely to support the government. There was now no question that King would be able to govern comfortably, as he had not been able to do in either of his previous terms.

The Aftermath

The next morning's newspapers revealed the scope of the new government taking shape in Ottawa. LIBERALS LEADING FIELD, the Halifax *Herald* headlined. The Winnipeg *Tribune* forecast LIBERAL-PROGRESSIVE COALITION PROBABLE while the Toronto *Star* proclaimed KING TO HAVE OVER 60 MAJORITY. Two things were evident: the scope of Mackenzie King's victory, and the disintegration of the Progressive party as a cohesive movement for social reform. The party had already broken into three factions, Progressive, Liberal-Progressive and United Farmers of Alberta. The outcome of the election left none of the factions in a position to influence the Liberal majority, a fact quickly recognized by Progressive leader Robert Forke. He eagerly accepted King's invitation to join the cabinet as minister of immigration. For Conservatives, the defeat left supporters pondering the future of the party. The veteran Winnipeg Tory, Robert Rogers, warned the party's future is "the concern of the party's rank and file" and decisions on policies and leadership could not be left to the parliamentary caucus. Conservative candidates had out-polled the Liberals in English Canada but the party was doomed by its losses in Quebec; it elected eighty-seven candidates outside Quebec compared to just sixty-eight Liberals. In the popular vote, the Liberals gained barely one percentage point more than the Conservatives – forty-six to forty-five per cent – but picked up a quarter of a million more supporters.

A week after the election, Lord Byng and his wife prepared to return to Britain, his tour as Governor General complete. Raised to a Viscount, Byng became Commissioner of the London Metropolitan Police and was promoted to the rank of Field Marshall. After his death in 1935 Lady Byng returned to live in Canada during World War II. The debate over the "King-Byng affair" went on for decades but most historians have concluded that the Governor General acted entirely properly in rejecting Mackenzie King's advice. It is now widely agreed that Byng was inescapably correct in his decision to provide the leader of parliament's largest party with the opportunity to form a government. Eugene Forsey, one of Canada's leading consti-tutional experts, argued the issue exhaustively in his 1943 work, *The Royal Power of Dissolution of Parliament in the British Commonwealth.* In his autobiography Forsey tells how he sat in the public gallery of the House of Commons throughout the customs scandal and was present when the King government was defeated. "I had not, even then, the slightest doubt that Lord Byng's refusal of Mr. King's request for dissolution of Parliament was completely constitutional, and indeed essential to the preservation of parliamentary government."[5] Forsey was of course correct. More graphically, it could be said that King's creation of a constitutional crisis was more con job than reality, and that Canadians fell for his shrewdly calculated appeal to national honour.

The two parties had gone into the election with relatively equal support. King's victory came as a result of his ability to hold together the disparate wings of the Liberal party – Quebec, farmers, unattached progressives, Catholics generally and small business entrepreneurs – while sketching out for voters the framework of a more independent and self-sufficient Canada. It came to be said of Mackenzie King that he never did anything by full measure when a half-measure was possible, and his use of the issue of Royal prerogative exemplified that approach. The election of 1926 stands as a turning point in the growth of Canadian nationalism. Constitutionally, it set a clear limit on how far the Crown could intercede in government without drawing a public rebuke. It more clearly defined the role of the Governor General as the representative only of the monarch in Canada, not of the British government. King declined to exploit his victory by pressing for radical reform of the Empire, preferring the slow progression of the Dominions toward increased independence. At the 1926 Imperial Conference King refused to support the demands of the Irish Free State and South Africa for written recognition of their independence. He helped draft a compromise declaration that established the Dominions as "autonomous communities within the British Empire, equal in status, in no way subordinate one to another in any aspect of their domestic or external affairs, though united by a common allegiance to the Crown, and freely associated as members of the British Commonwealth of Nations."

For Arthur Meighen the 1926 election marked merely a reversal, not a permanent setback, in his leadership of the Conservative party. He would become leader again one day but for now it was time to pass on the gavel. The millionaire Calgarian, Richard B. Bennett, won the party leadership at a convention in 1927 and went on, three years later, to defeat King just as the Great Depression began to strangle the economy. The election of July 23, 1930, saw Bennett pick up seats all across the country and especially in Quebec. There, the job losses of a sagging economy were sufficient to add twenty seats to the Tory total, just enough to give Bennett an overall majority of one hundred and thirty-seven in the two hundred and forty-five seat House of Commons. Mackenzie King was back to ninety-one seats, which came as a "great surprise." He had looked forward to "coming back stronger" than before. Finally, however, he concluded that "Bennett is going in only for a short time, or at best for one parliament." King would be glad to be out of office while the depression tore at the nation's economic vitals. The government would be helpless to deal with the poverty and deprivation about to sweep Canada and the Western world.

CHAPTER EIGHT

The Saskatchewan Election of June 15, 1944

THE ISSUES

In the Canadian province hardest hit by the Great Depression of the 1930s, the plight of farmers and fears of a return to depression-era conditions dominate the 1944 campaign. The CCF party's dream of establishing a socialist bastion in Saskatchewan – promising public healthcare and government-sponsored industrial development – arouses fierce opposition from business and the old-line parties, with the Liberal government asking voters for "another chance." Election of the CCF brings to power the first democratically-elected socialist government in North America and paves the way for country-wide medicare.

THE PERSONALITIES

CCF (COOPERATIVE COMMONWEALTH FEDERATION)

Thomas Clement Douglas,
Provincial leader and former MP for Weyburn, Sask.
M.J. Coldwell, Federal leader and MP for Rosetown-Biggar, Sask.

LIBERAL PARTY

William A. Patterson, Provincial leader and Premier
James G. Gardiner, former Premier, federal Minister of Agriculture

THE RESULTS

	SEATS	POPULAR VOTE
CCF	47	211,364 (53 %)
Liberal	6	140,901 (35.5 %)
Progressive Conservative	–	42,511 (11 %)
Other	–	3,026 (0.5 %)

Photo: www.canadianheritage.ca ID #21018, National Archives of Canada PA-36222,

*Tommy Douglas, Baptist minister turned politician, mesmerized
Saskatchewan voters with his call for a "New Jerusalem."*

LITTLE PINK HOUSE ON THE PRAIRIE

The Sasatchewan Election of 1944

Prairie farm homes sit far back from country roads, often sheltered by birch or poplar trees and close by a ravine where a small creek will have offered early settlers fresh water in all except the driest weeks of the Saskatchewan summer. When settlers from Europe and the United States arrived to claim their quarter-section homesteads, they found soil that was phenomenally fertile. Crops were bountiful, the price of wheat was on the rise, and the sod huts that originally sheltered homesteaders were soon replaced by frame houses built of wood lumbered in Ontario or British Columbia. Then, in the nineteen thirties, a cruel conjunction of fates came close to destroying prairie society. While the world moved inexorably toward global war, a combination of worldwide depression and unrelenting drought – the rains failing summer after summer – radicalized the people of the prairies. It often brought tragedy as well as deprivation. Ed Bates, a small town Saskatchewan butcher, saw his customers vanish as farmers quit coming to his village to shop. Bates took his wife and his son Jack to Vancouver, hoping to re-establish the family there. Their efforts failed and when they applied for welfare, they were denied because they were new to the city. Returning to Saskatchewan, they tried to go on relief in Saskatoon but again were rejected, being told they had to return to the town where they'd once lived. Too proud to go home in quest of welfare, distraught and emotionally disturbed, Bates and his wife decided to rent a car and kill themselves by carbon monoxide poisoning. Ed and his wife survived the attempt but their son Jack died. They were both charged with his murder. The community rallied to their support, believing that real responsibility for young Jack's death rested on the shoulders of politicians rather than the parents. A defence committee was formed and a coroner's jury found Bates and his wife innocent of their son's death. A decade later, most had forgotten the Bates case but all of Saskatchewan remembered the hardships of the depression. Farmers still on the land, townspeople, and soldiers overseas were united in a common goal: to win the war and ensure that their country never returned to the awful conditions of the depression. It was a sentiment that a young Baptist minister, Tommy Douglas, captured in a short sentence that he repeated, as if a mantra, over and over: "Surely, if we can produce in such abundance in order to destroy our enemies, we can produce in equal abundance in order to provide food, clothing and shelter for our children."

Douglas, who was not yet forty years old, had already spent nine years at Ottawa as the MP for the Weyburn district in southern Saskatchewan and was now leading the Cooperative Commonwealth Federation – the CCF – in its assault on the provincial Liberal machine that had controlled Saskatchewan since its formation in 1905. If the times had been normal, Liberal Premier William A. Patterson would have called the election as much as two years earlier, but not for a long while had times been normal in Saskatchewan. The last election in 1938 had produced another comfortable majority for the Liberals, thirty-eight seats to ten for the CCF, with two Social Crediters and two independents filling out the assembly at Regina. Patterson had come to realize, as the war dragged on and farmers slowly recovered from a decade of near-destitution, that his government had squandered its popularity. It was arranged for one of the independent members to put forth a motion to extend the life of the legislature – due to the "war situation" – into a sixth year. That would run out in early July, so the announcement that an election would at last be held on the fifteenth of June, 1944, came as no surprise.

The story of Tommy Douglas and his family's arrival in Canada in the early years of the twentieth century is not much different than that of many British immigrants to this country. New people in a new land, they provided an English veneer to a society that was becoming increasingly diverse and included eastern Europeans, Scandinavians, and settlers from the United

States, all seeking a new future in what was being boastfully described by railway promoters and land agents as the "last, best West." First to leave the family home at Falkirk, Scotland was Thomas Douglas senior, a veteran of the Boer war, who reached Canada in 1910 and soon found work in the booming frontier town of Winnipeg. Six-year-old Tommy, his two younger sisters and his mother followed soon after. They went back to Scotland during the first world war where young Tommy got his first job in a whisky distillery. The end of the war saw the Douglas' return to Winnipeg where Tommy endured his first great crisis – an attack of osteomyelitis which put him in the hospital and almost cost him his right leg. A prominent surgeon making the rounds with a group of interns noticed Tommy and believing he could save the boy from amputation, offered to operate without charge. The Douglas family had neither insurance nor the money to pay for the treatment, and Tommy would always remember his close call with the world of private medicine. Recovering, Tommy began visiting the recreation center at the All People's Mission in north Winnipeg. There he met the man who would profoundly influence his most important life decisions, Joseph S. Woodsworth, the Methodist minister at All People's and the founder and leader of the Independent Labour party.

Under the influence of Woodsworth, Tommy Douglas had little difficulty reconciling his rapidly developing political instincts to the social mission of the Protestant churches of the growing West. Casting about for a place to extend his education, Tommy Douglas chose to go to Brandon College, founded by missionary Baptists, where he was able to mix regular academics with theology, earning a bachelor's degree. It was also where Tommy met his future wife, Irma Dempsey. He later received a master's degree from McMaster University in Hamilton, Ontario, and in 1929 became a minister at Calvary Baptist church in Weyburn. It was an adventure for both of them, and doing the rounds of rural parishioners Tommy and Irma soon learned to love the vastness of the Saskatchewan horizon, the fields of grain, the grasslands, the coulees with small streams and clumps of trees, the dry air, blisteringly hot in summer and frigid in winter, the life surging from the soil each springtime.

The Mood of Saskatchewan

Saskatchewan's voters carried with them varying degrees of despair, anger and hope as they contemplated their lives following a decade of depression and five years of war. The onslaught of the depression, which struck stock values, corporations, jobs and family savings with equal severity, hit Saskatchewan with the force of a prairie tornado. It wasn't enough that the economic collapse of the nineteen thirties drove down grain prices. The weather was especially dry in the prairie West in those years, causing one of the most severe draughts ever recorded. Crops shriveled in the heat and the meager harvest was worth next to nothing by the time it was brought into the grain elevators across Saskatchewan. It was a sad come-down from the days when the province boasted of being the "bread basket" of North America.

Farm income in Canada peaked at nearly four hundred million dollars in 1929. In four years it dropped to sixty-six million dollars. Per capita income in Saskatchewan fell more than seventy percent, from nearly five hundred dollars to just one hundred and thirty-five dollars. By 1933, the worst year of the depression, two-thirds of Saskatchewan's farm population was destitute. The double assault of economic collapse and massive crop failures created a survival culture that would shape the behavior and attitudes of prairie Canadians for the rest of their lives. Those caught up in the hard times would live out their years distrusting the political status quo, practicing the habits of thrift learned in poverty, and determined to do whatever was necessary to ensure their children would have a chance at the abundance they knew their country was capable of producing. In Saskatchewan, a new party led by a charismic personality offered a hopeful alternative to the discredited policies of old-line Liberals and Conservatives. The fact that the CCF was ideologically a socialist movement was less important than that it seemed to offer practical solutions to the problems of meeting the farm mortgage, getting better prices for the crops, and being able to go to a doctor without worrying about how to pay the bill.

Canada's first rural revolt against the political status quo took place in Ontario in 1919 when the United Farmers of Ontario won office, as surprised at their victory as the Liberal government which it defeated. When the fires of rebellion failed to spread there, the West became the crucible of Canada's newly-developing social democratic movement. Nurtured in the strong tradition of farm cooperatives for marketing of wheat and other products, the prairies gave rise to first the Progressive party movement in the nineteen twenties, followed by the Cooperative Common-wealth Federation, or CCF, in the nineteen thirties. A protest movement of a different sort, Social Credit, found fertile soil in Alberta, seeded by the charismatic personality of William Aberhart. Farmer radicalism, whether it found expression on the right or the left, stemmed from a culture quite different from that of the urban labour movement which was strong in the West only in Winnipeg, the site of a general strike in 1919, and in Vancouver where miners, loggers and dockworkers were building their own trade union base. The two sides had great difficulty in finding common goals. Woodsworth, the saintly minister from the slums of north Winnipeg, leader of the independent labourites and a force in the early days of the Progressive movement, cultivated support among a number of activists, chiefly from Saskatchewan. They were all school teachers and would all turn out to be future leaders in the CCF: Clarence Fines, a future provincial treasurer; M.J. Coldwell, the future leader of the federal party; George Williams, who would become an early leader of the provincial CCF; and John H. Brockelbank, who would play a prominent role in a Saskatchewan CCF government. They all pushed a "unite the left" movement of farmer and labour political parties. The United Farmers of Canada (Saskatchewan Section), the remnants of the failed Progressive party, and various independent labour groups became the seedbeds of the CCF. A group of left-wing scholars calling themselves the League for Social Reconstruction, organized by Frank Underhill and Frank Scott, professors at McGill University, and supported by Graham Spry, editor of the *Canadian Forum* magazine, provided the intellectual framework for the new movement.

Following a conference of labour groups in Calgary in 1932, the CCF came into existence in 1933 at a founding convention in Regina. It elected Woodsworth as leader but the convention's highlight was the issuance of what was grandly called the Regina Manifesto. It advocated the "eradication" of capitalism and offered the classic socialist cures of social assistance for the poor, public ownership, economic planning and massive public spending on slum clearance, hospitals and schools, and rural electrification.

"We aim to replace the present capitalist system, with its inherent injustice and inhumanity, by a social order from which the domination and exploitation of one class by another will be eliminated, in which economic planning will supersede unregulated private enterprise and competition, and in which genuine democratic self-government, based upon economic equality will be possible."

Since the formation of Saskatchewan in 1905, it had been governed by a Liberal party machine whose grip was broken only once, in 1929, when a "co-operative government" of Conservatives, independents and Progressives replaced the regime of Premier James G. Gardiner. Another force in Saskatchewan at the time, the Klu Klux Klan, helped the Conservatives secure that victory. The KKK's literature was given out at the Conservative convention, its anti-French and anti-Catholic themes invoking prejudice toward the small French-speaking settlements of Saskatchewan. The Conservative success helped pave the way for the federal Conservative victory of 1930 when Richard B. Bennett, a transplanted New Brunswicker living in Calgary, defeated Mackenzie King's Liberals. Provincially, the Conservative coalition soon fell apart under the pressures of the depression and in the 1934 provincial election, Gardiner was returned to office winning all fifty seats in the legislature. He quickly established himself as the undisputed political boss of the province, ruling by patronage and controlling relief, road jobs, and the civil service. His cohorts were known as "The Highwaymen," for the control they had over both contracts and jobs on highway construction.

In that election, Tommy Douglas ran unsuccessfully as a Farmer-Labour candidate. The next year, after becoming leader of the CCF youth wing Douglas was tapped to contest the federal riding of Weyburn in the 1935 federal election. The approach came just as Douglas was debating his future, torn between moving to Milwaukee where he had been offered a ministry handy to the University of Chicago, where he wanted to pursue his Ph.D. When a Baptist official indicated Douglas's future in the church might be limited if he kept up his political activity, his response was "You have just got the CCF a candidate." His commitment to the social gospel of the church was now unswerving. Douglas used his position with the Weyburn Ministerial Association to push for higher relief payments and raised money to have fruit and vegetables that had been scheduled for dumping shipped in from British Columbia. Recalling those times later, he said "I learned a very hard lesson. You have to take a stand. Either with the sheep or with the fellow who's shearing them."[1]

In the 1935 federal election Douglas was able to put to use much that he had learned from his previous run. His opponent was a prominent Liberal, E.J. Young, who had worked on the royal commission investigating the spread in prices between what the producer received at the farm gate and what the consumer paid at the grocery store. It might have been an opportunity for Young to show sympathy for the problems of both, but he chose instead to speak in support of the meat packers and big retailers like Eaton's and Simpsons. Young had gone so far as to state in the House of Commons that Canadians must learn to accept a lower standard of living. That did it with penurious townspeople and stricken farmers. The campaign produced a minor scandal when Young's supporters broke into Douglas' headquarters and stole the proofs of a brochure that was ready for printing. Tipped off, the RCMP paid a visit to the local Liberal party president, a high school vice-principal, who confessed that his workers had committed the crime. Douglas beat Young by three hundred votes, becoming one of only eight CCFers elected across Canada.

As a new MP, Douglas turned his attention to learning the ropes at Ottawa, attending to the problems of constituents, and arguing CCF policies in the House. When Woodsworth resigned at the outbreak of World War II, ill and broken-hearted, the only member of the Parliament to vote against Canada entering the war, Douglas became a close confidante of the new leader, M.J. Coldwell. Both were re-elected in the wartime 1940 federal election. In Saskatchewan, the CCF was experiencing acrimonious times under its leader George Williams. In the 1938 election Williams, influenced by the "common front" tactics of European parties that put together coalitions of socialists and communists to oppose reactionary governments, tried to arrange saw-offs with Conservatives and Social Creditors. The CCF ran only thirty candidates and the strategy was a dismal failure, with many in the party never forgiving him. After the outbreak of war the CCF began to make dramatic gains across the country and in the Gallup Poll of September 1942 it reached a high water mark of 29 per cent support, one point ahead of the Liberals and Conservatives. In 1943 the party came within a whisper of winning the Ontario election, going from none to thirty-four seats. David Lewis, national secretary, was making a name for himself by articulating the vision of a brave new post-war world in such books as "Make This Your Canada."

Williams joined the Canadian Army's Princess Louise Dragoons in January 1941 and was posted overseas, still holding the dual positions of president of the party as well as leader. In July, when the president's post came up for renewal, many in the party concluded it was time for a change, and saw Douglas as their best hope for gaining power. Tommy Douglas was elected president and in 1942, in a three-way contest between himself, Williams, and J.H. Brockelbank, Douglas became provincial leader and named Brockelbank as House leader. Douglas had been nine years in Ottawa and now was back on home ground, ready to make the run for the Premier's office.

Douglas thought it was mainly personal jealousies that had been holding the party back. Williams had run the CCF in Saskatchewan as virtually a one-man party, elbowing M.J. Coldwell aside and keeping the key posts of leader, organizer and publicity chief in his own hands. Douglas set out to transform the CCF from a loose assemblage united by common ideology into an organized and disciplined political machine. He quickly created a shadow cabinet among CCF MLAs. Critics were ordered to learn everything about their areas, and to hound the government unmercifully. Douglas saw his system as a good training ground for future cabinet ministers. He divided the province into regions and gave MLAs responsibility for the ridings in their area. In addition, each member of the party executive was put in charge of a committee to handle finance, organization, publicity, youth activity and so on. Douglas was able to shake up the organization and streamline it because he had no personal enemies. "My main job was to get everybody working together like a symphony orchestra," he would later recall. Youth and women were targeted as two key areas of potential strength. The CCF Youth Movement was stronger in Saskatchewan than in any other province. Women, especially farm women, were prominent in the party structure and the CCF had more active women workers than either of the two old parties. Still a long way from exercising real influence, the women workers organized whist parties, rummage sales and dances, putting precious nickels and dimes in the party's coffers.

Douglas wanted an organization that would be democratic as well as effective. As in all parties, there was often tension between volunteers and the elected members. In a system unique to the CCF, Douglas agreed to face re-election annually as leader. "I'm the only Premier in Canada who must seek re-election once a year before my own supporters," he said after taking office.

The Campaign and the Candidates

By the time the election was called for June 15, 1944, Tommy Douglas had the CCF riding associations running smoothly and the central office in Regina working efficiently under a small but dedicated band of workers. "If he (Premier William Patterson) had called the election in '42 or '43 we would have had a close call, either way. By the end of '43 the tide had turned and nothing could save him," Douglas would later declare.[2]

Whether Patterson sensed this or not, one of his first decisions was to stay out of the riding of the former CCF leader, who was now a Captain in the Canadian Army serving overseas. It was a mark of respect for Williams' military service, Patterson said, to leave the rural Wadena riding uncontested by the Liberals. Williams returned home in May aboard a hospital train, announcing he was too ill to campaign. Six other MLAs on active service, but still in Canada, had to fight to hold their seats.

The prospect of winning in Saskatchewan, combined with favourable polls across the country, spurred the spirit of CCFers. The party was the official opposition, not just in Saskatchewan but in British Columbia and Ontario as well, and CCF members were making their presence felt in Ottawa despite their small number. Douglas had already prepared his letter of resignation as an MP, and had put it the hands of his friend Stanley Knowles, the CCF MP for Winnipeg North. Knowles gave it to the Speaker of the House as soon as the election was called.

When Douglas signed off on the party platform he chose as its theme "Humanity First," promising to devote seventy per cent of the province's budget to social services. The theme demonstrated both the earnestness of the CCF and the widely-held view that governments in general were not all that devoted to the interests of humanity, preferring to put the needs of big money and big business first. A 16-page pamphlet sent to farms across Saskatchewan promised to stop foreclosures and farm evictions, and put a moratorium on debts to mortgage companies and banks. Unions would be free to organize and the province would take over responsibility for education, paying teachers higher wages. The CCF promised a complete system of socialized health care with everyone receiving medical, surgical, dental, nursing and hospital care "irrespective of their economic status."

The CCF's intention was to "replace the present capitalist system with its inherent injustice and inhumanity by a social order from which the domination and exploitation of one class by another will be eliminated."

The CCF campaign derided the free enterprise system for having "left people to starve amidst plenty." Free enterprise had "staggered from boom to depression (and) produced an ever-increasing concentration of power in the hands of a few individuals and corporations. To permit its continuation after the war would be a tragic defeat for democracy in domestic affairs." The indictment went on:

"Burdened with provincial, municipal and farm debt, our people live in a state of insecurity. Educational services are inadequate and our teachers are miserably underpaid. Thousands cannot get adequate medical, dental and hospital services. Our old and physically handicapped people live on pensions that are a disgrace. We must act now if our province is to be saved from complete economic and social collapse."

The CCF platform also zeroed in on more specific planks: co-operate with Ottawa to win the war, keep veterans on full pay until they find jobs, end foreclosures against farmers, build manufacturing plants run by co-ops, enforce collective bargaining, raise the minimum wage, and abolish patronage in the civil service.

The Liberals did everything they could in Saskatchewan in 1944 to demonstrate that governments are seldom defeated, but rather commit suicide as a result of arrogance, stupidity or obstinance. In a tired echo of their six years of limited accomplishment, Liberals pleaded in brochures and newspaper ads, "Please Give Us Another Chance." Premier Patterson hoped the strong political machine that he'd inherited from Gardiner, and which had fallen into disrepair during the war, could be resurrected for the campaign. Policy was something that only dreamers worried about, the Liberal machine would get out the vote just as it had in the past.

The Liberal platform put winning the war as the government's first concern, and promised a fund to help finance post-war reconstruction. Farmers were promised access to markets at profitable prices, protection against crop failure, promotion of soil and water conservation, and independent ownership and operation of farms. The government would promote "the largest possible measure" of free trade between nations, establish floor prices for farm produce, and work toward "complete insurance against crop failure." There would be more money for schools. There was already free medical care for TB, cancer and polio patients and the Liberal government's new Saskatchewan Health Insurance Plan – passed by the Legislature but not yet in operation – would provide hospital access for all.

The Conservatives never held much hope of winning the election, but their platform promised "the attainment of fair prices for farm products by expanding foreign trade and a policy of full employment for all willing to work." The careful restraint made it clear there was a considerable belief that many people without jobs were that way because they didn't want to work. Farmers were promised that rural electrification would be the subject of "a complete study of the whole problem."[3] The Conservative platform made much of the achievements of John Bracken, the former Progressive party premier of Manitoba who was now federal leader of the newly-named Progressive Conservative party. It proudly endorsed his "progressive and sound agriculture policy." Better salaries for teachers, revision of the curriculum and the paving of two main east-west roads across the province were other highlights of the Tory platform.

After five years of war, most farmers were relatively well off but apprehensive for the future. Many had diversified into hogs and cattle, for which there was great demand, and the return of seasonal rain helped boost the grain crops. Douglas took pains to boil CCF rhetoric down to terms that would appeal to ordinary voters. He campaigned mainly on ending farm evictions and launching socialized medicine. Douglas promised a fall session of the legislature to bring in the new laws the CCF would enact. The choice before the public, he said, was between conditions "as they were before the war: a period of free enterprise and all the poverty it caused, or a change to a commonwealth of social justice."

One problem Douglas faced was that many of the CCF candidates had been selected by poorly-attended nomination meetings in 1942, when an election seemed imminent. A half dozen of the candidates were well into their seventies. Aside from being faithful party followers, most had few qualities that might appeal to voters. Douglas had the ticklish task of getting them to relinquish their nominations in favour of new and younger candidates.

Many of the charges the Liberals levied against the CCF were unfounded, but their attacks were rooted in CCF policies that raised serious questions about the party's commitment to private property, including farmland. In a desperate attempt to find ways to protect farmers against bankruptcy and loss of land, the CCF had early on adopted the "use-lease" policy of their Farmer-Labour predecessors. In order to save a farmer from eviction, the government would assume public ownership of his land, paying off mortgage companies in government bonds, and leasing the land back to the farmer. He could "use the land but would not have title to it." The use-lease policy was never accepted by farmers and it was dropped as CCF policy in 1938. It took many years to live it down and in the 1944 campaign Douglas went out of his way to reassure farmers that the idea had been abandoned. Instead, farmers were promised protection against evictions and crop seizures, as well as a moratorium on debt repayment and suspension of mortgage payments in years when the crop failed.

For all its commitment to policy, the CCF campaign revolved around just one feature – the personality of Tommy Douglas. His humour, optimism and stirring message made him, in the words of Grace MacInnes, the daughter of Woodsworth, "the living symbol" of a better future. Douglas drove from afternoon picnics to evening meetings, interrupted by visits to radio stations willing to broadcast his talks. Stopping in small town hotels at night, he wrote speeches for the radio by hand, staying up until two or three o'clock in the morning. He was scrupulous about handing them in the next morning; the War Measures Act, still in force, required texts to be submitted to radio stations in advance. The speeches focused on just two issues, health care and the plight of the farmer. Douglas promised to face down eastern banks and mortgage companies who wanted to throw farmers off the land, and to diversify the economy by jump-starting new industries. Douglas and the one or two supporters who travelled with him collected contributions for gas money and advertising at every meeting, financing the CCF campaign on a hand-to-mouth, day-to-day basis.

Douglas' cheerful spirit, infectious smile and amusing stories put his listeners in a good mood to hear the CCF message, but it was his plea for justice and decency that moved his audiences. Douglas loved to tell his Mouseland story, where he had a colony of mice choosing between black and white cats at each election. No matter which group was elected, the mice continued to have a bad time. Until one day, a radical in their ranks suggested, "Let us elect mice." Another favourite story involved visiting a farmhouse around lunchtime with an offer to help with the chores. Douglas would be assigned the easiest job: to turn the handle on the cream separator. It would make him think how farmers supplied the milk, workers turned the handle, but the cream went to the bosses. And when they got a stomach ache from overindulgence, the whole thing would be shut down, with a depression as a result.

Never forgetting his commitment to the social gospel of his church, Douglas campaigned in a largely Protestant province at a time when Christian values were important to most voters. At almost every meeting, he made a point of evoking those values by repeating these words from the British Labour party hymn:

"I shall not cease from mortal strife
Nor shall my sword rest in my hand,
Till we have built Jerusalem
In this green and pleasant land"

The CCF will always be remembered as the first champion of medicare, but the real struggle to establish publicly-funded medical insurance was still twenty years in the future. Although health was a provincial responsibility, the federal government was already mapping plans for a comprehensive national publicly-funded insurance system. The CCF expected that the federal government would pick up a large part of the tab, allowing it to launch both medical and hospital insurance. Saskatchewan had a long history of cooperative health care and many municipalities had operated Union Hospital Districts providing free hospital care since the nineteen twenties. One community, Swift Current, had already served as a testing ground for a fully socialized healthcare system. Doctors who were forced to go on relief during the depression, were given salaries of fifty to seventy-five dollars a month to stay in their communities, giving rise to a Municipal Doctors System. It was never more than a makeshift system, and many doctors soon moved away. By the middle of the war only four hundred were left to serve a population of nearly a million people. The Liberal legislation to establish public health insurance was generally supported by the doctors, on condition they would continue in private practice. The CCF, in contrast, advocated a completely socialized health system, with doctors drawing salaries from the government.

Late in the campaign came the great news of the invasion of Europe. The Allies landed in Normandy on D-Day, the sixth of June, driving all mention of the election from the papers and the radio. CANADIANS IN THICK OF IT AS ALLIES SMASH INLAND, the Regina *Leader-Post* headlined. A citizen's reconstruction committee reported with some jubilance that Regina families would be digging into their bankrolls to spend an accumulated nineteen million dollars on post-war shopping, including ten million for new homes, as well as new furniture and cars.

Most people relied on Saskatchewan's three daily newspapers for news of the campaign. The two largest newspapers, the Saskatoon *Star-Phoenix* and the Regina *Leader-Post*, were owned by Sifton family interests friendly to the Liberal government. The day after the election was called, the Regina *Leader-Post* argued politely that the CCF had been unable to pick a serious flaw in the government's record, meaning "either the program has been without mistakes or the CCF has not been competent to find them." That tone soon changed and later editorials claimed that the CCF would simply abolish democracy and be done with it. In response, Tommy Douglas pledged to hold elections every four years in June, a pledge he kept as long as he was premier. On the eve of voting, the *Leader-Post* warned that a CCF win would "start Canada on the road to strife and devastation that has been followed by European countries" and that Douglas as Premier would usher in a "stultifying dictatorial system." Surveys in Saskatchewan by the Gallup Poll reflected the growing national support for the CCF. In mid-campaign, a Gallup survey predicted a CCF victory but the Saskatchewan newspapers refused to print it. Instead, the *Leader-Post* came out with a survey of its own five days before the vote reporting "the consensus of opinion of a number of electors" that the Liberals would be re-elected. This all led Edward B. Joliffe, the leader of the Ontario CCF, to declare on a campaign visit to Regina that newspaper editorials had become so irresponsible that they had lost their influence. "What is being said about the CCF by the Saskatchewan press is too silly to take seriously."

With the smell of a Liberal defeat in the air, the campaign grew nastier. Hubert Staines, a Liberal cabinet minister, denounced the CCF as "a proper cesspool and a political sewer." The only difference between it and the Nazi party, he thought, was "its lack of the swastika and the goosestep." Mortgage and insurance companies joined the cry, warning that in the event of a CCF victory they would foreclose on any farmer behind in his mortgage payments. Douglas promised emergency legislation to deal with any such move. The major debate of the campaign took place not between two provincial party leaders, but between Tommy Douglas and Walter Tucker, the federal Liberal MP for Rosthern. It was framed as a traditional debate, with a resolution affirming it was in the interests of Saskatchewan to elect a CCF government. The debate took place in the small town of Watrous, not in a studio, with Douglas upholding the affirmative. He argued that the main issue of the election was whether to go forward with government social and economic planning, or go back to the economic conditions of the past ten years. Tucker was "scornful of CCF promises," claiming the four chief planks advocated by the party were either already in effect or were ultra vires – beyond the constitutional capacity of the province.

Harold Winch, a radical CCF member of the British Columbia legislature, stirred the campaign with intemperate comments about how a CCF government would deal with obstruction from the business community. "If those who oppose the people's government do not abide by the laws enacted they will be treated as criminals and handled by law enforcement bodies," he warned. Winch also called Premier Patterson a liar, leading the Liberals to run half page newspaper ads denouncing Winch as "the wild-eyed socialist from B.C. The Liberals are going to win. That is what is making Mr. Winch mad." Jimmy Gardiner, meanwhile, was still the big gun of Saskatchewan Liberalism. His swing around the province attracted large crowds, including two thousand who stayed until midnight at his last meeting, in Yorkton. There, he told a rambunctious audience that under the CCF people "would become chattels of boards who operate just as heads of big estates in Europe, as heads of large corporations."

The final meeting of the CCF campaign was at Stoughton, a village outside Weyburn. Douglas didn't get home until after midnight and was up at dawn on election day. Everything would depend on the rural polls, and the good weather was a Godsend – there'd been a winter blizzard on the day of the 1940 federal election and farmers weren't able to get to the polls. After a day touring the polls, Douglas went back to the small house he and Irma were renting for a quick supper while he listened to the early returns on the radio. The outcome was never in doubt. Douglas rushed back to his campaign office in the Weyburn Legion Hall to enjoy the victory with his election workers. Douglas had won Weyburn handily, by a margin of more than two thousand votes out of the ten thousand cast. Even Douglas' ten-year-old daughter Shirley (later Shirley Sutherland, married to actor Donald Sutherland and a life-long advocate of the public health plan pioneered by her father), took a turn at the mike: "It's been a great victory for all of us." Douglas knew the magnitude of the challenge he faced: "A province with the second highest per capita debt, the second lowest per capita income. I had no illusions that I was starting on a honeymoon. But I wasn't alarmed. When you are young you think you can lick anything. I kept remembering what the farmers had said. If you can just save our farms, if you can just do that much."[4] In Regina, street parties broke out spontaneously and people marched to the offices of the *Leader-Post*. Most cheered, but others came into the streets in tears. They'd believed the anti-CCF propaganda and feared the new government would expropriate their property and seize their bank accounts. Forty-seven CCFers had been elected and only six Liberals, among them the now former premier, William Patterson. He had managed to hold his rural seat of Cannington.

The next day, banner headlines across Canada recorded the CCF victory. LANDSLIDE FOR CCF, the Regina *Leader-Post* declared. Its editorial said the result "will go into the record as one of the sharpest upsets in the history of Canadian politics." It added: "The issue in the election was socialism. The CCF was born a socialist party, grew to maturity as a socialist party, and has continuously preached socialism. The fact it suppressed its socialism in the campaign does not prevent them from implementing the socialism they have temporarily submerged."

The Aftermath

The Saskatchewan legislature building, overlooking Lake Wascana, an artificial body of water created to soften the harsh environment of the capital district, was now the "little pink house" on the prairie. Just eleven years after its founding and ten years since it had first contested a provincial election, the CCF was in power. Mackenzie King, the Prime Minister, confided to his diary that the CCF victory was "no surprise." It was clear to him that "Douglas as a man of high ideals is a better leader in the minds of the rural people. The result does not cause me much concern for federal politics except that it shows what organization can do and we have not the organization we should have."

The national CCF, buoyed up by the win in Saskatchewan, scheduled its convention for Montreal that fall and Douglas was expected to be the main attraction. But he passed up the convention to visit Canadian soldiers in Europe. Douglas knew how difficult it would be to create a socialist state in Saskatchewan; there could be no nationalization of the banks or railways. It was, however, within the province's power to legislate more and bigger crown corporations, to extend social welfare programs, and to promote income redistribution through higher corporate taxes and royalties on natural resources. Douglas and his cabinet set bold goals for the province.

Douglas' pool of potential ministers differed greatly from other Canadian cabinets; the CCF had elected mostly farmers and school teachers, rather than businessmen and lawyers. He could count on the warm relations he'd established with party leaders to overcome what dissension had existed following his victory over George Williams. Williams agreed to be minister of agriculture but the most capable members of the new CCF caucus were arguably Clarence Fines and Woodrow Lloyd. Fines, a Regina school principal now representing the Biggar riding, became Provincial Treasurer and minister in charge of government organization. He'd been one of the few CCFers who had been confident of victory, predicting 48 seats. Lloyd, who had been president of the Saskatchewan Teachers Federation, became minister of education. He would eventually succeed Douglas as Premier. John H. Brockelbank, another school teacher, was named to Municipal Affairs. The only lawyer in the new government, Jack Gorman, the former mayor of Moose Jaw, became Attorney-General. J.T. Douglas, a farmer and no relation to Tommy, was given highways and public works. Two new departments, Welfare and Cooperatives were established, headed by a farmer and a former co-op agent, respectively.

Douglas set to work immediately on the CCF's legislative program. The first bills brought to the House that fall extended free hospital and medical care, increased pensions and mother's allowances, and revised the labour law to make it easier for unions to organize. Free school books were provided to students. But the most important priority, in Douglas' mind, was the new leg-islation to protect farmers. Douglas had pledged in the campaign to end farm foreclosures by mortgage companies; there had been one hundred and eighty evictions in 1943 and forty-five in the first two months of 1944. The CCF's Farm Security Act was passed early in the session. It protected the home quarter section against foreclosure and suspended mortgage payments in any year of crop failure (defined as one when income fell below six dollars per acre). More radically, it also proposed to wipe out interest payments for those years of crop failure. Mortgage companies railed against the new law and called on the federal government to use its power of disallowance, as it had done against Social Credit leader William Aberhart in Alberta. Mass meetings followed and in radio broadcasts Douglas declared that the battle for democracy had not been ended with war's end. "We have simply moved the battlefields from the banks of the Rhine to the prairies of Saskatchewan." Surprisingly, Ottawa blinked and chose not to use disallowance. Instead, the mortgage industry appealed to the Supreme Court of Canada which in 1947 ruled the crop failure clause to be beyond provincial powers; interest was exclusively a matter of federal jurisdiction. An appeal to the Privy Council failed and the battle over interest went on for years. A decade would pass before the government would finally give up.

The CCF had targeted patronage appointments in the campaign, claiming the civil service was filled with Liberal hirelings. Once in office Douglas made few changes in the upper ranks of the civil service. This was a great disappointment to true believers who felt Douglas was abandoning socialism by keeping on the old crew of bureaucrats. Soon, however, a new batch of technocrats began to make their way to Regina to begin building a public service that would become respected as one of the most professional in Canada.

Douglas' highest ambition was to establish publicly-funded hospital and medical care. This would be a historic breakthrough and if achieved in Saskatchewan, would inevitably spread throughout the rest of Canada and perhaps even the United States. His first step was to get the Saskatchewan Hospital Insurance program into operation, financed by five dollar per person premiums and municipal taxes. "It will be necessary to have the whole-hearted co-operation of the public to make the plan work," Douglas told the Legislature. By and large Douglas got that co-operation but because of the failure of the provinces to reach a cost-sharing agreement with the federal government, the CCF had to put medicare on hold. Instead, Douglas settled for a pilot program in the Swift Current region, where a joint hospital-medical insurance scheme was launched, funded by a local health tax with help from the provincial sales tax.

Private health insurance, often set up and promoted by groups of doctors, penetrated Saskatchewan slowly but steadily throughout the nineteen fifties. In Douglas' view, the inroads being made by private insurance illustrated how urgent it was to get a full-fledged public medicare plan going. His opening came when the new federal Conservative government of John Diefenbaker agreed to pay fifty per cent of the cost of public medical insurance. With medicare as the central plank of the CCF platform, the 1960 election became a bitter contest between Douglas and the Liberals under former CCFer Ross Thatcher. Thatcher had the support of almost all Saskatchewan doctors who were convinced the CCF plan would put them under government control, both financially and professionally. Douglas tried to simplify the issue: "Instead of the doctor sending the bill to you, he will send it to the medical plan. There's nothing very complicated about that." His arguments won over the public and that year the CCF was re-elected with forty per cent of the popular vote and thirty-eight of the legislature's fifty-four seats.

Believing that his crusade had triumphed, Douglas resigned as Premier in 1961 to become the federal leader of the CCF's successor, the New Democratic party. In 1962, with Woodrow Lloyd in the Premier's office, Saskatchewan at last brought in its plan for socialized medicine. Under a plan set to go into effect on the first of July of that year, doctors would have no choice but to participate, likely ending up as salaried employees of community health clinics. It was an unrealistic option that the province's doctors would never accept. Older doctors who had learned to live with cooperative insurance and municipal funding, might have been receptive to the CCF plan but by now they were retired, replaced by immigrant doctors who were refugees from British socialized medicine. Saskatchewan's medical profession decided on drastic action – an all-out doctor's strike in every community across the province. Within hours of the plan becoming law, hospitals closed their emergency wards and doctors abandoned their offices except for a handful that were told to be available for extreme emergencies. On the very first day of the strike, a baby died in its mother's arms as the frantic parents drove from town to town trying to find a doctor who would serve them. The death didn't move the strike leaders, nor did it much influence the public. Keep our Doctors committees sprang up around the province. The government responded by flying in foreign doctors, many from Britain. Strike leaders called the new arrivals "the garbage of Europe" and warned that the government would soon be forcing Catholic hospitals to perform abortions. Strike leaders initially refused to meet with the government despite assurances of Premier Lloyd that the government was willing to consider changes in the legislation. After a rally on the grounds of the legislature attracted only a few thousand supporters – rather than the forty thousand that had been expected – it became clear to the doctors that public support was slipping away. Ironically, it took a British psychiatrist brought in by the government as a mediator just five days to settle the strike. Doctors would be allowed to opt out of the plan if they wished, and those who stayed in would be paid on a fee for service basis. The walk-out ended after twenty-three days, having split Saskatchewan and left a trail of bitterness on both sides. But medicare was here to stay, and before many years the Saskatchewan model would be copied in every Canadian province.

From the time the CCF took office in 1944, Douglas and his cabinet hoped to diversify Saskatchewan's economy through government ownership of new manufacturing industries. Existing Crown corporations were expanded and new ones were launched. These included the Saskatchewan Power Corporation (electricity and natural gas), Saskatchewan Government Telephones, Saskatchewan Government Airways, the Saskatchewan Government Insurance Office, and the Saskatchewan Transportation Company (bus lines). The government, in return for loan guarantees, bought stock in the Interprovincial Steel and Pipe Co (IPSCO). New marketing boards were established for timber and furs. Other ventures, not all successful, included a tannery, a woolen mill, a box factory, a shoe factory, a sodium-sulphate plant, a seed-cleaning plant, fish-filleting plants and a brick yard. More successfully, the potash industry was developed under government leadership.

The rout suffered by the federal CCF in the general elections of 1957 and 1958, the first bringing to office the Conservative government of John Diefenbaker and the second giving Diefenbaker the largest majority in Canadian history, left the CCF once again with only eight MPs. The outcome shook the party to its core. With McCarthyismn rampant in the United States and its influences reaching into Canada, anything that smacked of socialism was linked in the minds of many with Russian Communism. The more pragmatic of the party's leaders, especially David Lewis, saw an opportunity to move beyond the CCF's traditional socialist base to build a true labour party based on the formal allegiance of trade unions. The party had to be rebuilt from top to bottom. Lewis helped to pave the way by getting the CCF at its 1956 convention in Winnipeg to pass a declaration substituting social democratic reform for the hard line of socialism. Replacing the Regina Manifesto, the Winnipeg Declaration asserted that the aim of the CCF was "the establishment in Canada by democratic means of a co-operative commonwealth in which the supplying of human needs and enrichment of human life shall be the primary purpose of our society." While sketching out what was still a noble goal, the Winnipeg Declaration effectively put an end to socialism as a political force in Canada. It was a natural step to organize a new party supported by the country's two major English-language labour unions, the Trades and Labour Congress (TLC) and the Canadian Labour Congress (CLC). The new party's organizing convention in Ottawa in 1961 chose the name New Democratic Party and it took only a brief leadership skirmish for Tommy Douglas to defeat one of the surviving federal CCF members, Hazen Argue, for party leadership. The leadership contest was almost overshadowed by a divisive debate on the future of Quebec. With Quebec's "Quiet Revolution" about to get underway, there was much discussion in political circles of the concept of Canada being composed of two nations, English and French, representing the two founding parties of Confederation. The NDP latched on quickly to the new idea, formally recognizing the right of the French-speaking community to use the word "nation" to describe itself. Embracing the "two nations" concept of Canada was too much for the scholarly constitutional expert Eugene Forsey, a staunch CCF supporter. He left the convention, never again to support his old comrades in arms.

The New Democratic Party has never lived up to the hopes of its founders. In its first election in 1962 the party suffered a devastating blow when Douglas was defeated in a Regina constituency. It was in the middle of the controversy over medicare and the province's doctors had thrown both money and influence into the election. In conceding defeat that night, Douglas reached back into Scottish mythology to tell a national television audience, in the words of a sixteenth century Scottish rebel:

"I am hurt, but I am not slain,
I will lay me down and bleed awhile
And then I'll rise and fight again …"

Douglas did rise to fight again, winning a by-election in Burnaby-
Coquitlam in British Columbia. By 1971, a decade later, he'd had
enough. The NDP leadership passed at last to David Lewis whose
campaign against the "corporate welfare bums" helped reduce
Pierre Trudeau's government to minority status in the 1972
election. Douglas carried on as the NDP's energy critic until
resigning his seat in 1976. Weakened by cancer, he died on
February 24, 1986. At his memorial service the Prime Minister,
Brian Mulroney and the Liberal leader, John Turner, led a standing
ovation for him. The NDP would go on, its best performance
coming in the 1988 free trade election when, with Ed Broadbent
as its leader, it would capture forty-three seats and more than
twenty per cent of the vote. The NDP would never, however,
return to the era of hope and fervour when the CCF's goal was the
"New Jerusalem" that would liberate the tired workers, farmers
and urban middle class for whom Douglas had dedicated his life.
The greatest accomplishment of Tommy Douglas remained the
victory in Saskatchewan, an election that stands as a turning point
for having brought the left to power for the first time in Canada,
and set the stage for universal public health care that would one
day become the most cherished of Canadian values.

CHAPTER NINE

The Federal Election
of June 11, 1945

THE ISSUES

Fearful of the growing popularity of the socialist CCF, Mackenzie King's Liberal government offers Canadians a broad plan of social welfare and postwar reconstruction, while the Progressive Conservatives campaign against King's prosecution of the war and demand conscription of troops to finish the fight against Japan. The Liberals successfully blunt the left-wing appeal of the CCF and use the election to begin a "Gentle Revolution" of social reform, erecting a "safety net" of health care, pensions, jobless protection and support for post-secondary education.

THE PERSONALITIES

THE LIBERAL PARTY
William Lyon Mackenzie King, Prime Minister
Brooke Claxton, Minister of National Health and Welfare
Clarence Decatur Howe, Minister of Reconstruction

PROGRESSIVE CONSERVATIVE PARTY
John Bracken, Leader
Gordon Graydon, Progressive Conservative House Leader
George Drew, Premier of Ontario

CO-OPERATIVE COMMONWEALTH FEDERATION (CCF)
Major James Coldwell, Leader
David Lewis, Party Secretary

THE MINOR PARTY LEADERS
Solon Low, Social Credit
Maxime Raymond, Le Bloc Populaire
Tim Buck, Labour Progressive Party

THE RESULTS

	SEATS	VOTES
Liberal Party	127	2,146,330 (40.9%)
Progressive Conservatives	67	1,435,747 (27.4%)
CCF	29	816,259 (15.6%)
Social Credit	13	214,796 (4.1%)
Others*	9	632,796 (11.1%)

Winning the 1942 Conscription referendum paved the way for King's re-election in 1945.

MACKENZIE KING
AND THE GENTLE REVOLUTION

The Federal Election of 1945

Official dispatches arriving in Ottawa early on the morning of Monday, May 7 1945, confirmed the news that had been expected for the last several days: the end of the war in Europe, unconditional surrender of Germany and all of its armies, ships at sea, and the remnants of its powerful air arm, the Luftwaffe. General Dwight D. Eisenhower, the Supreme Allied Commander, had taken the surrender of German military leaders at a schoolhouse in Reims, France, and V-E Day was to be proclaimed the next day, May 8. Before that could happen, however, an enterprising American war correspondent had broken the embargo on the formal announcement. By the time the news was relayed officially to Prime Minister Mackenzie King in his suite at the St. Francis hotel in San Francisco, where he was attending the founding meeting of the United Nations, Canadians were already celebrating the end of the fighting.

The victory over Germany overshadowed all else this bright spring day, including campaigning for the federal election to be held June 11. So far, Canadians had paid little attention to the campaign. Preoccupied with the ending of the war and the return to civilian life of a million men and women, few voters had given much thought or attention to the arguments that would be put to them during the coming month.

Certainly, the election was the last thing on the minds of 8,000 sailors on shore leave in Halifax that day. They gave the city a memento of the last six years in which their presence had been barely tolerated by a testy and prudish civilian populace. Infuriated at the closing of liquor stores and pubs on this day for grand celebration, the sailors smashed into every beer saloon and liquor store in which a drink could be found. Before the day was out, the looting had spread to nearby towns, two sailors had been killed, and an entire ward of the Royal Canadian Navy hospital filled up with the injured, most of whom had fallen drunkenly onto broken glass. By the time Mayor Alan Butler imposed a curfew at eight o'clock, damage had reached five million dollars and a thousand troops had been needed to restore order. Finance Minister James L. Ilsley, the MP for Digby-Annapolis-Kings in Nova Scotia, was ordered to break off his electioneering and begin an investigation of the disturbance. After a tour of the city, he appointed Justice R.L. McKellock of the Supreme Court of Canada to conduct an inquiry.

Other Canadians took the end of the war in Europe with more equanimity. The shrill blast of factory whistles brought most war work to a halt, and parades, memorial services and community sing songs assembled spontaneously in a thousand communities. Across the country, there was little of the emotional explosion that would come three months later with the collapse of the Empire of Japan, but for most Canadians, the real battle was over on May 7.

These events were already unfolding when an aide with an "important message" awakened Mackenzie King in his San Francisco hotel room at 7 a.m, Pacific Daylight time. "I then turned on my side and uttered a prayer of thanksgiving and of rededication to the service of my fellow men," he would note later in his diary.[1] The Canadian Premier (the term Prime Minister was not yet widely used) spent part of the day preparing notes for a radio broadcast to the nation the next day, V-E Day. In it, he warned that Germany's surrender was no time for exultation: "The hard struggle for peace must go on long after the guns cease firing." He also found time to ponder the speech he would make in Vancouver on May 16 to open his Liberal party's campaign, and to telegraph the Liberal association in Prince Albert, Saskatchewan of his willingness to stand for re-election there.

With Mackenzie King in San Francisco was his Minister of Justice from Quebec City, Louis St. Laurent, as well as the leader of the CCF, M.J. Coldwell, and the House leader of the Progressive Conservatives, Gordon Graydon. King had pointedly ignored Conservative party leader John Bracken in when he made up the invitation list for the Canadian delegation; he was contemptuous of the former Manitoba premier for his failure to seek a seat in Parliament on taking over his party's leadership in 1942, and saw no reason to let Bracken share in the aura of the the new world organization. Also in San Francisco, although not an official member of the Canadian delegation, was John Diefenbaker, just completing his first term as the Conservative MP for Lake Centre, Saskatchewan.

But it was not the supposedly rejuvenated Conservatives who King feared as he looked ahead to the election and Canada's emergence from World War II. King's real concern was the socialist CCF, which had formed the government of Saskatchewan the previous year and constituted the official opposition in British Columbia, Manitoba and Ontario. The CCF was offering Canadians a vision of a bright new world, a post-war era of socialism and security from which the mind-numbing poverty of the depression of the 1930s would be permanently banished. Having seen Canada marshal its people and resources to fight the war, becoming a world industrial leader and demolishing unemployment in the process, Canadians were demanding economic security and steady jobs after the war. Many were convinced that only the CCF, with its platform of nationalization of the banks and the big corporations, was committed to the economic reforms needed to achieve full employment.

For a brief time midway in the war, the CCF had even led the Liberals and Conservatives in the opinion polls, a political phenomenon that had arrived only recently in Canada with establishment of the Canadian Institute of Public Opinion as a spin-off from the work of the pioneer pollster, Dr. George Gallup in the United States.[2] While it was true that by January, 1945, the CCF had eroded to third place, it still had the support of 22 per cent of the voters. It was to fend off this threat that despite misgivings about the cost, Mackenzie King had accepted with hardly a murmur the proposals of his principal secretary, Jack W. Pickersgill, for a broad program of post-war social reform. It had all been put together in the famed Marsh report, by McGill

University professor Leonard Marsh, himself a former CCFer. The centrepiece of the program was the family allowance to be paid directly to mothers (and in their own names), starting at five dollars per month for each child under six and rising to eight dollars for teenagers to age 16. Parliament passed the Family Allowance Act in 1944 and registration for the "baby bonus" was already under way, with payments to begin on Dominion Day, July 1.

Canadians didn't recognize it as they prepared for an election in the Spring of '45, but they were about to unleash what can now be seen as a Gentle Revolution; a social transformation profoundly reshaping the social structure of the country and setting it apart ideologically if not economically from the United States. The policies advanced in the 1945 election set the framework for programs that would be adopted in varying degree by all Canadian political parties. They were founded on the concept of a comprehensive welfare state offering a social safety net ensuring health, education and opportunity for all citizens. The economic thrust of Canada's Gentle Revolution, with emphasis on such practical provisions as state health and unemployment insurance, universal old age pensions, social assistance, and subsidized post-secondary education, would by the 1960s and 70s metamorphose into the social engineering of bilingualism, multi-culturalism, human rights legislation, environmental protection and, finally, legislated gender equality. Government spending would soar, ultimately delivering a day of reckoning in the 1990s when the realities of deficit financing would force governments and taxpayers to rein in the cost of the country's collective dream.

The Gentle Revolution, however, would irrevocably change Canada from the narrow and parochial country it had been before the upheaval of depression and war. Gone soon would be the inward-looking Waspish establishment that dominated Canada economically and culturally, submerging the non-Protestant and non-Anglo minorities to an existence at survival's edge. It would stamp the Canadian character with clearly distinguishable new qualities, leading to the pluralistic, permissive society of the early 21st century, condemned by some as creating a nation of dependency, but supported by most as a kinder, gentler and more compassionate version of the unbridled free market of corporate capitalism that permeated life in the United States. The magic of Canada was that the country's political system, rather than blindly repudiating the mistrust and discontent that built up in the years between the wars, was able to respond with policies to rebuild social harmony and create a new confidence in the future.

The Politics of War

By the end of the war, Canadians were prosperous but apprehensive. The government had carefully managed the economy, limiting price increases, restricting consumer spending, marshalling labour resources, and overseeing the erection of a new industrial apparatus that built planes, ships and munitions that helped the Allies win the war. A cadre of economists, civil servants and businessmen poured into Ottawa to carry out the Keynesian policies of fiscal management that had been wholeheartedly adopted in Western capitals. Clearly, there was to be no return to the unregulated free enterprise economy of the hungry thirties. Canadians had fresh memories of the disastrous failure of Conservative Prime Minister R.B. Bennett to cope with depression hardships. They'd put Mackenzie King back in power in 1935, when the Liberals campaigned on the slogan of "King or Chaos," winning 173 of 245 parliamentary seats. The Conservatives were left with only 40, probably more than they deserved. The newly-formed Social Credit party, recently swept to power in Alberta, elected 17 MPs with barely half the votes gained by the CCF, which won only seven seats.

Mackenzie King made no attempt to launch a Canadian "New Deal" after the 1935 election. He had witnessed Bennett's frantic but failing efforts to nudge his cabinet toward Rooseveltian reform in the dying months of the Conservative regime, and his own innate conservatism held him back from trying radical measures. King also recognized that the British North America Act severely restricted the power of the federal government in the field of social welfare. The legal committee of the British Privy Council ("the wicked stepfathers of Confederation," as Eugene Forsey would call them),[3] had drastically altered the original intent of the BNA Act with rulings that made the provinces virtually sovereign powers in the fields of social legislation and trade. The effects, among others, would be to make the federal government powerless to bring in unemployment insurance in the 1930s.

It was left to the onset of World War II to rescue the Canadian economy from the turgid backwater into which it had drifted. On Sept. 10, 1939, a hastily assembled Parliament voted to declare war on Germany, thereby demonstrating Canada's independence from Britain's declaration a week earlier. The Rev. James S. Woodsworth, leader of the CCF and "the saint of Canadian politics" was the only English-speaking MP to dissent. This act of conscience effectively ended the political career of the aging and ill Methodist minister who had spent most of his life in the cause of socialism. It fell to the party's national chairman, M. J. Coldwell of Saskatchewan, to state the CCF policy which favoured economic aid, but not conscription of manpower.

In this, the CCF was at one with the Liberals and Conservatives in a common acceptance of Quebec's resistance to sending its *habitants* to foreign wars. For the Conservatives, Bennett's successor Dr. Robert J. Manion of Fort William, Ont., was fully aware that his party's only hope of appealing to Quebec rested on its ability to erase the memories of World War I, when Sir Robert Borden brought in disaffected Liberals to a Unionist government that imposed conscription. Manion himself had been elected as a Liberal Unionist in 1917 and had lost his seat in 1935, having served only briefly as Minister of Railways and Canals in the Bennett government.

The Prime Minister had promised the Conservative leader that "there would be no general election until after the next session – that is, the January session." But King soon found an excuse to set aside that commitment. He got it from Mitchell

Hepburn, the erratic Liberal Premier of Ontario with whom he'd been feuding for years. On January 18, 1940, Hepburn and most of his MLAs had voted to support a motion by the provincial Conservative leader, George Drew, condemning the federal government's war record. King seized on the vote like manna from heaven, and when the MPs assembled on January 25, expecting to debate the war plans of the Liberals, they were told that Parliament was being dissolved and an election would take place on March 26. The Opposition cried that democracy was being betrayed at home while Canadians were being sent to war abroad; government was ruling by order-in-council, the action of the Ontario legislature meant nothing to the federal parliament, and King had clearly broken his promise that he would submit his performance to another session of the House before going to the people. "Of his two favourite maxims, 'Parliament will decide' and 'the people will decide,' he chose the one that suited his own purposes."[4]

The campaign that followed was filled with innuendo and personal abuse. Dr. Manion called for a National Government, but was unable to explain how non-Conservatives would be included. Having failed to win the confidence of the business establishment, Manion got little financial backing for the Tory campaign. Mackenzie King chose to stay in Ottawa, making free-time election broadcasts on the CBC stressing "there is but one issue – it is Canada's war effort." He boasted of having already sent a fully equipped division to Europe, with a second soon to follow. At home, a War Supply Board had been set up to oversee a smooth transition from a peacetime economy. The CCF campaign consisted largely of a defence of parliament against King's bureaucratic methods, and a call for guarantees against war profiteering. The election gave Mackenzie King the greatest victory of his career – 51.5 per cent of the popular vote and 181 seats in Parliament. The Conservatives were unable to improve on the 40 they had elected in 1935, while the CCF, which put up only 96 candidates, returned eight MPs, just one more than had been elected five years earlier.

By now, Mackenzie King was ready to fulfill the spirit of a non-partisan war effort, and he quietly wound down the Liberal party organization. Dr. Manion resigned just as German armies moved into the Low Countries and France in May of 1940. The Conservative party chose R. B. Hanson of Fredericton, N.B., and MP for York as temporary leader. After one session, he resigned and the party asked Senator Arthur Meighen, twice a short-term occupant of the Prime Minister's office, to take over the leadership, setting the stage for one of the most bizarre political episodes of wartime Canada.

Of all the Conservative opponents that Mackenzie King might find himself up against, it was Arthur Meighen whom he most detested and feared. "Meighen will be for railway amalgamation, have the CPR and other big interests back of him and Imperialist jingoes in Canada and Britain alike … life day by day will be made intolerable by his attacks, misrepresentations and the like."[5] But Meighen would first have to get a seat in the House. After much deliberation, he agreed to the resignation of the Tory member for the Toronto riding of York South, Alan Cockeram, who was on active service. February 9, 1942, was set for three federal by-elections: York South; Quebec East, where the distinguished lawyer Louis St. Laurent would stand for the Liberals; and Welland, Ont.

Meighen looked unbeatable in York South; the largely Anglo-Saxon riding that had voted consistently Conservative was not likely to spurn the former Prime Minister, especially after it was announced there would be no Liberal candidate, out of respect to the tradition of party leaders being acclaimed in by-elections. The CCF, however, felt bound by no such restriction and nominated Joseph Noseworthy, head of English at Vaughan Road Collegiate. Noseworthy had run a poor third to Major Cockeram in 1940. In a campaign studded with intrigue (Norman Lambert tapped Liberal finances for a $1,000 contribution to the CCF), and misjudgement (Meighen attacked only the Liberals, ignoring his CCF opponent), Noseworthy rolled to an unexpected victory, beating the former Prime Minister, 16,408 votes to 11,952.

One of the factors in Meighen's defeat was his strident call for conscription; it alerted Mackenzie King to the realization that his pledge not to conscript men for overseas service could yet cause him serious political trouble. The way to disarm Meighen, King decided, would be through a plebiscite. Accordingly, the Speech from the Throne opening Parliament on January 22, 1942, revealed that voters would be asked if they would release the government "from any obligation arising out of any past commitments restricting the methods of raising men for military service."[6] It disarmed Meighen of his best by-election issue. When the plebiscite was held on April 27, every province except Quebec voted overwhelmingly to permit conscription; 2,945,514 "yes" votes across Canada, to 1,643,006 "no"; it had carried by 63.7 per cent. But in Quebec, urged on by the anti-war *Ligue pour la Defénse du Canada*, the vote was 71.2 per cent the other way. King immediately repealed the clause of the National Resources Mobilization Act restricting compulsory service to home defence. On June 10, the Prime Minister told the House of Commons, in his famous phrase, "not necessarily conscription, but conscription if necessary," that compulsory service would be implemented at some future date only if the need for troops could not be met by voluntary means.

For the Allies, mid-1942 marked some of the bleakest days of the war; the United States and Russia were now fighting side with Britain and the Dominions, but the Japanese were reaching out across Asia and the Pacific toward Australia and the sub-continent of India, while German armies marched through the Ukraine and pressed northward toward Moscow and Leningrad. The Canadian Army was still being held in reserve in Britain for future battles and for the moment, there was no need of reinforcements.

Arthur Meighen continued to call for compulsory service, but others in the party recognized the need to begin to think about the kind of policies that Conservatives would promote under a new post-war leader. With the approval if not the enthusiastic support of Meighen, about 150 Conservatives met in Port Hope, Ont., to draw up resolutions nudging their party closer to centre, hopefully to avoid annihilation in a square-off between the Liberals and the CCF. The "Port Hopefuls" backed ideas such as low-cost government housing and a national contributory health insurance program (the term "medicare" had not yet been coined). When the party gathered in Winnipeg in December, 1942, to choose a new leader, front-runner John Bracken, the Liberal-Progressive Premier of Manitoba, won on the second ballot after letting it be known he would change the name of the party to Progressive Conservative.

John Bracken, tall, angular and austere, came to politics through the farmer revolts that decimated the old parties from Ontario to Alberta in the early 1920s. When a leaderless United Farmers of Manitoba defeated the Liberals in 1922, Bracken gave up his presidency of the Manitoba Agricultural College, bringing just the prestige and the profile to give a stamp of respectability to the new government. As Premier, he soon gained a reputation for efficiency, and in 1932, having swallowed up the remnants of the Progressive party, engineered a merger with the Liberals and recast the party as the Liberal-Progressives. In 1940, convinced that party politics should be put aside in wartime, he created a coalition of all parties in the Manitoba legislature. Bracken, perhaps mindful of Meighen's rejection in York, opted against trying to get into Parliament through a by-election. He had conceded to Mackenzie King that he was not a strong speaker "and would find the House of Commons difficult." Bracken left it to the Conservative caucus to pick Gordon Graydon, the MP for Peel, Ontario as House Leader, and began to tour the country to build support for the party.

Danger on the Left!

While John Bracken spent his time visiting schools, curling rinks and county fairs, and Mackenzie King was preoccupied with the expanded responsibilities of running a wartime administration, the

CCF found itself the unexpected beneficiary of the social and political ferment that came with the approach of the end of the war. If the York South by-election "ushered in the Golden Age of Canadian Socialism,"[7] business and financial interests were as quick to recognize that the post-war election could mark the end of the capitalist era in Canada.

The unpredictable Mitchell Hepburn resigned as Premier of Ontario in 1942, paving the way for the momentous provincial election of August 4, 1943, in which the CCF came within a few seats of gaining power. Winning a plurality of the votes – 40 per cent – the CCF elected 34 members to 38 for George Drew's Progressive Conservatives. Five days later, the CCF won two of four federal by-elections (a third going to a candidate of the Communist Labour Progessive party) and the struggle for post-war political control was clearly on. Buoyed by its victories, the CCF topped the Gallup Poll that came out in September, giving the party the support of 29 per cent of the voters, with the Liberals and Progressive Conservatives tied at 28 cent, and Social Credit at 15 per cent. The CCF led all the parties in Western Canada, causing alarm to both Liberals and Conservatives. That alarm would prove to be well founded just nine months later when the CCF would win the June 15, 1944 Saskatchewan election, bringing to office North America's first socialist government.

The CCF victories jarred Mackenzie King. He regarded himself as Canada's leading social reformer, having spelled out his views 20 years earlier in his reformist textbook, *Industry and Humanity*. He soon realized that that the agonizingly slow pace he had held to in the past would have to be quickened if he was to deal with this new challenge to Liberal hegemony. It was time to reactivate the National Liberal Federation. On Sept. 24, 1943, in the first meeting in four years of the Federation's Advisory Council, practically the entire post-war policy of the Liberal party, which became the basis for the Gentle Revolution, was affirmed. It was built around the ideas of King's principal secretary, Jack Pickersgill, and a small group of senior civil servants. Pickersgill had put a detailed list of social welfare initiatives in writing in a long memorandum to King in mid-August, 1943. He argued that farmers and labour alike feared "a post-war depression with ruinously low prices and mass unemployment. The Liberal party should ... seek by positive, concrete measures to remove this fear of the future." The immediate establishment of children's allowances paid by the State could head off demands by the trade unions for higher wages, Pickersgill wrote. Because the "baby bonus" would not be directly paid by employers, it would not "cause upward pressure on prices at all comparable with the pressures exerted by wage increases."[8]

The Pickersgill memorandum also called for a floor under farm and fish prices and programs to promotoe nutrition, housing and public development. "Domestically, it would put the other political parties on the defensive; internationally it would put Canada in the forefront of social progress. It would give the future to the Liberal party." By the end of the 1944 session of Parliament, the Liberal government was able to claim that every one of these initiatives was underway. New departments had been established for Veterans Affairs, Reconstruction, and National Health and Welfare. An Industrial Development Bank had been set up to make business loans, and the National Housing Act expanded to increase the supply of mortgage money. Registration of children for family allowances would begin the day after adjournment of Parliament. The government also promised to support national health care and contributory old age pensions, subject to provincial cooperation.

While the Liberal party turned left to meet the new CCF challenge, the long dormant right wing of the Conservative party was reasserting itself. Hard-line Tories, as well as a few right-wing Liberals, financed a squad of free lance propagandists in a crude, but largely effective, campaign to fan anti-socialist sentiment. One tactic was to try to make socialism synonymous with hated Naziism. The faint logic of this claim was based on the CCF's admission that it was a national movement, and socialistic, and therefore, said its critics, stood for "National Socialism" – and everyone knew the full name of the Nazis was the National

Socialist German Workers' Party. The Canadian Underwriters' Association told insurance salesmen to warn their customers that the CCF would seize life insurance policies and savings. The Canadian Chamber of Commerce scrapped the agenda of an Executive Board meeting to discuss propaganda schemes to "combat the menace of socialism." The Property Owners' League of Ontario warned of the need to defend free enterprise from the CCF. Banks and insurance companies extolled the virtues of individualism and free enterprise in their advertising.

The former general manager of the Canadian Broadcasting Corporation, William Ewart Gladstone Murray, marshalled the mounting anti-socialist alarm into a concerted propaganda drive. With the help of mining magnate J. P. Bickell, he set up a "Responsible Enterprise" committee, and soon donations were pouring in that would finance a burst of pamphleteering, advertising and speakers' bureaus. Murray's example was soon followed by Burdick A. Trestrail, a Missouri-born free enterpriser who financed his company, General Relations Services Limited, with fees paid by the "Society for Individual Freedom (Opposition to State Socialism)." The Society, in turn, was funded by corporate donations. A book by Trestrail, *Stand Up and Be Counted* was published to counteract such CCF propaganda as David Lewis' appeal for the new social order in his book, *Make This Your Canada*. The Society ran a public opinion poll in Toronto asking citizens whether they opposed state socialism – "the kind of system practised in Russia and Germany." But even Trestrail had difficulty matching the hysteria of another Toronto businessman, Montague Sanderson, who ran a firm of pest exterminators. Sanderson spent $75,000 of his own money on ads warning against the "Communist-CIO-CCF dictatorship" that "would exterminate democratic government by violence."

But before Mackenzie King and his cabinet could pre-empt the CCF's promise of a better post-war world, a fresh crisis over conscription had to be dealt with. The advance of the Allied forces through Italy and France in the fall of 1944, in which the Canadian Army came close to fulfilling its propaganda role as "a dagger pointed at the heart of Berlin," came with heavy casualties. Col. J. L. Ralston, the Minister of National Defence, learned during his annual visit overseas that casualty rates were running so high that 15,000 additional Canadian infantrymen would have to be sent overseas before the end of the year. He demanded that the NRMA home reserve draftees – "zombies" they were now called – be ordered to Europe. King, dreading the political consequences of conscription, sacked Ralston and replaced him with the commander of the First Canadian Army, Gen. A. G. L. McNaughton. A desperate campaign by McNaughton to persuade more draftees to enlist fell far short of the needed number. It was at this point that Prime Minister King executed one of the most careful compromises of his career: He ordered 16,000 of the conscripts, just barely enough to meet the Army's immediate needs, sent overseas. The cabinet held, with only C. G. "Chubby" Power of Quebec, the Minister of National Defence for Air, resigning in protest. By now, the Progressive Conservative pro-conscription campaign was in full flight, with John Bracken and other party leaders condemning the government for failing to protect Canada's overseas volunteers by not sending all of the conscripts to the battle zone. For the first time in the war, public opinion in English Canada turned against King, carried along on a strong strain of anti-Quebec sentiment. In Quebec, meanwhile, nationalist groups such as le Bloc Populaire (an outgrowth of the anti-plebiscite Ligue pour la Defénse du Canada), were rallying against the Liberal party. Maurice Duplessis' Union Nationale had defeated the provincial Liberals in the August Quebec election, raising the spectre of a Conservative-nationalist alliance of the type that destroyed Laurier in World War I. There was rioting in Montreal and Quebec City, and Home Army conscripts were said to be in mutiny in the West.

The resignation of a Liberal backbencher opened up the Ontario riding of Grey North for McNaughton in a by-election on Feb. 5, 1945. The new Minister of National Defence was opposed by the mayor of Owen Sound, W. Garfield Case, for the Conservatives and Air Vice Marshall A.E. Godfrey, for the CCF.

The idea of the Opposition parties running candidates against his new minister displeased King: "That surely is allowing personal hate and ambition to override all thought of country at a time of war," King wrote in his diary. The issue of reinforcements dominated the campaign. When Bracken charged that conscripts bound for Britain had thrown their rifles and ammunition overboard (only one was proven to have done this), what little public support McNaughton had soon evaporated. He lost badly, 6,097 votes to 7,333 for Case, and 3,118 for Godfrey.

When the 1945 Parliamentary session opened on March 14, Conservatives stepped up their attack on the government's failure to provide adequate reinforcements, even though the end of the war was obviously not far off. House leader Gordon Graydon pressed for the use of conscripts in the Pacific if the war were to end first in Europe. But Mackenzie King was thinking further ahead. The coming United Nations conference in San Francisco, he confided to his diary, "will change the whole trend of the campaign from the conscription issue in a general election to leadership in peace in the post-war world." He shared this view with the Liberal caucus two days after the opening of the House: the campaign would be fought "on the peace issue and the social issues." The conscription crisis had been ridden out; the Liberals would soon be offering Canadians their own version of a country freed from war and economic insecurity, even if it meant a revolutionary degree of government power over a peacetime economy.

The Spring of '45

In 1945, after a long winter of the deprivations of the depression and the sacrifices that went with the war, spring offered more than just the spring of a new year to Canadians; for many it seemed like the very spring of life itself. In point of fact spring came early to much of Canada that year. The weather averaged 12 degrees above normal in Toronto in March. The country was reading Bruce Hutchison's *Unknown Country*[9], absorbing its lyrical description of the season as "racing eastward on the hot breath of a Chinook wind." But if the spring of '45 held a special promise of new life, Canadians were still burdened with the fetters of the old. Wartime rationing, price and wage controls, and compulsory savings remained in effect. Bureaucrats in the Emergency Shelter Administration controlled the country's housing and in the cities, newlyweds were being allotted only rooms without housekeeping facilities. Teams of high school girls were recruited for farm work at 30 cents per hour. Wartime productivity had peaked in 1944 when 675,000 Canadian workers turned out $2.5 billion worth of goods, compared to the $2.3 billion produced by 848,000 in 1943.

The question was being asked, what would the workers and soldiers do after the war? Perhaps the answer would be to re-build the country; in Toronto it was announced that $60 million worth of new public buildings – hospitals, schools and universities – were on the drawing boards for the city. The Toronto Stock Exchange was in its heyday as North American's biggest penny mining stock emporium, a virtually unregulated, reckless forum of speculation. Mail order ads in the newspapers offered such soon to be forgotten issues as Transterra at 45 cents. The Toronto Maple Leafs managed to beat the Detroit Red Wings four games to three for the Stanley Cup after the Leafs' goalie, Frank McCool, had shut out the Wings in the first three games. Hugh McClennan had just published *Two Solitudes*, giving Canadians a revealing glimpse of the deep division between French and English Canada. A small town school teacher interviewed at an education convention extolled the virtues of city life. Only in the big city could he "have a glass of beer without someone putting in a complaint ... Sometimes I wish I were a doctor or a lawyer and had a little freedom."

Canada in the spring of '45 still wore an aura of rustic simplicity, despite its new-found industrial strength. Even with wartime prosperity, the twelve million Canadians lived frugal lives, harbouring their savings, haunted by the fear of a return to the hardships of the 1930s. Entertainment came from the radio and the local movie house and dance hall; weekends at the cottage or vacations by the sea were unknown to all but a tiny minority.

It was a country physically unscarred by conflict, but indelibly soul-seared by the hardships of the years between the wars, and the losses it had endured during the wars. Now, Canadians were determined to stake their claim to the good life: education, jobs, cars and new houses. Whichever party seemed best able to deliver that good life would gain their vote on June 11. This longing for economic security and a better way of life overshadowed the more narrow issues of the election as the parties moved into the campaign after V-E Day.

The CCF platform for the 1945 election demanded "that Canada shall go forward to a new life and not back to the old evils." A million and a half new jobs would be needed after the unconditional surrender of Germany and Japan; the CCF proposed to achieve this by socializing banks, processing plants, and other big corporations "which are monopolistic in character or are being operated to the detriment of Canadian people." The CCF planned to use public funds for housing and slum clearance, and promised lay-off pay to supplement the unemployment insurance of war workers until they found new jobs. The CCF also advocated appointment of a Canadian as Governor-General (seven years before Vincent Massey would become the first Canadian to occupy the office), and urged adoption of "a distinctive national flag and national anthem." Canadians were promised a new status as citizens of Canada, not just as subjects of Britain.

The platform adopted by the National Liberal Committee stressed that steps had already been taken "to see that every Canadian after the war shall have a wide-open chance to make a real success of his life." The Liberals would aim for 900,000 more jobs than existed in 1939, and a 60 per cent increase in foreign trade. "Money must serve the needs of humanity. The people of Canada shall have economic freedom," the platform proclaimed. Family allowances would pump $250 million a year into "the hands of people who need it most." Re-elect Mackenzie King's government, it promised, and returning veterans would get $750 million in gratuities to launch them on civilian life. There would be low-interest loans to farmers, floor prices for farm and fish products, a system of contributory old age pensions with a lower age limit and no means test, annual vacations with pay for workers, and reduced taxation "to give Canadians prosperity, employment and freedom."

The Progressive Conservatives, convinced that the election would see the defeat of Mackenzie King and the installation of either a Tory or a CCF government, also tried to move to the left. Bracken's Charter for a Better Canada pledged the party to policies "which will assure jobs for workers at decent pay, a square deal for farmers, restored confidence to business men, a national development plan for Canada, social security for all." The Conservatives promised that returning soldiers would not be demobilized, except at their request, until they had jobs. There would be federal grants to education to enable high schools to train students in agriculture, mining, forestry and fisheries. There would be a contributory health insurance scheme, and a program of subsidized low-cost housing. Amendments were promised to the BNA Act in recognition of the fact "the nation has outlived its constitution." But the Conservative party, Bracken's statement added, "stands four square for private enterprise and individual freedom. It is against socialism and state control of enterprise."

The Campaign and the Candidates

The United Nations conference opened in San Francisco on April 25. The fact that it would keep Mackenzie King out of the country for the first month of the campaign bothered him not a bit. King's broadcast to Canada on V-E Day, he thought, was "worth more than two weeks' campaigning on party matters." The June 11 election date had been set at a cabinet meeting April 12, within hours of word being received that Ontario Premier George Drew had announced an Ontario election for the same date. C. D. Howe, by now Minister of Reconstruction, suggested that holding the federal vote on the same day as the Ontario election would deprive Conservatives of any momentum they might gain from an expected provincial win. Drew promptly advanced the date of the Ontario polling by a week, to June 4. Mackenzie King's final preparation for the federal election was to bring in six backbenchers to replace departing cabinet ministers. Prominent in the new crop were Paul Martin from Windsor, Ont., Douglas Abbott of Westmount, Que., and Lionel Chevrier, from Stormont in Ontario.

In San Francisco, King had a "beautiful suite at the St. Francis hotel looking out over a small park." But he found "the whole business very trying," and concluded that he disliked San Francisco "intensely because of it having no boulevards or parks;" he thought it was a noisy place, and the weather "uncertain." None of these reactions were unreasonable for a man of 70; he could be expected to fret over his speeches and find the drafts prepared for him to be "wholly inadequate." He railed at Pickersgill for "impertinence" in suggesting that once having ordered the Canadian Ensign to replace the Union Jack atop Ottawa flag poles in celebration of victory, King would keep it there. It would be by a resolution of Parliament and not by "an arbitrary act of a Prime Minister" that Canada would settle the question of a national flag, King said.

M. J. Coldwell and Gordon Graydon were still in San Francisco on nomination day, May 14, when a record 965 candidates filed to contest the 245 House of Commons seats. Mackenzie King was readily nominated again in Prince Albert, Saskatchewan, where he faced three opponents including a strong CCF challenger, E. L. Bowerman. Gen. McNaughton was nominated in another Saskatchewan riding, Qu'Appelle, where the CCF put up Mrs. Gladys Strum, was one of the early pioneers among Canadian women politicians. John Bracken was nominated to run against a Liberal incumbent in Neepawa, Manitoba.

The Liberal election machine by now was making little use of the traditional party apparatus; the National Liberal Federation had been allowed to virtually wither away. What was left was in the hands of Agriculture Minister James C. Gardiner and Halifax lawyer J. Gordon Fogo, who had been given the party chairmanship over the head of the NLF president, Sen. Wishart Robertson of Nova Scotia. Fogo, a partner in Finance Minister Ilsley's law firm, had spent most of the war in Ottawa working for various government boards, and the Department of Munitions and Supply. C. D. Howe tapped into war contractors, especially in Toronto, for the bulk of the party's financing.[10] His Toronto finance co-chair, businessman Peter Campbell, reported in May that $700,000 had passed through his hands, with more to be raised. The fact that he had lists of contractors supplied by the Munitions Department made his task somewhat easier. Gardiner, meanwhile, was calling on his traditional sources in Montreal, including the CPR, for contributions.

Mackenzie King kept close watch on the Liberal election machine through both Pickersgill and his parliamentary assistant, later to be Minister of National Health and Welfare, Brooke Claxton. Claxton had demonstrated his natural bent for organization when he won the Montreal seat of St. Lawrence-St. George in the 1940 election. His campaign had the professional help of Cockfield Brown, then the largest advertising agency in Canada. It made use of such innovative techniques for that era as regular opinion polling. It was at Claxton's behest that Cockfield Brown was retained as the party's advertising agency in 1943. The appointment had been eagerly sought by several agencies, not for the fees it paid (none) but for the government contracts that could be expected after the election.

In 1944, the agency surveyed voters in 43 ridings, finding that if an election were held then, the CCF would have won 18, the Conservatives 13, and the Liberals only 12 of the seats. But more important, the survey tested a variety of campaign slogans, the first time this had been done for a Canadian campaign. The favoured slogan among Liberal supporters was "Bring Victory Home," but when the election was finally called, this had been updated to "Unity-Security-Freedom ... Vote for a New Social Order." The ad man on the Liberal account, H. E. Kidd, had $175,000 to spend on the national campaign and he devised a mix of newspaper ads, billboards, posters and pamphlets that played up leading Cabinet personalities and aggressively sold both the government's record and its plans, especially family allowances, and support for new housing. "Liberal Family Allowances Provide Food, Health, Security," one poster boasted.

A second agency, Walsh Advertising, handled Liberal party publicity in Ontario. Its president, W. George Akins, set up shop in room 286 of the King Edward Hotel and pumped out a stream of bulletins to assist local candidates. The May 9 bulletin included a canned speech, to be "phrased according to a speaker's own style," written by a "recently-discharged Squadron Leader of the RCAF." The author was probably James Sinclair, who would win the North Vancouver riding for the Liberals, become a long-time cabinet minister, and the father-in-law of a future Prime Minister, Pierre Trudeau. The speech painted an idyllic future for Canada's war veterans: "while nothing is too good for the boys who have fought and sacrificed for their country, it provides a lot of sat-isfaction to know the utmost is being done by the Liberal government to make their restoration to peacetime duties as helpful and happy as is possible ..."

The Progressive Conservatives also were into large-scale political advertising, and for the first time, the party com-missioned its own ad agency, McKim Advertising. The strategy the agency came up with was a bold one for the era – to build the campaign around the personality of John Bracken. He would be given Lincolnesque attributes of humility, sincerity and foresight. The Conservative attempt to run a "leadership campaign" was felt to be necessary to counteract Liberal propaganda, especially in the West, that Bracken was little more than a mouthpiece for monied Tory interests in the East. Conservative advertisements played up "John Bracken – the Man," "John Bracken – The Worker," "The Farmer," and cast him in roles designed to appeal to every kind of voter. One, headed "Security and Opportunity for Women," promised "a genuine new deal for women" including "equal pay for equal work," and cleverly suggested "perhaps the fact that (John Bracken) is a family man himself influenced him as he shaped these policies." There was no need to mention King's status as Canada's most famous bachelor. But King had almost the last word on the Conservative advertising program, telling the Ottawa *Journal* on June 9 that the Tories had sold John Bracken as if he were "a new breakfast food, or a new brand of soap." The hefty Conservative advertising campaign reflected the party's ability to once again attract large donations, especially in Eastern Canada. Over $550,000 had been raised in Montreal and Toronto by the end of May. The Conservatives would spend "at least $1,500,000 in the election."[11]

In comparison, the CCF campaigned on a shoe-string, spending barely $80,000. But for free-time CBC broadcasts – 21 quarter-hours were allotted to the Liberals, 15 to the Conservatives and 14 to the CCF – the CCF would have been crippled in getting its messages to the voters. It also had to try to repel a vitriolic ad campaign from B. A. Trestrail's Society for Individual Freedom. "The CCF stands committed to complete 'State Socialism,' 'State Socialism' stands for control by the 'State' of all production, distribution, finance, education, employment, etc ... no such program can be attempted except under rigid regimentation that spells DICTATORSHIP." M.J. Coldwell charged that Trestail spent a million dollars, but Trestail claimed the campaign had cost "less than one-eighth" that amount.

While the CCF tried to answer the allegations of Trestrail and other right-wing voices, the party's natural constituency – the labour vote – was wooed by an unlikely combination of Liberals and Communists. The Communist Party of Canada, outlawed at the onset of war, resurrected itself as the Labour Progressive party and set about trying to duplicate the feat of European parties in establishing links with centrist governing parties such as Canada's Liberals. The LPP called for a "Liberal-Labour" government and in many ridings its members worked for Liberal candidates. One beneficiary of this strategy was Paul Martin, the Liberal MP since 1935 for Essex East, who had his own powerful machine based on thousands of carefully-cultivated personal contacts.

The Prime Minister spent nomination day on the train from

San Francisco to Vancouver, and it was in the crowded ballroom of the Hotel Vancouver on May 16 that he made his first speech of the campaign. Thirty minutes of it were broadcast on the CBC and King found it "indeed a real pleasure to broadcast for such a splendid audience." He told Canadians he was appealing to them "in terms, not of promises, but of performance," and that they would have to decide whether to allow "the affairs of our country in its national and international relations" to be carried on by "the tried and trusted administration you know" or turned over to "unknown and untried hands." King sought to head off the expected Conservative attack on conscription by stressing that the election should be decided on no single issue. After the speech, he would note in his diary, he was especially glad he had been able "to get through without having to touch upon problems of the Japanese war. That point was not mentioned to me in the course of my whole visit."

The next day, the Prime Minister returned to his train for a 24-hour trip on the Canadian National Railway to Edmonton. "Around six o'clock I got up and looked out at the scenery for a time. Canada looks beautiful. Indeed going through the mountains all morning has been a wonderful inspiration." In Edmonton, the party had arranged a dinner for 450 Liberal supporters; the failure to call a public rally led the Edmonton *Journal* to ask, "What's the matter with Mr. King? Is he afraid to face the public?" The first half hour of King's speech again was broadcast, and while arguing that only the Liberals could lead Canada at the peace table, he began to sharpen his attacks on John Bracken. He zeroed in on the fact that Bracken had chosen to stay out of Parliament. "I have been in Parliament all these years and I haven't been devoting my time as an organizer for a political party." In Edmonton, where Trade Minister J. A. MacKinnon and Mrs. Cora Casselman (who had accompanied King to San Francisco) were standing for re-election, the real opposition to the Liberals came from the Social Credit party. In a province that strongly supported free trade, King stressed that Canada's prosperity was dependent on world trade and accused Social

Credit of being "no less protectionist than the most old-fashioned Tories."

For King, his western tour was a journey of re-discovery, from which he drew solace at any demonstration of support. As his train passed the farm village of Duck Lake, Saskatchewan, a notable event occurred: "There, when I stood at the back of the car, from a very humble shack, in one of the fields, a couple of women came to the door and shouted: Mackenzie King, Mackenzie King, and began to cheer. It really touched me very much to hear that welcome from the place from which it came." In Prince Albert, King received a "splendid reception" at the station, but he was unhappy at being kept on his feet for two hours at a ladies' reception. He was tired now, and had made no preparation for the speech he must give that night at the Armouries.

"When I got up to speak, I found the minute I opened my mouth that I was done out ... I had no joy in what I was saying. Indeed I realized that I had made the mistake I had been seeking to guard against, not having time for rest and being overcrowded." The Prime Minister spent four days in the riding, visiting small towns where he would declare a holiday for the school children. He concluded that he would hold the seat. "I really love being with the people, especially these simple, humble, honest and genuine folk."

King's largest meeting of the election so far came in Winnipeg on May 23. He worked at "fever heat" all afternoon writing his speech, and when the last revisions were at last typed, had no time for a final reading. But in it, he captured the essence of the Liberal campaign theme: "We cannot expect, and we do not want to continue, in peacetime, government spending on a wartime scale or anything approaching it. Neither do we want to go on spending public money on those things that work for death and destruction. If, however, it is possible to become prosperous in a time of war, through the employment war affords by the demand it creates, for those things which serve the ends of death and desolation, surely it should be possible, by a demand for those things which serve the ends of life and happiness, to achieve a like or even greater prosperity."

After five weeks away from Ottawa, King arrived back in the capital May 26, having committed his impressions of the campaign to his diary. "My feeling at the end of the tour from Vancouver to Ottawa is that the party's prospects are much better than I had believed they were when Parliament dissolved ... Unless some unforeseen situation develops, I believe we will have an overall majority and that I, myself, will be returned for Price Albert ..." In this judgment, Mackenzie King was relying solely on his political insight, having foresworn spiritualist séances for the duration of the war. But he was always acutely aware of good omens; his obsession with clocks was never far from his mind and on entering the Ottawa Auditorium for his final campaign rally on June 8, he would note later, "the hands were in a straight line at 10 to 10 p.m."

John Bracken's campaign was hard-edged and unrelenting, but by focussing on the conscription issue he failed to come to grips with the post-war social issues that were the main concern of voters. In Charlottetown on May 11, Bracken insisted that "people want it made known that Canadians will not weaken in their share of the fight against aggression till every enemy with designs against our allies is beaten to his knees." He told the audience in the Forum that "national unity has been sacrificed upon the altar of expediency. Needless friction has been cultivated between the great races." He would try to bring together the provinces to "the end that their problems will be fairly and har- moniously resolved within the Federal system that is our con- stitution."

All but oblivious of the fact that the war had ended in Europe and the fighting that had to be done in the Pacific was mostly in the hands of Americans, Bracken harped on the government's "cowardly manpower policy" in speech after speech. In Chapleau, Ontario, he condemned the policy of sending only volunteers to the Pacific as a last-minute bid to regain "the lost vote of Quebec."

CCF canvassers were knocking on doors within a few days

of the election call, but M. J. Coldwell did not leave San Francisco until May 19, after having delivered the party's first free-time broadcast on the CBC. Coldwell set out the five-point CCF program for post-war recovery. He said the party's goals were attainable through "social ownership and control of giant monopolies; conversion of government-owned war plants to peacetime production; planned programs in housing, slum clearance and regional development." Knowing that the CCF would be the target of anti-socialist campaigns, Coldwell also spoke of a "grave and disturbing report" that a group led by "big corporate and financial interests" from Toronto would unleash a "flood of vicious propaganda" against his party. Like King, Coldwell began his cross-country tour in Vancouver. His speech there on May 22 would be re-worked for audiences in every province: fewer than 100 capitalists controlled Canada's economic destiny and these "free enterprisers are already talking of recurring periods of depression and unemployment ... only the CCF program can prevent these economic and social disasters."

The CCF's best hopes were in the West, especially Saskatchewan where the party held power, and in Ontario, where membership grew rapidly after it became the Official Opposition in 1943. But when the results of the Ontario election came in on June 4, the CCF bubble had burst; the party elected only eight candidates, to 66 Conservatives and 14 Liberals. The anti-CCF campaign of Trestrail and Murray had achieved its objective of undermining public support. A more significant cause of the party's disastrous finish, however, might have been the political ineptness of its Ontario leader, E. B. Joliffe. He'd been unable to back up his campaign charges that George Drew was operating his own private political Gestapo in connivance with the Ontario Provincial Police. The charges seemed irresponsible, and Joliffe's failure to document them led to a public backlash.

For Mackenzie King, the most difficult region he had to deal with was, as always, Quebec. His rallies in Quebec City and Montreal were both successful; in Montreal this unilingual Prime Minister "was given a great reception when I got up to speak and again when I used a few words of introduction in French." In Quebec City, he paid tribute to Louis St. Laurent, recruited at mid-war as Minister of Justice, and in many ways he considered the meeting "the greatest triumph" of the campaign. By now, it was evident that the threatened mass desertion of Liberals in Quebec would not take place; even P. J. A. Cardin, the former Minister of Public Works, had come quietly back to the fold after abandoning plans for a *Front Nationale* party that would have challenged the Liberals in every riding. What nationalist opposition the Liberals faced came from *le Bloc Populaire*, which continued to fight any form of conscription while demanding greater provincial autonomy and more seats in Parliament for Quebec. But this Bloc was an essentially federalist party, and the other planks in its platform – a distinctive Canadian citizenship and the use of French in the armed forces and the diplomatic service spoke to the timidity of Quebec nationalism at the end of the war. The fact that the PC organizer in Quebec, Paul Lafontaine, admitted to giving Tory support to 33 independent candidates was seized on by Liberals in English Canada; it gave Mackenzie King an opportunity to compare himself with Wilfrid Laurier and to inveigh against a repeat performance of the 1911 "unholy alliance" of Tories and Quebec nationalists.

Mackenzie Ring expected to win 130 seats on June 11; he had made this prediction to the Governor General at lunch two days before election day. As King received the results at Laurier House on election night, it was soon clear that while he was not far wrong in his forecast, the outcome would put the Liberals dangerously close to falling below the 123 seats needed for a majority.

The first report the Prime Minister heard, from Cape Breton South in Nova Scotia, put the CCF's Clairie Gillis in the lead. This was followed by news that David MacLaren was running behind his Conservative opponent in Saint John. Both reports proved correct; Gillis won and MacLaren lost, but in the end, the over-all results for the Maritimes were exactly the same as in 1940: 19 Liberals, six Conservatives, one CCF.

Mackenzie King had hoped for 50 seats in Quebec and he did

even better; 53 Liberals, plus eight independents, most of whom would support the government. Only two Conservatives were elected; J. T. Hackett took Stanstead from the *Bloc* and a self-styled Independent Conservative, G. H. Heon, won Argenteuil from a Liberal. The *Bloc Populaire* elected two candidates, leader Maxime Raymond and J. I. Hamel. One communist, the LPP incumbent in Montreal-Cartier, Fred Rose, who would later go to jail in the post-war Soviet spy scandal, was returned.

Even with the Liberal near-sweep of Quebec's 65 seats, both Conservatives and the CCF held hopes of winning enough seats in Ontario and the West to form a minority government. For a time, it looked as if the Conservatives might do just that, capturing 48 of Ontario's 82 seats. But the CCF's high hopes of creating a post-war socialist government were demolished by the Ontario results; not a single CCF candidate was elected, as the party's vote dropped to 260,00 from the 390,000 it had received in the Ontario election just a week earlier. The Conservatives held all their Ontario seats and gained 23 more; Toronto went Tory except for Spadina, held for the Liberals by David Croll, a former provincial Minister of Labour. Even York South, won by the CCF in the by-election that saw the defeat of Arthur Meighen, returned to the fold with the member who had stepped aside for Meighen, Lt. Col. Alan Cockeram, winning easily. The Liberals held their three Windsor area seats, and 31 others throughout the province. LPP leader Tim Buck was beaten in Toronto Trinity.

Buoyed by these results, Conservative optimism turned to gloom with returns from Western Canada's 72 ridings. Bracken failed utterly to swing western voters behind him; only five Conservatives were elected in the three prairie provinces. Bracken won Neepawa to gain a second Tory seat in Manitoba. John Diefenbaker held Lake Centre in Saskatchewan, and two new candidates, Arthur L. Smith and Lt. Col. Douglas Harkness, won in Calgary. British Columbia returned five more Conservatives. The CCF, building on its provincial strength in Saskatchewan, managed to elect 18 members there, including M. J. Coldwell in Biggar. It also gained five seats each in Manitoba and British

Columbia. Social Credit clung to its Alberta power base, and among the defeated Liberals was Mrs. Casselman in Edmonton East. The new Social Credit leader, Solon Low, carried Peace River without difficulty. Only 19 Liberals were elected in Western Canada, ten of them in Manitoba, two each in Saskatchewan and Alberta, and five in B.C. Squadron Leader James Sinclair was one of these, winning in Vancouver North.

The Prime Minister left Laurier House at 11 o'clock, having heard the Canadian Press concede him the election, to go the CBC for a victory broadcast. There, he met John Bracken. "He put out his hand to shake hands and extended his congratulations. I thanked him but said nothing more." King "reluctantly" repeated the hand-shake for the benefit of photographers but refused to take part in the making of a theatre newsreel. "I do not need to sacrifice my self-respect by immediately treating the whole political scene as if it were part of some circus." Of Bracken, he thought, "it will not be too long before the party will get rid of him."

The final result was 127 Liberals, 67 Progressive Conservatives, 29 CCF, 13 Social Credit, two Bloc Populaire, one LPP, and six independents. The Conservatives gained 27 seats from the Liberals and one from the CCF; the CCF ten from the Liberals and three from the Conservatives. King had his majority, but a narrow one, gained in part by winning the largest share of the military vote, 118,537, to 109,679 for the CCF and only 87,530 for the Conservatives, who had built their campaign almost entirely around the need to reinforce the Army with conscripts.

It would be another week before Mackenzie King would receive confirmation of his own defeat in Prince Albert, due largely to the soldier's vote having gone against him. "This town liberated by the Canadian Army," a sign posted by a wag declared. At one point on election night, convinced he had been beaten, King concluded he would have to resign as Prime Minister; he hoped he might be able to get the job of chairman of the Ottawa Federal District Commission. "It was like a tiny shock." But that forlorn thought had left his mind long before the final returns would show he had lost his seat, 7,779 votes to 7,923. A similar fate befell Gen. McNaughton, the Minister of National Defence, loser to Gladys Strum of the CCF in Qu'Appelle. McNaughton, and David MacLaren of Saint John, were the only ministers King lost. King would finish his years in Parliament as the MP for Glengarry, Ont., elected in a by-election later that summer against the token opposition of an independent candidate. It was the fifth riding he would represent.

The Aftermath

Despite the closeness of the 1945 election, Mackenzie King's victory was a remarkable one in that it was fashioned from a careful balancing of the conflicting attitudes of Quebec and English Canada toward the war, and a deep concern by all Canadians for the problems the country would face at home and abroad after the war. It marked King's third successful campaign in a row, and the seventh in which he had led his party since becoming leader in 1919.

The 1945 election, however, was no mere re-affirmation of the status quo. The political ferment that preceded the election perhaps even more than the campaign itself, made it clear that Canadians would demand the fruits of the better world that had been denied them in the 1930s, and for which they had fought in the 1940s. The Liberal party read the mood of the voters with remarkable accuracy. Simply put, it was to deliver social and economic reforms equal to those promised by the CCF. If Canadians could not achieve reform under free enterprise, they would turn to socialism.

At the end of World War II, Canadians were eager to venture into the unknown in pursuit of their vision of a bright new world. The Conservative party's inability to look anywhere but backward, exemplified by its making conscription an issue even though the war was for all intents and purposes over, obscured the fact that it also had developed a progressive social program The CCF, by insisting on socialism as the only vehicle that could take

Canada into an era of economic growth and social security, faced the impossible task of overcoming the campaign of fear that been mounted by business-backed free enterprise groups. But the social design formulated by the CCF, based on government intervention in the private sector and massive spending in the public sector, had sufficient appeal to force both the Liberals and Conservatives to fashion similar, though non-socialist, alternatives. By co-opting these policies more skilfully and with more apparent conviction than could John Bracken and the Progressive Conservatives, Mackenzie King gave the Liberal party a legacy that would enable it to dominate Canadian politics for decades to come.

True to Mackenzie King's prediction, the Conservatives would soon replace John Bracken, with George Drew becoming leader in 1948. But by then King, too, was ready to give up his long hold as Liberal party leader and Prime Minister. On November 15, 1948, Louis Stephen St. Laurent was sworn in as his successor, having won the first Liberal leadership convention in 29 years. The social welfare politics and the new methods of economic management instituted by Mackenzie King and the Liberals for the turning point election of 1945 would set the framework for the governing of Canada for the rest of the century.

CHAPTER TEN

The Newfoundland Referendums of June 3 and July 22, 1948

THE ISSUES

Britain's oldest North American colony, Newfoundland, emerges from World War II and a long tradition of distress and destitution, searching for prosperity and a better future. But first, its people must make a historic decision – whether to continue under autocratic and colonial commission rule, return to an earlier system of democratic self-government (with economic union with the U.S. a possible result), or join Canada as a tenth province, fulfilling the destiny it had rejected at the time of Confederation.

THE CHOICES

Newfoundland and Labrador voters are offered the three choices on June 3. Commission government, the least popular option, is dropped from the ballot for the second referendum on July 22.

THE PERSONALITIES

CONFEDERATE ASSOCIATION
Joseph (Joey) R. Smallwood, journalist and broadcaster,
General Secretary and Campaign Manager
F. Gordon Bradley, lawyer, Chairman of National Convention, President

RESPONSIBLE GOVERNMENT LEAGUE
Major Peter Cashin, Founder

ECONOMIC UNION PARTY
Chesley (Ches) Crosbie, St. John's businessman, leader
Geoffrey W. Stirling, Publisher, *The Sunday Herald*, co-founder

THE RESULTS

June 3 Referendum

For Responsible Government . . . . .69,400 (44.6 percent)
For Confederation . . . . .64,066 (41.1 percent)
For Commission Government . . . . .22,311 (14.3 percent)

July 22 Referendum

For Confederation . . . . .78,323 (52.2 percent)
For Responsible Government . . . . .71,334 (47.7 percent)

Premier-to-be, Joseph Smallwood, signing the Confederation with Canada document, December 1948. He held office as Liberal premier until 1977.

SCHEMES AND DREAMS:
THE MISSION OF JOEY SMALLWOOD

The Newfoundland Referendums of 1948

Canada's day begins with the mists of dawn clinging to the sheer rock face that climbs out of the cold waters of the Atlantic ocean, leaving but a ninety-metre opening of submerged rocks and hidden shoals at the entrance to St. John's harbour. Above the harbor, from the shops of Water street to the mean neighbourhoods clinging to Signal Hill and in the hodgepodge of streets criss-crossing this eastern shore of Newfoundland's Avalon Peninsula, the city is busy hours before most people have awakened across North America's seven time zones. So it was on the morning of July 22, 1948, when for the second time in seven weeks the citizens of Britain's oldest colony were voting on the form of their government and the shape of their future. Today's referendum was a run-off of sorts, with but two options on the ballot – to join the Canadian Confederation as the country's tenth province, or return to the system of Responsible Government that Newfoundland had known before being pushed to the brink of bankruptcy in the nineteen thirties. A third choice, to return to colonial administration under the appointed Commission that had run Newfoundland's affairs since 1934, was eliminated in the island's first referendum, on the third of June. The fact that an option to join Canada was even on the ballot was something of a miracle. Newfoundland's ruling merchant class had no interest in having to cope with the fresh competition that would surely follow the island's joining Canada. They put their influence behind either the Responsible Government League, or the rival Economic Union Party. The two differed only in that the Economic Unionists would use responsible government to pursue a customs union and free trade with the United States. Without the commitment of Joey Smallwood to the mission on which he was fervently bent – and the complicity of colonial officials in London who were desperate to get the bankrupt colony off

Britain's hands – the three hundred and fifty thousand descendents of pioneering English, Irish and Scottish settlers making up the population of Newfoundland and Labrador would not have the option of this choice today.

As North America's closest point of contact with Europe, Newfoundland has always stood as a sentinel in the north Atlantic, first visited by Vikings who left behind traces of settlement a thousand years ago. They were followed by Portuguese and other fishermen lured by the immense stocks of cod, now largely extinct, that filled the waters off Newfoundland's Grand Banks. The arrival of Europeans led to a similar fate for the island's original inhabitants, the Beothuk Indians. The last of them were dead by the end of the nineteenth century, wiped out by a combination of famine and killings, some just for the sport of it, as if they were sub-human. For two centuries, the British forbade settlement in Newfoundland as a means of protecting the economic interests of England's western port cities, especially Bristol, from which fishing fleets would sail every spring. When permanent settlement finally got underway, it was under a form of mercantile feudalism marked by vicious treatment of poor, uneducated immigrants from the lower working classes of England's West Country and southern Ireland. Newfoundland's colonial status was not confirmed until 1824, with representative government arriving six years later followed by the advent of responsible government in 1855. Newfoundland was invited to join the other British North American colonies in Confederation in 1867. After sending delegates to both the Charlottetown and Quebec conferences, the old colony backed off from joining the new Dominion and in the "Confederation election" of 1869, anti-Confederates won a landslide victory. A Newfoundland ditty of the time went:

> Our face towards Britain, our back to the gulf,
> Come near at your peril, Canadian wolf.

The grinding poverty and perilous lifestyle of most Newfoundlanders created, over the generations leading up to the referendums of 1948, an attitude of both fierce independence and meek acceptance of whatever fate might bring. Poverty, malnutrition and disease ran rampant, especially in the outports, the thousand or so tiny villages strung along the coastline where electricity was unknown and visits from a doctor were annual, or rarer, events.[1] The depression of the nineteen thirties destroyed fish values and the colony fell into virtual bankruptcy, unable to pay interest on a hundred million dollars of debt. A Conservative party government of Frederick Alderdice petitioned London in 1932 to be rescued from financial debacle. A three-man Royal Commission – a Briton, a Canadian and a Newfoundlander – studied the matter and decided the answer was to replace the democratically-elected assembly with a Commission of Government. It took office in 1934 and was still running the island's affairs when pressure began to build after World War II for Newfoundlanders to re-take control of their destiny. The war had brought a welcome economic revival. There were better markets for fish, and when the U.S. got leasing rights to a naval base and was permitted to open airstrips in Newfoundland in return for sending fifty destroyers to Britain, many got jobs with the military. At the peak, there were ten thousand U.S. and six thousand Canadian troops on the island. It didn't help a lot; most Newfoundlanders still led lives of far less comfort than people in Canada. In 1948, four hundred and fifty years after its discovery, this tenth largest of the world's islands had only ninety-four miles of paved road, was served by just one hundred and forty-four doctors and seventeen dentists, and had the highest rate of tuberculosis in North America. It had no university, and was giving its old-age pensioners one hundred and twenty dollars a year to live on. A married couple got the same amount as a single person.[2]

The wartime presence of the U.S. in Newfoundland worried the Canadian government. Canadian High Commissioner Hugh L. Keenleyside – the Commonwealth version of an ambassador – was sent to St. John's in 1941. He reported back that the "vested interests" feared the return of popular government and while many of the "educated and informed" favoured Confederation, they were keeping quiet. Prime Minister King approached the issue with his usual caution. In 1943 he stated that "if the people of Newfoundland should ever decide that they wish to enter the Canadian federation, and should make that decision clear beyond all possibility of misunderstanding, Canada would give most sympathetic consideration to the proposal." In the careful words of diplomacy, it was as bold a come-on as Canada was likely to give. A few months later King had on his desk a high-level report from his Department of External Affairs arguing that Canada would have vital defence and civil aviation interests in Newfoundland after the war. It was time to advise Britain, the report added, of Canada's readiness to "consider seriously the incorporation of Newfoundland."

In London, the British Dominions Office – successor to the Colonial Office – was working on a reconstruction plan for Newfoundland. Postwar Britain could ill afford to continue to subsidize its financially beleaguered colony and the Labour government was horrified at the prospect of diverting hundreds of millions of pounds from its social welfare agenda to keep a Commission of government afloat in St. John's. In an irony of history, the man who had served as secretary to the royal commission that brought an end to responsible government in Newfoundland in 1934 – Sir Peter Clutterbuck – was now Britain's High Commissioner to Canada. Both sides recognized a practical but very political stumbling block: how could Newfoundland agree to Confederation without there first being a return to responsible government? And once responsible government was restored, who could be sure Confederation would follow? The solution would be a popularly-elected national convention that would recommend to London the possible forms of future government. The options would then be put to the people in a referendum. In a memorandum to the British cabinet the minister for the Dominions Office, Lord Addison, cautioned that there must be no hint of the British-Canadian desire to accomplish Confederation. Once the way was cleared for the national convention, any initiative for Confederation would have to be left entirely to Newfoundlanders. Shades of the New Brunswick election of 1866![3]

The Undernourished Dreamer

There would have to be a strong new voice for Confederation for this strategy to succeed. The situation called for someone who could be an authentic advocate for Newfoundland, able to both overcome the caution of the Canadians and satisfy the British colonial powers that Confederation was a realistic option. It needed a man with a mission. Thus there came to Joey Smallwood – born Joseph Roberts Smallwood on Christmas Eve, 1900 – the opportunity to fulfill the mission that he had become convinced was to be the chief work of his life, to bring to Newfoundlanders the benefits he was convinced union with Canada would provide. A spindly man who looked undernourished and sickly for most of his life, Smallwood was part visionary, part schemer and dreamer, part confidence man; dutiful husband and father with a strong social conscience; a man many would denounce as a charlatan and a trickster although none dare deny his role as a nation-builder.

Smallwood's Newfoundland roots did not go as deeply as most island residents of the time. His grandfather had arrived from Prince Edward Island to build a fairly prosperous life around a lumber mill he operated, followed by a shoe-making business in St. John's. For a time, the Smallwood name was one of the most famous in Newfoundland, especially after his grandfather had a large wooden shoe hung out on a cliff overlooking the Narrows advertising Smallwood leather fishermen's boots. His father, a life-long alcoholic, never amounted to much and it was only through the generosity of an uncle that Smallwood received what formal education he did as a student at the town's leading private school, Feild College. Young Joey didn't stay there long, dropping out after a dispute with a fellow student, giving him the time and the necessity of taking up newspapering as a craft, first as a printer's devil and then as a subscription order-taker before landing a job as a reporter on the St. John's *Telegram*. By this time, Smallwood was a dedicated socialist, a credo that took him to Boston and then New York where he worked for the socialist daily, the *Call*. This was at a time when the Socialist party was a serious player in American politics, running such notables as Eugene Debs for president. Smallwood could have had a job on the New York *Times* but he chose instead to get mixed up in a scheme to make movies in Newfoundland, the first of a life-long series of entre-preneurial failures. Back in New York, Smallwood survived by sleeping on park benches, living in flop houses, and eking out an existence as a penniless journalist while preaching the socialist cause at union halls and open air rallies. He never lost his love of his homeland, always carrying with him a large cardboard map of Newfoundland and going every week to Brooklyn to meet the Red Cross boat arriving from St. John's, in hope of finding someone he knew.

Smallwood returned to Newfoundland for good in the mid-nineteen twenties, organizing unions, working for various papers and for a time publishing his own newspaper in Corner Brook, the *Humber Herald*. He thought it would be a spring-board to get elected as the Liberal member of the Assembly for the local district. After having made himself "known to just about every living soul" in the district, Smallwood wrote to the Liberal leader, Sir Richard Squires, to tell him of his ambition. To his shock, he got a letter back announcing that Sir Richard – now in Opposition after a term as Prime Minister – would run in Humber himself and would like Smallwood as his campaign manager. Bitterly dis-appointed, Smallwood burned off his rebellion with a ten-mile walk to a nearby outport and back. He then wired Sir Richard: "Not for any other man would I do this but I will step aside and manage your campaign as well."[4] Squires was re-elected in 1928 and when the Liberals sought another term in 1932, Smallwood was a candidate in Bonavista South where he felt he had a chance among the riding's voters of mixed religious persuasion. Church affiliation was and remained a crucial element in Newfoundland politics for many years to come, and Smallwood, a nonconformist baptized in the Methodist church, was unacceptable to Anglicans. As it turned out, Smallwood's Liberal connection was more damaging than any religious association. With the depression already biting Newfoundland hard, the Liberals were swept from office, retaining only two seats in the Assembly. Smallwood presciently forecast that whatever government was elected, it would last no more than six months.

In the hardest years of the depression, Joey Smallwood managed to support his growing family – three children had been born to he and Clara Oates – from a series of labour union jobs. He walked seven hundred miles of Newfoundland railway line to organize a union for section hands, and endured dangerous boat trips to isolated harbours to organize a fisherman's union. These efforts were only a prelude, however, to his real interest: to write and publish the first encyclopedia ever devoted to the island, *The Book of Newfoundland.* With the financial support of St. John's businessman Chesley Crosbie, Smallwood hired writers, ad salesmen and subscription takers to peddle what would be a five-volume work. The first two volumes were published in 1937, but again Smallwood found himself without a regular income. The answer was to talk John Currie, the publisher of the the St. John's *Daily News* into paying him twenty dollars a week to write a human interest column about Newfoundland and its history. Smallwood called it "From the Masthead" and signed it under the name of "The Barrelman." Its popularity led a local radio station, VONF, to give him fifteen minutes a night to tell stories and historical tid-bits about the island and its people. He was able to convince a local business to pay him thirty dollars a week for the privilege of buying the air-time to sponsor the show. Over a six-year period, Smallwood broadcast six nights a week, making his name a household word in the lonely outports as well as in the cities and towns that dotted Newfoundland's coastal inlets. Life as The Barrelman, however, left him with time on his hands. Smallwood filled it by taking up farming, first with a chicken farm on the outskirts of St. John's, and later with a piggery, financed in part by Ches Crosby, that he operated near Gander where a large air base had been established. While living at Gander, he would sometimes hitch free rides with the RCAF Transport Command to Toronto or Montreal. It was while returning from Toronto where he'd gone to buy animal feed that Smallwood read in the Montreal *Gazette* of Britain's decision to allow Newfoundlanders to elect a National Convention that would arrange a referendum on the future of the country. At long last, he thought as he wandered the streets of Montreal, Newfoundlanders would be given the opportunity to settle their own fate. "I was going to be in it. All the King's horses and all the King's men wouldn't stop me. All of my work and training up to that moment made my entry inevitable. But on what side?"[5]

Smallwood had seen just enough of Canada to convince him that he should carefully examine what Confederation might offer. He wrote to Prime Minister King and each of the nine provincial premiers, explaining his intention to seek election to the National Convention and asking their assistance in making "a careful study" of the effects of joining Canada. After weeks spent reading the material that came back, Smallwood was a confirmed believer in Confederation, subject only to Newfoundland being able to negotiate beneficial terms of union. In this, he was encouraged by a retired judge and former leader of the Newfoundland Liberal party, Gordon Bradley. "Confederation with Canada is our only hope, our only salvation," Bradley had told Joey. Satisfied this was the case, Smallwood prepared a series of eleven articles that he managed to have published as letters in the *Daily News*. They attracted comment throughout the island, and helped Smallwood to a comfortable victory in the district of Bonavista Centre. He went into the convention with the prestige of having won the largest majority of any of the forty-five delegates. Smallwood was the only avowed Confederate among them.

Days and Nights of the National Convention

In preparation for the convention, Smallwood and Bradley made a trip to Ottawa and between the two of them, paved the way for a future request to Canada for terms of union. Smallwood and Bradley understood that Confederation would not only restore democracy to Newfoundland, but would give the island three political venues: the provincial House of Assembly, the House of Commons in Ottawa, and the Canadian Senate. The two agreed that Smallwood would take the Premier's job and Bradley, who wanted no part of the St. John's scene, would stand for the House of Commons and once elected, would serve as the province's chief federal minister.

The National Convention was called to order in the Lower Chamber of the Colonial Building on September 11, 1946. Smallwood and many other delegates were put up at the only decent hotel on the island, the Newfoundland Hotel, and the daily afternoon debates were often extended informally into the evening over drinks of rum and Scotch, the two favoured libations of the day. The entire proceedings were recorded on wax discs, and rebroadcast every night from nine until midnight. Officially, the tasks of the convention were to examine the state of Newfoundland's economy and determine whether the island had become self-supporting, and then recommend to the United Kingdom what forms of government should be submitted to the people in a referendum. Ten committees were set up to look at every aspect of Newfoundland life; Smallwood was named to the committees for education, health, and welfare. He had a deep interest in these issues, but his mind was focused on achieving Confederation and he would have to somehow bring the convention around to supporting his position. On October 28, Smallwood introduced a resolution calling for a delegation to be sent to Ottawa to find out the conditions Ottawa might set for federal union. The delegation, pointedly, would have no authority to make a deal, simply to find out and report back to the convention.

Smallwood supported his resolution with a stirring speech, but it won over few delegates. "Compared with the mainland of North America, we are fifty years, in some things a hundred years, behind the times. We live more poorly, more shabbily, more meanly. Our struggle is tougher, more naked, more hopeless. Confederation I will support if it means a lower cost of living for our people. Confederation I will support if it means a higher standard of life for our people. Confederation I will support if it means strength, stability, and security, for Newfoundland." Smallwood had touched many nerves, and he had awakened the ardour of proud Newfoundlanders. Delegate after delegate tore into him, accusing him of political bribery, of being a traitor and a Quisling. The vote, twenty-five to eighteen, seemed to have spelled the death knell of Confederation for Newfoundland. Yet, Smallwood was not in the slightest discouraged. He thought nothing could now keep back discussion of Confederation. He was convinced it was a cause that wouldn't die.

One reason Confederation wouldn't die was that neither London nor Ottawa were prepared to allow it to expire. While debate in the convention dragged into 1947, the new British governor, Sir Gordon Macdonald, a close friend of Prime Minister Clement Attlee, made it clear that he shared Atlee's view that union with Canada would be the best solution for Newfoundland and for Britain. On March 1, 1947, the convention agreed at last to send two delegations: one to London and the other to Ottawa. Gordon Bradley headed the London mission but he was almost the only one of its seven members who supported Confederation. The others, especially Peter Cashin and Ches Crosby, were strong advocates of responsible government. Their hopes were dashed when London advised them that financial support and responsible government didn't go together; the two just didn't mix. In contrast the Ottawa delegation which set out after the return of the London mission, found a warm welcome, both politically and in the weather in the Canadian capital. Gordon Bradley also headed that mission and clad in tweed suits and woolen underwear suitable for the cool Newfoundland climate, suffered from the heat even after Smallwood convinced him to buy a linen suit and boxer shorts. Discussions in Ottawa dragged on, partly because Smallwood felt delay would help turn the tide for Confederation. When the delegation finally returned to St. John's it came not with terms of union, but a set of "black books" in which the Canadian government described how the federal system worked and what Ottawa did for the provinces. The terms of union under which Ottawa would accept Newfoundland as a province, along with a letter from Mackenzie King, were conveyed to the convention on November 6. First, however, the convention had to dispose of an economic report submitted by Peter Cashin on behalf of the finance committee. It argued that Newfoundland had again become solvent, thus justifying a return to responsible government. When the convention got around to Gordon Bradley's motion to receive the Canadian communication, Bradley had fallen ill and it was left to Smallwood to make the argument for the Canadian offer. Debate raged until the Christmas adjournment on December 12 and resumed on January 5, 1948. It was finally agreed on January 15 that the terms from Ottawa would be put into the record, and the convention turned to considering the forms of government which should be placed on the referendum ballot. A motion that the ballot include responsible government and the commission form of government passed easily, on the understanding that it did not preclude discussion of other forms of government. The convention's chairman, John McEvoy, then asked members for their individual preference. Twenty-nine pronounced in favour of responsible government; none spoke up for commission government.

The next day, Smallwood went before the convention with a motion recommending that Confederation be added to the choices to be placed on the ballot. Perhaps letting on more than he should, Smallwood predicted that Newfoundlanders would have the opportunity to vote for Confederation even if his motion was defeated by "a mere majority of this convention." He then made a savage, albeit eloquent, attack on Newfoundland's establishment made up largely of merchants, bankers and resource companies.

The opponents of Confederation, he charged, were led by parasitic monopolists who represented "a new race of traders (which) has arisen in our midst." The country was being run by "twenty millionaires along Water Street" and it was time to put a stop to their depredations. Another two-week debate, capped by an all-night session January 27-28, ended shortly after five o'clock in the morning with Smallwood's motion convincingly defeated, twenty-nine to sixteen. The convention dissolved the next day, but the furor over Smallwood's speech had hardly begun. Bradley went on the air with a speech written for him by Smallwood denouncing "the twenty-nine dictators" for denying Newfoundlanders the right to vote for, or even against, Confederation. In less than a week Smallwood received thousands of telegrams as well as petitions signed by almost fifty thousand people, demanding Confederation be put on the ballot. He took every last one of them to Governor Macdonald and asked that they be forwarded to London. The Governor never actually sent the telegrams and petitions, but he did file a lengthy report describing them. On March 11, word finally came from London. The official announcement, read over the Newfoundland Broadcasting Corporation, advised that His Majesty's government was of the view that Confederation, as well as the commission form of government and responsible government, should appear on the referendum ballot.

The Campaign and the Cause

Acting on instructions from London, the Commission government set June 3 as the date of the referendum and arranged for ballots to offer the three options to voters. There would be voting in each of the thirty-eight districts that had elected members to the national convention. The voting age for women was lowered from twenty-five to twenty-one, the same as for men. There was no public funding and no formal organization for the referendum; it would be up to Newfoundlanders to campaign as they would. No thought was given to setting spending limits. A last-ditch effort to keep Confederation off the ballot failed when a petition from thirty-two St. John's lawyers, arguing that inclusion of the option was unconstitutional, was ignored when it was presented to the United Kingdom parliament.

Working almost around the clock, Smallwood had already taken the first steps to organize a Confederate Association. He'd arranged for a campaign headquarters in the back of Bartlett's barber shop on Water Street, just down from the cheap apartment where he was living. Long conscious of his bedraggled image, Smallwood managed to buy some double-breasted suits and outfitted himself with white shirts and colorful bow ties. The Confederate Association held its inaugural meeting in the ballroom of the Newfoundland Hotel on March 26. As planned, Gordon Bradley was elected president and Smallwood was given the position of campaign manager. Smallwood would confide in his memoirs that it was a post that would make him a "dictator" for the campaign. No fewer than one hundred and fifteen vice-presidents from around the island were named that night. A number had to be dropped when it turned out they were actually anti-Confederates. Money was a problem for Smallwood at the start, coming mostly from small donations and promissory notes given by friends. Within a fortnight, the first issue of a new paper, *The Confederate*, was on the streets singing the glories of Canadian family allowances, pensions and the lower food prices that Confederation would bring. Well-written and brightly laid out, fifty thousand copies of the weekly paper were given away free across the island to be read avidly in towns and outports. Even anti-Confederates appreciated its witty articles and caustic cartoons. The latter were a contribution of Canada's leading cartoonist of the day, Jack Boothe of the Toronto *Globe and Mail*. Smallwood gave Booth crude sketches of the cartoons he wanted – even down to describing the appearance of various characters – and the accomplished illustrator turned them into biting caricatures of Newfoundland personalities. Smallwood later claimed that he wrote ninety per cent of the content and only grudgingly conceded that Harold Horwood and Gregory Power, who had come on board as organizers, also had contributed to *The Confederate*.

Smallwood also used radio broadcasts and public rallies to get across the glories of Confederation. He hired a small float plane to take him to the outports where he would summon locals by shouting through two loudspeakers fastened to the wing as the plane descended into a harbour. Many had never seen an aircraft and the novelty of Smallwood standing on a pontoon, clinging to a strut as he addressed the villagers gathered on the shore and in small boats, was etched into the memories of thousands of Newfoundlanders. No one had ever before cared enough about them to come and speak to them in person. On parts of the island served by rail and roads, Smallwood's transportation was more conventional. He travelled with a car and a sound truck playing Newfoundland airs. It was as if a circus had come to town and Smallwood's rabble-rousing skills came to the fore in these appearances. He would get parents to allow their children onto the platform beside him, the better to put across his message that the seven dollars that Ottawa would send directly to their mothers every month for every child would put clothes on their back, school books in their hands, and food in their stomachs. Against this appeal, Peter Cashin could only thunder that family allowances were "the most immoral and corrupt enactment that has ever stained the pages of the statutes of Canada."

Smallwood soon realized that he would need real money to finance a winning campaign, and he turned to Canada for the funds. A Montreal heiress to the Redpath sugar fortune, Lady Amy Roddick, is said to have been Smallwood's first contributor. Senator Gordon Fogo, the National Liberal treasurer, turned over a list of generous Liberal donors – including liquor companies and big importers – to Smallwood's friend Ray Petten. Back home in Newfoundland, future Senate seats were sold off at ten thousand dollars a crack. Not all received their reward; in at least one case a donor ran afoul of Canadian tax law and another passed on before getting his seat. According to Smallwood biographer Richard

Gwyn, the Confederates amassed a campaign fund approaching one hundred and fifty thousand dollars.

The anti-Confederates failed to raise much much money or properly organize themselves, even though they represented the best of Newfoundland society. All the top St. John's families, the Crosbies, Herders, Bowrings, Cashins and Outerbridges, were backers of either the Responsible Government League or the Economic Union Party. None were prepared, however, to part with a lot of their wealth or even give a lot of their time to the cause of Newfoundland independence. The most effective of the lot was Peter Cashin, a major in the Newfoundland Regiment in the first world war, and a leading St. John's businessman and politician. Cashin had been a Conservative member of the House of Assembly and served as Minister of Finance in the last Newfoundland government. He'd been out of Newfoundland during most of the nineteen thirties, returning in 1942. Cashin was elected to the national convention where he argued for responsible government, becoming head of the League when it was launched in February, 1947. Concentrated almost entirely in St. John's, the League accomplished little and soon became caught up in personal rivalries among members of the city's establishment. Its newspaper, *The Independent,* displayed little of the flair of *The Confederate.* Its editorials argued that heavy Canadian taxation would take back any social welfare benefits that Newfound-landers might receive.

In November, 1947, a splinter group encouraged by Geoff Stirling, the aggressive young owner of the *Sunday Herald,* set up a "Union With America" party. Stirling, who was only twenty-six, was born in St. John's, educated in Florida, and had been working in Honduras when he got the idea of putting out a tabloid in his home town. He bought up sixty tons of newsprint from Smallwood's defunct paper, *The Express,* and by offering a sprightly diet of gossip, court reports and cheesecake, soon had the largest weekly on the island. The United States had become hugely popular as a result of the strong American presence on the island during the war. Thousands of Newfoundlanders had gone to the "Boston States" for work, and the new party hoped to cash in on the widespread pro-American sentiment. Stirling, supported by another young St. John's entrepreneur, Don Jamieson, soon realized they needed heftier support. They went to Ches Crosbie, who agreed to become leader of the party on condition it change its name to the Economic Union Party and focus on a customs union and free trade, rather than outright incorporation into the U.S. which Crosbie knew could never be accomplished. The name change took effect on March 20, just ten days after the London announcement that Confederation would be on the ballot. For all the warm sentiment that Newfoundlanders felt toward the U.S., however, the question of economic union was not on the ballot and there was no chance it would be put there. The party ran an enthusiastic campaign under the theme of "For a Brighter Tomorrow," seeking to capitalize at resentment against paying high tariffs on imported clothing, food and furniture. It was only the EUP's failure to gain any significant recognition from the U.S. that made its ideas seem slightly eccentric, if not wildly implausible. Smallwood derided the whole thing as "comic union." But he took the threat of the EUP seriously enough to offer the premiership to Crosbie, who declined. It was not surprising as Crosbie, a lively man in private, would become tongue-tied and flustered in public. Aside from draining energies away from the Responsible Government League, the EUP may have actually helped the Confederate clause by splitting the establishment and clouding the issue of responsible government.

The voting on June 3 revealed a deep division among Newfoundlanders, geographically, economically and socially. After two days of counting, an indecisive result was tallied:

Responsible government	69,400
Confederation	64,006
Commission of government	22,311

The urbanized Avalon peninsula had voted heavily for responsible government – sixty-seven percent to twenty-five per cent for

Confederation and only eight percent for commission government. The rest of the island had gone fifty-four percent for Confederation, twenty-six percent for responsible government, and only twenty percent for commission. Smallwood had worked his magic on the outports, but in St. John's and other towns, Confederation was still viewed with skepticism. Another vote was ordered for July 22, with the contest between responsible government and Confederation.

Religious differences had come to the fore in the last days of the first referendum, pitting Catholics against Protestants with often bitter results. Religious distinctions have always been important in Newfoundland, creating a sharp cleavage between the southern Irish settlers who brought their Roman Catholicism with them, and the west country English who sprang from Anglican or Methodist and other nonconformist stock. Lacking a strong government, the entire society revolved around sectarian institutions. This not only split the community along denominational lines, but severely drained local resources for the support of separate schools, hospitals and other community services. Six denominations – Anglican, Pentecostal, Seventh Day Adventist, Salvation Army, Roman Catholic and the United church – ran their own school boards who divvied up the annual education budget. In the main, Catholic church leaders strongly opposed Confederation. The Archbishop of Newfoundland, Edward Patrick Roche, feared that "a simple God-fearing way of life" would be contaminated by the Protestant morality of much of Canada, encouraging divorce and mixed marriage.[6] What had been a small parish paper, *The Monitor*, was sent island-wide to counter Confederate arguments. It condemned the placing of Confederation on the ballot as a political crime, saying no consideration had been given to the social and religious implications of union. On the other side, the Orange Order, that long-established fanatical wing of Irish Protestantism, had a strong following in Newfoundland. Even moderates such as Gordon Bradley counted themselves as members.

Under the emotional strain of the new campaign, appeals to prejudice became more blatant. On the weekend following the June 3 vote, the *Sunday Herald* reported, apparently unwittingly, that for the first time Roman Catholic nuns had left their convents and gone out to vote. When he read this, Harold Horwood got Joey Smallwood's permission to buy up hundreds of copies and send them to Orange Order lodges around the island with the offending article duly circled in blue pencil. Orange leaders hit the roof. Local Lodges forced the calling of a special convention on the pretext that "the Roman Catholic church is attempting to dominate Newfoundland." The convention was held in Grand Falls the week before the July 22 vote. It had letters sent to all Orange Lodges, signed by the Grand Master, urging Orangemen to "use every effort" to overcome Catholic efforts to influence the outcome of the referendum.

Both sides calculated that the second referendum would turn on the twenty-two thousand votes that had been cast for Commission government. Considering there had been no campaign in support of the status quo, it was surprising that Commission had received so many votes. Smallwood thought it indicated a "plague on both your houses" from many voters, distrustful of returning Newfoundland to political control, and skeptical of the promises held out for Confederation. It all meant that Smallwood would have to work much harder, and he did. Accompanied by two husky body guards recruited from His Majesty's Penitentiary, Smallwood set out to repeat his canvas of the island. This time, however, the Confederates paid more attention to St. John's, and scheduled a huge rally at the Armoury a few nights before the referendum. Feelings by this time were running so high that a mob of anti-Confederates gathered at the front door, ready to assault Smallwood on his exit. He fled through the back door to a waiting car, escaping to a small outport hotel. Smallwood's wife and family had been moved out of town to an undisclosed location the day before. In two days, Joey made fifty-six speeches in fifty-six outports. The advantages of Confederation were still the main theme of his talks, but a new element was injected when it was decided to attack the advocates of responsible government as anti-British and pro-republican.

The defection of a number of St. John's establishment figures to the Confederation cause lifted the spirits of Smallwood and his supporter in the last days of the campaign. Sir Leonard and Lady Outerbridge were among the most prominent, followed by members of the Bowring, Munroe and Winter families. Two of the three members of the Commission of government spoke publicly for Confederation.

Thursday, July 22, 1948 dawned as a typically cool Newfoundland summer day. The voting was even more orderly, if that was possible, than it had been seven weeks earlier. In a number of polls it was noticed that fewer ballots were being cast; the offshore fishing season had opened and some ten thousand fishermen were out on the Grand Banks. This worried Joey Smallwood, who knew that despite his new respectability in St. John's, his greatest strength was still in the outports. He also worried about the Catholic vote, but doubted whether much could be done about it. That night, St. John's and its suburbs once again gave responsible government an early edge. But as the votes were tallied in the outports it became clear that a majority, however thin, would be registered for Confederation. The outcome would be confirmed the next morning when the last of the ballot boxes were opened:

Confederation	78,323
Responsible government	71,334

Twenty-nine districts had gone for Confederation, only nine (including most of the St. John's polls) had stayed loyal to responsible government. The Roman Catholic vote remained largely anti-Confederate. The fishermen out on the Grand Banks who missed the vote probably accounted for the fact the Confederate majority had not been larger. Despite this, the turn-out reached a remarkable eighty-five percent. Joey Smallwood had fulfilled his mission. By a margin of seven thousand votes or almost five percent – 52.24 to 47.76 – Newfoundlanders entrusted their future to him and his cause. Doubts, however, lingered. Canadian newspapers concentrated on the narrowness of the outcome. The Halifax *Herald* headline the next day read:

SLIM CONFEDERATION MAJORITY
INDICATED IN OLD COLONY VOTE
Union With Canada Still Not Certain

Ches Crosbie, leader of the EUP, called on his members to accept the decision of the majority, but his was a lonely voice in post-referendum Newfoundland. Both St. John's newspapers, *The Evening Telegram* and the *Daily News*, urged the formation of a provisional government to review the "old colony's" options. It would do the work of the national convention all over again. Joey Smallwood couldn't understand the indecision. "What is Canada to do?" he asked the press. "Is she just to ignore our majority in the popular vote and the sweeping majority we had by districts? Can she ignore the proposed terms of union?" In Ottawa, an ever-cautious Mackenzie King was asking himself the same questions. King dithered until, as famously recounted by his assistant Jack Pickersgill, he was made aware that Smallwood's majority was greater than King had gained in every election but one. On July 30, the announcement came from Ottawa: Canada would "be glad to receive with the least possible delay authorized representatives of Newfoundland to negotiate the terms of union." Gaining Newfoundland would provide a fitting legacy to King's career, then about to come to a close.

The Aftermath

Confederates cheered, anti-Confederates mourned the outcome of the referendum. Smallwood and his supporters celebrated at a rowdy day-long picnic held on a meadow outside Spaniard's Bay, a village fifty miles from St. John's. Anti-Confederates lowered the Union Jack to half-mast, wept, and got drunk. Once sober, they plotted ways to stave off union with Canada. The Responsible Government League declared the referendum illegal, and asked that its results be set aside. They demanded a meeting with Mackenzie King, but were denied. Six former members of the Newfoundland Parliament went to court to argue that Confederation was unconstitutional; they lost at both the Newfoundland Supreme Court and at the Privy Council in London. Peter Cashin, still the only effective opponent of Confederation, organized a petition signed by fifty thousand Newfoundlanders and took it to London. There, he addressed a meeting of British MPs and arranged for the petition to be presented to the House of Commons. It was received, and filed away to be forgotten. The Newfoundland bill sanctioning union with Canada passed the House comfortably, two hundred and seventeen to fifteen.

The terms of union discussed by the informal delegation that had gone to Ottawa in 1947 were only provisional. It now became necessary to send an official mission to Ottawa. The Commission chose one of its own for this task, Albert Walsh, a leading lawyer who would later become Chief Justice of the Newfoundland Supreme Court. Smallwood was included, of course, along with Gordon Bradley, Ches Crosbie, and other prominent figures such as businessman Gordon Winter and John McEvoy, the last chairman of the national convention. On the Canadian side, the team negotiating Confederation included King's "minister of everything," C. D. Howe, and the up-and-coming young economics advisor, Mitchell Sharp. The key to the talks was settling on a grant formula for Newfoundland. Both sides recognized that a massive infusion of money would be needed to bring the island's services up to Canadian standards. Transitional grants were set at forty-three million dollars, to be paid over twelve years. Pensions of all kinds would be moved up to Canadian levels and Canada guaranteed that the ferry and coastal freight services would be maintained at current levels. More important, Newfoundland would benefit from the huge annual transfers that have-not provinces received each year from Ottawa. All in all, it would amount to a one-billion dollar a year windfall for the new province. The talks went on from October 6 to December 11. In the end, the only hold-out was Ches Crosbie, who insisted the terms did not make Newfoundland financially secure.

As the fateful day for Confederation came closer, jockeying for political standing grew fierce. Joseph Smallwood had no challenger for the premiership, and Gordon Bradley had agreed to become Newfoundland's chief political representative in Ottawa. It was taken for granted the Confederate leaders would all join the Liberal party. Louis St. Laurent had succeeded Mackenzie King, and he agreed to give Bradley a cabinet post, pending his election in one of the six new seats set aside for Newfoundland. There was much debate as to what position Bradley would fill; it had to sound important even if it wasn't. Because Newfoundlanders knew that the job of Secretary of State was an important one in the American cabinet, it was decided to give Bradley the same title, and he was sworn to that position the day Newfoundland officially joined Confederation, on April 1, 1949. In St. John's, ceremonies the night before saw the Commission of Government transfer its authority to the newly-knighted Sir Albert Walsh who had been named Lieutenant-Governor. He swore in a new provincial government headed by Joseph Smallwood as Premier. Not a single member of his cabinet had ever before occupied high office. Simultaneous broadcasts from Ottawa and St. John's heralded the occasion. Listeners heard the bells of the Peace Tower play "the Squid-Jiggin' Ground." Prime Minister St. Laurent saw it as a "day which will live long in North American history, a ful-fillment of a vision of great men who planned the nation of Canada more than eighty years ago."

Smallwood recognized he would need a well-organized Newfoundland branch of the Liberal party to sustain him in power. He set out creating one with the same enthusiasm he'd given to campaigning for Confederation. A train was hired to bring delegates in from Port-aux-Basques and other towns across the island, and more than a thousand met in the St. John's Armoury to found the new party. Smallwood was elected leader of the provincial wing and Bradley the head of its federal wing. A provincial election was called for May 27, 1949, resulting in the election of twenty-two Liberals, five Progressive Conservatives and one independent, Peter Cashin. It was the first of sixteen elections in which Smallwood would lead the Newfoundland Liberal party. He would boast that with but two exceptions, he also selected and appointed every Newfoundland federal Liberal candidate in the first seven federal general elections held following union.

Until Smallwood was finally defeated by the Progressive Conservatives in 1971, he managed Newfoundland as virtually a one-party fiefdom, turning aside all challengers and ignoring all criticism. He closed down hundreds of outports, moving people to larger communities. His efforts at economic development, however, often had disastrous results. Power from the Churchill Falls hydro development in Labrador was sold to Quebec for a niggardly price, enriching that province as it re-sold the electricity to New York State. Pulp mills, hydroponic tomato projects and other schemes meant to create employment and generate taxes were dismal failures. His greatest wound, Smallwood would admit, was suffered when he had to prefer charges of fraud against his economics advisor, Alfred Valdmanis, who got four years in prison for taking bribes to arrange government support for dubious schemes. After his government's defeat, Smallwood lost the Liberal party leadership to Ed Roberts, then formed his own rump party, the Liberal Reform party. He won four seats in the 1975 election, just enough to hand victory to the Conservatives, and finally resigned his seat in 1977. Richard Gwyn describes Smallwood as "the great white whale of Newfoundland imagination," a man who challenged his countrymen to realize their backwardness, and helped them find a way to overcome it. In one of his last speeches, to the Empire Club in Toronto in 1983, Smallwood held to his view that because of Confederation, "Newfoundlanders are better fed, better clothed, better housed, better educated and healthier than we ever hoped to be."

The Newfoundland referendums of 1948 were a turning point both for the colony and for Canada. The result was divisive and controversial, and it would not have come about without the leadership of Joey Smallwood, nor without collusion between London and Ottawa. It did not put an end to Newfoundland nationalism, which remains strong. Had the referendums gone the other way, would Newfoundland have been able to develop economically without the infusion of the billions of dollars it has received from Canada? Would it be better off, morally and socially? Those who point to the success of Iceland as a prosperous, independent state feel that Newfoundland, left to its own destiny, would have managed its resources better than it has done as part of Canada. There is no doubt, however, that Newfoundlanders today are firmly wedded to Confederation. The Royal Commission that reported in 2003 on Newfoundland's place in Canada found that the people of Newfoundland and Labrador are proud to be Canadians, but their participation in Canada "has come nowhere close to reaching its full potential." The commission rejected separatism but also called for changes in the partnership with Canada, especially in the management of fisheries and off-shore oil.

Joseph Roberts Smallwood, affectionately known as the last Father of Confederation, fell victim to a stroke on September 24, 1984. He had just published the third volume of his life's final work, the *Encyclopedia of Newfoundland and Labrador*. His memoir, *I Chose Canada*, was published in 1973. He died in his sleep on December 19, 1991, and his body lay in state at the Colonial Building, the old legislature where Smallwood first dreamed his dream of Confederation. His funeral was so large that it had to be held in the most spacious church in St. John's, the Catholic Basilica of St. John the Baptist, once the home of his most ardent anti-Confederate opponent, Archbishop Roche.

CHAPTER ELEVEN

The British Columbia Election of June 12, 1952

THE ISSUES

The entry of Social Credit as a new political force in British Columbia, taking advantage of popular discontent over health services, poor working conditions in the natural resource industries, and resentment toward Ottawa, inflames public opinion following the collapse of the Liberal-Conservative Coalition government, in office for a decade. Emergence of Social Credit as a conservative populist force under a former Tory, W.A.C. Bennett, offers an alternative to the socialist CCF. The outcome completes the transition of the political culture of Western Canada, entrenching a deeply-felt anti-Ottawa sentiment.

THE PERSONALITIES

SOCIAL CREDIT:
William Andrew Cecil Bennett,
MLA for South Okanagan and presumptive Social Credit leader
Tilly Jean Ralston, ex-Conservative MLA and supporter of W.A.C. Bennett
Lyle Wicks, President of the B.C. Social Credit League

LIBERAL PARTY
Byron "Boss" Johnson, Liberal leader and Premier, former Coalition leader
Gordon Wismer, Attorney General in the Johnson government

PROGRESSIVE CONSERVATIVE PARTY
Herbert Anscomb, Progressive Conservative party and
Opposition leader, ex-Coalition Minister of Finance

THE CCF PARTY
Harold Winch, Leader of the B.C.
Cooperative Commonwealth Federation (CCF)

THE RESULTS

	SEATS	VOTES
Social Credit	19	203,932 (30.2%)
CCF	18	231,756 (34.3%)
Liberal	6	170,674 (25.3%)
Progressive Conservative	4	65,285 (9.7%)
Labour and other	1	4,007 (0.5%)

*Premier W.A.C. Bennett, centre, recruited veteran Einar Gunderson
and young attorney Robert Bonner as ministers in his new
Social Credit government.*

W.A.C. BENNETT
AND THE POLITICS OF PLUNDER

The British Columbia Election of 1952

In clusters of twos and threes, Bibles under their arms, the newly-sworn cabinet ministers of a party that had never before elected a single member to the British Columbia Legislature, paraded up the long curving driveway to the Legislative Building overlooking Victoria's Inner Harbour. The three thousand roof-top light bulbs that give the building its dramatic nighttime sparkle were unlit now, with morning sunshine glistening on the lawns. Early risers among the tourists stopping at the Empress Hotel on this August Saturday are already enjoying the city's downtown public gardens, photographing its totem poles and visiting such attractions as the "Birdcage," the frail wooden house that was home to British Columbia's first parliament. The last passengers have disembarked from the overnight ferry from Vancouver.

The march to power of the newly-elected Social Crediters, led by 51-year-old William Andrew Cecil Bennett, a maverick populist who had bolted from the ranks of the provincial Progressive Conservatives, was almost anti-climactic to the months of political turbulence that had gripped British Columbia. Derided by his critics as impetuous and unreliable, seen as an opportunist who had found in Social Credit a white horse on which to ride to power, Bennett had brought down the entire political establishment of the province. He vanquished the established parties of both right and left by mobilizing a massive protest vote that completed the West's journey of alienation from the politics of old-line Canada. The rejection by Westerners of the eastern-dominated parties could be traced back to the election of Manitoba's farm-based Progressive movement in the 1920s. It spread to Alberta with the advent of a United Farmer regime, followed in the 1930s by the first incarnation of Social Credit under "Bible Bill" Aberhart, before veering leftward in Saskatchewan in the 1940s under the CCF government of Tommy

Douglas. Now it was the turn of the west coast province, and British Columbians were demonstrating in spectacular fashion their ability to confound conventional wisdom by choosing the new and untried over the familiar but discredited brand of politics they'd known in the past.

Bantering among themselves on that walk up the driveway, only Bennett and Tilly Jean Ralston, the new minister of education and the sole woman in the cabinet, had previous legislative experience. She had sat in the Coalition government with Bennett, and followed him across the floor as an independent. Only she and Bennett knew that she was dying of cancer. The other nine ministers, all political neophytes, included an ebullient Pentecostal evangelist from Kamloops, Phil Gaglardi, as minister of public works; a Vancouver streetcar conducter, Lyle Wicks, who was now minister of labour; and two school teachers from the Kootenays, Robert Sommers who had been given two ministries, lands and forests as well as mines, and Wesley Black who Bennett named as his Provincial Secretary. The two most qualified members of Bennett's team, his Attorney General, Robert Bonner and his minister of finance, Einar Gunderson, hadn't yet been elected. Bennett had wisely tapped them from the worlds of law and accounting, promising he would get them into the Legislature through early by-elections.

The outcome of the election had hung in the balance for fifty days after June 12, while recount after recount went on to determine winners under the cumbersome transferable balloting system that was being used in B.C. for the first time. When it finally emerged that the upstart Social Credit party had won the most seats – edging out the CCF nineteen to eighteen – the Lieutenant Governor of B.C., shipbuilder Clarence Wallace, a stalwart Liberal, found himself obliged to invite Bennett to take power. How had it come about that the province's three entrenched parties, Liberals, Conservatives and CCF, had all been upstaged by this rebel from the Okanagan who had walked out of his Tory caucus, flirted with forming his own United Progressive Party, and then had taken up the cudgels for a splintered, dispirited and disorganized Social Credit faction that had won barely two per cent of the vote in B.C.'s last election?

The 1952 British Columbia election was driven by more than just dissatisfaction of voters with the Coalition government of Liberals and Conservatives that had held office since 1941. With an economy that relied almost totally on the extraction of natural resources, eight out of ten British Columbians were dependent for their livelihoods on the forests, fisheries and mines. As usually occurs in frontier territories, a small group of influential players representing large corporations, acting with the acquiescence of government, controlled the exploitation of B.C.'s riches and managed the distribution of its rewards. It was the plundering of these resources that had given rise to a class-based political struggle over the division of the spoils, rather than over whether B.C.'s lands and water could much longer sustain virtually uncontrolled exploitation. Twenty years earlier, a leading historian described Vancouver as "an eager, grasping, acquisitive community ... all the time extending its economic power until it held most of the province in fee."[1] Little had since changed. The population of B.C. at mid-century was nudging the million mark, half born outside the province, mostly engaged in trades and labour which made for aggressive union growth. Lacking strong traditions or a shared past, most British Columbians felt themselves in thrall to the natural resource companies, who in turn were vulnerable to the fluctuations in the demand of export markets for lumber, minerals and fish. Trade unions fought for higher wages and more jobs for workers, small operators demanded access to lands reserved for large corporations, and farmers, merchants and ordinary citizens wanted improvements to roads, ferries and railways. A politician who could offer to meet all these needs – who would use the instruments of government to accelerate, rather than diminish, the plunder of the province's natural wealth – would not lack for support. In W.A.C. Bennett, British Columbians found such a man.

The Start of a Saga

"Wacky" Bennett (his initials were translated into a term of mild opprobrium by media critics) was elected in the first year of B.C.'s Coalition government. He was a product of small town Canada, a civic booster from Kelowna in the fruit-rich Okanagan valley where he'd been a merchant, president of the board of trade, a faithful family man, dedicated church-goer, and a teetotaler. Bennett was regarded as a jovial sort with a chubby pleasantness about him; he learned to wear well-tailored suits to disguise his ample paunch. Born in New Brunswick, he had followed his father to Alberta's Peace River country. Their relationship was difficult, and before long Bennett struck out on his own in Edmonton. Finding work with a hardware wholesaler, young "Cece" took advantage of an opportunity to become a partner in a hardware store in the small Alberta town of Westlock. He soon married May Richards and started raising a family. In 1930, he sold out to his partner and headed to British Columbia, where May had relatives in Victoria. Bennett scoured the countryside for a business to buy, ending up in Kelowna, then a town of five thousand, where he was able to take over a hardware store for the cost of its inventory.

Bennett's interest in politics went back to his youth in New Brunswick and a family of staunch Conservative heritage. He remembered the 1911 federal election when, as a boy, he helped light the bonfire that local Tories built to celebrate the defeat of Wilfrid Laurier. In Kelowna, Bennett became active in the local Conservative association and in 1941, was elected the MLA for South Okanagan. That year, the Liberal government of Duff Pattullo was returned as a minority, holding twenty-one seats to fourteen for the CCF, twelve for the Conservatives, and one independent, self-styled Labour party leader Tom Uphill from the Interior coal mining town of Fernie. The Conservative leader, R.J. "Pat" Maitland, suggested a coalition government of the three main parties as a wartime strategy. Feeling vulnerable after the Japanese attack of December 7 on Pearl Harbour, the Vancouver business community liked the idea of coalition, but neither they nor CCF leader Harold Winch were interested in having the socialists in bed with the free enterprise Liberals and Conservatives. When Premier Pattullo resisted, rebellious Liberals organized a special convention in Vancouver and succeeded in ousting him. By Christmas, a Coalition government of Liberals and Conservatives had been sworn in, with former finance minister John Hart as Premier, and Maitland in the finance portfolio.

Bennett eagerly embraced the Coalition but thought it should be entrenched in a formal merger of the two parties. At war's end in 1945, the Coalition easily won re-election, thirty-six seats to ten for the CCF. On the death of Maitland, Herbert Anscomb, to whom Bennett had never warmed, became head of the B.C. Conservatives. Disillusioned with provincial politics, Bennett resigned to run as the federal Conservative candidate in the Yale riding. He lost to the CCF's O.L. Jones and found himself back in Kelowna operating his now expanded chain of hardware stores. By the 1949 provincial election, Bennett's fill-in at Victoria had tired of the job and Bennett was again nominated in South Okanagan. His easy victory mirrored the Coalition landslide of that year, when the government carried sixty-one per cent of the popular vote, winning thirty-nine seats – twenty-eight Liberals and eleven Conservatives. The CCF was elected in only seven. Bennett's victory emboldened him to run against Anscomb for the Conservative leadership. He wooed convention delegates with apples rather than liquor and lost badly, 450 votes to 167. But the setback did little to distract him from the stubbornly ambitious, self-interested course he'd set out on when he first entered politics.

All through the 1950 and 1951 sessions of the Legislature, Bennett tugged at the tether of his party's control. Left out of the cabinet, he continued to urge the closest collaboration between the governing parties, even advancing a name for a newly merged party; he would call it the United Progressive Party. He was urging new legislation to expand the government's control over natural resources, especially a publicly-owned hydro authority. Bennett also put forth the idea of a single transferable ballot as a more democratic method of choosing a government. Voters would rank candidates in their order of preference. If no candidate won at least fifty per cent of the vote on the first count, the lowest-ranking candidate would be dropped, with those ballots reallocated according to each voter's second choice. The process would continue until some candidate emerged with a majority. Ironically, the government accepted both of Bennett's proposals, warmly embracing the transferable ballot as a tactic that would freeze out the CCF, especially if Conservatives and Liberal voters gave each other's candidate their second choices.

But it was the first great postwar experiment in social welfare, publicly-managed, compulsory hospital insurance, which became the Achilles heel of the Coalition. Set up with great fanfare, the B.C. Hospital Insurance Corp. quickly found itself the target of public opposition over constantly increasing premiums, the addition of co-payment charges, and a mounting debt. On March 15, 1951, Bennett delivered an hour-long indictment of Coalition policies, and crossed the floor of the House to sit as an independent. Within two weeks, Tilly Rolston would follow him. For the rest of the year, Bennett pondered his future. He was realistic in his view that forming a new party would be difficult. Slowly, another idea began to germinate; perhaps the nascent Social Credit movement in British Columbia could be fashioned into a viable challenge to the old line parties and the CCF.

Bennett was not uncomfortable with much of the philosophy of Social Credit, although he had no interest in either its underlying monetary theories or the narrow, often racist attitudes of many of the original diehard Social Crediters. The evangelical Christian background of the movement, stemming from the time of Alberta evangelist William Aberhart's adoption of the theories of Socred founder Major C.H. Douglas, would cause Bennett no difficulty. What impressed him most about Social Credit was the way in which Aberhart's successor as Premier, Ernest Manning, was presiding over a conservative government that was managing with spectacular success Alberta's two great resources, oil and natural gas. Returning home when the House adjourned for

Easter, Bennett found a groundswell of support for an alternative to the old line parties. A thousand voters turned up for an accountability meeting in Kelowna, with Bennett getting a strong endorsement for his abandonment of the Coalition.

Through the summer of 1951, Bennett felt his way cautiously, realizing many Social Crediters were reluctant to embrace a former Tory who might use the party to achieve his own ends. Lyle Wicks, the Vancouver streetcar conductor who was president of the fractious Social Credit League, took a somewhat warmer stance. He wrote to Bennett congratulating him on leaving the Coalition: "It is a rare thing in the political arena to see a man assert his convictions to the extent that he is prepared to leave the Party of his choice rather than stifle his conscience."[2] Bennett met shortly after with Wicks, and began to cultivate other Social Credit figures such as Eric Martin, who had led a veteran's sit-down in the old Hotel Vancouver, forcing authorities to make it available for public housing. By the end of the year, Bennett felt ready to make his move. On December 15, he issued a statement from his home saying he believed that the best thing for B.C. would be a government similar to the Social Credit government of Alberta. He'd decided to join the Social Credit movement.

As the parties prepared for the 1952 session of the legislature, it was becoming increasingly clear that the Coalition was coming apart. The very magnitude of its 1949 landslide led both parties to believe they could win and hold power on their own. At the same time, their federal cousins were uncomfortable with the cozy provincial alliance. By now, Byron "Boss" Johnson had succeeded John Hart as Premier, with Herbert Anscomb retaining the Finance portfolio. As a Tory, Anscomb used his position to wage war on the federal Liberals over national fiscal and tax policies. Taking advantage of Anscomb's habit of announcing government policies to the media before they'd cleared cabinet, Johnson fired him. Other Conservatives in the cabinet walked out, making it inevitable that the two parties would face off against each other in the next provincial election. The break-up of the Coalition set the stage for a lame duck session of the legislature. Premier Johnson ended it on April 10 and a writ was issued for an election on Thursday, June 12.

With an election at hand and Social Credit facing the voters without a leader, Bennett still had to convince many party faithful of his sincerity to their cause. The opportunity came at a hurriedly called convention in New Westminster, where delegates would have to decide on the party leadership. Bennett told them that when he'd joined the Social Credit movement, he'd joined it "hook, line and sinker." His fervor greatly impressed the Social Crediters, especially when, after the convention decided to name only a campaign leader instead of a party leader, Bennett declined to stand for the post. It went instead to the Rev. Ernest Hansell, a Socred MP from Alberta. Bennett and the party were taking a calculated risk; Social Credit would go into the upcoming election campaign without a party leader, although Bennett was clearly both its most visible personality and its greatest asset.

Party Politics: Policies and Personalities

Party politics came late to British Columbia, but its politicians have always been colorful. After joining Confederation in 1871 on a promise of a transcontinental railway within ten years, B.C.'s governments for many years were made up of independents. None was more memorable than the self-styled Amor de Cosmos ("Lover of the Universe"), born in Nova Scotia as plain William Smith. He came to B.C. with his new name after taking part in California's 1849 gold rush, launched the *British Colonist* in Victoria, and used it to heap scorn on the colonial government. De Cosmos went on to become the province's second premier (1872-74). It was not until 1901 that party lines became firm, with Liberals and Conservatives putting forth full slates for the 1903 election, the province's tenth. Richard McBride, an early-day populist known affectionately as "the People's Dick," led the Conservative party to victory that year, winning twenty-two seats to seventeen for the Liberals, three socialists and one independent.

He was re-elected three times and held office until 1915. McBride was the longest-serving premier before W.A.C. Bennett and the first premier born in the province. He ended his days as B.C. agent general in London.

Gold, forests and railways dominated the politics of B.C.'s first century. It was the pursuit of gold and other minerals that brought the first wave of immigrants to the B.C. mainland. Once gold panning was exhausted and mining had become a serious business, adventurous men lured by prospects of riches found themselves part of a powerless labour class dependent on a few large operators for work in the mines and forests. Farming was confined to small stretches of land in the narrow valleys intersected by the north-south mountain ranges running up and down the province, from the Coast mountains to the Rockies. Even salmon fishing required a considerable investment and by 1901 six large firms were hauling in nearly half the catch. The railway builders, from William Van Horne of the Canadian Pacific to Mackenzie and Mann of the Pacific Great Eastern and the Canadian Northern, were accustomed to receiving both large land grants and government subsidies. By 1913, more than twenty million acres, much of it at the core of new town sites along the rail routes, had been granted to railway promoters. The parcels automatically became the most valuable tracts in the province, to be resold to settlers at land boom prices. In a single session, McBride's government passed bills giving support to six railway projects. Money that didn't end up in politicians' pockets was used by the promoters to buy up shares in their own companies, or invest in mines and timber schemes.

True to its name, British Columbia for many years attracted mostly British immigrants. Many had strong trade union backgrounds, giving rise to the early building trades and mine and forest workers' unions. Early in his tenure, McBride recognized the growing strength of labour by mandating an eight-hour day in the coal mines. The labour movement, seeing Asian immigration as a threat to jobs for whites, helped plant a strong strain of racism in B.C. politics. Chinese workers and native Indians were disenfranchised as early as 1874. Japanese were added to the list in 1905, Hindus in 1907, and Doukhobors in 1931. Not until after the Second World War – which saw thousands of Canadian-born Japanese interned in B.C. camps – were these restrictions abolished. The lumber camps were filled by mostly Canadian-born workers. From 1903 to 1907 alone, McBride's government issued over fifteen thousand licenses to cut nine million hectares of Crown forest land – three-quarters of all government land in the province. The rush to exploit the forests might have completely denuded B.C.'s hinterlands, but pressure from a growing conservation movement led to appointment of a royal commission of inquiry in 1909. Only a few of its conservation recommendations were acted on, and the 1912 Forest Act was concerned with achieving "full" use of forest resources by encouraging access to high-quality, old-growth Douglas fir at low fees. Successive governments saw it as their job to promote the growth of forestry. Regulations were kept to a minimum, unlimited cutting was allowed, and there was virtually no reforestation. Timber licenses, once obtained could be freely sold, enabling pioneer lumber barons such as H.R. MacMillan to gain control over vast tracts of prime forests. By the Second World War, operating under thirty-year old rules, B.C.'s forest industry was reaching an impasse. The best timber lands were spoken for, harvesting rates had tripled, and reforestation was lagging. A second royal commission appointed in 1943 called for policies to ensure "sustained yield" – "a perpetual yield of wood of commercially usable quality." The recommendations put the Coalition to test. One of the last acts of Premier John Hart's government in 1947 was to pass a new Forest Act setting up a fresh system of forest management licenses, later renamed tree farm licenses. Stricter controls were put on cutting and replanting. But fees remained low, continuing a long tradition that has stretched into the present.[3]

The Campaign and the Candidates

British Columbians basked in a comfortable Pacific climate and scenic grandeur, enjoying a growing postwar prosperity as the 1952 election got underway. There was nervousness and uncertainty, however, about whether the new prosperity would last and what the consequences might be if an economic downturn caused job losses for woodsworkers, miners and fishermen. Two old line parties, Liberals and Conservatives; a traditional opposition, the socialist CCF; and now a newcomer without a leader or a clear set of policies, Social Credit, contested for the support of three quarter of a million voters. The campaign brought out a deep vein of populist protest against the trite generalities and conventional assumptions of British Columbia politics, which only Social Credit was in a position to exploit.

Premier Byron Johnson's Liberals, freshly anointed as a minority government after the break-up of the Coalition, found themselves caught between incumbency and opposition; able neither to claim credit for Coalition successes, nor vigorously attack what had gone wrong. An overconfident Johnson was sure the new transferable ballot would bring him victory. He told intimates to expect voters to give Liberals their first choice and Conservatives their second, "1-2 for free enterprise." The new Opposition leader Herbert Anscomb had an easier target, and campaigned as the "only united free enterprise party and therefore the only party equipped to provide the province with able and stable government." He boasted that "never before in the history of British Columbia has a political party presented the people with candidates of such excellent calibre." Harold Winch, bumped as Opposition leader when the Coalition broke up, still saw the CCF as the only alternative to the old line parties. His socialist rhetoric was designed to cement the party's core vote while reaching out to marginal voters discontented with the government's handling of hospital insurance and natural resources. Social Credit had the advantage of clear targets in all parties, and no record to defend. It didn't hurt that Alberta was prospering under a regime of oil and

Social Credit. With Bennett as putative leader, stalwarts such as Lyle Wicks, Eric Martin, Peer Paynter and William Chant were quickly nominated by newly formed riding associations. Most candidates, however, were unknown and inexperienced, reflecting the deep discontent that ran through the ranks of small town shopkeepers, ranchers and fruit growers, school teachers and workers across British Columbia. They raised their own funds (despite rumors of money from Alberta) and put out poorly printed pamphlets often riddled with typographical errors. It all reinforced Social Credit's image as a people's movement.

The state of the forest industry and the conditions affecting British Columbia's other natural resource producers were, as always, perennial issues. In the six weeks leading up to the voting, the threat of a strike by the thirty thousand members of the International Woodworkers of America (IWA) hovered over the province. All parties, but especially Social Credit and the CCF, advocated more aggressive natural resource development under terms that would increase public revenues. A more emotional issue affecting almost every voter raged around the British Columbia Hospital Insurance Service, a pioneering foray into publicly-financed medicare that was intended as a great social advance but was creating seething resentment. Brought in by the Coalition government, the plan was compulsory and was to be financed through premiums. When these turned out to be inadequate, the government imposed a co-insurance charge for every hospital stay, infuriating the public. The media played up the few cases of uninsured who were denied hospital admission. The Liberals were forced onto the defensive, answering charges of incompetence and heartlessness. Johnson seemed to be sleepwalking through the campaign, committing a series of tactical blunders that almost made it look as if he was courting defeat. When he learned from hospital insurance commissioner Lloyd Detwiler that the new co-insurance charges had generated a three million dollar surplus – evidence that the government had the plan under financial control – Johnson ordered the information suppressed, fearful it would bring demands for a cutback in premiums. He defended the hospital insurance scheme and predicted that similar plans would be in place across Canada and in many states within five years "because of the inability of people to pay huge hospital bills." It was late in the campaign before he realized that the real threat to his party's re-election was Social Credit. Over Johnson's signature, full page newspaper ads warned that "Voting for leaderless individuals could result in hopeless chaos such as this province has never before experienced. All parties concede the Liberals will have the largest group ... Anything else is bound to result in confusion, confiscation and frustration."

The Premier's most effective campaigner was probably Gordon Wismer, the outgoing attorney general, despite the fact the two were frequently in disagreement over the government's handling of hospital insurance. Wismer liked to boast that he hadn't forgotten a face in forty years in politics. "Sure, we've made mistakes," he would tell anyone who listened, "but our record is unequalled in the good things that we have accomplished for British Columbia."[4] Wismer did his best to repair Liberal fences, taking arduous trips up the B.C. coast and into the Interior. Travelling by ferry, train and car, he attended eight rallies in eight days, proclaiming on his return to Vancouver that he'd found "an upsurge of Liberalism in the hinterlands." To the independent loggers who crowded into his meetings in towns such as Terrace, Smithers, Burns Lake and Williams Lake, Wismer admitted that small operators had been unfairly treated in the granting of forest management licenses. He promised a new Liberal government would correct things.

The Liberals were the first to complete their slate of nominations. As their 48th candidate, they put up country editor Stan Orris of the Grand Forks *Gazette* against CCF incumbent Rupert Hagen. Orris had lost to Hagen when he ran against him as an independent in 1949. In many ways, Byron Johnson's appeal to B.C. voters was almost quaint. In an election eve interview with the Vancouver *Sun*, Johnson couched his appeal in the language of respectable middle class concern for the poor. "Liberalism offers a way of life that is acceptable to the masses of the people," he intoned. The party backs free enterprise but "places special emphasis on the state's responsibility to care for the under-privileged and less fortunate people."

Anscomb, like Johnson, underestimated the threat of Social Credit, deriding the Socreds as "a headless brigade from over the mountains." He thought it preposterous that British Columbians were being asked to vote for a "leaderless group whose philosophies are beyond all comprehension." He urged Conservatives to plump for their candidates by voting only for the Tory. Winding up his campaign in his home riding of Oak Bay, the leafy and com-fortable Victoria suburb he'd represented since 1933, Anscomb claimed the Liberals had become deeply divided, with Johnson in disagreement with Wismer and others over hospital insurance and resource policy.

The strongest critic of Social Credit was CCF leader Harold Winch, who saw in Social Credit a Canadian form of fascism that was raising "the ugly head of totalitarianism in B.C." CCF audiences ate it up, but because Winch was well known for extreme statements, most voters shrugged off his charges. Winch had earlier gotten himself into trouble by asserting that corporate executives who didn't obey a CCF government would be hauled off to jail. Fiercely dedicated to social democratic aims, Winch sat for the working class riding of Vancouver East. His father, veteran English socialist E.E. Winch, represented the next door con-stituency of Burnaby. Winch vowed to nationalize the B.C. Electric hydro system and promised a publicly-owned automobile insurance plan, similar to the B.C. hospital plan. "Both Conservatives and Social Credit," Winch argued, "are out to wreck hospital insurance by placing it in the hands of private insurance companies." The CCF will take "practical steps to make people greater partners in the development of provincial resources," he told the Vancouver *Sun*. Speaking in the CCF stronghold of Courtenay on Vancouver Island, Winch attacked the meagre tax revenue the government was earning from mining companies, which he put at $1.4 million a year. It cost almost a million dollars just to run the Department of Mines, leaving less than half a million "to go toward running British Columbia's business." Under a CCF government, Winch promised, "We are going to see that the people of this province become the rightful partners in the development of this natural wealth."

The momentum that was building behind Bennett and Social Credit went largely unnoticed and unreported almost until voting day. After securing his own nomination in South Okanagan, Bennett set out to visit every Interior community he could reach. Having traded in his luxury Packard car for a more modest Chevrolet, he drove himself to campaign rallies in the small towns of the upcountry. Sometimes sleeping by the side of the road, in the morning he'd refresh himself at a service station and then go into town to canvass the merchants, meet local Social Credit supporters, give an interview to the weekly paper, and line up arrangements for the night's meeting. As the meetings grew in size and fervor – the crowds often displaying an equal measure of religious zeal and political fervor – the Socreds managed to nominate a candidate in every riding but the far north district of Atlin. The candidate whose nomination caused the most stir, next to Bennett, was Tilly Rolston in the well to do riding of Vancouver Point Grey. After sitting as an independent following her exit from the Coalition, she switched to Social Credit in what the Vancouver *Sun* described as a "well-kept secret up until the very night of her nomination." Of Social Credit, she said "I don't know what it's all about, but I'm all for ya!" Perhaps typical of Social Credit candidates was Cyril Shelford, a large, raw-boned rancher from the Burns Lake country who was brimming over with resentment at what he saw as the government's neglect of the north country. David Mitchell, writing in *W.A.C. Bennett and the Rise of British Columbia*, describes a nomination scene in the Omineca riding where Shelford arrived fresh from his ranch with manure on his shoes. "Don't worry," he told his supporters, "I've just come from the Liberal meeting."[5]

Bennett realized better than most that British Columbia's electorate was deeply fragmented along geographical as well as ideological lines. The CCF had won thirty-five per cent of the vote in 1949 but Bennett was convinced that this support was rooted more in protest than in deeply-held socialist convictions. Having lived mostly in small towns, he understood the conservative climate of rural B.C. and recognized that the province contained distinct geographical voting blocs – the independent-minded, conservative thinking small town and ranch voters of the Upcountry beyond the Fraser valley; a core bloc of urban professionals and unionized workers in Vancouver and its developing suburbs; and the tradition-minded voters of Vancouver island, many of them retired and mostly of British descent.

At every turn, Bennett repeated his mantra that Social Credit would bring "a new, better and more honest government." Presciently, he claimed that Social Credit would win such a smashing victory that it would destroy the provincial Liberal and Conservative parties "for fifty years." He attacked the compulsory nature of hospital insurance and promised to put it on a voluntary basis. All of this was done without much reference to Social Credit theories of monetary reform, a subject that Bennett cared little about and knew was beyond provincial jurisdiction. Even E.G. Hansell, as campaign leader, skirted Social Credit's "funny money" ideas although he did go as far as to attack the "great monetary power" of secret forces that were more powerful than governments. Hansell's final appeal to voters ran along with the statements of the party leaders in the Vancouver *Sun*. He cited four main planks to the Socred platform: integrity of government and opposition to patronage, favouritism and self-interest; elimination of compulsion (especially in hospital insurance); support for free enterprise; and an insistence that "the natural wealth of British Columbia belongs to the citizens and should be developed to return them their fair share of that wealth."

In an era before election polls and phone-in radio shows, the B.C. media covered the election sparingly, but at least one journalist detected the surge to Bennett and his candidates in the last week of the campaign. Writing in the Vancouver *Sun* on June 7, Ron Haggart observed: "The Battle of Hospital Insurance and a new appreciation of the strength of Social Credit have emerged in the final lap of one of British Columbia's longest political campaigns." That long campaign came to an end under cloudy skies on Thursday, June 12, with some eight hundred thousand voters eligible to mark the new transferable ballot, as well as vote on plebiscites on daylight saving time and the sale of liquor by the glass. Voting started slowly, but by day's end more than a half million voters, sixty-eight per cent of those eligible (down from seventy-four per cent in 1949) had marked their ballots in their order of preference for the candidates. It took some voters ten minutes to complete the task in Vancouver's two and three member ridings. Delays and indecision at the polls merely set the stage for the longest night in B.C.'s election history, and by the time beleaguered vote counters retired for the night it was clear that an electoral explosion had occurred. The CCF seemed within grasp of forming a minority government; it was leading in twenty-one seats with Social Credit ahead in fourteen. The two opposition parties had between them come out on top in thirty-five of B.C.'s forty-eight seats, leaving the Liberals leading in only nine seats and the Conservatives in a mere three ridings. Tom Uphill, as usual, stood atop the polls in Fernie but even he did not have a majority. Of the five candidates declared elected on the first count, three were Social Crediters: W.A.C. Bennett in Kelowna, gas station operator Ken Kiernan in Chilliwack, and rancher turned novelist Ralph Chetwynd in Cariboo. The other two seats had gone to the CCF, with leader Harold Winch and native Indian Frank Calder in Atlin each winning more than half their riding's vote. Now, the desperately ill-prepared election staff around the province would have to wait three weeks for absentee ballots before tackling second and in some cases third counts that would finally confirm the government British Columbians had chosen. The Vancouver *Sun* headlined the results the next day:

Election of New B.C. Gov't Hangs on July Ballot Count

Completion of the second count on July 3 awoke British Columbians to a full realization of the spectacular defeat they'd inflicted on the Liberals and Conservatives. Ten Social Crediters and nine CCF candidates had been elected, but only one each from the old lines parties. That kept the CCF narrowly ahead of Social Credit, twenty seats to seventeen. Premier Johnson was ousted in New Westminster, beaten by the CCF's Rae Eddie, and Herbert Anscomb lost his Oak Bay seat to former Victoria mayor Archie Gibbs, a Liberal. Adding in the candidates who were in the lead but lacked a majority, the count was CCF twenty, Social Credit seventeen, Liberal six and Conservative four. Tom Uphill had won Fernie, on the strength of CCF and Social Credit vote transfers. Bennett received the returns at home in Kelowna. No longer able to contain himself, he put out a news release the next day forecasting victory: "I am confident that when the final election results are in, Social Credit will form the new Government of British Columbia and will open a new era of stability and progress for our Province." In another week, when third counts were completed, he would be proven right. Social Credit gained two more seats while the CCF lost two, producing Bennett's final nineteen-eighteen margin of victory. The regions had split much as Bennett had expected. Social Credit did especially well in the Interior, picked up the better off ridings in the Vancouver area, but failed to elect a single member on Vancouver Island. Bennett suggested, perhaps as a joke, that some Island MLA resign to make way for a government member.

It was now clear that British Columbians had voted massively in protest against the Coalition partners. An analysis of voting transfers showed that in thirty-one out of thirty-three ridings where either the Socred or CCF candidate was dropped, their supporters' second choices had gone to the other party.[6] Liberal and Conservative voters showed the same pattern. Ironically, the transferable ballot achieved what it designers had hoped for: the defeat of the CCF. What had not been foreseen was the arrival of Social Credit as a populist alternative. Had the traditional "first past the post" voting system been in effect in B.C. in 1952, the CCF would have formed a minority government with just thirty one per cent of the vote, compared to twenty-seven per cent for Social Credit. Even on the final count, the CCF outpolled the Socreds by four percentage points.

With Social Credit waiting in the wings to form a government, it was time to choose a leader. The party's candidates, successful and defeated, met in the Hotel Vancouver to elect their chief. After singing O Canada and O God Our Help, they voted almost unanimously for the obvious choice: W.A.C. Bennett. Only then did Bennett proceed to Victoria, taking a suite at the Empress Hotel where he awaited the inevitable call from Lieutenant Governor Wallace. As Bennett gathered his prospective cabinet ministers around him he knew that Johnson had recommended that he be called on to form a government. Still, Wallace dithered and it was not until the afternoon of August 1 that the Lieutenant Governor finally invited Bennett to Government House. On arrival, he was told that a decision could not yet be made; with Tom Uphill's support, the CCF would be tied and after all, the CCF had gotten the most votes. Bennett, according to biographer David Mitchell, then produced a letter from Uphill indicating his support for Social Credit. Wallace broke off the meeting, promising a phone call within the hour. Bennett returned to the Empress and forty-five minutes later the phone rang; he was being summoned with his cabinet for a swearing in at nine o'clock that evening. Chief Justice Gordon Sloan, who had just settled a six-week strike of the International Woodworkers of America, conducted the ceremony. William Andrew Cecil Bennett was now the twenty-fourth Premier of British Columbia.

The Aftermath

Few British Columbians realized they had elected a regime that would fundamentally change the way public administration was conducted in the province. The inexperience of Premier Bennett's ministers, combined with the religious zeal and unsophisticated social attitudes of that party's core adherents, projected a distorted image of the radically different approach to government that

Social Credit would follow. Cartoonists and columnists portrayed the Premier as a happy but devious leader of a band of black-suited puritans intent on policing morality and stamping out vice, oblivious to the social revolution sweeping the country through the 1950s and 1960s. In fact, the Bennett government applied itself mainly to promoting economic development, which in the case of British Columbia meant intensive exploitation of natural resources, to the point of plundering its wealth for short-time benefit. The three chief aims of the government were to build an infrastructure of highways and railways to move resources to market, to create a power grid of massive power dams to supply industry with all the electricity it would need, and to maintain a political environment conducive to capital investment and job creation. W.A.C. Bennett succeeded spectacularly in extracting the wealth of the province's forests, mountains and rivers, leading British Columbia into a period of unparalleled prosperity. In the longer term, he was less successful in that his government did little to prepare B.C. for the day when wood, minerals and fish would become low-cost commodities on the world market, available globally from the cheapest source, usually overseas. The party's chief 1952 election promise to make hospital insurance voluntary was soon forgotten as British Columbia, in tandem with other provinces, moved toward a comprehensive and universal medical insurance system.

While Bennett brought many able people into public life, his autocratic style and his insistence on direct personal control of every facet of government gave B.C. the appearance of a personal fiefdom. Bennett personally checked the province's finances first thing every morning, finding out what revenues had been collected and how much had been spent the day before, just as he had tracked cash flow when he ran his hardware store. Putting together a cabinet of political neophytes (except for himself and Tilly Rolston) he instructed them to learn the details of their departments and to expect to be held accountable for their operations. Bennett moved quickly to overcome two glaring omissions among the nineteen Social Crediters elected in 1952: a lawyer who could serve as attorney general, and someone with sufficient experience in the business world to become a credible minister of finance. Bennett filled the first gap by turning to a young Vancouver lawyer, Robert Bonner, who'd been active in Conservative politics. His choice for minister of finance was a former Alberta government accountant, Einar Gunderson, who Bennett had known from his days in Edmonton. They proved to be effective choices and both were easily elected in by-elections in the interior ridings of Similkameen and Columbia. Bennett knew that his minority government could not survive for long, and he planned carefully for the legislative impasse that would allow him to go back to the people for a stronger mandate. The opportunity came shortly after meeting the Legislature for the spring 1953 session. His commanding appearance and his rapid-fire delivery – a stuttering staccato of promises, claims and accusations – left opposition leaders exhausted in trying to keep up with him. After surviving a budget vote when the Liberals supported the government, Bennett chose to test the Opposition over a school-financing bill that favoured rural areas at the expense of urban school districts. The so-called Ralston formula brought the desired result; the government fell on a vote of twenty-eight to seventeen, and Bennett had his new election.

In the general election of June 9, 1953, Bennett campaigned on a "pay-as-you-go" platform, promising to wipe out the public debt and bring political stability to British Columbia. Under a slogan of "Social Credit or Chaos," he was able to transform the movement from the upstart band of unknowns it had been a year ago, to the only cohesive political party in the province. All three opposition parties went to the voters with new leaders. CCF leader Harold Winch had left in a fury of frustration, to be replaced by the decent but untried Vancouver school principal, Arnold Webster. The Liberals turned to a Vancouver MP, Arthur Laing, and the Conservatives put their trust in an unknown insurance agent from Nanaimo, Deane Finlayson. For the second time in a year British Columbia went through the suspense of an election based on the single transferable ballot, but this time the outcome was far more decisive. Thirty Social Crediters were elected or leading on election night, compared to seventeen CCF. The final result produced a legislature of twenty-eight Social Credit, fourteen CCF, four Liberals, one Conservative, and Tom Uphill in Fernie. It was the last election to use the transferable ballot; Bennett's new Social Credit majority returned to the old first-past-the-post system at first opportunity.

Although Bennett found himself commanding a majority in the assembly, he lost two of his most faithful supporters. Einar Gunderson, hailed as a financial wizard for his work on Social Credit's first budget, and good friend Tilly Ralston, were both defeated in the three-member riding of Vancouver Point Grey. Bonner won there, along with Liberal leader Arthur Laing. To make matters worse, Gunderson also lost a later by-election in Victoria, although he remained for years an influential advisor to the government, sitting on the Boards of several B.C. crown corporations. With Gunderson's defeat, Bennett assumed the Finance portfolio himself, further tightening his grip on control of the administration.

Bennett liked to boast that the movement of people to the "Pacific slopes of North America represented the greatest mass movement of peoples in history." The facts fell slightly short of the rhetoric, but British Columbia did gain a half million new residents in the 1950s, a growth of almost forty per cent. He saw the province's great rivers as an immense source of power that would meet the needs of the burgeoning industry and new settlers. The Canadian and U.S. governments were already into negotiations over the Columbia river when Bennett came into office. He was determined to enrich B.C. beyond the terms agreed on by Ottawa, and to back up his demands he announced plans for a second, all-British Columbia project, to dam and tame the great Peace river in the province's northeast. Bennett would say later that his "two rivers" policy was his greatest achievement of his decades as Premier.[7] Ignoring the fact that Ottawa had already made a deal with the U.S., Bennett extracted a one-time payment of two hundred and seventy-three million dollars from President

Lyndon Johnson in return for granting the U.S. the right to one-half of the power to be generated downstream from the three big Canadian dams. The Columbia's huge Duncan lake dam was dedicated in August, 1967. Opening of the W.A.C. Bennett dam (the Premier was not one to wait to pass from the scene before lending his name to public structures) followed a month later on the Peace river, anchoring a 925 kilometer transmission line to Vancouver. Did British Columbia squander its water resources in the Columbia river deal? The issue has been argued endlessly, but it is undeniable that left undeveloped, the power potential of the great stream would still be flowing away to the ocean day after day, yielding little or no benefit to British Columbia.

Scandal touched Bennett's government twice during its twenty-year reign. Both occasions involved cabinet ministers, the more serious that of forests minister Robert Sommers who went to jail for accepting bribes (although it was never established that any company had received a forest management licence as a result). The highways minister, the colorful Phil Gaglardi, was accused of various improprieties including land speculation, and flying his family around on government aircraft. Bennett defended him for years, but finally had to sack him. Like other politicians, Bennett changed policies when he saw it an advantage to do so. His ceaseless railing against socialism "('the barbarians are at the gates," he declared before one election), did not prevent him making dramatic political reversals. He stunned his business friends by taking over the B.C. Electric Co. to create a publicly-owned hydro system and buying the CPR and Black Ball ferry systems that ran between Vancouver and the Island to create B.C. Ferries. He also took over and expanded the Pacific Great Eastern railway, renaming it B.C. Rail and extending its lines into new northern communities. By transferring provincial liabilities to crown corporations, Bennett was able to declare British Columbia debt-free; an accomplishment he celebrated by burning a barge loaded with $70 million of bonds and sinking the whole lot into Okanagan Lake. The flaming arrow he fired at the barge fell harmlessly into the water but a Mountie who had been placed discreetly on board with a torch soon had the raft ablaze.

"Wacky" Bennett went often to the people – every three years on average – and was re-elected six times before, with age and public discontent catching up with him, his government fell to the CCF of David Barrett in 1972. "I feel very sorry for Mr. Barrett," he later said. "He entered his position without knowledge. He provided car insurance at less than cost. Anyone can get popular giving away ice cream cones."[8] The Barrett interregnum lasted only three years, and in 1975 Social Credit was returned to office under the leadership of Bill Bennett, son of W.A.C. Bennett. The prophetic declaration that the senior Bennett had made in 1952 that the Liberal and Conservative parties would be out of office "for fifty years" stands as one of the most prescient political observations of Canadian history. He died at his home in Kelowna on February 23, 1979, at the age of 78. It was not until after two more Social Credit premiers, most notably Bill van der Zalm, had left the party's reputation in tatters that the west coast establishment would regroup under a reborn Liberal party in the 1990s. By his almost single-handed victory in the 1952 election, and his overwhelming re-election the next year, W.A.C. Bennett brought British Columbia to a turning point that saw the birth of a unique west coast political culture. Fuelled by the spark of alienation then lighting fires in the West, it helped to ignite the flames of the anti-Ottawa sentiment that has since burned steadily on western horizons. No Western provincial government has since been compliant to the pressures of Ottawa or the policy dictates of Central Canada. Nor is such a government likely to emerge in the future anywhere west of Lake Superior.

CHAPTER TWELVE

The Federal Election
of June 10, 1957

THE ISSUES

The Liberal government's controversial use of closure to give a U.S. syndicate
an $80 million loan to build the Trans-Canada natural gas pipeline, contrasted
with its niggardly improvements to social services at a time of budget surpluses
– a six-dollar a month increase in old age pensions being a prime example –
makes the Liberal party's governing style the main issue in the election. It is
brilliantly exploited by Conservative leader John Diefenbaker – Dief the Chief
– who is twice re-elected before his government collapses after reneging on a
nuclear defence agreement with the United States.

THE PERSONALITIES

LIBERAL PARTY
Louis St. Laurent, MP for Quebec City, Prime Minister
Lester B. Pearson, MP for Algoma, Ontario, Minister of External Affairs
C. D. Howe, MP for Port Arthur, Ont., Minister of Reconstruction

PROGRESSIVE CONSERVATIVE PARTY
John G. Diefenbaker, MP for Prince Albert Sask., Leader of the Official
Opposition
Léon Balcer, Gordon Churchill, Donald Fleming, David Fulton, Howard
Green, Douglas Harkness, Conservative MPs

THE CCF PARTY
M. J. Coldwell, MP for Rosetown, Sask., Leader

SOCIAL CREDIT:
Solon Low, MP for Peace River, Alberta, Leader

THE RESULTS

	SEATS	VOTES
Progressive Conservative	112	2,572,926 (38.9%)
Liberal	105	2,702,573 (40.9)
CCF	25	707,659 (10.7%)
Social Credit	19	436,663 (6.6%)
Other	4	186,159 (2.8%)

Prime Minister John G. Diefenbaker proudly displaying
the Bill of Rights of 1958. He made passage of the Bill
a priority of his new government.

DIEF THE CHIEF:
THE MAGNIFICENT FAILURE

The Federal Election of 1957

It was an election that shattered the bedrock of Canadian politics, and the reverberations lasted for a decade before the political landscape returned to something resembling its normal shape. In 1957, John G. Diefenbaker refashioned Canada's founding political party in his own image – populist, erratic and unpredictable – vanquished his detractors, and against impossible odds defeated one of the most strongly-entrenched governments ever seen in Ottawa. John Diefenbaker's electoral success, surprising in 1957 and overwhelming in 1958, swept aside the Liberal fiefdom which Canada had known for an uninterrupted twenty-two years. For his Progressive Conservative party, the price of success was the repudiation of right-wing orthodoxy and the abandonment of the fiscal caution for which it was known from its earliest days. In their place Diefenbaker, the ultimate outsider within the corridors of power, set out to pump public money into the economy at a furious pace. In his first parliamentary session as Prime Minister he raised old age pensions, gave cash grants to farmers, extended unemployment benefits, launched a winter works program, cut small business taxes and took one hundred thousand people off the tax rolls. The new Tory fiscal profligacy led to an unprecedented six straight deficit budgets during Diefenbaker's three terms in office. It set the stage for ever-mounting spending by successor governments, both Liberal and Conservative, before the final squelching of deficit financing in the 1990s. The man known as "Dief the Chief" would confuse and confound the U.S. over Canada's stance on nuclear defence, drag Canada back from the cusp of technological supremacy in aerospace, and preside obstinately over a moribund economy. His proudest achievement, a Canadian Bill of Rights, proved so ineffectual it is now all but forgotten. Diefenbaker, without peer as a campaigner, secured the greatest electoral victory in Canadian history up to his time by entrancing Canadians with his "vision" of a new frontier in the North, and his dream of "one Canada" where all citizens, including those of neither English nor French origin, would stand as equal and unhyphenated Canadians. How did this furiously determined prairie lawyer, filled with resentment and envy toward those he saw as his enemies, overcome the failure of five successive election defeats and the disdain and distrust of his own party's establishment, only to fail again – magnificently – at the apex of his power?

All parties approached the 1957 election realizing that the Liberals of Louis St. Laurent would be difficult, if not impossible, to dislodge. St. Laurent had shown exceptional competence in leading the government since replacing Mackenzie King in 1948. The fatherly Quebec City lawyer, now 75, was brought in by King in 1942 following the death of his French Canadian lieutenant, Ernest Lapointe. Entering the House of Commons through a by-election in Wilfrid Laurier's old seat of Quebec East, St. Laurent was put straight into the ministry of justice and groomed from his arrival to take over as PM on King's retirement. The succession firmed up the Liberal tradition of alternating between English and French leaders that had been set when King succeeded Laurier. As Prime Minister, St. Laurent easily won back-to-back majorities in 1949 and 1953 while the country enjoyed the benefits of the great postwar boom that would lead to the decade being dubbed "the fabulous fifties." War veterans found jobs plentiful and thousands had enrolled in universities, thanks to educational grants from a grateful nation. They were now out in the marketplace fuelling a consumer spending boom, buying houses, automobiles and refrigerators as quickly as builders could put up frame homes and manufacturers could organize assembly lines. The children born since the war, the first products of the baby boom, were enjoying a cosseted childhood of material comfort unknown to any previous generation. Only the shadow of the deepening cold war, with civil defense exercises and warnings about the threat of instant annihilation in nuclear war, marred the decade-long party on which most Canadians were by now fully embarked. For admirers of royalty, of which there were many in Canada at the time, a new Queen Elizabeth was on the throne, offering hope of a new Elizabethan age for what was left of the Empire and the Commonwealth.

The great Liberal majority of 1949 – 193 seats out of 262, leaving only 41 for the Conservatives, 13 for the CCF, ten for Social Credit and five for various independents – slipped somewhat in 1953 but the results hardly dented St. Laurent's comfortable margin. By winning a fourth straight mandate, the Liberal party that year came back to a parliament which many in the government had come to look on as a nuisance and interference to their natural right to govern Canada. The Liberal majority had dropped slightly, to 171 seats in the now enlarged 265 seat House. The Conservatives managed to add only ten seats to their total, while the CCF contingent rose to 23 and Social Credit to fifteen. For St. Laurent, dubbed "Uncle Louis" by a perceptive journalist, the cabinet that served him were family, just as, in his view, were all Canadians. His was a corporate style of governance and he saw himself as chairman of the board with able associates responsible for each branch of the company. In fact, St. Laurent's grip was slipping but the success he'd attained in two elections squelched any whisper of criticism. While the Liberal front bench contentedly surveyed the abbreviated Opposition sitting across the aisle, the PC leader and former Ontario premier, George Drew, struggled to find meaningful issues on which to challenge the government. He was unable to capture the public's imagination over noisy engines on Trans-Canada Airlines planes. Even the discovery of horses on the payroll of Camp Petawawa, a Canadian Army base, failed to seriously embarrass the minister of defence, Brooke Claxton. Drew attacked the Liberals over their continued budget surpluses but the public didn't mind that finance minister Walter Harris was able to cut personal income taxes by nearly a quarter of a billion dollars. Paul Martin, at health and welfare, was stitching together the long-promised Liberal social security net, while Lester Pearson, the minister of external affairs, was advancing his own and Canada's reputation abroad. Jimmy

Gardiner, the agriculture minister, still held Saskatchewan in thrall, at least at the federal level. Meanwhile, presiding over all of the government's ambitious development programs was Clarence Decateur Howe, the architect of Canada's war-time industrial explosion, still minister of trade and commerce and head of the department of defence production. He was better known as the "minister of everything."

Howe, the American-born ultimate bureaucrat whose hard-driving style was responsible for much that the King and St. Laurent cabinets had achieved economically, carried within himself the seeds of the government's ultimate downfall – hubris and arrogance. These qualities were first clearly displayed in the debate over the extension of the Defence Production Act in 1955. Passed during the Korean war, the Act gave the minister sweeping authority to expropriate private property and to force defence suppliers to accept whatever terms the government chose to offer. With the Korean war over for two years, the government introduced an amendment to eliminate the sunset clause that would have seen the law die on July 31, 1956. Drew and the Conservatives launched a determined filibuster to prevent its passage and eventually forced the government to limit renewal to a further three-year term. Howe didn't like it, complaining "I've more to do than spend my time amusing Parliament."

There was worse to come – the bitter debate over the government's eighty million dollar loan in 1956 to American investors who had formed Trans-Canada Pipe Lines Limited. This was to be the towering monument to C.D. Howe's career, a vital link in nation-building equal to the construction of the CPR. It would carry the new gold of Alberta natural gas to markets in the United States and Ontario, but the syndicate licensed to build it needed the government loan to complete its financing. In order to meet the construction deadline the loan had to be approved in Parliament by June 7. Nobody objected very much in principle to either the building of the line or even the loan. It was the way the cabinet rammed the bill through the House, using not just closure but "closure within closure" – stopping debate on each individual clause of the bill – that caused an uproar in Parliament and across the country.

Even with the government's time controls, the Opposition was able to force seventy votes, twenty-four of them to appeal rulings by the Speaker, Réné Beaudoin, between May 14 and June 5. M.J. Coldwell, the CCF leader, compared the antics to what had gone on in the German Reichstag. When Donald Fleming, the Toronto Tory MP who led the attack on the bill was "named" and ejected from the House, five hundred cheering supporters greeted him at the airport when he returned home that night. The fight, he told the crowd, was "for the democratic rights of Canadians yet unborn." A Canadian ensign, the national flag of the time, was draped over Fleming's vacant parliamentary desk. The debate might have sputtered out, except that in an arcane parliamentary ruling, Speaker Beaudoin first accepted, and then reversed, a ruling he'd made on a letter published in the Ottawa *Citizen* by Eugene Forsey, the constitutional expert. A CCF member, Colin Cameron, had cleverly suggested that Forsey's criticism of the Speaker's behaviour constituted an attack on the dignity of Parliament. The Speaker agreed, and took steps to have Cameron's motion debated the next day. Horrified members of the cabinet were seen descending on the Speaker's home that evening. When the House sat on June 1, a day that became known as "Black Friday" for the Canadian Parliament, Beaudoin had a sudden change of mind. He ruled that Cameron's motion had actually been out of order and that the House should return to the time before the motion was put. The clock would be turned back, nothing had transpired to interrupt the pipeline debate. The House erupted in bedlam. Opposition members swarmed into the aisles shaking their fists at the Speaker, while Liberals sang what had become their new anthem, "I've been working on the pipeline." Diefenbaker managed to restrain himself and stayed at his desk. That night, he told a friend, "At last I understand the meaning of revolution."[1] After the use of closure on third reading, Trans-Canada got its check in time for its deadline but ironically, had to delay construction by a year because of a steel strike in the

United States. The debate stiffened the spirit of the Opposition but it also exhausted Drew. He resigned in ill health after having to break off a Bermuda holiday to enter hospital in Toronto. In December, 1956, Conservative faithful gathered in Ottawa to choose his successor.

Conservatives at a Crossroads

The convention came on the heels of the greatest international crisis since the Korean war, the seizure of the Suez canal by Britain, Israel and France. The incident split Canadian public opinion and hurt the Liberals when Lester Pearson moved a resolution at the United Nations to form a UN Emergency Force to displace the invading troops at Suez. Most notably, St. Laurent raised the hackles of anglophiles with his declaration that "the era when the supermen of Europe could govern the whole world is coming to an end." Pearson was equally rash when he asserted that Canada would not be a "colonial chore boy" who stood around shouting "Ready, Aye, Ready." Pearson was awarded the Nobel Peace Prize in 1957 for his efforts, but a large segment of public opinion, especially in the Conservative party, felt the government had betrayed the mother country. The linkage to Britain still had powerful attraction to Tory voters.

John George Diefenbaker saw himself as the personification of all those who by their ethnicity, station in life or social views were anathema to the leadership of his party. His first political affiliation, ironically, was as secretary of the Liberal association in rural Wakaw, Saskatchewan, where Diefenbaker had opened his first law office. He would claim his name was put forward without his permission and this is likely true, given the fact all of his known political activity was as a Conservative. What is more abundantly true is that from the time when he first stood as a sacrificial Conservative candidate in Prince Albert in 1925, Diefenbaker found himself at odds with many of his party's positions. In that election, he thought it "preposterous" that the outgoing Tory Prime Minister, Arthur Meighen, refused to support Western farmers in their demands for lower freight rates and the building of a Hudson Bay railway. At a time when most Canadians were identified by their ethnic origin – there was no Canadian citizenship until after World War II – Diefenbaker had set out "to bring an end in this country to discrimination on a basis of race, creed or colour." He was so sensitive about being called a Hun for his Germanic name that during his university days in World War I he obtained a letter from his professors attesting that he was of Canadian birth.

Diefenbaker in fact possessed two distinguished family lineages and on his mother's side his Scottish forebears had helped Lord Selkirk pioneer early settlements in Canada. John was born in Neustadt, Ontario in 1895. His school teacher father moved the family to the prairie West in 1903 and John grew up in lower middle class respectability on a harsh and often unforgiving frontier. He served with the Canadian Army in England in World War I, but was never sent to the front. Returning home, he earned a law degree from the University of Saskatchewan. Tall, angular and lean, polite almost to a fault, Diefenbaker became known in the small towns around Prince Albert for his willingness to take on unpopular cases defending "bohunks" or other eastern European immigrants. With this background, Diefenbaker's position in the largely anglophile Conservative party was never a comfortable one, despite his often asserted loyalty to Canada's British heritage and his willingness to take on impossible tasks. He was beaten by none other than Mackenzie King in the 1926 election that restored the Liberals to power. He lost the Prince Albert provincial seat in the Saskatchewan election of 1929 that put a Conservative government in office just in time for the Depression. This may have been a fortuitous defeat, in that the Tories were helped into office with the active support of the Ku Klux Klan. Diefenbaker then ran for mayor of Prince Albert, losing in 1933. In 1936, he became leader of the provincial party, a hopeless task that he surrendered only after the Conservatives were annihilated in the 1938 provincial election. Five attempts to win office, five straight defeats. "I wanted to … relinquish my political obligations, and to devote the rest of my life to the practice of law."[2] This all changed in 1940 when Mackenzie King unexpectedly called a winter election, ostensibly to gain a mandate for the prosecution of his wartime policies. The election gave the Liberals a great victory and reduced the Conservatives to only thirty-nine seats. One of them, surprisingly, was Lake Centre in Saskatchewan, captured by John Diefenbaker. He'd accepted the nomination only after the duly-chosen candidate stepped aside, telling a rural nominating convention that Diefenbaker would be the best candidate. Diefenbaker's formidable reputation as both a criminal and a civil lawyer, and as a champion of the underdog, undoubtedly contributed more to his victory than his party affiliation.

For seventeen years, Diefenbaker shuttled between Prince Albert and Ottawa, defending people charged with crimes ranging from arson to murder – his first murder jury acquitted the accused partly because it was Diefenbaker's birthday – and acting in a variety of cases involving civil rights and liberties. He defended the Jehovah's Witnesses when that church was outlawed in 1940. Remembering how German and eastern European immigrants had been imprisoned and denied the vote in World War I, he criticized the forced removal of Japanese Canadians from the west coast in World Wear II. Diefenbaker was one of only two Tory MPs who argued in caucus in favour of the family allowances brought in by the Liberals in 1945. In 1948, he argued successfully against a Conservative plan to campaign for outlawing of the Communist party. One of Diefenbaker's most famous trials concerned his defence of a railway telegrapher in the Canoe River train disaster in British Columbia, where twenty-one soldiers bound for Korea had been killed, along with four railwaymen. He successfully defended John Atherton, the telegrapher charged with manslaughter, by arguing that a garbled message blamed for the crash was more likely the result of ice and snow on the telegraph lines than any oversight by the telegrapher. Emotionally, however, he won the case by showing that Atherton was being scape goated for larger errors by the Army and the railway.

Diefenbaker entered Parliament as a member of a leaderless

party, due to the defeat of Tory leader Dr. R. J. Manion in the 1940 election. Arthur Meighen, brought back as a temporary fill-in, quit after failing to win the York South by-election in 1942. At a convention held in Winnipeg the former Liberal premier of Manitoba, John Bracken, defeated four rivals and promptly rechristened the party as the Progressive Conservative party of Canada. One of the defeated rivals was Diefenbaker. He knew he had no chance of winning and would have dropped out after the first ballot but for the convention chairman's insistence on "mis-pronouncing my name in every reference he made to me, making it as strongly German as it was possible to make it." Diefenbaker was re-elected in 1945 and when Bracken's failure to substantially improve the party's standing led to his resignation and another leadership convention in 1948. Diefenbaker was again a candidate. George Drew, the Ontario premier, won handily on the first ballot, with Diefenbaker second and Donald Fleming, the Toronto MP, a distant third. Diefenbaker still had not earned the approval of the party establishment. He felt he received a frosty reception at Drew's victory party: "I walked into that gathering and it was as if an animal not customarily admitted to homes had suddenly entered the place."[3]

Diefenbaker held to his resentments as firmly as ever during Drew's leadership and when he was passed over for the post of deputy House leader, he considered quitting politics entirely. He might well have done so, except for the pipeline debate and the animosities it stirred in him. Then came Drew's resignation, and an informal poll of the Tory caucus suggesting Diefenbaker could be the favourite to replace him. Diefenbaker went back to Prince Albert to clean up some law office business before plunging into his campaign. On his way back to Ottawa he recruited Gordon Churchill, the widely respected Winnipeg Tory MP, and happily accepted an offer of support from Alistair Grosart, the Toronto advertising man who'd managed George Drew's campaigns. In Quebec, he recruited Paul Lafontaine, the scion of an old Quebec family, but also had to deal with the enmity of the province's top Conservative operative, Léon Balcer, who had the backing of most of the province's 342 convention delegates. Much was made of the fact that Diefenbaker had himself nominated by Major-General George Pearkes of Victoria, and seconded by Hugh John Fleming, the Conservative premier of New Brunswick, rather than by a French-speaking Quebecer. This slighting of Quebec would not be forgotten but it did not affect the outcome. Diefenbaker took the leadership on the first ballot with 774 votes. Donald Fleming finished second, far back at 383, followed by David Fulton of British Columbia, 117. "We will be the next government," Diefenbaker solemnly told the convention. "We have an appointment with Destiny."

The House assembled on January 8, 1957, for the final session of the St. Laurent era. The usual courtesies were extended the new Leader of the Opposition. Then it was on to the Throne Speech debate and a few weeks later the presentation of the budget. Neither offered much to excite the public, giving Diefenbaker the opportunity to criticize the government for lacking a vision for national development. A new national policy – harkening back to the catch phrase of Sir John A. Macdonald – was needed, in the rhetoric of the new Opposition leader. His sharpest criticism, however, was reserved for the niggardly six dollar a month raise in the old age pension that the Minister of Finance, Walter Harris, provided for in the budget. It seemed a pittance when the budget was projecting a quarter billion dollar surplus. The session dribbled to an end on April 12, 1957. It was soon announced that the Prime Minister had been to see the Governor-General, Vincent Massey – the first Canadian-born to occupy the office – and that an election would be held on June 10. Not much was expected from the campaign; the parties would duly name their candidates and go forward with their campaigns but little, in the opinion of the well informed, was likely to change as a result.

The Campaign and the Candidates

The Conservative establishment that had tried to stop John Diefenbaker from gaining the leadership would rather, he thought, have the party remain in opposition than have it win under him. National Director Bill Rowe quit in a huff a few days after the leadership convention. Diefenbaker was able to get Alistair Grosart to take on the task part-time. Grosart was soon working full time for the party, assisted by another Toronto ad man, Dalton Camp. Diefenbaker was in better shape in his parliamentary office, where all of Drew's appointees, including his private secretary Derek Bedson, stayed on. Others came forward to help Diefenbaker gear up the party apparatus, organize fund-raising, plan publicity and tours, and put campaign strategy in place. Fred Davis, who had been the official photographer for the Dionne Quints, joined as campaign photographer. George Hogan, the 28-year-old scion of the Toronto auto dealership family, signed up as tour manager.

Diefenbaker was acutely conscious of the need to cast the Conservative party in a new light. He understood that his campaign strategy would have to break sharply with Conservative tradition if it was to offer voters new reasons to turn away from the Liberals. To his good fortune, he was given two key elements that lifted his campaign out of the ordinary, an appealing slogan and an imaginative vision. The slogan dreamt up by Grosart's team, It's Time for a Diefenbaker Government, promised the complete break with the past that voters seemed to be seeking. The vision was a romantic and mostly impractical, but nonetheless appealing dream of a "New Frontier Policy" that would make Canada a great new northern powerhouse by tapping the rivers and the resources of the North. It had been formulated by a young economist, Dr. Merril Menzies, and brought to Diefenbaker by Menzies' brother-in-law, Prince Albert physician Glen Green. Diefenbaker saw immediately that Menzies' ideas provided the framework for a reincarnation of John A. Macdonald's National Policy, updated to fit modern circumstances. In the paper that was passed on to Diefenbaker, Menzies had written that Canada's original development was "given shape and direction" by Macdonald's policy of tariff protection and domestic development. In Menzies' words:

> Since then we have had no national policy – and we have had no transcending sense of national purpose, no national myth, no unifying force ... Liberal policy has no character, no vision, no purpose – with appalling consequences to our parliamentary system and national unity. Regionalism in many vital respects is growing not diminishing ... Time is running out and only the Conservative party can stem this complacent drift ... The present drift can only be stemmed by a new unifying force, a new national policy, a new national myth.

> That is why I have proposed a new national policy – the New Frontier Policy, a new national strategy – that of "Defense in Depth"; a new national myth – the "North" in place of the "West" which "died" a quarter of a century ago."[4]

Diefenbaker had already spoken of the need to develop the North: On February 11, 1957 he told the House: "I can see cities developing there as they are developing today in Norway, if only the government would catch the vision of the possibilities." He enthused about Menzies' ideas, although he found many of the specific proposals – such as a new province to be carved out of the southern Yukon and parts of the Northwest Territories – too audacious even for him. It was the inspirational language and the more modest plans to develop the North's hydro and resources potential that held Diefenbaker's attention. He brought Menzies on board as his economics advisor and put him to work drafting speeches that would spell out the vision, starting with his official campaign launch that had been scheduled for Massey Hall in Toronto on April 25.

The Gallup poll was still reporting the Liberals ahead, but support was down to 46.8 per cent, with the Conservatives at 33 per cent and ten per cent favouring the CCF and others. Diefenbaker fretted constantly about his own prospects in Prince Albert. "Gee it would be my end if I got defeated personally and I would be *out* for sure," he wrote in February to his brother Elmer in Saskatoon. "I wish you would spend some time up there and make a survey of the situation."[5] The situation was that local Liberals saw Diefenbaker's 1953 victory as an upset in this long-held Liberal riding and were sure they could prevent it happening again. They nominated a popular local dentist and former president of the Saskatchewan Liberal party, Dr. R.E. Partridge. The CCF also thought it had a chance. Three hundred supporters turned out to nominate R. N. Gooding, and to hear the CCF MP from Saskatoon, Roy Knight, attack the Conservative party for its "Bay Street" bias. Knight treated Diefenbaker gently, focusing on the difficulty he would have in controlling the PC right wing. That didn't bother the Diefenbaker supporters, who were again setting up Diefenbaker clubs all over the riding. It was a technique that had worked in 1953 and brought in people who were more comfortable under a Diefenbaker banner than the PC flag. His campaign office was set up in the basement of the Lincoln Hotel on Central Avenue, and Diefenbaker spent a week main streeting in Prince Albert and visiting the nearby towns that were part of the riding. His chief country organizer, Art Pearson, signed up fifteen hundred people to staff country polls on election day.

The campaign kick-off in Toronto's Massey Hall on April 25 rekindled what had been a dwindling Conservative heritage in Canada's largest English-speaking city. It was in that same hall that every Conservative leader since Sir Charles Tupper had rallied his supporters, but never was there a more enthusiastic gathering than the one that greeted Diefenbaker. A huge blue and white banner stretched across the stage, repeating the slogan, "It's Time for a Diefenbaker Government." The Premier of Ontario, Leslie Frost, chaired the meeting. He hailed Diefenbaker as "a great Canadian, a man of the people, and the next Prime Minister of

Canada." For forty minutes, Diefenbaker held the rapt attention of the audience. He lambasted the "six buck boys" who were neglecting the needs of pensioners, promised to cut taxes, bring in more immigrants, and treat all Canadians the same. The main part of his talk, however, was drawn from the three speech drafts he'd been given, with the suggestion that he should use the one he liked best, or parts of all three. In true fashion, Diefenbaker charged off on his own but it was the passages from Merril Menzies' draft, about a New Frontier Policy (a full three years before John F. Kennedy memorialized the phrase) that caught the imagination of his listeners. More than the words, it was the way in which they were delivered that had listeners by turn laughing, gasping, and howling in derision at the ghastly mistakes of the Liberals. Drawing on the skills he had honed in countless courtroom appearances – right hand on hip, as if to hold back the lawyer's legal robes, left arm pointing to every listener – his voice rising and falling, jowls shaking, in turn mocking and pleading, Diefenbaker laid out his promise to fulfill the "sacred trust handed down to us in the tradition of Macdonald":

> "We intend to launch a National Policy of development in the Northern areas which may be called the New Frontier Policy. Macdonald was concerned with the opening of the West. We are concerned with developments … in our Northern Frontier in particular. The North, with all its vast resources of hidden wealth – the wonder and challenge of the North must become our national consciousness. All that is needed, as I see it today, is an imaginative policy that will open its doors to Canadian initiative and enterprise."

Diefenbaker left Massey Hall charged with electric enthusiasm. Accompanied by his wife Olive and six aides, he embarked on one of the most grueling campaign schedules – visiting 130 constituencies over the next thirty-nine days – that any leader had ever tackled.[6] The *Globe and Mail* thought he was wasting his time making dozens of minor addresses instead of a handful of major ones. After winning over friendly audiences in Ontario, Diefenbaker headed to his beloved West, where his message to "ordinary Canadians" was that they would soon have somebody who understood their needs making laws for them. He unveiled his "One Canada" dream for a rambunctious crowd of six hundred farmers in Carmen, Manitoba, and later addressed an overflow crowd of a thousand in Dauphin, a town of 2,300. So it went across the prairies. In Regina, he brought a crowd of nine hundred to its feet with a promise to build the south Saskatchewan dam and use its power to turn an arid landscape into an oasis. Alberta welcomed him as a conquering hero, then it was on to British Columbia where hundreds of supporters turned out in every town he visited. The nine hundred who filled the Penticton high school auditorium cheered him as he promised, "We will form the next government of Canada." In Victoria, he told nearly four thousand at his largest rally so far that "An aroused public opinion has the Liberals running scared." Neither Diefenbaker nor his entourage knew it, but it was all just rehearsal for a gigantic rally in Vancouver on Thursday, May 23. On that damp and mild spring evening a crowd of more than two thousand jammed the sidewalks outside the Georgia Street Auditorium, unable to get into the the hall where three thousand early arrivals were impatiently awaiting "Dief the Chief." He and Olive arrived in a convertible and as Diefenbaker stepped from the car he was handed a microphone. "This is a great inspiration," he shouted, "thank you from the bottom of my heart." Then it was into the Auditorium where he gave his greatest speech of the 1957 election. At the podium, Diefenbaker paused for what seemed like a long time as the audience cheered his arrival. Finally, he leaned into the microphone and began: "Across this country Canadians as a whole will agree that something is happening. The Liberals are realizing that Canada is aroused as it has not been for many years, and people everywhere are asking what shall the future of this nation be?" He raised his head and looked around the auditorium. The audience was standing and cheering. "Give 'em hell, John!"

they shouted, "Give 'em hell!"[7] For the rest of the speech, waves of laughter, applause and cheering rolled up from the seats. Newspapers across the country the next day reported Diefenbaker's hugely successful rally in Vancouver. It was becoming evident that the election had turned into much more of a contest than anyone, especially the Liberals, had expected.

Almost no one in the entire Liberal party seemed to have any real understanding of the difficulty Liberal candidates were having in defending the government's record against the relentless and often exaggerated criticism of Diefenbaker and his leading candidates. Davie Fulton was ranging through the small towns of British Columbia, adding fuel to the fires that Diefenbaker had set ablaze on his tour. Donald Fleming in Toronto, Gordon Churchill in Winnipeg, William Hamilton in Montreal, and J.C. Van Horne in New Brunswick led the Tory onslaughts in their regions, reporting back to Grosart that poorly-managed Liberal campaigns were having little effect on the voters. It was St. Laurent's plan that the government would run on its record and while it would not claim perfection, it would make the perfectly sound argument that no one else could have done any better in managing Canada's affairs. He even told listeners that if they thought someone else would do a better job they should vote for them, "although I don't know where you'll find them."

The Liberal campaign was launched with a rally for St. Laurent in Winnipeg on April 29. Ironically, there had been a suggestion that the Prime Minister should go to the North and speak of plans to develop that part of Canada, but it was rejected – the trip would be too expensive, too tiring for St. Laurent, and it would take too much time. Instead, St. Laurent travelled leisurely – and free of cost – by train to the Manitoba capital where a half-filled auditorium, lethargic and only slightly interested in what he had to say, awaited him. He spent an hour on the stage delivering what amounted to a report on the government's stewardship over the past four years. St. Laurent recounted the economic growth Canada had enjoyed, defended his government's role in the pipeline debate, and took credit for gaining Canada a new level of respect in the world. "No government in Ottawa could take the credit for the great things that Canadians have done and are doing," St. Laurent said, "but the present government has certainly helped." It was not an evening of high emotion. St. Laurent tried to laugh off charges of dictatorial conduct over the pipeline debate. He said the debate had been "nearly as long as the pipeline itself, and quite as full of another kind of natural gas." A minor blunder became a major gaffe when St. Laurent criticized Diefenbaker for obscuring his Conservative connections by featuring his name in large print in posters and ads, while playing down his PC affiliation. When Alastair Grosart read of this in the newspapers, he had the stories sent out to PC candidates, urging them to play up their membership on the Diefenbaker team. It was also said, although never substantiated, that Grosart had copies of the speech sent in plain envelopes to every Liberal candidate and soon the refrain was being heard across the country that Diefenbaker wasn't really a Conservative. It was just what Diefenbaker's supporters wanted coming from mouths of Liberals.

St. Laurent moved across the prairies by train and after meetings in Calgary and Edmonton, travelled to Vancouver for a rally marked by outburst from hecklers, some of whom had to be ejected by the police. After an overnight yacht voyage to Vancouver Island St. Laurent drove along the new Malahat Highway from Nanaimo to Victoria, where he planned a major foreign policy address. His speech had been written by officials in the Department of External Affairs and it sounded like it, a sort of diplomatic position paper "carefully designed to avoid saying anything that could possibly be considered as breaking new ground."[8] St. Laurent argued that Canada had opposed the British-French intervention at Suez in order to save the Commonwealth and prevent a split between the United Kingdom and the United States. The speech was not well received in this most pro-British part of Canada and Liberal organizers were soon on the phone to Mike Pearson to ask him to come to town and try to repair the damage. Stopping in Saskatchewan en route back east, St. Laurent resolutely refused to take a stand in support of the South Saskatchewan dam, the one thing people wanted from Ottawa more than anything else. Even Jimmy Gardiner, the agriculture minister, was for it but that was not enough to bring St. Laurent around. "I'm sure that this project offers many benefits but I'm not prepared to give a definite answer until I can tell Parliament that I'm certain the nation would get more out of it than it would put into it."

The only region where the Liberals continued to draw substantial support despite declining crowds at rallies was in Quebec. St. Laurent was their native son and short of a calamity, they would be voting *rouge* on June 10. He opened his Quebec campaign with a meeting at the Capitol theatre in Quebec City on May 13. Although small, it was only half-filled. St. Laurent reminisced about his sixteen years in Ottawa, letting on that he wouldn't really know what to do if he ceased being Prime Minister. Most of his talk was about national unity, something he'd not said much about so far. The Liberal party was the only party capable of ensuring unity, since it was a truly national party with "principles equally acceptable to all the population of Canada." His speech, although given with much sincerity, revealed how lacking the Liberal campaign was in enthusiasm and excitement. The dry details of government statecraft, delivered with an over-abundance of statistics, were poor substitutes for the colorful call to arms that Diefenbaker was sounding throughout the land.

For John Diefenbaker's Conservatives, Quebec offered bleak prospects; Diefenbaker was much influenced by a paper by Gordon Churchill that argued the Tories were wrong to have tried so hard there in past elections. Splitting party funds fifty-fifty between Quebec and the rest of Canada didn't make sense, Churchill wrote, because that left the Conservatives with inadequate resources to fight for ridings in English Canada that they had a better chance of winning. Churchill's advice was taken in 1957 and while Quebec wasn't totally neglected, it didn't get the attention it had received in past campaigns. Faint stirrings of support among Union Nationale cabinet ministers offered some fresh hope and in his appearances in Quebec Diefenbaker managed to speak a little French, but with execrable results.

The Struggle for York-Scarborough

Canada's cities were growing rapidly in the nineteen fifties, pushing out into new suburbs that had been farm land a few years before. They were filled with young, optimistic families who were realizing the dreams that war and depression had denied their elders. Nowhere was the surge to the new suburbia more dramatic than north and east of Toronto, where between 1951 and 1957 the population of the riding of York-Scarborough, stretching from the shore of Lake Ontario to the dairy barns of York county, doubled to nearly one hundred and seventy thousand, making it one of the largest in the country. The rivalry here between Liberal incumbent Frank Enfield and his Conservative challenger Frank McGee, crystallized the larger campaign that the two parties were waging across Canada.

Enfield, a thirty-six old lawyer, war veteran and former school board trustee, was renominated by acclamation for the seat he'd won by fewer than seven hundred votes in the 1953 election. The fact he'd used his parliamentary frank – the free mailing privilege enjoyed by MPs – to send out invitations to his nomination meeting was seized on by McGee as a "typical Liberal tactic," highlighting once again their arrogance. For McGee, a descendant of the assassinated Father of Confederation Darcy McGee, winning the campaign was almost a career necessity. His boss at the big Robert Simpson department store, where the thirty-one-year-old McGee was a buyer of boy's jeans, thought his interest in politics indicated something less than a total commitment to his job. He'd get his job back if he lost, but his chances of promotion would be doubtful. McGee ran anyway and with a strong speech at the PC nominating convention, beat out two other unknowns. He was wildly cheered when he told the thousand or so Tories in attendance that "the government is made up of men whose ears are so full of the sound of their own voices they can no longer hear the heartbeat of the nation."[9]

The York-Scarborough candidates ran on local as well as national issues. At all-candidate meetings McGee attacked the government's tight money policy which was making it difficult to obtain mortgages. He criticized the lack of home mail delivery in the new sub-divisions. Enfield's response was to blame land speculators, saying they had "made a killing at the expense of the building industry and the Canadian people." He called for the federal government to buy land, sell it to home builders at cost, and make direct loans for home building. Such proposals flew in the face of the government's housing policies, and probably did Enfield little good. Like other Liberal candidates, Enfield had the uneasy task of defending the government's use of closure in the pipeline debate. "No one argues it (the pipeline) was not necessary and that takes the sting out of it," Enfield thought hopefully.

All the candidates – including the CCF and Social Credit nominees who had little impact on the campaign – relied on personal canvassing to reach voters. McGee hired a housekeeper for eighty dollars a month while he and his wife set up a campaign office in their basement. He had the help of thirty to forty canvassers who would go door-to-door every evening, ringing every fourth doorbell. The other main way of talking to voters was neighborhood coffee parties. By the end of the campaign, McGee admitted to losing seventeen pounds before "running out of steam." He managed to gain an unusually high profile for a local candidate, partly because his father-in-law worked for a local daily. McGee also had his own ideas and one he took to Toronto *Telegram* publisher John Bassett resulted in a full-page article, A Candidate on Your Doorstop. Friendly photos of the candidate being awakened by pillow-swinging children ran alongside a story hailing McGee as "a possible future Prime Minister." It made for good reprints that McGee's team distributed to every home in the riding. A hundred metal McGee signs, four feet by eight feet, were set up at key locations throughout the riding, while Enfield relied on lawn signs. McGee also got good publicity from a visit by John

Diefenbaker, when two thousand voters turned up at a reception for the Chief. Clearly, something was happening in the Toronto suburbs. A week before the election a telephone survey of one hundred and twenty people, taken at the behest of political scientist John Meisel, showed McGee beating Enfield, thirty-one to eighteen among the decided voters. Meisel thought the poll either inaccurate or too small a sample to trust, and put it aside.

The Final Wrap-up

All the parties shared in free-time broadcasts on radio and TV, which for the first time played an important role in the campaign. St. Laurent, however, resisted the blandishments of the electronic medium. In the three speeches he recorded for TV he refused to follow a teleprompter, scorned the use of make-up, and read his speeches from a text, seldom raising his eyes to the camera.

The long campaign came to a close with fresh indications of a Liberal victory. On June 7, the Gallup Poll gave the Liberals the support of 43.5 per cent of decided voters, enough to assure re-election by a comfortable majority. John Diefenbaker's frenetic campaigning had raised the level of Tory support to 37.5 per cent. The next day, *Maclean's* magazine, widely regarded as the family magazine of Canada, went to press sure of a Liberal victory. Although it wouldn't be on the newsstands until after the election, the lead editorial began: "For better or for worse, we Canadians have once more elected one of the most powerful governments ever created by the free will of a free electorate …"

That same evening the final Liberal rally at Maple Leaf Gardens in Toronto was planned as a huge celebration that would lift party workers for the final drive to get out the vote on Monday. The hallowed hockey arena was dressed with huge red and white pictures of St. Laurent, while Liberal heavyweights Mike Pearson, Walter Harris and Paul Hellyer occupied the stage and ten thousand loyal supporters waited to hear the Prime Minister. St. Laurent had barely begun speaking when a teen-age heckler, William Hatton, strode onto the stage carrying the PM's poster. Suddenly, the boy tore it into pieces and dropped it at St. Laurent's feet while the Prime Minister looked on, startled. The chairman of the meeting, fearing an attack, rushed forward. In the resulting melee, the boy fell to the concrete floor, banging his head. The crowed gasped, then sat in silence while attendants rushed to help him to his feet before escorting him from the hall. It was a discouraging omen of what was to come.

As this was happening, Diefenbaker was flying back to Prince Albert for a final weekend of campaigning. He was met with a cavalcade of 158 cars that escorted him to the campaign headquarters in the Lincoln Hotel. There was another procession that night to the Orpheum Theatre where Diefenbaker held his last rally. "When we form the government," he proclaimed, "we will inaugurate a highways to resources program. We will give cash advances on farm-stored wheat. When we form the government, we will reduce taxation to a fair and reasonable level. We will return power to the people from an all-powerful government with an all-powerful majority." The cheers of the crowd were deafening. On Monday, Alastair Grosart flew out from Ottawa and Elmer Diefenbaker came up from Saskatoon. Election day was cool and wet in Prince Albert. After voting, Diefenbaker returned to the small house he and Olive had rented, while Grosart worked the phones to pick up the early returns from Eastern Canada. St. Laurent had returned to Quebec City for the weekend. He did some light campaigning on Sunday, was up early on Monday, voted and visited the polls, then rested in the afternoon. Joined by his family and a few close friends, he was settled in his living room by seven o'clock to watch the returns on television.

The first results from Newfoundland forecast a long night of upsets. Progressive Conservative candidates were leading in both St. John's seats. The only Liberal to retain a comfortable majority on the island was Jack Pickersgill, party brain-truster and adviser to both King and St. Laurent, re-elected in Bonavista-Twillingate. Two Liberal cabinet ministers, Milton Gregg and Robert Winters, were trailing their PC opponents in New Brunswick. Conservatives were taking seat after seat in Nova Scotia, ending up with all but two ridings. All four Prince Edward Island seats went Tory. Only in Quebec were Liberal fortunes holding, although PC candidates were on their way to winning nine ridings, five more than in 1953, thanks to timely intervention by ministers of the Union Nationale government. Ontario that night presented an entirely different picture, where the Conservatives would increase their seats from thirty-three to sixty-one, sweeping aside powerful cabinet ministers with ease. After the defeat of Paul Hellyer and Walter Harris came the stunning news that an unknown CCF school teacher, Douglas Fisher, had beaten C.D. Howe in Port Arthur. Among front-line cabinet ministers, only Paul Martin and Mike Pearson survived the Tory onslaught. Pearson had taken to heart the advice of a constituent about his international achievements: "That was a fine thing but it won't help you much around here if you don't get us a new post office."[10] In York-Scarborough, John Meisel's pre-election survey only hinted at the scope of Frank McGee's victory over Frank Enfield: a twenty-thousand vote majority, the largest in Canada.

With the polls beginning to close in Western Canada, the Liberals were holding a meager six seat lead, ninety-seven to ninety-one, leaving voters in the West to decide who would be Prime Minister. Workers at Diefenbaker's headquarters were overjoyed and incredulous at the national results; they went wild when they heard Diefenbaker had chalked up a sixty five hundred vote majority over the CCF's Robert Gooding. The local radio station invited listeners to hurry to the airport to see off Diefenbaker, who was boarding a Canadian Pacific Airlines Dakota to fly to Regina where he would go on CBC –TV. There, he gave a low-key, almost somber summation of the election results.

> "My fellow Canadians (an opening that would become
> a trade mark of his future speeches): This is a moment
> not for elation but dedication. The complete results are
> not yet known but I feel that at this time I must express
> my deep gratitude and appreciation to all of those

whose votes today were cast on behalf of the Party which I have the honour to lead …

I shall honour the trust you the Canadian people have given me. I shall keep the faith – and maintain the spiritual things without which political parties cannot lead a full life. I ask your prayers. With God's help I shall do my best. 'He who would be chiefest among you shall be servant of all.'"

Louis St. Laurent also was subdued when he went on TV from the CBC studio in the Frontenac Hotel in Quebec City. Tired and looking every bit his seventy-five years, he observed that while the outcome of the election was still uncertain, the "necessary action" would be taken once the results were final. As the long night wore on, the West fulfilled all of Diefenbaker's expectations. Manitoba elected eight Conservatives, five CCFers and just one Liberal. In Saskatchewan, Jimmy Gardiner hung in with a slim victory but he was one of only four Liberals to last the night. The CCF's M.J. Coldwell was elected in Rosetown, one of ten socialist candidates to win in Saskatchewan. The Conservatives took three seats, counting Diefenbaker's. Alberta sent thirteen Social Crediters back to Ottawa, along with three Conservatives and one Liberal. British Columbia split three ways, with seven CCF, seven PC, and six Social Credit. Just two Liberals were elected there. Among the beaten was Jimmy Sinclair, the minister of fisheries, who would become better known as the father-in-law of a future Prime Minister. When all the returns including the military vote were tallied, the final seat count would be Conservative 112, Liberal 105, CCF 25, Social Credit 19, others four.

When Diefenbaker returned to Prince Albert at midnight two thousand people cheered his touch down at the airport. The next morning, he went down to the local barber shop for a haircut. He and Elmer flew to Saskatoon to see their mother, then went off fishing at Lac la Ronge with travelling reporters and a few aides. The Diefenbakers left Prince Albert on Thursday and after an overnight flight, reached Ottawa the next morning to await the resignation of the Prime Minister and the call from Governor General Massey to form a new government.

The Aftermath

The Liberal party had been routed even though it had gained the larger share of the popular vote – 41 to 39 per cent for the Conservatives. Some cabinet ministers including Jimmy Gardiner argued the government should meet Parliament, present a legislative program and look to the small parties for support. St. Laurent hesitated, fearing a repetition of 1925 when Mackenzie King vainly sought a new election rather than resign. A radio commentary by a McGill University professor, Jim Mallory, helped make up his mind. In a CBC talk Mallory had declared that any attempt by the Liberals to carry on would lead to a constitutional crisis. St. Laurent ordered a copy of the broadcast and after reading it, issued instructions for the government's departure. On Monday, June 17 he resigned, to be immediately replaced by Diefenbaker. The new Prime Minister's first task was to attend the Commonwealth Conference in London, and then to form a cabinet, a task that went on until October 9, a few days before the opening of Parliament. The important posts went to long-time Conservatives, with Donald Fleming taking finance; Howard Green, public works; George Hees, Solicitor General; David Fulton, national revenue; Gordon Churchill, trade and commerce. Diefenbaker recruited Dr. Sydney Smith, president of the University of Toronto, as minister for external affairs.

The first session of Canada's first minority government in over thirty years gave Diefenbaker the opportunity to fulfill many of his campaign pledges. Old age pensions were raised to $55 a month, $150 million was sent to western farmers. A federal-provincial conference was set up to plan for national hospital insurance. A score of other legislative initiatives followed. Personal and corporate taxes were reduced and one hundred thousand low income earners were taken off the tax rolls entirely.

Money flowed in an uninterrupted stream – for housing, for exports, for disabled veterans. Gordon Churchill led a fifty-man trade mission to Britain with instructions to protect Canada's markets there in event of the UK joining the European Common Market. Satisfaction with the new government was high among Canadians as the year ended.

The Liberal party, struggling to adjust to its new role in opposition, held its fourth leadership convention since Confederation. Lester Pearson, now more often known as Mike, quickly became the early front-runner and on January 16, 1958, defeated Paul Martin and one unknown candidate on the first ballot. Returning to the House of Commons, painfully aware the Liberals were not ready for another election, Pearson offered a bizarre want-of-confidence motion that he knew would fail to gain the support of the CCF or Social Credit. Arguing that Conservative policies had plunged the country into a string of economic woes, Pearson demanded the government resign and allow the Liberals to return to office without an election. In all Canadian parliamentary history, probably no greater political faux pas had ever been committed. It gave Diefenbaker a heaven-sent opportunity to demolish Pearson and complete the rout of the Liberal party. Rising from his seat in indignation, Diefenbaker spent two hours skewering the new leader of the Opposition and his arrogant demand that the government resign. By the time he was finished, Pearson was ready to slink from the House, only too aware that his daring ploy had dangerously misfired. Ten days later Diefenbaker was given dissolution by the Governor General and a new election was ordered for March 31. The campaign that followed smacked more of a triumphant coronation than a general election. Contributions flowed like a rip tide to the Conservative coffers, enabling the party to launch a flood of advertising and publicity. In Quebec, Maurice Duplessis ordered his agents to bring candidates, recruits and money to the PC cause. Diefenbaker's northern vision was updated with a newer vision, this time of the "One Canada" that he would create when the nirvana of a re-elected government was realized. As crowds jammed into Diefenbaker's rallies across the country, placards showing two footprints exhorted voters to "Follow John," a simple, stark message borrowed from a Vancouver candidate, car dealer John Taylor, who had used it to good effect in 1957. The result was the greatest majority ever attained up to that time: two hundred and eight seats. Liberals were reduced to a rump of just forty-nine members, twenty-five of them from Quebec. They would sit alongside a corporal's guard of eight CCF. Social Credit was wiped from the electoral map. The Conservatives had won almost four million votes, compared to fewer than two and one-half million for the Liberals.

The 1958 election vaulted John Diefenbaker to the peak of his power. For a time, his authority in Parliament and his influence in the country eclipsed that of all who had occupied the Prime Minister's office before him. His departure five years later, in dismay and defeat, was equally unmatched by his predecessors. All that was ahead of him when Parliament came back May 12, 1958 to hear the government was planning the biggest public spending program since the war. It would include his much-loved South Saskatchewan Dam project, more money for the unemployed, new airport and harbor construction, and a start on his visionary "Roads to Resources" in the North. The minister of finance, Donald Fleming, followed up with a budget that provided for a $400 million deficit. Overlooked, however, was the fact that $10 billion dollars worth of wartime Victory Loans and other government bonds would fall due over the next five years. Nothing had been put aside for this purpose. "This was rather disturbing news," Diefenbaker would recall. The solution was a massive Conversion Loan at record interest rates of four and one-half per cent. The loan was well received in financial quarters where hefty commissions stood to be earned, but the net effect was to lift interest rates across the economy, contributing to a growing economic malaise.

There was more economic distress ahead: the firing of Bank of Canada governor James Coyne. In 1961, Coyne refused to increase the money supply, something that would have made it easier for the government to achieve its social and political objectives. This was followed by the foreign exchange crisis of 1962 when the dollar had to be frozen at ninety-two and one-half cents. It led the Liberals to issue cartoon versions of a "Diefenbuck," little realizing that a far more drastic devaluation of the dollar would occur under a Liberal regime thirty years in the future. A week after the June 18, 1962 election when Diefenbaker found himself once again in a minority position in Parliament, he was forced to announce an austerity program of the type usually resorted to by third world countries. A quarter of a billion dollars worth of election promises, including the building of a causeway to Prince Edward Island, had to be dropped. The International Monetary Fund was tapped for a $1 billion loan and import tariffs were increased, all to shore up Canada's financial reserves. The inability to anticipate these developments was due in large part to Diefenbaker's style of management. He would routinely deflect Opposition attacks with sudden announcements of new initiatives about which his cabinet colleagues knew nothing. One time it would be a plan to Canadianize the British North America Act, another to implement the recommendations of a royal commission on the future of Canadian magazines and newspapers.

The slow unraveling of Diefenbaker's political success came soon after the 1958 election when he failed to either recognize or understand how to deal with the suddenly enlarged pool of support the Conservatives had found in Quebec. While he was putting French on government checks, he pushed for the return of the 'Dominion of Canada' title which had fallen into disuse under the St. Laurent government. Worse, in the eyes of many Quebecers, he proposed to remove from the census the one question that gave them the opportunity to assert their French identity: "What is your origin on your father's side?" Diefenbaker, anxious to promote his concept of One Canada, ordered it be replaced with the simply declaration, "Canadian origin." After much protest the original question was restored. Of less trivial consequence was Diefenbaker's apparent inability to find qualified Quebecers for his cabinet. Of the forty-two French-speaking MPs elected from the province in 1958, a mere half dozen were taken into cabinet. Most observers thought Diefenbaker chose badly from those available to him. Aside from his selection of Major General Georges Vanier as Canada's first French-speaking Governor General, no Quebecers were appointed to significant positions while Diefenbaker was prime minister.

Back to a Minority

The Diefenbaker government's return to minority status in the election of 1962 marked the greatest reversal of electoral fortunes suffered by any Canadian party up to that time. From a peak of 207 seats, the Progressive Conservatives fell to 116 while the Liberals were successful in 100 ridings, Social Credit elected thirty and the NDP sent nineteen MPs to Ottawa. Diefenbaker governed uneasily as a result, confronted with a growing economic distress in many parts of the country – there were three-quarters of a million unemployed – and a public perception that while he had been a great opposition leader, he was ineffective in managing the affairs of Canada. This was especially evident in the government's relations with the United States on defence matters. A committed Canadian nationalist with strong bonds to Britain, Diefenbaker felt a deep distrust of American foreign policy and never warmed to John F. Kennedy, who was equally unimpressed with the Canadian leader. Diefenbaker's ultimate failure, leading directly to his final downfall and the election of the Pearson Liberals, resulted from his inability to mount a coherent defence policy that Canadians could trust and Americans would respect.

Canada's approach to defence and international security long reflected the country's willing dependence on the U.S. nuclear shield. This was complicated, however, by an insistence on maintaining an independent Canadian stance on issues in which the country had a direct stake, and the preservation of a voice of its own in world affairs. Many prime ministers have been tested on their skills to meet both realities; Mike Pearson faced castigation from Lyndon Johnson for his public utterances on the Viet Nam war, Pierre Trudeau was derided with obscenities by Richard Nixon, and Jean Chrétien earned the enmity of George W. Bush for not supporting the U.S. invasion of Iraq. All three, however, kept their cabinet together and gained, rather than lost, public support. In the situation that developed following the Cuba crisis of October, 1962 Diefenbaker dithered between a neutralist nuclear policy and a grudging but only partial fulfillment of Canada's obligations under the North American Air Defense Agreement (NORAD). It won him neither the support of Canadian voters or acceptance from the American administration.

The defense crisis of 1963 can be traced back to one of the most controversial of Diefenbaker's decisions in his first term in office – the scrapping of the CF105 Avro Arrow jet fighter. The price tag to build one hundred of the faster than sound interceptor aircraft had been put at $780 million. There seemed little chance of selling the Arrow to the U.S. or other countries, and there was growing evidence that aircraft of this type might soon be rendered obsolete by the new intercontinental ballistic missiles. The 1959 cancellation cost the jobs of fourteen thousand workers at Avro's plant at Malton, outside Toronto. It sent the best brains of the Canadian aerospace industry to the United States. More than forty years later, the Arrow remains a symbol of the technological supremacy Canada might have enjoyed had the government possessed the global economic vision, and applied the necessary financial resources, to sustain a project of such magnitude. Contrary to the conventional wisdom of the time, ballistic missiles did not replace fighter aircraft. It is likely that lucrative markets would have been found for the Arrow had Canada been able to summon the vision – the very quality that Diefenbaker felt he had in abundance – to stay the course.

Without the Arrow, Canada turned to the United States for new fighter aircraft. But military attention was turning away from airplanes and toward missiles and with the Cold War at its height, the U.S. developed a solid-fuel rocket, the surface to air, nuclear-tipped Bomarc B. Canada agreed to take fifty-six of the missiles for a new base in North Bay, Ontario. It would be better to bring down Russian nuclear bombers over the Arctic wastes than have them shot down over southern Canadian cities, which would be the case if Bomarcs were fired from U.S. bases further south. In announcing the deal to the House of Commons, Diefenbaker said "the full potential of these defensive weapons is achieved only when they are armed with nuclear warheads."

When it came time to accept the warheads, however, Diefenbaker resisted. Because U.S. law required nuclear weapons to be under control of U.S. citizens at all times, it would be necessary to have American soldiers in charge of the Bomarcs in North Bay, a condition the nationalist-minded Diefenbaker could not accept. American impatience grew when, after President Kennedy had identified the presence of Russian missiles in Cuba, Diefenbaker – apparently not entirely convinced – called for an on-site inspection by an international body "to ascertain what the facts are." It was known that Diefenbaker's cabinet was split on acceptance of nuclear arms, with the minister for external affairs, Howard Green, opposed to nuclear armament and the defence minister, Douglas Harkness, strongly in support. Mike Pearson, sensing the opportunity to skewer Diefenbaker, changed his own position on nuclear arms. At a conference of the York-Scarborough Liberal association he made a dramatic call for Canada to accept the warheads for "those defensive tactical weapons which cannot effectively be used without them but which we have agreed to use." Pearson's flip-flop upset many Liberals, including two prospective Quebec candidates, Pierre Trudeau and Jean Marchand. They both refused to stand as Liberal candidates in 1963. Strategically, Pearson's pronouncement forced the split in the Conservative cabinet into the open. He later declared that the making of his pro-nuclear speech "was when I really became a politician."[11]

Shortly after, the American State Department intervened with an unprecedented commentary on the domestic affairs of a friendly country by declaring that Canada "has not yet proposed any arrangement sufficiently practical to contribute effectively to North American defense." The blunt statement gave Diefenbaker the opportunity to tell Parliament that Canada would remain an ally of the U.S. but would not "accept external domination or interference in the making of its decisions." The emotional turmoil of these rapid developments quickly became unmanageable. On February 3, Douglas Harkness resigned his defence portfolio, the next day a Liberal non-confidence motion brought down the government, and by the end of the week newspapers that had long supported Diefenbaker, including the Toronto *Globe and Mail*, were calling for his resignation. Diefenbaker's response to all this was to argue that Canada had simply taken a stand for nuclear non-proliferation: "... in the interests of disarmament ... the nuclear family should not be increased so long as there is any possibility of disarmament among the nations of the world."

While idealistic, Diefenbaker's arguments could not be sold to a Canadian public that saw the American nuclear shield as the sole defense against Russian attack. By agreeing to take the Bomarc and then reneging on the nuclear warheads, the Canadian government had assembled a $685 million dollar weapons system – almost the cost of the ill-fated Arrow – that was described by Diefenbaker biographer Peter Newman as "the most impressive collection of blank cartridges in the history of military science." With an election called for April 8, defections from the cabinet continued – George Hees and Pierre Sevigny were the next to quit, then several other ministers announced they would not stand for re-election. Defence policy was a central issue of the election, but not by any means the sole one. Politicians, the media and the public were engrossed with the antics of a government stumbling through a half-crazed political twilight zone of wild exaggerations, bitter personal accusations, and contorted twists of policy, leaving the Prime Minister's supporters confused and his critics mystified. The *Canadian Annual Review* saw the spectacle of "a nation apparently hovering on the brink of financial collapse, a government rejected by two-thirds of the electorate refusing to meet Parliament, a defeated ministry borrowing millions of dollars and levying new taxes by unusual means ..."

After six years of brilliant but ineffectual leadership, Dief the Chief met defeat in 1963 with the loss of a further twenty-one seats, most of them going to the Liberals. Lester B. Pearson became Prime Minister of a minority government of 129 Liberals, facing an Opposition of 95 Conservatives, 24 Social Credit (mostly from Quebec under the banner of *Ralliement des Creditistes*), and 17 NDP. Back as Leader of the Opposition, Diefenbaker conducted a remarkable guerrilla defence and ably attacked Pearson's initiatives during an opening "Sixty days of decision."

Under Pearson, 26 nuclear-tipped missiles were installed at North Bay but by the late 1960s they were phased out, a useless asset in an era of intercontinental ballistic missiles. For the 1965 election, when Pearson vainly sought a majority, Diefenbaker had won back most of his lost media support and actually managed to pick up two seats while holding the Liberals to an equal gain, still short of a majority. Diefenbaker had won his Prince Albert seat again and would be re-elected four more times, for a total of 13 successive victories, even after resigning the leadership in a bitter coup that divided the party in 1966. He was witness to the efforts of two successors, Robert Stanfield who was unable to beat Pierre Trudeau, and Joe Clark who briefly headed a Conservative government in 1979. Diefenbaker died in Ottawa on August 16, 1979, at eighty-three, but not before meticulously planning his funeral arrangements. After a two-thousand mile train journey across the country he was buried in Saskatoon. Joe Clark said in his eulogy that "John Diefenbaker opened the politics of our country to those to whom it had always been closed. He gave politics a lively reality to those to whom it had seemed remote. He brought daylight to a process too long obscured in shadow and mystery."

John Diefenbaker was the last Prime Minister of the old Canada, the Canada that took shape on the frontier plains of the West, in the mean manufacturing towns of Ontario and Atlantic Canada, the lumbering camps of British Columbia and the sheltered homes of *les habitants* of Quebec. He was intensely loyal to the monarchy, a paragon of moral rectitude, and oblivious to the social and technological changes that were sweeping Canada. He was the last Prime Minister able to be away from Canada on a leisurely tour of world capitals, as he did for six weeks in 1958. He bitterly fought Pearson's introduction of the nation's most distinctive symbol, the Maple Leaf flag. The achievement of which he was most proud, a Bill of Rights guaranteeing basic freedoms in matters under federal control, had little more than symbolic value and never measurably broadened the rights of Canadians. That had to be left to the Charter of Rights and Freedoms. The 1957 election was a turning point that opened up the Canadian political establishment to outsiders like Diefenbaker who by their ethnicity or position in life had previously found the barriers to high office insurmountable. He rescued the Conservative party from stuffed shirts and Colonel Blimps, but failed miserably – and magnificently – at the art of government.

CHAPTER THIRTEEN

The Federal Election of June 25, 1968

THE ISSUES

Pierre Elliott Trudeau's promise to create a Just Society – a vaguely-defined concept that seems to proffer solutions to all of Canada's problems – helps to fuel Trudeaumania, catapulting the charismatic new leader of the Liberal party into the role of a public idol. Trudeau's vision of a bilingual Canada competes with the two nations/deux nations formula for national unity embraced by elements of the Progressive Conservative and New Democratic parties. The outcome equips Trudeau to pursue his goal of a new Canadian constitution anchored by a charter of rights and freedoms.

THE PERSONALITIES

LIBERAL PARTY
Pierre Elliott Trudeau, Prime Minister and Leader of the Liberal Party
Jean Marchand and Jean Pelletier, the other two of the "three wise men"
recruited by Lester B. Pearson to the Liberal party in 1965
John Turner, Minister of Consumer Affairs, later Minister of Finance

PROGRESSIVE CONSERVATIVE PARTY
Robert Stanfield, former Nova Scotia premier,
leader of the Official Opposition
Dalton Camp, former PC President instrumental in the forced resignation
of John Diefenbaker

NEW DEMOCRATIC PARTY
Tommy Douglas, former Saskatchewan premier, leader of the NDP

SOCIAL CREDIT:
Solon Low, MP for Peace River, Alberta, Leader

THE RESULTS

	SEATS	VOTES
Liberal Party	155	3,696,875 (45.5%)
Progressive Conservative	72	2,554,765 (31.4%)
New Democratic Party	22	1,387,389 (17.0%)
Ralliement des Créditiste	14	359,885 (4.4%)
Others	1	135,924 (1.7%)

*Pierre Elliott Trudeau's glamour and the infectious novelty of his
candidacy captured the imagination of Canadians in 1968.*

CHARISMA, THE CONSTITUTION AND THE CHARTER: THE VISION OF PIERRE ELLIOTT TRUDEAU

The Federal Election of 1968

Four hundred thousand Montrealers were out this pleasant June evening, the night before the federal election, to watch the parade celebrating St. Jean Baptiste Day, the national holiday of French Canada. A day that had originated as a pagan tribute to the summer solstice and had been observed in New France since 1615 had become known, in the wake of the Quiet Revolution that was reshaping Quebec society, for its heady mixture of nationalistic pride and youthful exuberance. The parade travelled six miles along Sherbrooke Street, the broad boulevard sweeping across the island of Montreal from the English enclaves at its west end to the French working class districts of the east end. At the reviewing stand set up outside the municipal library at Lafontaine Park, the new Prime Minister, Pierre Elliott Trudeau, waited with the Premier of Quebec, Daniel Johnson and the mayor of Montreal, Jean Drapeau for the first contingents to come into sight. Trudeau had enjoyed a quiet dinner with his mother, Grace Elliott Trudeau in her Outremont home. It had been a brief enough respite from the accolades of adoring crowds who during the election campaign had showered affection on him to a degree experienced by no politician in the country's history. When Trudeau stepped out of the library and onto the reviewing stand at 9:34 p.m. to take his seat beside Archbishop Gregoire of the Roman Catholic church, his view of the approaching parade was blocked by a wall of TV scaffolding and lights set up across the street. What Trudeau and the others could not immediately see was a series of pitched battles taking place between police and several hundred separatist demonstrators carrying the blue-and-white *fleur des lis* flag of Quebec. They were throwing themselves against police barricades, hurling tomatoes and other missiles and shouting

"Québec aux Québecois" and *"Tru-deau au pot-eau"* (Trudeau to the gallows). As the parade arrived in front of the stand and a band paused to let a police van carrying prisoners move by, the uproar of exploding firecrackers, police sirens, and a wave of pop bottles – some containing paint, kerosene or acid – showering down on the nearby crowds suddenly made it clear that Trudeau's presence had goaded a militant fringe to a dangerous level of violence. When a bottle sailed into the reviewing stand, its arc caught in the eye of a TV camera transmitting live coverage, Premier Johnson departed hurriedly from his seat, followed by the mayor and his wife and most of the other official guests. A Mounted Police guard threw himself on the Prime Minister, then covered Trudeau's head with a raincoat and tried to pull him from his seat. Trudeau briefly stood, flung out his arms, then planted himself firmly in his seat, his elbows on the front railing and declared, "I'm not leaving. I must stay."

Trudeau did stay, until the end of the parade well after eleven o'clock, exhibiting the kind of personal courage he'd shown as a young man, whether as a lone voyageur into the forested reaches of northern Quebec or as a backpacker trekking across Europe and Asia, skirting revolutions and wars, arrested in Palestine as a suspected Israeli spy, attacked by river pirates in India, or escaping China on the last American boat to leave Shanghai before the Communist takeover. TV images seen across Canada that night depicted Trudeau standing almost alone against a separatist mob. The coverage embarrassed many in Quebec but it reinforced the views of other Canadians that the new Prime Minister was someone who would "keep Quebec in its place." Morning newspapers on election day told of what had been the most violent clash in Montreal since the conscription riots of World War II. "Hundreds arrested in separatist riots," bannered the Montreal *Gazette*. It reported injuries to 43 policemen and the arrest of 292 demonstrators. Among those detained was Pierre Bourgault, founder of the separatist movement, *Ralliement pour l'indépendence National du Québec* (RIN).

The dramatic finale to the 1968 election campaign added an

extra touch of the bizarre to what had been a new and quite different political experience for most Canadians. The arrival on the federal scene of the charismatic new personality of Pierre Trudeau coincided with – and drew encouragement from – the mood of optimism that filled Canada toward the end of the nineteen sixties. The long post-war economic boom had spread prosperity throughout the country. Most families were living comfortably on the income of a single wage earner, while the newly liberating social attitudes sweeping the Western world seemed to promise new freedoms and privileges to anyone adventurous enough to claim them. The Centennial celebrations of 1967 and the success of Expo in Montreal, following on the unveiling of Canada's new Maple Leaf flag in 1964, all combined to foster a new nationalistic spirit. As Canadians looked south at the violence that had overtaken public dialogue in the United States – the upheaval of the Vietnam war and the assassinations that spring of Robert F. Kennedy and Martin Luther King – they congratulated themselves on living in a saner society where differences could be settled by ballot rather than by bullet. A new generation of leadership had taken over the stage in Canada, offering a positive change from the tired and discredited debates that had wracked a Parliament divided by the strident partisanship of the followers of John Diefenbaker and Mike Pearson. A new Canada was emerging with new leaders who would bring rational analysis and thoughtful discourse to the political scene. Little did Canadians realize they were about to enter on some of their country's most traumatic and divisive years.

The five years of Prime Minister Pearson accustomed Canadians to minority government, but also tested the public's patience for rancorous debate over petty scandals and the personal antagonisms that made cooperation between the government and the Opposition impossible. After winning the 1963 election, Pearson set out on "sixty days of decision" determined to overcome his minority position through decisive action on the key elements of his platform. He achieved reasonable success in improving relations with the Kennedy administration. The first

Liberal budget, however, drafted by the new minister of finance, Walter Gordon, with the assistance of advisors from his management consulting days in Toronto, was a catastrophe. A proposal to put a thirty per cent tax on the sale of shares of Canadian companies to non-residents caused havoc on the stock market. When the measure was withdrawn during trading hours, speculators reaped a fortune. Meanwhile, letter bombs were going off in the mail boxes of Westmount and other English districts of Montreal, a reminder that Canada was not immune to the tumult of the 1960s that was leading to violence in other countries. Hoping to find new strategies to deal with English-French relations, Pearson appointed a royal commission to study the state of bilingualism and biculturalism. He went before the convention of the Canadian Legion to announce plans for a distinct Canadian flag, a proposal that drew dark mutterings from most of the old soldiers. Some saw it as a sop to Quebec but when Parliament finally adopted the maple leaf flag – after 270 speeches over thirty-three days – a prospective Liberal candidate in Quebec, Pierre Trudeau, declared that French Canada did not give a "tinker's damn" about it. The Bi and Bi commission report in February, 1965 caused earnest concern among the political and intellectual classes with its declaration that Canada was "passing through its greatest crisis in its history." Clearly now, in Pearson's view, new French-Canadian voices were urgently needed in Ottawa, especially in light of the unhappy failure of several of his Quebec ministers to survive personal and political scandals.

The first choice of Pearson and his advisors was the Quebec labour leader, Jean Marchand, who had created the province's modern trade union movement and had spent a lifetime battling reactionary elements in the Maurice Duplessis government. They'd long wanted to bring Marchand to Ottawa and had given him federal exposure by appointments to the Bi and Bi commission and to the advisory council of the Unemployment Insurance Commission. Still, Marchand was reluctant to plunge into federal politics without the involvement of his two closest friends, Gerard Pelletier and Pierre Trudeau. Their relationship went back fifteen years to the bitter strike of asbestos miners in 1949, where Marchand as the leader of the strikers, Pelletier as a young journalist reporting the strike for *Le Devoir*, and Trudeau as a footloose young lawyer back from five years of study and travel abroad, came together in the grungy mining halls and open pits of the asbestos works around the town of Asbestos, Quebec. While Marchand plotted union strategy and Pelletier reported on the appalling working conditions and low wages of the miners, Trudeau gave stirring speeches to the strikers to explain their rights and urge them not to give in on their demands. In a book he edited about the strike, Trudeau called the event "a turning point in the entire religious, political, social and economic history of the Province of Quebec."[1]

The Road to Leadership

Marchand's insistence that Pelletier and Trudeau be invited to run for the party in 1965 led to considerable reflection among influential Quebec Liberals. Pelletier, by now editor-in-chief of Quebec's largest newspaper, *la Presse*, could be a considerable catch but Trudeau was a lesser known quantity. For most of the 1950s Trudeau had been a gad-fly on the Quebec scene, blocked by the Roman Catholic church and Duplessis in his efforts to get a teaching appointment to the University of Montreal. He'd put in two years in Ottawa as a junior civil servant in the Privy Council Office, edited the intellectually anti-clerical magazine *Cite Libre*, written widely on Quebec social and economic issues, and as a qualified lawyer, took on civil rights cases that interested him, often without charge. In 1961, with a new Liberal government in office in Quebec, Trudeau finally gained an appointment as an associate professor of law at *Université de Montréal* where he settled in to lecture on constitutional law and write papers on the superiority of federalism over Quebec nationalism, which he considered parochial and backward. Trudeau also managed to earn the enmity of many Liberals with his attack on Pearson's 1963 flip-flop over nuclear arms. After denouncing Pearson as "the defrocked Priest of Peace" and belittling the "anti-democratic reflexes of the spineless Liberal herd," Trudeau campaigned that year for his friend Charles Taylor, leader of the NDP in Quebec. By 1965, however, Pearson was ready to accept Jean Marchand's conditions and seats were found for all three in the election of November of that year. Fatefully, no French-speaking riding seemed to want Trudeau and so he ran in the English-speaking enclave of Mount Royal, where he was easily elected. At Marchand's urging, Pearson appointed Trudeau as his parliamentary secretary and in April, 1967 named him Minister of Justice. It was a post which would prove to be a perfect match for Trudeau's interest and intellect, and the ideal positioning for his accession to Liberal party leadership.

The social ferment of the 1960s put the criminal justice system at the focal point of change, and Trudeau plunged into his duties with energy and enthusiasm. He was a dashing figure around Parliament, and drew a scathing dressing down from John Diefenbaker for showing up in the House in an outfit that included sandals and an ascot. Issues that Trudeau had debated academically were suddenly matters over which he could exercise some control. Reform of the criminal code, easing of Canada's then rigid divorce laws and abolition of the law against homosexuality were all high on the agenda of the new minister and his department. Trudeau's first major public pronouncement, however, was on the constitution and was delivered to the annual meeting of the Canadian Bar Association in Quebec City on September 4, 1967. Despite being Centennial year, 1967 saw heightened tensions between Ottawa and the provinces on such issues as revenue-sharing and provincial rights. Ontario Premier John Robarts had staged his own Confederation of Tomorrow conference in Toronto and Pearson had proposed a federal-provincial conference for early 1968 to discuss adoption of a constitutional bill of rights that, unlike Diefenbaker's rights bill, would be binding on both the federal and provincial governments. Trudeau seized the Bar association meeting to put individual rights and language equality atop the constitutional agenda:

If we reach agreement on the fundamental rights of the citizen, on their definition and protection in all parts of Canada, we shall have made a major first step towards basic constitutional reform.

Part of those fundamental rights, Trudeau argued – in addition to traditional rights such as freedom of speech, the press, religion and assembly – should be the right to live and work in either of the two official languages of Canada.

If we are able to reach agreement on this, we will have found a solution to a basic issue facing Canada today. A constitutional change recognizing broader rights with respect to the two official languages would add a new meaning to Confederation. Without these rights we cannot assure every Canadian an equal opportunity to participate in the political, cultural, economic and social life of the country.

Perhaps more important, as Trudeau made clear in a press conference the next day, was the need to ensure equality of French and English right across Canada, not just in Quebec. Two nations, special status, and of course separatism were all unacceptable. "I think particular status for Quebec is the biggest intellectual hoax ever foisted on the people of Quebec and the people of Canada. The more you increase the powers of Quebec, the more you reduce the presence of Quebec at Ottawa." The speech put Trudeau in conflict with much of the conventional wisdom of the day, and signaled the clear course on which he would set sail throughout his public life – instead of special treatment of Quebec, a renewed federalism entrenching the equality of French and English throughout Canada. It was a daring concept that would bring bitter condemnation from the extremes of both language groups, those English who wanted to confine French to Quebec, and those French who wished to build a wall around their province, without regard for the fate of their compatriots outside Quebec.

Constitutional reform, then as always, was somewhat of an arcane subject to most Canadians. Divorce, homosexuality and abortion were something else, and the new Justice Minister moved quickly to reform laws in all these areas. Divorce reform had always been considered too sensitive to attempt, especially in Quebec where the Catholic church still stood so solidly against divorce that a special act of Parliament was required to dissolve a marriage. Adultery had to be proven, a provision which often forced couples to resort to perjured evidence. Trudeau expressed the distinction between civil law and moral standards when he told Parliament, "it would be a mistake for us to try to legislate into this society concepts which belong to a theological or sacred order." The bill broadening the grounds for divorce was passed quickly by Parliament and when Trudeau was asked the next day if he would soon bring in other amendments to the Criminal Code, he leaped at the opportunity. Shortly before Christmas 1967, Trudeau introduced amendments lifting the prohibition on homosexual acts between consenting adults, and providing for abortion in cases where a committee of physicians could agree that a pregnancy was affecting a woman's physical and mental health. In a news conference Trudeau held to explain details of the bill, he uttered one memorable line that became the Canadian "sound bite" of the decade: "There's no place for the state in the bedrooms of the nation." With that single, unequivocal statement Trudeau captured the imagination of the country. Here was a figure of authority demonstrating a contemporary attitude, speaking in the language of the people. It marked the emergence of Trudeau's personality into the public consciousness, and it came only days before Pearson announced his retirement.

The new public figure that was emerging might have been an image cut to fit the cloth of a swinging new decade,. In fact Trudeau's personality had matured by early middle age – he was forty-eight when he won the Liberal leadership – and he had "come to power with a coherent and painstakingly developed political philosophy."[2] As Canadians first became aware of Trudeau, however, it was the colorful aspects of his personality that turned them on – his overt sexiness, his informality, his athletic grace and his insouciance – and which magnified his impact on the public and the media. Trudeau was not handsome in the conventional sense and his high cheek bones and narrow eyes gave him a somewhat exotic countenance, suggesting an air of inscrutability, or perhaps great wisdom. He was physically slight (his presence enlarged by the television cameras) and spoke gently, his English and French both perfectly formed, erudite and unmistakable, carrying a cold force of logic and delivered with a level of confidence bordering on arrogance. While the more obvious elements of his biography soon became well known, Trudeau succeeded throughout his life in retaining a shield of privacy over his inner life, despite the often public displays of emotional excess exhibited by his wife Margaret, or his all too apparent desolation over the loss of his youngest son, Michel, swept away by an avalanche in the snowy mountains of British Columbia.

From his birth in Montreal on October 18, 1919, Pierre Trudeau received an upbringing that offered him the advantages of considerable wealth in a social milieu that challenged him to excel intellectually and personally. His family environment was warm and secure and from his birth, he grew accustomed to hearing both English and French spoken around him. The Quebec heritage of his father Charles-Emile Trudeau, ran deep into history, back ten generations to Etienne Truteau, a sturdy French carpenter who arrived in the New World at the age of seventeen in 1659. The family stayed on the land until his father, given a university education and a bent for business, turned from practicing law to founding an automobile owners' association and running a string of gas stations. Imperial Oil paid the elder Trudeau $1.4 million for the business in 1932, at the depth of the depression. It assured a comfortable life for his wife, the former Grace Elliott, the daughter of a mixed French-Scottish marriage, and his three children, Suzette, Pierre and Charles, the youngest. Two years later, on a trip to Florida to watch the spring training of the Montreal Royals, a baseball team of which Pierre's father was a part-owner, Charles Trudeau caught pneumonia and died at the age of forty-six. The loss of a father at the age of fifteen had to be traumatic. It encouraged Pierre to dedicate himself to personal achievement, whether at school, in athletics such as swimming and canoeing, or in challenging authority. Like most Quebec youth, he refused to enlist in World War II and in one flash of irresponsibility, rode around on a motorcycle wearing a spiked helmet from an old German army uniform. His first involvement in politics came in the 1940 federal election when he campaigned unsuccessfully for the future mayor of Montreal, Jean Drapeau. It was a time of tumult, when a tightly-knit group of young Quebecers was establishing relationships that would last throughout their lives, often from rival political camps.

Trudeau's education, from age twelve to twenty, came at the Jesuit-run Collège Jean de Brébeuf, an elite classical school where he is remembered as much for rebelliousness and mischief as for academic achievement. He took his BA to *Université de Montréal* where he earned a law degree and worked briefly for a local firm before setting off to see the world in 1944. In two years at Harvard Trudeau studied economics and government, leaving with a master's degree in political economy. Then it was on to Paris and the political science and law faculties of the Sorbonne, followed by study at the London School of Economics. He spent a total of eight years at various universities, but still wasn't ready to come home. Travels through Europe and Asia led to many hazardous encounters in out-of-the-way places – the Arab-Israeli conflict, civil war in Burma, the Vietnamese rebellion against the French Empire, the partition of India and Pakistan and the Communist revolution in China. It all gave Trudeau an exceptional appreciation of the consequences of nationalism when wedded to ethnic, social or religious beliefs. "I tempted fate. I used to deliberately put myself into some pretty tricky situations just to see how I would handle them."[3]

When Mike Pearson announced on December 14, 1967, that he would resign following a leadership convention in the Spring, many well-known cabinet ministers were seen as possible successors, including Paul Martin, Mitchell Sharp, Robert Winters, Paul Hellyer and the up and coming young John Turner. Quebec Liberals were anxious and uncertain, convinced they needed to put up a candidate but not entirely confident they had someone who could win. Initially, attention focused on Jean Marchand but his self-doubts about his health, his relatively poor English, his limited understanding of constitutional law – something of paramount importance at this point – all led to the view that Pierre Trudeau would be the stronger candidate. Trudeau took off for a two-week holiday to Tahiti where he would meet the woman he would later marry, Margaret Sinclair. On his return to Montreal he had a long dinner at Café Martin with Marchand and Gérard Pelletier. They put it to him that he should run. Trudeau thought his federalist reputation, and now his bills to legalize abortion and homosexuality, would hurt him in Quebec. They told him they could deliver the Quebec delegation, but Trudeau would have to win over English Canada. First, however, Trudeau had to get through the constitutional conference called by Pearson for late January. As Minister of Justice, he would be handling the main item on the agenda, the proposal that he had carefully nurtured for a Canadian Charter of Human Rights.

The conference turned into an icy confrontation between Trudeau and Daniel Johnson, the premier of Quebec, and adjourned without taking concrete action other than to set up committees to study various ideas for constitutional reform. Even Pearson thought Trudeau had gone too far in rejecting any special constitutional status for Quebec. In fact, Trudeau was being consistent with positions he'd expressed ever since getting involved in federal politics, first at the Canadian Bar Association convention and most recently at the convention of the Quebec Liberal party. There, he'd told a thousand delegates that on constitutional issues, it was a choice between "more rights for French-Canadians or more power for the province of Quebec." He went on: "Personally, I believe it is not a particular status in Confederation for the government of Quebec but an equal status for all French-speaking Canadians in all of Canada that will bring enduring unity to our country." Trudeau was drafting a new political architecture that would prove equally irritating on both sides of the language divide: one nation with two languages or ultimately, two separate nations.

In addition to the encouragement Trudeau was receiving from his long-time allies in Quebec, significant support was turning up in Ontario. Two Ontario MPs, Robert Stanbury of York-Scarborough and Donald Macdonald from Toronto Rosedale, along with an Ontario provincial member, Tim Reid of Scarborough East, formed a "Draft Pierre Trudeau for Prime Minister" committee. They had considerable backing among Ontario's academic community, including Professor Ramsay Cook of the University of Toronto and Professor William Kilbourn of York University. After a survey of Stanbury's riding members showed a preference for Trudeau over all the other candidates, the committee appealed to him to come to the annual meeting of the Ontario Liberal Association. There, they rented the Ontario Room of the Royal York hotel for a press conference and reception. Although Trudeau had not yet declared his candidacy, the room was thronged by both press and delegates. If there was any doubt about Trudeau's appeal, this event made clear the immense enthusiasm and excitement that a Trudeau candidacy would create. Still, Trudeau held off and it was not until after meeting privately with Pearson that he told a small group of dinner companions in the parliamentary restaurant on February 15 that he would go for the leadership.

A parliamentary foul-up almost threw the Liberal leadership campaign off the rails before it really began, and it severely damaged the prospects of Mitchell Sharp, the minister of finance. With Pearson in the West Indies to accept an honorary degree, a debate in the House on a bill to impose a surtax on high incomes went against the government, 84 votes to 82. Sharp had allowed a vote on third reading even though many Liberal members were absent at the time. Defeat on a money bill normally leads to the resignation of the government, but the Liberals were in no mood to go into an election on the eve of Pearson's retirement. Returning to Ottawa shocked and enraged (as he told a CTV interviewer), Pearson and his advisors concocted a motion stating the House did not regard the vote as a vote of non-confidence. After eight days of debate, and with all Liberal MPs present, the government was upheld, 138 to 119.

The debate gave Trudeau the opportunity to take the offensive by attacking the Opposition for exploiting "obsolete rules" and prolonging the debate at a time when "decisions must be taken much more rapidly, not only on behalf of the nation but on behalf of justice." The statement drew catcalls from the Tories and the NDP. Staring coolly across the floor, Trudeau commented:

> "When people yell like animals, one cannot hear very well the questions asked. If somebody wants to ask me questions I will answer them, but to bawl like a herd will not do very much for the decision."

His put-down set the style for many Trudeau ripostes. When Premier Johnson renewed his attack on the federal government's constitutional proposals, asserting that Trudeau was fostering "backward and retrograde attitudes" toward Quebec, he added that it was just the kind of attitude that could be expected of a "Lord Elliott." Other people would try to use Trudeau's mixed parentage to challenge the legitimacy of his views, and on every occasion Trudeau would turn the exchange to his advantage. "I think this shows how afraid he is of the people of Quebec becoming interested in federal politics," Trudeau said. "If they do, then he knows he won't be lord and master over all Quebec. I think he's playing a desperate game which I think will backfire."

Trudeau often fell into his law professor lecture role, but it didn't seem to make any difference to those who heard him. An elemental chemistry was already at work and he was making contact with his listeners in ways that went beyond the content of his words. It was the beginning of the most remarkable demonstration of personality politics the country had ever seen. This new, fascinating figure soon was being depicted on t-shirts and sweaters and his picture was being displayed in store windows. Many copies of Trudeau's book, *Federalism and the French Canadians*, were bought although not that many were actually read. Trudeaumania was especially rampant among women and young people, two constituencies not normally given to a great interest in politics. Thousands of anecdotes were told of people waiting hours to meet Trudeau for a moment or two and enjoying the unforgettable experience of shaking hands – or kissing – while exchanging a few words. The St. Lawrence Hall in Toronto was the scene of one of the most frenzied rallies when five thousand jammed the old building to hear Trudeau speak for half an hour before answering questions from the media. To the question, "How badly do you want to be Prime Minister?" Trudeau responded with a quotation from Plato: "A man who wants to be very badly head of the country should not be trusted." It drew the warmest applause of the evening and was widely and favourably repeated on air and in print.

The news media fed what seemed to be an insatiable public interest, providing long feature articles, in-depth TV reports and on-the-street radio interviews. Nor was the coverage confined to Canada; newspapers in the United States and Britain were also reporting on this unusual new personality, "a national leader so lucid and contemporary, so impatient with the platitudes and deceits of public life and so clear sighted about the future, that he could make politics not only relevant but exciting to a generation alienated from the political process."[4] While even normally Conservative-supporting newspapers were recounting Trudeau's capture of the public imagination, newspapers in Quebec remained generally immune to the allure of this new personality. Quebec editorialists worried that Trudeau's rejection of any special status for the province made him unacceptable to the political-intellectual class. Many Quebec Liberal MNA's campaigned against Trudeau for this reason. From many pulpits there was heard criticism by the Catholic clergy of Trudeau's liberalizing reforms.

The Liberal convention opened in Ottawa on April 4 with a CBC poll that put Trudeau far ahead of his rivals. It caused Mitchell Sharp to withdraw and throw his support to Trudeau. When Trudeau arrived on the afternoon train from Montreal, he was mobbed by news reporters and delegates before being driven in a caravan to Parliament Hill. There, he went to his office before crossing the street to the National Press Building for a news conference. It was as much a celebration as an interview. Asked whether he would be giving up his Mercedes if he moved to 24 Sussex Street, Trudeau replied, "Are you talking of a car or a girl? I'm not going to give up either." The convention, like most political party meetings, revolved around cocktail parties, barbeques and beer fests but Trudeau's event for delegates at the Chaudière Country Club, near Hull, surpassed them all. All roads were jammed and when Trudeau arrived a flying wedge had to be formed to escort him into the building. An orchestra was playing twist tunes, a popular dance of the time, and Trudeau exhibited his ballroom as well as his oratorical skills. Premier Joey Smallwood arrived from Newfoundland in time to declare that Trudeau as leader would win the Liberals another million votes.

The speeches to the convention Friday night drew a huge television audience. While other candidates were led to the podium by bands and demonstrating supporters, Trudeau's team opted simply to surround him with hundreds of delegates carrying burnt orange Trudeau posters and banners. Supporters as well as friendly members of the public had been told to get there early and to spread out throughout the Lansdowne Park arena. As Trudeau strode to the platform the entire arena seemed to rise en masse, waving signs and chanting "Tru-deau! Tru-deau!" He stood at the microphone, waiting for the tumult to subside, and with downward motions of his hands encouraged people to resume their seats. His call for a "just society" seemed to be embraced by almost everyone in the hall:

> "For many of us, the world of today stands on the
> threshold of a golden age. By building a truly just

society, this beautiful rich and energetic country of ours can become a model in which every citizen will enjoy his fundamental rights, in which two great linguistic communities and people of many cultures will live in harmony, and in which every individual will find fulfillment. Liberation is the only philosophy for our time, because it does not try to conserve every tradition of the past; because it does not apply to new problems the old doctrinaire solutions, because it is prepared to experiment and innovate and because it knows the past is less important than the future."

Claude Ryan, the *Le Devoir* editor who had endorsed Paul Hellyer after criticizing Trudeau as "dangerously rigid and haughty" on Quebec, thought that Trudeau's speech had won him the convention. He told the CBC-TV audience: "Around his speech there was an aura of victory. The speech made a real impact on the delegates. It was a good presentation of modern liberalism." When the voting took place Saturday afternoon, however, it took four ballots before Trudeau could gain a majority over his closest competitors, Robert Winters and John Turner. The final count was Trudeau 1,203, Winters 954 and Turner, who had refused to drop out although he had no prospect of winning, 195 votes.[5] A swelling chant, "Trudeau Canada, Trudeau Canada" swept over the arena. That night, in response to the invitation Trudeau issued in his televised acceptance speech to "join the celebration" at the Skyline Hotel, some twenty-five thousand people jammed the hotel's lobbies and filled the streets outside. The doors had to barricaded against the surging crowds.

The Conservative Change of Guard

The bitter struggle in the Progressive Conservative party to replace John Diefenbaker came to a head at the party's 1966 meeting in the chandeliered ballroom of the Chateau Laurier hotel in Ottawa. There, the president of the party and a former architect of Diefenbaker's triumphs, Dalton Camp, won his own re-election and then gained passage of a motion expressing support for Diefenbaker but stipulating that a leadership convention be held in 1967. There was a deeply-felt mood within the party that western populism was no longer popular, even in the West, and that a more coherent approach to managing the country's affairs was needed if the Liberals were to be defeated in the next election. Many Conservatives saw an opportunity to bring an end to the personal bitterness of the Diefenbaker-Pearson rivalry and go to the people with a new face who would appeal to uncommitted voters as well as traditional Conservative supporters. Diefenbaker, accepted none of that and insisted on running for re-election. He faced an array of opponents. The former minister of justice, Davie Fulton, spoke early from British Columbia of his intention to run. The Premier of Manitoba, Duff Roblin, was seen as a strong candidate. The grandson of an earlier Manitoba premier, he was thought to be able to retain Western votes, while appealing to Quebec on the strength of his fluent French and his recent lifting of the prohibition on the use of French in Manitoba schools. The odds on a Roblin victory changed, however, with the entry of Nova Scotia Premier Robert Stanfield. The heir to an underwear fortune, Stanfield had achieved a remarkable revival of Conservative fortunes in his native province. First elected as one of only eight PCs in 1949, Stanfield formed a government in 1956 and won three subsequent elections. The other major candidate was George Hees, the peripatetic ex-minister of trade and industry under Diefenbaker, seen as something of a glamour boy but actually possessed of keen political insights and virtually unlimited energy. In the voting that took place in the hot and humid Maple Leaf Gardens in Toronto on September 9, 1967, Stanfield required four ballots to finally defeat Roblin, 1,150 to 969. Diefenbaker had dropped out after placing an embarrassing fifth. The photo op of the convention was the picture of Stanfield calmly munching on a banana while awaiting the results. If the photo was seen as a demonstration of Stanfield's humanity, it projected another, less attractive quality: the essential plainness of the man.

The delegates soon packed their bags and left Toronto but the legacy of the convention was yet to be realized; it lay in the Conservative party's apparent acceptance of the concept of Canada as consisting of two nations, English and French, with Quebec holding the jurisdictional right to the future of French language and culture in Canada. It first took root in a Conservative party "Thinker's Conference" held the year before at Montmorency Falls, near Quebec City. The idea was seen by many Conservatives as a way of overcoming the traditional distrust of the party in French Canada. It came to the fore when Marcel Faribault, a prominent Quebec Conservative and advisor to Premier Johnson, told the meeting that "the question of two nations is no longer debatable in the Province of Quebec." If Canada was to ever have a new constitution, he said, it would have to include "the recognition that there are in this country two founding peoples." He explained that in French this could only be articulated as *deux nations*, although in English that could mean two founding races or people. The conference bought into the idea and in its constitutional report, it declared that "Canada is composed of the original inhabitants of this land and the two founding nations *(deux nations)* with historic rights, who have been, and continue to be joined by people from many lands." The very idea of *deux nations* infuriated John Diefenbaker who with his "One Canada" obsession saw the term as denoting two countries, independently governed. He told the convention: "They say I don't understand the meaning of 'nation,' that it means something different in French than in English. Laurier said it was one nation, Cartier said it was one nation. I'm not going to go back one hundred years or more and borrow a policy that proved to be wrong in order to get votes in 1967." Stanfield was more cautious. He did not directly reject *deux nations* but he described it as ambiguous and managed to put off further discussion by promising it would be taken up at a future policy convention.

The Campaign and the Candidates

The Liberal leadership contest became the perfect launch pad for the election campaign. For a time, it obliterated the Conservatives and the NDP from the media and from the thoughts of Canadians. After a short Easter holiday in Florida, Trudeau returned to Ottawa ready to put together his cabinet, and determined – although only a few advisors were aware of this – to call the election as soon as possible. The new cabinet that was sworn in on Saturday, April 20 contained few surprises. Three veterans were lost immediately: Robert Winters had told Trudeau he would be leaving politics, Paul Martin agreed to go to the Senate, and Judy Lamarsh, the only woman minister, had made it clear she had no desire to serve under "that bastard" Trudeau. The cabinet dropped from twenty-seven to twenty-four, with only three new faces – supporters Donald Macdonald from Toronto and Gérard Pelletier from Montreal, and John Munro from Hamilton, Ontario. Parliament met the following Tuesday, its members expecting to spend the afternoon congratulating Trudeau, paying respects to the outgoing Prime Minister, and questioning the new cabinet on its spending and policy intentions. Robert Stanfield had prepared a gracious speech for the occasion. Mike Pearson also had prepared a short speech: "I think it was a good one. I never got a chance to use it."[6] Trudeau rose after the opening formalities, thanked everyone who had sent him messages of congratulations, and abruptly announced that Parliament had been dissolved. A general election would be held on June 25.

There was no need for a two-month campaign; the time frame had been set decades before in election laws written when travel throughout the country was arduous and communication was largely person-to-person. Campaigns would be shorter in the future, but for now the parties concentrated on getting ready, renting planes and buses, finishing off advertising plans, and drafting speeches for the leaders. The Conservative leadership, including campaign manager Eddie Goodman, the Toronto lawyer, and the national organizer, Gene Rheaume, a former MP for the Northwest Territories, met with Stanfield in Toronto. Dalton Camp, the former party president who was getting ready to run in the Don Valley riding, was not asked to attend. Stanfield feared retribution from those still loyal to Diefenbaker and he was anxious to show that he was his own man, not beholden to Camp. From the start, Tory organizers knew they would have difficulty competing with the image politics driving Trudeaumania. Stanfield, warm and charming in private, retreated into aloofness with large crowds and became hesitant when confronted by the media. "You walk out and they shove a bunch of microphones in your face and in thirty seconds you're expected to produce a profound and intelligent answer to what may be an extremely complicated issue."[7]

Trudeau had no such problems with the media. He went straight from the House to a press conference where he justified holding an early election, before he had put out any policies or added further to the legislative record he'd established as justice minister. "Many changes have occurred in Canada since the last general election," he said. "One intangible but important phenomenon is the change in attitude of many Canadians towards the nature and the future of the country." On the Just Society, he promised "I will use all my strength to bring about a just society to a nation living in a tough world." He didn't want to make the election a personality contest: "I don't want the Liberal party to be elected on something called 'Trudeauism.'" Stanfield scoffed when he heard this, and when he followed Trudeau to the podium at the National Press Building he took the Prime Minister to task for going to the people with "no record, no policy, and no proof of his ability to govern the country." He thought the government should at least present an outline of how it would deal with the country's problems: high interest rates, housing, unemployment, a weak dollar. Of the swinging new image of the Prime Minister, Stanfield wondered if Trudeau wasn't like a "swinging gate that had become stuck." For the New Democratic party, its 63-year-old leader Tommy Douglas had no desire for a "blind date" with the charismatic new Prime Minister. Having sat in Parliament on and off since 1935, Douglas had little time for someone who had spent less than an hour in the House as the Prime Minister. "Platitudes about a just society will not suffice," he told the press.

An election campaign is partly about political process. It involves setting up attack lines, identifying the themes that will play to best effect, and finding chinks in the other side's armament. It also requires skillful management of a small corps of professionals and thousands of volunteers, and a strategy for dealing with the media. In 1968, the Liberal party found itself with a leader of profound intellectual capacity and with a deep understanding of the public policy issues with which the government would have to deal. Trudeau did not, however, understand or appreciate the intimacies of party politicking, as the organizers of the campaign would soon discover. John Nichol, the Vancouver businessman and president of the Liberal party who co-chaired the campaign with Jean Marchand, struggled to get Trudeau to participate in the necessary rituals of meeting local officials and volunteers. Trudeau detested cocktail parties where he would have to indulge in small talk with strangers. It took a shouting match and Nichol's threatened resignation to get Trudeau to do a tour of Western cities. He wanted to cancel the trip because he was tired and anyway, was ahead in the polls.[8]

Trudeau's inclinations meshed comfortably with Liberal party strategy; the campaign would be built on impressions and attitudes, not policy promises. Trudeau stayed on this course even though his one written policy document, The Just Society, set out specific commitments. Its chief points were that everyone must have the motivation and means to participate fully in society, regardless of the region or group from whence they came. There would be a Department of Regional Development to assist less affluent regions. Consumers would be protected by a Consumers' Code. There would be a task force on urban issues and urban development would be a keystone of the Just Society. Dealing with the galloping cost of real estate would be a priority. More effective solutions would have to be found for air and water pollution. "An expanding economy and a fairer distribution of our national wealth are fundamental to our concept of the Just Society." As a party platform, it was one on which almost any party could run. Its broad principles met little argument; the test would be in the measures the government would adopt to translate its high hopes into reality.

In mid-May, Trudeau boarded his campaign jet (Stanfield satisfied himself with a 1950s' era DC-7 turboprop) and began to caress the Canadian electorate. His tours had been well planned by William Lee, the former executive assistant to Paul Hellyer, and Trudeau proved himself superb in doing in public what he refused to do in private: to set out his ideas about the country and to gain an adoring acceptance of everything he talked about. It didn't seem to matter whether the audiences heard or understood all his words, because the country was caught up in Trudeaumania, a new political phenomenon which one observer likened to a kind of mass auto-eroticism. Trudeau seemed to represent the Camelot that America had lost and Canada would yet enjoy.

If there was a starting point for the Trudeaumania epidemic, it might have been his arrival on Parliament Hill for his very first cabinet meeting after being chosen leader. A seventeen-year-old girl emerged from the waiting crowd and asked Trudeau whether she could kiss him. "Why not? It's spring," he answered. She pronounced the kiss as "fantastic." From his first foray into the Northwest Territories – where Trudeau threw a proffered bearskin over his shoulders and danced for the photographers – the media were entranced by his energy and informality. In Edmonton, five thousand people clutching, pushing and shouting demonstrated their delight at being in Trudeau's presence. A photo of Trudeau doing a backflip into a swimming pool at an Oakville, Ontario motel made front pages across the country. Wherever he went, the crowds were enormous. In Toronto, fifty thousand people surged into Nathan Phillips Square at City Hall for the largest and most exuberant rally of the campaign. Crowds were six to eight deep along Bay Street as a 25-car cavalcade led by trumpeter Bobby Gimby and 115 children singing the Expo theme song, "Ca-na-da" escorted Trudeau to the Square. In

Montreal, forty-five thousand turned up for Trudeau's main rally. In tone, they were no different than the dozens of smaller events the Liberals organized across the country. The formula was always the same: Trudeau would be met at the airport by an adoring clutch of supporters and would be driven, usually in a convertible, to a shopping mall where a waiting crowd would give him an enthusiastic hearing. In later years, Trudeau would continue to exhibit an uninhibited public behavior that contrasted sharply with the thoughtful, often shy demeanor that was a truer reflection of his personality. He would point a middle finger at hecklers, slide down banisters, dance a pirouette behind the Queen's back, or twist a tie around his neck in a mock self-hanging. What Canadians experienced in the campaign of 1968 fell far short of the classic case of political charisma where a population, influenced by personality characteristics of physical appearance, gestures, style of life and mannerisms, grants a leader unquestioned loyalty. That condition more properly fits a Castro, Stalin, Mao or even a Gandhi, not the leader of a western democracy. It could be credibly argued, however, that Trudeau did possess something approaching the "gift of grace," the early Christian measure for the meaning of charisma.

For all the adulation of the crowds, Trudeau's short speeches were more of a lecture in civics than partisan political orations. He promised to create a more "participatory democracy" and talked about the need to "shape our history and our industrial policy in a way which is conducive to progress." He became more animated when speaking of his vision of a charter of rights, saying "We have set out as the first priority a declaration of human liberties, a chart of fundamental human rights." All of these ideas were cornerstones of his Just Society "in which citizens have a role and feel that their share of all social benefits is a just share ..." He spoke most passionately of federalism and his conviction, as he argued in his seminal work, *Federalism and the French Canadians,* that the powers enjoyed by Quebec should be no greater than any other province:

"How can a constitution be devised to give Quebec greater powers than other provinces, without reducing Quebec's powers in Ottawa? How can citizens of other provinces be made to accept the fact that they would have less power over Quebec at the federal level than Quebec would have over them? How can Quebec be made the national state of French Canadians, with really special powers, without abandoning at the same time demands for the parity of French and English in Ottawa and throughout the rest of the country?"

It was on this issue that the only serious debate of the campaign occurred, and it put the Progressive Conservative party in a difficult position. Stanfield recruited Marcel Faribault as his star candidate, believing he would attract a solid following without upsetting voters elsewhere in Canada. There was hope at Conservative headquarters that Faribault and his allies in the *Union Nationale* would bring the PCs thirty-five or forty seats in Quebec, enough to deny Trudeau a majority. In fact, Faribault's agreement to stand for the PCs in Gamelin, an east end Montreal riding, gave Trudeau a perfect target to attack the Conservatives on *deux nations*. Stanfield had gone on record that his party viewed the term "purely in a sociological sense" and that any new rights that might be extended to Quebec would be offered to all the provinces. Trudeau, speaking to 1,200 businessmen at a Montreal Chamber of Commerce luncheon, tied the idea of special status to demands by Premier Johnson for the right to act internationally on matters of provincial jurisdiction, such as education. To Trudeau, the idea of Quebec sending its own delegations to international conferences, as it had done for francophone education meetings in Gabon and France, was a terrible one. It would mean "Quebec can act as a sovereign state in matters of its own jurisdiction." This would lead to "the disintegration of Canada and also the disintegration of other countries and of international law itself." Stanfield's response, in a speech in Halifax, was that Trudeau was trying to "destroy" Premier

Johnson and that even if he succeeded, other forces in Quebec including the provincial Liberals, would take up the argument for special status. On this issue, ironically, the parties had reversed themselves since 1965. Then, the Liberals were sympathetic to special status while John Diefenbaker campaigned for "one Canada." It was expected that national unity issue would lead to fireworks in the televised debate of the party leaders on Sunday evening, June 9 but the entire two-hour affair was something of a let-down. Many observers thought Tommy Douglas had performed the best of the lot.

The New Democratic party, under the influence of Quebec academics committed to the party's brand of social democracy, had also accepted the principle that Canada's two founding peoples constituted two sociological groupings, each with inherent political rights. There was no better place for Trudeau to attack the NDP than in Douglas' B.C. riding of Burnaby-Seymour. In a visit, he charged the NDP with promoting one policy in Quebec and another in the rest of Canada. "In Quebec they are talking about two nations and about special status, and in the rest of the country they are talking about one nation and no special status – and they think the Canadian people do not know about this." Trudeau made certain his own message was consistent throughout the country. He unveiled his six-point charter for bilingualism, based on the recommendations of the Bi and Bi commission, in Sherbrooke, Quebec. "We talk of two official languages in Canada and we talk of one nation and we talk about it in every province."

An early Gallup Poll put the Liberals ahead, 43 per cent to 34 per cent for the Conservatives, a lead that grew but slowly throughout the campaign. The Trudeau phenomenon had apparently captured the public's imagination early on; if it held up a majority government would be assured. Each party added thousands of new recruits; in Toronto Davenport Liberal membership spiraled from 150 to more than five thousand. The riding's nominating convention was moved from a neighborhood hall to the Coliseum building of the Canadian National Exhibition.

In Vegreville, Alberta, three thousand Conservatives balloted all night before nominating Don Mazankowski at five in the morning.[9] Some of the most raucous nominating meetings took place in Quebec where *Le Ralliement des Créditistes,* a populist Quebec version of Social Credit headed by Réal Caouette that had won twenty seats in 1963 but only nine in 1965, put up seventy candidates. Social Credit, by now a waning force in the West, managed to run 31 candidates in Alberta and B.C. In a clear sign of the party's decline, former national leader Robert Thomson stood for re-election as a Conservative in Red Deer, Alberta. The NDP set out ambitiously to match the Liberals and Conservatives and remarkably, ended up contesting all but one of 264 ridings.

June 25 dawned as a beautiful early summer's day across Canada. By the time the polls closed on the west coast, more than eight million Canadians, the largest number ever, had cast ballots. The Liberal party booked a double suite for Trudeau in the Chateau Laurier and it was there that he watched the returns, accompanied by the Pearsons and clutch of party organizers. Spending much of the evening alone in a small bedroom working on the statement he would make later that night, Trudeau watched apprehensively as the first returns came in from Newfoundland and the other Atlantic provinces. Things were not developing as they should; despite Joey Smallwood's fierce support, Liberals lost six of their seven Newfoundland seats, holding only Burin-Burgeo, the fiefdom of broadcaster Don Jamieson. Conservative winners included Frank Moores, a future premier of the province. Prince Edward Island was another wipe-out, all four seats going Conservative. Less surprising were the Nova Scotia results where loyalty to Bob Stanfield gave the Conservatives ten of eleven seats. The only Liberal survivor was Allan McEachen, the minister of health and welfare, re-elected in Cape Breton-Highlands-Canso by a margin of just over six hundred votes. New Brunswick, long a Liberal stronghold where the party enjoyed strong Acadian support, split its ten seats equally, a pick-up of one for the Conservatives. It was the only Atlantic province where the Conservative vote fell below fifty-one per cent. Coming out of the Atlantic region, the Conservatives were triumphant in 25 of 32 seats.

The Maritime results were received nervously by the Liberals gathered at the Chateau Laurier. Would Trudeau's magnetism be enough to overcome the opposition to his strong federalist stance? Claude Ryan had urged the readers of *Le Devoir* to vote Conservative – "All things being equal it is necessary to prefer the candidates of Conservative leader Robert Stanfield to Prime Minister Trudeau" – and the recruitment of Marcel Faribault had brought several other star-quality candidates into Tory ranks. It wasn't enough to deter Quebecers from supporting one of their own, in much the way they'd rallied behind Wilfrid Laurier in every election between 1896 and 1917. The 56 seats the Liberals would win there this night, however, were one less than they'd captured under Pearson in 1965. This was no help to the Conservatives, who retained only four of their eight seats. Faribault was beaten decisively in Gamelin where a travelling salesman standing for the Liberals won by a better than two-to-one margin. The defeat of two of the ablest Conservative MPs, Heward Grafftey in Missisquoi and Roger Regimbal in Argenteuil, was put down to the loss of the English-speaking vote. The spoiler of the night was Réal Caouette and his *Créditistes* who bounded back to win 14 seats, a big improvement from 1965. Their support came from a mostly rural slice of disaffected voters who cared little about constitutional issues and were mistrustful of Trudeau's promise of a Just Society. On the island of Montreal, the Liberals took 65 per cent of the popular vote, infuriating Quebec nationalists who saw the city slipping away from its francophone heritage. Trudeau carried Mount Royal by a 20-to-one margin. Liberal leadership contender Eric Kierans edged out the NDP's best hope, Quebec leader Robert Cliche, by 2,500 votes in Duvernay. Other NDP hopefuls who lost that night included two well-known literary figures, Laurier LaPierre and Charles Taylor. The list of Liberal wins went on: Gérard Pelletier in Hochelaga, Jean Chrétien in Saint-Maurice, Jean Marchand in Langelier, Bud Drury in Westmount.

The results came tumbling in from Ontario as the Quebec returns were still being absorbed. If Trudeaumania had failed to ignite the Maritimes, and had merely maintained the status quo in Quebec, it burned furiously in Ontario and especially in Toronto. Of Ontario's 88 seats, 64 went Liberal against 17 Conservative, six NDP, and one independent. Not a single Tory was elected in the Metro Toronto area, as the Liberals took almost half the popular vote. Dalton Camp, beaten in Don Valley by Robert Kaplan, said he'd lost not to his opponent but to Trudeau. John Turner captured his new seat, Ottawa-Carleton, by a 17,000 vote margin. The only Conservative to survive the Trudeau landslide in the Golden Horseshoe was Lincoln Alexander in Hamilton West, the first black to be elected to the House. The Conservatives lost Michael Starr's Oshawa seat to an up and coming young university professor standing for the NDP, Ed Broadbent. It was the worst Conservative performance in history, even dipping under their previous low of 22 Ontario seats in 1874.

With the Liberals verging on a majority – 127 elected heading into Manitoba – the results from the West came as a bonus. In 1965, only a single Liberal had been elected in all 48 of the prairie ridings. Tonight, with three seats eliminated by redistribution, tight three-way contests were being fought all over the plains. In Manitoba, discontent over tax increases by the provincial Tory government helped the Liberals win five seats, leaving the other five in Tory hands. Former Conservative premier Duff Roblin was among the defeated. The NDP elected three members, including the venerable Stanley Knowles in Winnipeg North Centre and a well-regarded young Winnipeg academic, Ed Schreyer, in Selkirk. Saskatchewan returned six NDPers, five Conservatives and two Liberals. Only in Alberta did Conservative strength persist, with fifteen Tories elected to four Liberals. Don Mazankowski proved to be one of the biggest Tory vote-getters, carrying Vegreville with ten thousand more votes than his Liberal opponent, the mayor of the town. Not a single Social Crediter was elected. Although the prairie split favoured the Conservatives with 25 seats to 11 Liberals and nine NDP, Trudeau found himself assured of a majority even before the polls closed in British Columbia and the Yukon. Sixteen victories in B.C., plus the lone North West Territory seat won by a Liberal, simply fattened Trudeau's majority. In the process, Ray Perrault, a former provincial Liberal leader, beat NDP leader Tommy Douglas by 138 votes in Burnaby-Seymour. In Kamloops-Cariboo, Liberal Leonard Marchand became the first native Canadian MP to be elected, defeating Davie Fulton. Erik Neilsen carried the Yukon for the Conservatives by 62 votes. The new House would have 155 Liberals, 72 Conservatives, 22 NDP, and 14 *Créditistes*. The one independent, Lucien Lamoureaux, would become Speaker.

Robert Stanfield conceded defeat long before Trudeau went on television just before midnight. The Tory leader was gracious as always, but John Diefenbaker could not resist the opportunity to issue a bitter judgment: "The Conservative party has suffered a calamitous disaster." None of that mattered to the excited crowd awaiting Trudeau when he descended to the lobby of the Chateau Laurier to face TV cameras and reporters. A wilted red rose in his lapel, he pledged to work to "build a stronger, more prosperous and just Canada." The work would begin immediately, he said:

> "For me (the election) was a great adventure of discovery. The election has been fought in a mood of optimism and of confidence in our future. We have seen an unexpected upsurge of interest and involvement. But it was also a mood of tolerance. There is a strong desire amongst Canadians not only to make it possible for both language groups and our many cultural communities to coexist in all parts of the country without assimilation, but to take advantage of our diversity."

Newspapers headlines the next day told the story. GO, GO TRUDEAU – AND HE DID, bannered the Toronto *Star*. Peter Newman, the paper's Ottawa editor, wrote in a front page column that "Trudeau's resounding victory yesterday was plainly a mandate to settle the national unity crisis in Canada." Canadians had cast their ballots, Newman added, "for the only party leader who was able to state – and reiterate – a clear and firm position on the French-English dilemma."

The Aftermath

For all that Pierre Trudeau's charismatic appeal attracted more voters to the Liberal party – its share of the popular vote rose to 45.5 per cent from 40.2 per cent in 1965 – the results were uneven across the country. The new government had to live with only spotty support in the West and almost no representation in Atlantic Canada. Trudeau thought his own role had been "a little overplayed by the media" and he promptly set out on a technocratic reordering of how government should function. Studies were commissioned and experts brought in, but the changes entrenched power even more solidly in the PMO – the Prime Minister's Office – and alienated many conscientious MPs in all parties. One review led to an early reduction in Canada's commitment to the North Atlantic Treaty Organization. It reflected the Canadian view at the time that the country had no real need for a strong military, a de-emphasis that continued through the end of the century. Of more concern to the government in its first term were the twin issues of bilingualism and the constitution, the two forces that had motivated Trudeau to enter federal politics. The promised Official Languages Act was passed in 1969, enshrining official bilingualism at the federal level and launching a massive program to teach French to English-speaking civil servants. Not all welcomed the opportunity. The act also changed the packaging laws of the country and created resentment, especially in the West, to finding French on corn flakes boxes at breakfast. The first real effort to achieve constitutional reform ended in failure when the Victoria Charter – so named for the conference in that city in 1971 – floundered when Premier Robert Bourassa, under pressure from advisors such as Claude Ryan, withheld approval despite the fact Quebec would have enjoyed a veto over future changes. The failure to replace the

British North America Act with a made in Canada constitution so discouraged Trudeau that he vowed to take the constitution off the political agenda. The government's other main initiatives in its first term reflected the trend to bigger and more expensive government common in the 1960s across North America and in Europe. A Department of Regional Economic Expansion was created to help establish new industries in underdeveloped regions, especially Quebec and the Maritimes. There were new programs to make work for young people right across the country. All these measures ramped up government spending.

The defining moment of Trudeau's first term came in October 1970 when a small band of separatist terrorists calling themselves the *Front de Liberation du Québec* (FLQ), kidnapped the British trade commissioner in Montreal, James Cross, then seized the Quebec minister of labour, Pierre Laporte. Only later would it be learned that these extremists, some of whom had been trained in Palestine and Jordan, had committed over 200 political actions in the previous decade, including bombings and bank hold-ups, causing at least three deaths by bombing and two by gunfire. The country seemed on the verge of chaos and the term "apprehended insurrection" came into the language as fear grew that Quebec harbored a well organized underground movement capable of unimaginable outrages. While provincial politicians panicked and some Quebec intellectuals theorized about the merits of establishing a provisional government, Trudeau acted. In a nationwide broadcast, he told Canadians he had imposed the War Measures Act to deal with "violent and fanatical men attempting to destroy the unity and the freedom of Canada."

> "If a democratic society is to continue to exist, it must be able to root out the cancer of an armed, revolutionary movement that is bent on destroying the very basis of our freedom. The War Measures Act gives sweeping powers to the Government. It also suspends the operation of the Canadian Bill of Rights. I can assure you that the Government is most reluctant to

seek such powers, and did so only when it became crystal clear that the situation could not be controlled unless some extraordinary assistance was made available on an urgent basis."

The FLQ's response was to strangle Laporte and stuff his body in the trunk of a car. Several hundred people suspected of separatist sentiments were arrested; all were eventually freed without being charged, and the members of the cell were taken into custody in a deal that allowed them to go into exile in Cuba. Trudeau was criticized severely by civil rights advocates. When a CBC reporter demanded to know how far he would go to deal with the crisis, Trudeau's response was "Just watch me!" It was an answer that earned the respect if not the support of the entire nation. Eventually it would be realized that the FLQ was nothing more than a tiny rabble and had never constituted a serious threat. None of that was known at the time. Trudeau's actions, extreme though they may have been, were taken to defend the state against unknown danger. Thirty years on, the United States would find itself in a situation requiring drastic steps to combat terrorism; the American government's response bears some striking similarities to Trudeau's course of action.

Canadians breathed a sigh of relief when the crisis passed, but it did not make up for the growing dissatisfaction with Trudeau's autocratic style ("Why should I sell your wheat?") or his failure to deliver on the expectations of the Just Society. The 1972 election turned into a near disaster when Trudeau ignored the advice of political operatives around him and conducted a campaign that was both irrelevant and dull. The charisma was gone, Trudeau's pedantic lectures bored the voters, and the "election goodies" being offered across the country – including a new waterfront park and a second airport for Toronto – failed to impress. In Quebec, Claude Ryan's *Le Devoir* again endorsed Robert Stanfield and on October 30, after a campaign in which Stanfield benefited from a strong Conservative organizational effort and the NDP made much of an attack on "corporate welfare bums" by new leader David Lewis, Canadians rendered a split decision. For a time on election night the Liberals and Conservatives were hung in a deadlock at 109 seats each. It took almost two weeks for recounts to confirm the final outcome: 109 Liberals, 107 Conservatives, 31 NDP, 15 *Créditiste* and two independents. Sixty-four ridings had changed hands, most of them Liberal seats going to the Conservatives and NDP. Liberal losses included 28 seats in Ontario and 20 of their Western members. Only Quebec stayed loyal. The NDP went from 22 to 31 seats, winning the balance of power.

Liberal party operatives huddled in shock and dismay. Two of the most determined voices calling for a make-over of the party's election strategies were Jerry Grafstein, the clever Toronto communications lawyer and Gordon Dryden, of the briefly famous Unity Bank of Canada that had been conceived as a lender of first choice to ethnic borrowers. Joined by management consultant Jim Coutts and other insiders the group succeeded in bringing back to prominence another Toronto operative, Keith Davey. The consummate party organizer, Davey had been at Lester Pearson's side in the campaigns that defeated Diefenbaker, but had taken much of the blame for Pearson's failure to win a majority in 1965. Now, with Trudeau willing to accept advice from the pols, "the Rainmaker" was given a second chance. As Davey began to fuse together an effective new election team, Trudeau started giving lunches for Liberal delegations from around the country. He brought in defeated Toronto MP Martin O'Connell as his principal secretary and shook up his cabinet, giving each minister, in addition to their departmental duties, political responsibility for a group of ridings.

In Parliament, the minority government focused on legislation that would win the support of the NDP. There were generous tax concessions for most of the middle class, including a greatly expanded program of Registered Retirement Savings Plans. These soon became the main vehicle for private pension savings, thanks to enlarged tax deductibility. Another provision that would cost the government billions of dollars was the indexation of income tax against inflation, protecting taxpayers from being pushed into higher tax brackets. None of these measures were as fundamental as the introduction of unemployment insurance (1940), family allowances (1944), Old Age Security (1952), the Canada Pension Plan (1965), or medicare (1967), but they all helped restore the Trudeau government's popularity. Growing more comfortable, Trudeau began to taunt the Opposition in the House, accusing New Democrats of "hanging onto us like seagulls, claiming that they are really steering the ship."[10] The 1974 budget from John Turner, the finance minister at the time, was intentionally designed to provoke the hostility of the NDP and cause an election. When the government lost a vote of confidence on the budget, Pierre Trudeau became only the third Prime Minister in Canadian history (after Arthur Meighen and John Diefenbaker) to be defeated in Parliament. For two years, Canadians had enjoyed the dance of government generosity. Soon it would be time to pay the piper. Between 1968 and 1974, the government had roughly balanced its expenditures and the federal debt hovered around $18 billion. With spending rising and taxes dropping from 1973 on, that figure would rise to $200 billion by the time Trudeau would leave office in 1984. Under his successor, Brian Mulroney, the culture of entitlement built up over two decades – and later on, even more significant tax cuts to interest groups – would see the debt spiral to $500 billion.

The election held on July 8 1974 – the first summer vote since 1953 – generated a wave of good feeling for the Trudeau government. It was not exactly Trudeaumania again, but Canadians were pleased with the Prime Minister's more approachable style and the positive performance of the economy. The new Parliament had 141 Liberals, a comfortable majority, facing just 95 Conservatives, 16 NDPers and eleven Social Crediters. It was Robert Stanfield's third straight loss to Trudeau and again the defeat was to a degree self-inflicted, arising partly from Stanfield's vow to impose wage and price controls to curb the rising rate of inflation. "Zap, you're frozen," Trudeau mocked during the campaign. He had won the election handily – with his beautiful young wife, Margaret at his side during much of the campaign – but his personal life was beginning to intrude on his political concentration. Margaret, who never managed to summon the maturity needed in the spouse of a powerful public figure, took to a hospital bed for psychiatric counseling and Trudeau left MPs cooling their heels for three months before recalling Parliament. When he did, there was little in the way of meaningful legislation until, more than a year later in one of the great flip flops of modern Canadian politics, Trudeau imposed wage and price controls on a stunned public. The decision infuriated John Turner, who resigned as finance minister. The next blow came from Quebec, with the election of the Parti Quebecois on November 15, 1976. On a single day in late 1978, the government lost five by-elections. Finally, at the end of a full five-year mandate, Trudeau faced the electorate on May 22, 1979. Under a new and untried leader, Joe Clark, the Progressive Conservative party won 136 seats, just shy of a majority. The Liberals dropped to 114, the NDP went up to 26. "We will govern as if we had a majority," Clark told the country. It lasted nine months. By ignoring the six *Créditistes* who had been elected from Quebec, Clark's government fell in the vote on its first budget. Trudeau had by now submitted his resignation, but after frantic appeals from all corners of the Liberal party, he agreed to return. On the night of February 18, 1980, surveying the election results that would miraculously restore him to office, Trudeau told party supporters gathered at the Chateau Laurier, "Welcome to the 1980s." Then he quoted these words of poet Robert Frost:

> The woods are lovely, dark and deep
> But I have promises to keep
> And miles to go before I sleep

The greatest promise Trudeau had to keep was to himself; to use his new and unexpected lease on power to repatriate the British North America Act into a Canadian constitution, with a freedom charter that would establish the rights of the individual as paramount to the rights of government. First, however, came the struggle to win the Quebec referendum that Parti Québécois premier Réne Lévesque had set for May 20, 1980. The referendum, a vote to empower the Quebec government to negotiate "sovereignty-association" with Ottawa, demanded a simple yes or no answer to a convoluted question. Public opinion in Quebec seemed to be moving with the PQ, raising the prospect that a yes vote would shatter the uneasy truce emanating from Ottawa's recent moves to entrench bilingualism while relinquishing significant power to the provinces. Trudeau's intervention in the campaign proved decisive. Appealing to Quebecers to vote no, he pledged to accept a federalist victory as a mandate for constitutional renewal: "We will start immediately the mechanism of renewing the constitution, and we will not stop until it is done." When Quebec voted 60-40 to reject the sovereignist option, Trudeau called the premiers into a series of conferences to work out a new constitutional deal.

The struggle was bitter but short-lived. There were initial reversals. The British parliament rejected the federal government's request to proceed without the concurrence of the provinces. The Supreme Court of Canada held that at least "substantial" – although not necessarily "unanimous" – agreement of the provinces would be needed to legitimize Ottawa's intentions. When Trudeau called the premiers into session at the old railway station in the capital on November 2 1981, he confronted them with a new Constitution Act built around a Charter of Rights and Freedoms that clearly limited the privileges of both levels of government. It also provided what had been a long-elusive formula covering any future amendments; any changes would require consent of seven of the provinces having at least fifty per cent of the population. The provision actually gave Quebec less of a lever on constitutional change than the Victoria version that had been rejected a decade earlier by Robert Bourassa. After three days of interminable discussion, the English premiers had had enough. In a "kitchen accord" negotiated in the back halls of the conference centre, every province but Quebec accepted Ottawa's terms. Any province would be free to opt out of federal programs, and Quebec could excuse itself from any constitutional arrangement affecting language and culture, with full financial compensation. On the Charter of Rights and Freedoms, Trudeau reluctantly agreed to give the provinces a "notwithstanding" clause that could be used to exempt provincial legislation from the Charter for up to five years. In return, minority language education rights were guaranteed. In Trudeau's view, it was not perfect but he was prepared to accept less than perfection to bring a new Constitution into being. Lévesque left Ottawa infuriated and in despair. In separatist mythology, the circumstances around the after-hours agreement soon became known as the "night of the long knives,' a betrayal of Quebec's interests by its English-language provincial cousins.[11] In fact, Lévesque had simply been out-negotiated and out-maneuvered.

Living With the Charter

At a ceremony on Parliament Hill on April 17, 1982, Queen Elizabeth signed the proclamation of the new Constitution of Canada. "Today, at long last, Canada is acquiring full and complete national sovereignty," Trudeau said in the presence of the Queen.

> "The Constitution of Canada has come home. The most fundamental law of the land will now be capable of being amended in Canada, without any further recourse to the Parliament of the United Kingdom. We now have a Charter which defines the kind of country in which we wish to live, and guarantees the basic rights and freedoms which each of us shall enjoy as a citizen of Canada. The government of Quebec decided that it wasn't enough. It decided not to participate in this ceremony, celebrating Canada's full independence. I know that many Quebecers feel themselves pulled in two directions by that decision. But one need look only

at the results of the referendum in May, 1980, to realize how strong is the attachment to Canada among the people of Quebec. By definition, the silent majority does not make a lot of noise; it is content to make history."

Trudeau had coined another aphorism to add to the legion of those he'd already expressed.

The new constitution's paramount segment, the Canadian Charter of Rights and Freedoms, drastically altered the relationships between Canadians and their governments, and among themselves. Often criticized for allowing judges to makes rules that only Parliament should create, or for catering to disadvantaged groups – women, aboriginals, ethnic communities and others – in ways that might discriminate against majorities, the Charter in twenty years became "as Canadian as the beaver, the hockey puck and medicare."[12] If Canadian society has become more egalitarian, tolerant and open in the past two decades – which it assuredly has, although the virtues of these changes are argued by some – it is the Charter that has been primarily responsible. It is only necessary to recall circumstances in which Canadians found themselves before the Charter to appreciate its positive impact. No longer are accused persons required to prove themselves innocent (as the Narcotics Act once required); no longer can one spouse be denied equal treatment in marriage break-up (unlike the ranch wife who was left penniless after 25 years of helping her husband raise cattle); nor can established dentists, accountants and lawyers enrich their quasi-monopolies by preventing their peers from advertising their services. No longer are women denied the right to abortion, nor can the insane who have been acquitted of crimes be kept locked up indefinitely at the pleasure of a provincial cabinet. The murky concept of the "public interest" is no longer justification for denial of bail. The Lord's Day Act no longer keeps shops shuttered on Sunday. Public servants cannot be denied the right to support political candidates of their choice. Nationwide legal firms came into existence only after an Alberta rule prohibiting such networking was overturned. Quebec, which brought in its own Charter of Rights, has been especially affected. The landmark Supreme Court ruling on a province's right to secede – perhaps its most important decision under the Charter – established a precise legal framework for dealing with any future attempts to split the country. Whole sections of Quebec's French-only language laws were struck down. Governments have been forced into wholesale rewriting of their statutes to eliminate discriminatory sections. Other decisions driven by the Charter have been equally important, if on a less momentous scale. The Charter's focus on freedom of expression has even extended into the sphere of commercial rights, which had not been contemplated by its framers. The Charter has promoted a pan-Canadian vision of equality of rights, facilitated greater access to the justice system, and freed Canadians from an array of restrictive laws affecting their right to work, their personal freedom, and their control over their individual lives. It has become a cornerstone in Canada's striving for a more just society.

With the new constitution and the Charter which carried forward Trudeau's strategy to institutionalize bilingualism within a framework of individual rights now in place, the main objectives of his public life were accomplished. Trudeau enjoyed less success in the economic field. A short-lived National Energy Program taxed away the profits the Alberta oil industry had stood to gain from rising world prices – much to the advantage of eastern consumers—but decimated jobs and provincial revenues. The experience soured Alberta on Trudeau Liberalism to a degree from which the party has still not recovered. An attempt to impose onerous new tax measures on corporations failed when the 1981 budget of Finance minister Allan McEachen had to be watered down. Public spending continued to grow while tax revenues fell during the recession of the early 1980s. Trudeau's final attempt to add a global perspective to his legacy largely floundered when he set out in 1983 to travel around the globe presenting a set of proposals that he believed would ease international tensions and lessen the chances of the Cold War turning into a hot one. His peace offensive largely ignored, Trudeau retired to the Prime Minister's residence in Ottawa and on February 28, 1984, took his famous "walk in the snow" – the night of the city's worst storm of the year – and decided it was time, finally, to resign. He had been Prime Minister for 16 years; only John A. Macdonald and Mackenzie King surpassed his length of tenure.

Pierre Elliott Trudeau left office with the world, and Canada's place in it, presenting a vastly different set of challenges than when he won the election of 1968 as an exciting and charismatic new personality who seemed perfectly cast to lead an optimistic country into a new and brighter future. Trudeau aroused in Canadians aspirations and expectations that were wholly consistent with the characteristics of truly transformational leaders. He engaged Canadians as no politician has done before or since and in the process charmed, challenged and angered broad swaths of the electorate. His leadership continued to reveal itself long after his retirement, as in his intervention in the Meech Lake and Charlottetown debates, and his continued insistence that Quebecers needed no insulating barriers to protect their economic or cultural ambitions. In the words of one set of biographers, Pierre Trudeau "haunts us still."[13] If this is so, it is because instead of brokering compromise among the chief elements in Canadian society – a tactic for which at least one earlier Prime Minister would be most remembered – he insisted on the logic of rigorous analysis and the certainty of principled advocacy. His death on September 28, 2000 brought about, as sometimes occurs when principled leaders pass away, a renewal of Trudeau's charismatic endowment. The turning point reached in the 1968 election consolidated the emergence of the new Canada that had been taking shape since World War II. It vaulted the country from an age of post-colonialism into an era of post-nationalism, a geography in which Canada will struggle for many years to learn how it fits and where it belongs.

CHAPTER FOURTEEN

The Federal Election of November 21, 1988

THE ISSUES

Signing of the Canada-United States Free Trade Agreement leads to a dramatic confrontation between the Prime Minister, Brian Mulroney, and the Leader of the Liberal Party, John Turner. Outcome of the election will turn on the Progressive Conservative counter-attack against the charge that free trade is a "sell-out" of Canada's future. With Mulroney also pressing for constitutional change, the Meech Lake accord wins all-party agreement but Turner's approval of the deal is used by supporters of leadership rival Jean Chrétien to undermine him. Voting-splitting between the Opposition parties leads to a second Mulroney majority government, passage of the free trade pact, and its replacement by an enlarged North American Free Trade Agreement (NAFTA).

THE PERSONALITIES

PROGRESSIVE CONSERVATIVE PARTY
Brian Mulroney, Prime Minister, MP for Manicouagan, Que.
Don Mazankowski, Deputy Prime Minister, MP for Vegreville, Alberta

LIBERAL PARTY
John Turner, MP for Vancouver-Quadra, B. C. and Leader of the Opposition

NEW DEMOCRATIC PARTY
Ed Broadbent, MP for Oshawa, Ont., Leader

REFORM PARTY OF CANADA
Preston Manning, Leader

THE RESULTS

	SEATS	VOTES
Progressive Conservatives	170	5,625,288 (43 %)
Liberals	82	4,168,230 (31.9%)
New Democratic Party	43	1,661,745 (20.4%)
Reform Party and others	–	619,779 (4.7%)

Above: Brian Mulroney and Mila campaigning at Toronto's Harbourfront, 1984. Below: Mulroney and Turner confront each other in dramatic TV debate.

FREE TRADE II:
CANADA TAKES THE PLUNGE

The Federal Election of 1988

The powerful klieg lights bathing the television studio illuminated every crease on the faces of the three men standing at their lecterns. Brian Mulroney, John Turner and Ed Broadbent were waiting to begin the leaders' debate that has become the centrepiece of North American elections since John F. Kennedy and Richard Nixon first squared off in their presidential contest of 1960. The Prime Minister had spent the weekend at his official residence, 24 Sussex Street, preparing for this occasion. As always, he was boundlessly confident that he would be able to dispatch his chief rival, Liberal leader John Turner, just as he had done four years earlier in their first, memorable encounter. Ed Broadbent, the leader of the New Democratic party, was there almost at the sufferance of the two main antagonists; there had even been talk of it being a two-man debate. Elsewhere in the cavernous CJOH broadcast centre on this night of October 25, 1988, two hundred journalists had gathered to cover the debate in the same way six million other Canadians would follow it – by watching TV. The only difference was that the journalists' ranks would be infiltrated by politicians of all parties, there to "spin doctor" the event and convince the media their guy had won it all.

It was the half-way mark of the election and to this point, the efforts of the Liberals and New Democrats to focus on free trade had failed to lift either party in the opinion polls. An Angus Reid poll on September 26 had the Conservatives poised to win another majority; it gave the Tories 40 per cent of the decided vote, the NDP 31 and the Liberals 26. When Mulroney and the Progressive Conservatives won their first majority in 1984, ending John Turner's short reign as the successor to Pierre Trudeau, free trade had never been an issue. Turner, sworn in on June 30, 1984, sent Canadians to the polls on September 4. In a campaign that was more about Liberal patronage appointments than government policy, the glamorous sheen that had enveloped Turner through his years as Minister of Finance and Prime Minister-in-waiting dropped away to reveal a politician who was both rusty in handling the media and in meeting the public, and at times ill-informed about his party's policies. Mulroney, who had engineered the overthrow of his leader Joe Clark after Clark's defeat and the re-election of Pierre Trudeau in 1980, took every advantage of Turner's discomfort. His greatest moment came in the 1984 television debate when Mulroney demanded to know why Turner had found it necessary to make a score of patronage appointments just before the election. Turner's response, "I had no option" was based on the fact that if Pierre Trudeau had made the appointments before leaving office, the new government would have been reduced to minority status. "You had an option, sir," Mulroney insisted, "to say no and you chose to say yes ... that is an avowal of failure ... a confession of non-leadership and this country needs leadership." The exchange destroyed what credibility Turner had at the time. The TV debate was a crucial factor in the outcome that gave Mulroney the greatest majority in Canadian history, 211 seats against only forty Liberals and thirty New Democrats.

Remembering the impact of that exchange, the leaders prepared carefully for the two debates that would be held this time, one in each official language. Tonight's followed by 24 hours the French debate. All three leaders spoke French, Mulroney brilliantly, often laced with the argot of the streets learned from his school boy days in a tough Quebec paper-making town; Turner elegantly as befitted a man of his education and experience; Broadbent adequately if at times somewhat strained as he sought to convey the nuances of a particular position.

The debate began with Turner, who knew his personal ratings lagged behind both Mulroney and Broadbent, declaring that "What is at stake is not the popularity of a leader, but the future of our country." Mulroney counter-punched on the leadership issue: "What is at stake is in fact leadership, the leadership of Canada." For Broadbent, portraying himself as the common man, the election was about "our families, our children, our parents, our grandparents." The French debate didn't seem to change many voters' minds. Quebeckers were more concerned about coping with an unseasonable weekend snow storm that knocked out power to thousands of people in Montreal. The *Gazette* settled for a headline that summed up the lack of serious policy discussion: "You lack courage, Turner tells PM." He had criticized Mulroney for not having the courage to withdraw from free trade negotiations after realizing he was not going to get the deal he wanted.

Mulroney, pleased at how the French debate had gone, felt confident that tonight's three-hour session – a mix of one-on-ones interspersed with all three together – would also go well. Turner, who had rehearsed extensively, also felt he was ready despite some serious back pain and worry about a threatened revolt against his leadership. He'd been advised to save his strength for the final hour. After taking a break in his trailer parked behind the station, Turner returned to the studio for his final set-to with Mulroney. When Pamela Wallin, representing the CTV, asked how the two men would protect women whose jobs might be lost because of free trade, Mulroney answered by quoting an Economic Council of Canada study saying the pact would create 250,000 new jobs. Turner used the question to ask Mulroney why he'd declined to have a debate exclusively on free trade. He went on:

> "I think the Canadian people have a right to know why, when your primary objective was to get unfettered and secure access into the American market, we did not get it – why did you not put clauses in to protect our social programs in this negotiation that we will have on the definition of subsidies, where the heavy weight of the American republic will be put in against us. Why did that not happen?" Then he added, dramatically, "I think you have sold us out!"

It was the beginning of the most remarkable two and one-half minutes of Canadian political theatre:

"I happen to believe that, once you ..." continued Turner.

"Mr. Turner, just one second."

"Once any region – "

"You do not have a monopoly on patriotism," fired back Mulroney.

"Once – "

"And I resent the fact of your implication that only you are a Canadian. "

"I'm sorry," Turner replied, "I – "

"I want to tell you that I come from a Canadian family – "

"Once – "

"And I love Canada," added Mulroney.

"Once any – "

"And that's why I did it," Mulroney finished, "to promote prosperity – "

"Once any country – "

"And don't you – "

"Once any country yields its economic levers," Turner insisted.

"Don't you impugn my motives or anyone else's!" Mulroney interjected, but Turner was by now firing on all cylinders.

"Once a country yields its energy – "

"We have not done it."

"Once a country yields it agriculture, once a country –"

"Wrong again."

"—opens itself up to a subsidy war with the United States –"

"Wrong again."

"—in terms of definition, then the political ability –"

"You – "

"—of this country to sustain the influence of the United States, to remain as it is, a competitive nation, that – "

"Mr. Turner."

"—will go on forever, and – "

"Mr. Turner."

"—that is the issue of this election, sir."

"Mr. Turner, let me tell you something, sir. This country is only about one hundred and twenty years old, but my own father, fifty-five years ago, went himself, as a labourer, with hundreds of other Canadians and with their own hands, in northeastern Quebec, they built a little town and schools and churches and they, in their own way, were nation-building in the same way as the waves of immigrants from the Ukraine and eastern Europe rolled back the prairies and, in their own way, in their own time, they were nation-building because they loved Canada."

"I admire what your father did," Turner responded. "My grandfather moved to British Columbia. My mother was a miner's daughter there. We are just as Canadian as you are, Mr. Mulroney, but I will tell you this. You mentioned one hundred and twenty years of history. We built a country east and west and north. We built it on an infrastructure that deliberately resisted the continental pressure of the United States. For one hundred and twenty years, we have done it. With one signature of a pen, you have reversed that, thrown us into the north-south influence of the United States – "

"With a – " Mulroney interrupted.

"—and will reduce us, I am sure," Turner added, "to a colony of the United States, because when the economic levers go, the political independence is sure to follow."

The emotional vibrations of this riveting exchange were being felt in living rooms across the country. When Mulroney defended the Free Trade Agreement as only a "commercial document can- cellable on six months' notice," an astonishingly vapid statement, voters were concluding – as later polls would confirm – that Turner was winning the debate, even if he would not win the election. This was not, however, the message the Prime Minister heard later that night at 24 Sussex Street when he phoned allies across the country. In his final call at 1:30 a.m., he was told by a friend, "Well, you can sleep easy tonight – you won."[1]

The two and one-half minutes that it took for these exchanges dominated media headlines and coffee shop discussions for the next three weeks. They dramatically changed the contours of the 1988 election, transforming it from what might have been the routine re-election of a government of only middling popularity, to one of the major turning points of Canadian history. The election had reversed the traditional positions of the two major parties on free trade and its outcome would lead to a new and enlarged economic environment for every Canadian business, whether in the domestic market where foreign players would now be entitled to "national treatment" – competing under the same conditions as Canadian companies – or in the international market where Canadians would be on an equal footing with their U.S. rivals. Globalization was striking home, and while many Canadians were excited by the challenge, others were fearful.

Brian Mulroney was a late convert to free trade. When he challenged Joe Clark for the Conservative party leadership in 1983 he declared that "This country could not survive with a policy of unfettered free trade ... we'd be swamped." After wresting the leadership from Clark and becoming Prime Minister, Mulroney found that high ranking public servants were examining the issue seriously. They were worried about rising protectionism in the U.S. and the recent formation of the new European trade bloc. Free trade became a matter of public discussion when Donald Macdonald, the former Liberal finance minister, came out for it in the report of his Royal Commission on Canada's Economic Prospects. It was time, Macdonald said, for a "leap of faith" that would put Canada in a position to reap the benefits of integration with a larger and more buoyant marketplace. There are some who argue that Mulroney always allowed opportunity to outweigh principle, and this is why he so eagerly adopted free trade as a mantra for his government. As with most generalizations, this was not entirely true; Mulroney early on expressed opposition to capital punishment when the death penalty still had high support among right-wing conservatives. As the party's new leader, he spoke up courageously in support of bilingualism when Manitoba PCs were filibustering a French-language-rights bill in that province.

Mulroney had always displayed the characteristics of a gladhander; biographer John Sawatsky notes that he "shamelessly inflated his rhetoric and often took flight into hyperbole. He exaggerated automatically and constantly."[2] Growing up in the small town of Baie-Comeau, Quebec, of an Irish Catholic family in a town of French workers dominated by an English Protestant clique, Mulroney learned early on that charm could effectively substitute for connection. His ability to carry a tune got him noticed by Colonel Robert McCormick, the American newspaper publisher who owned the North Shore Paper Company where his father worked as an electrician. Having heard Mulroney in a church choir, McCormick invited the boy to sing for him whenever he visited. Sent to a Catholic high school in Chatham, New Brunswick, Mulroney went on to St. Francis Xavier university in Nova Scotia where he became involved in student politics and served as prime minister of the school's model parliament. He then spent a year at the law school of Dalhousie University in Halifax before transferring to Laval University in Quebec City. Mulroney could be brazen in his overtures to his elders; he shamelessly pursued John Diefenbaker and got to the point where he could call the Prime Minister on the telephone just to impress his friends. Contacts he made at school would last Mulroney throughout his life; Peter White, an advisor and fixer to Conrad Black, Sam Wakim, a key supporter, Michael Meighen, grandson of a prime minister whom he would one day name to the Senate, Lowell Murray, another future Senator appointee and constitutional advisor on the Meech Lake and Charlottetown accords. Another classmate was Lucien Bouchard.

Mulroney wangled an articling position with the prestigious Montreal law firm of Howard, Cate Ogilvy but almost lost it when he twice failed his Quebec bar exams, passing only narrowly on the third attempt. He was dropped into sensitive labour negotiations involving a bitter strike of longshoremen at St. Lawrence river ports and successfully represented the Shipping Federation before a commission of inquiry. Mulroney was then tapped to help one of the firm's best clients, Paul Desmarais of Power Corp., settle a damaging strike at *La Presse*, Quebec's largest newspaper. He had a devastating ability to cross-examine witnesses, which brought him to public attention when working on the Cliche Commission of Inquiry into corruption and violence in the Quebec construction industry.

By 1976, when Robert Stanfield stepped down as leader of the Progressive Conservative party, Mulroney was ready to try for the political big time. He ran for leader despite never having held a parliamentary seat and being almost unknown outside Quebec. After running second on the first ballot, he faded and was dropped after the third ballot, with Joe Clark coming from behind to win on the fourth ballot. After the convention, Mulroney took a job as president of the U.S.-owned Iron Ore Company of Canada. One of his main tasks was to close down the town of Schefferville, where the company had operated a smelter for many years. The defeat of the Conservative government over its first budget in 1979 forced Clark to put his leadership up for review. Despite protestations of his support, Mulroney worked assiduously to build a network to challenge him. At the leadership convention of 1983, Mulroney overcame an early lead by Clark and was elected leader on the fourth ballot. He quickly won a by-election in Nova Scotia, then came the 1984 election, Mulroney's landslide victory over John Turner, and four years of turbulent government. Mulroney moved quickly to abolish a number of Liberal programs and agencies, including the National Energy Program and the Foreign Investment Review Agency. Canada was again "open for business" while Deputy Prime Minister Erik Nielsen would conduct a rigorous review of all government expenditures. By 1988, however, the chief trademark of the Mulroney government, in the eyes of many Canadians, was the fact that no fewer than eight cabinet ministers had been forced to resign over various scandals. Patronage, over which Mulroney had attacked John Turner so effectively, reigned even more supreme in Ottawa.

In addition to both having been touched by patronage scandals, Mulroney and Turner shared characteristics that are common to highly successful people: abundant self-confidence, a high level of optimism, and deep faith in the rightness of their missions. Both had been raised in the Catholic faith. Their lives first intersected on a summer day in 1962 when Mulroney, then a law student working in the office of a Conservative cabinet minister, Alvin Hamilton, spotted Turner, the newly-elected MP for a Montreal riding coming down the steps of the Parliament Building's Centre Block. Mulroney leaped to introduce himself.

John Turner's mother, Phyllis Turner, was a miner's daughter from Rossland, British Columbia. She met and married John's father in England, then returned to Canada after his death in 1932. She later moved to Ottawa, secured a low-ranking civil service job and when John was sixteen, married a prominent B.C. businessman who would become Lieutenant-Governor. Turner enjoyed the affluence of his teen-age years and as "Chick" became a popular young man about campus at the University of British Columbia. He studied law as a Rhodes scholar at Oxford, went on to the University of Paris and back in Canada in 1954, passed his Quebec bar examinations without much difficulty. He practiced law in Montreal and in 1962, when the Diefenbaker government was coming apart, secured the Liberal nomination in the Montreal riding of St-Lawrence-St-Georges. Mike Pearson made him a minister without portfolio in 1965, promoted him to Registrar General in 1967, then quickly made Turner Minister of the new department of Consumer and Corporate Affairs. Turner was bright, young and dedicated, carrying responsibility for a new dimension of government, consumer protection. The post was ideal for his run at the Prime Ministership when Pearson retired, but he had neither the experience nor the organization to seriously challenge Pierre Trudeau. He hung in until the last ballot, his 195 supporters becoming known as the "195 Club." When Turner's Montreal riding was eliminated through redistribution, he switched to the Ontario riding of Ottawa Carleton in 1968, and promptly swamped his Conservative and NDP opponents, winning 66 per cent of the vote. Trudeau handed Turner his own previous ministry, Justice, giving him the task of putting the finishing touches to the new abortion legislation.

The relationship between Trudeau and Turner remained uneasy during their years together, foreshadowing the strains that would beset a future pairing in power, Jean Chrétien and Paul Martin. Impatient for a second chance to become Prime Minister and increasingly irritated by Trudeau's imperious style, Turner resigned suddenly late in 1975 and moved to Toronto. It was the opening of a glamorous new phase in Turner's private and public life, filling the role of Prime Minister in waiting while dispensing legal advice to the country's corporate elite. He watched the Trudeau administration decay through the late 1970s, but when Trudeau resigned following his 1979 defeat, Turner shrewdly held back from declaring his candidacy to succeed him. The sudden collapse of the Clark government gave Trudeau another chance and his re-election in 1980 kept Turner waiting another four years for a leadership convention. When it finally came, Turner was the choice of most Liberal party heavyweights as well as the rank and file. He beat Jean Chrétien on the second ballot, although as party president Iona Campagnola famously observed, Jean remained "first in our hearts." Returning to Ottawa as Prime Minister, Turner encountered a political environment quite different from the one he'd left a decade earlier. Gone were the trusting camaraderie of politician and press, the jock-to-jock talk in the hallways and over martinis, and the comfortable chauvinism of a male-dominated political hierarchy. Turner was nervous and rusty before the TV cameras and his "bum-patting" episodes during the 1984 campaign embarrassed himself and the party. Starting with a comfortable lead in the public opinion polls, Turner "marched his party to the worst political catastrophe in Canadian history."[3] He fought back from the Opposition side of the House for the next four years and now, deep into the most fateful campaign of his life, he had a chance to overcome the disappointments and distrust that had led to a near-rebellion within the Liberal party.

The Campaign and the Candidates

The media had been notified that on Saturday morning, October 1, Prime Minister Mulroney would announce the calling of the general election. Shortly after ten o'clock, in time-honoured ritual, he emerged from his visit with the Governor General at Rideau Hall to announce the vote would be held on November 21. "The key question for the electorate will be who best can manage change," Mulroney said, reflecting the direction he'd received from the public opinion polling of Allan Gregg. "We intend to run on our record of the past and our plan for the future. Four years ago, we inherited a Canada scarred by economic recession and divided by mistrust of the major partners of our federation. Today we have an economy that is a world leader in growth and job creation ... The free trade agreement with the United States will mean enlarged opportunity for our producers and businesses, more and better jobs for Canadians, especially our youth, and higher living standards for our people ... we are ready to be judged on our record." Only a few noted that the Prime Minister had spoken of free trade only in French.

Seven weeks was far more than was needed to debate the issues of the 1988 election, but John Turner and Ed Broadbent had to get into the fray immediately. Turner, with his wife Geills and two of their four children, answered the call of the Liberal campaign committee and made a hurried visit to Kensington Market, the polygot district in mid-Toronto of Portuguese, Chinese and Caribbean merchants, their sidewalk stalls filled to overflowing with fruits, vegetables and low priced shirts and trousers. "For two months I have been asking the prime minister to let the people decide, today he finally agreed," Turner told the hastily-assembled TV cameras. "This election is primarily about two things: an independent and sovereign Canada, which has never been so threatened as it is by the Mulroney trade deal, and fairness, particularly for low- and middle-income Canadians who have been hit by Tory tax increases over the last four years." Unlike many of the appearances Turner would make through the rest of the campaign, this first stop was short, effective and well-covered by the media.

How to handle the free trade issue was a major strategic problem for the New Democratic party in 1988. The dilemma was compounded by the fact that NDP popularity seemed to be holding quite steadily in second place, having slipped from a dizzying first-place ranking in the fall of 1987. While many in the NDP wanted an all-out assault on free trade because of their belief it threatened the jobs of unionized workers, Broadbent and his closest advisors were fearful that too much talk about free trade would hand the issue over to the Liberals. A Liberal vote could be perceived as the best way of stopping free trade. When Ed Broadbent left his Ottawa office to provide a photo opportunity at the Byward market, he spoke in symbolic terms of the need for Canadians to strengthen their institutions. It was code that New Democrats would understand, but other Canadians heard a different message – of the NDP commitment to a health care system that might be threatened by an American system "operated for profit rather than to service human needs." Broadbent headed west with this message in the first week of the campaign, drawing a large crowd in Edmonton where the NDP expected a breakthrough of two to three seats.

Also in Alberta, the first stirring of western rebellion against Brian Mulroney was beginning to take shape. Preston Manning, the economist son of the revered former premier of Alberta, Ernest C. Manning, was about to launch his Reform party on the slogan of "The West Wants In." Many Conservatives in the West were becoming dissatisfied over bilingualism and the pro-Quebec leaning of their party, as exemplified by the Meech Lake Accord. Mulroney's appointment of Don Mazankowski, the highly-regarded Minister of Transport from Vegreville, Alberta, as Deputy Prime Minister did little to help. The discontent flared into open defiance when Ottawa rejected a bid by Bristol Aerospace of Winnipeg to service CF-18 aircraft, instead giving a more costly contract to Canadair of Montreal. Manning, assisted by a young economics graduate, Stephen Harper, put together a platform in opposition to the Meech Lake accord, support for a "Triple E" Senate (equal, elected and effective), a lowering of interest rates, and calling for changes in the taxation system to favour western resource producers. Free trade was not a big issue for Reformers. Getting even was, and Manning would run in Joe Clark's own riding of Yellowhead, in the Rocky Mountain foothills west of Edmonton.

All through the first three weeks of the campaign, the Conservative re-election machine hummed smoothly, following a strategy crafted by a legion of advisors and a cadre of well-paid lobbyists and pollsters. At the top level, the Tory strategy group included former premiers William Davis and Peter Lougheed, insiders Peter White, Bernard Roy, Norman Atkins, Dalton Camp, and MPs Don Mazankowski and Bill Jarvis. They had crafted a careful schedule of photo opps and brief prime min-isterial appearances which would lead the media to charge that Mulroney was being kept in a "cocoon." A typical day on his first swing through southern Ontario had Mulroney articulating a theme from the campaign at a morning photo opp, giving a speech at noon to a friendly but non-partisan audience, and talking to a Tory rally in the evening. From Ontario, Mulroney flew first to St. John's to support Ross Reid in St. John's East, then to Halifax where Michael Forrestal, Howard Crosby and Stewart McInnes, the public works minister, received a boost from his appearance. The Halifax visit was intended to highlight the government's support for environmental protection, but the media gave more attention to what seemed to be Mulroney's lukewarm commitment to defending Canada's social programs – the very programs he had promised in 1984 to treat as a "sacred trust."

The Liberal brain trust had never intended that free trade be the central focus of the campaign; rather it was to be used as one more example of how Brian Mulroney could not be trusted. But when free trade was debated in the House on October 26, 1987, Turner put himself irrevocably in opposition to the pact: "We did not negotiate the deal, we are not bound by the deal, we will not live with this deal, and if the deal and the final contract reflects the principles and the general terms of the agreement we have seen, we are going to tear the deal up." After the U.S. and Canada formally signed the agreement in January 1988, Turner stepped up the tempo.

John Turner has always regarded himself as a free trader, and it was a twist of political fate that he would be most remembered for his campaign against it. His problem with the FTA was that he didn't see it as a true free trade agreement; he thought the many provisions allowing the U.S. to make trade policy outside the pact gave the U.S. an upper hand. His views were confirmed for him when six American Senators came to Ottawa in 1987 to pave the way for a final signing. Led by Democratic Senator Lloyd Bentsen of Texas, with the venerable Sen. Mike Mansfield of Missouri as the ranking Republican, the delegation breakfasted with Prime Minister Mulroney and then called on John Turner. It was agreed Turner would host a lunch in a committee room at the Parliament Buildings, and that other key members of the Liberal caucus would attend. As pre-lunch drinks were being served, Turner suggested they "get business out of the way and we'll have a more relaxed lunch." Turner told them he'd read all the documents and didn't think they set out a true free trade agreement. "I've been advised by some of my more moderate colleagues in the business community that we should sign the agreement, and we can then negotiate upwards," he said. Bentsen quickly responded, "That would be a very bad idea, it's take it or leave it. There's no post-agreement negotiations contemplated." At this, Turner recited the list of exclusions – anti-trust, countervailing duties, presidential discretion – and concluded by noting that even the dispute tribunals would be guided by American law, "as it may be amended from time to time." Again, Sen. Bentsen's response was quick in coming: "You've read the agreement correctly, they're deliberately not covered. The United States Congress will never, I repeat never, yield its jurisdiction over trade." By mid-summer, Turner was calling for an election on the issue. The agreement had the approval of the House but not the Senate, and Turner instructed the Liberal majority there to hold up passage until after an election. It was a controversial move, and it made it certain that free trade would dominate the campaign. He'd later say that holding up the bill "was the only constructive use of the Senate in a long time."

For John Turner, the weeks leading up to the debate were a nightmare of policy mix-ups, bad press, and an incipient palace revolt led by insiders such as Michael Kirby, Alasdair Graham, Alfonse Gagliano and the former Trudeau cabinet minister, Andre Ouellet. Turner had to defend himself against reports that candidates were quitting because they didn't think they would be able to win. Paul Martin, running in a Montreal riding, said "I believe in miracles" when asked if he thought he would be elected. What was to have been a major announcement by Turner of a program to provide 400,000 new day care spaces at a cost of $4 billion fell apart when insistent media questioning pushed the price tag up to $10 billion. A poll showing that the Liberals would be more popular under Jean Chrétien added further embarrassment. Growing discontent in the upper echelons of the party – much of it originating with Jean Chrétien's supporters, who bitterly opposed Meech Lake – reached Turner when his principal secretary, Peter Connolly, delivered the message that certain Liberals wanted him to step down midway in the campaign. Furious, Turner refused. "If our party had appeared more unified in the earlier days of the campaign I think we would have had a chance to win," Turner later recalled. "Jean Chrétien never really reconciled with me after the leadership convention of 1984, and even in the middle of the election campaign there were rumblings from certain sources that there was an attempt to overthrow me."[4]

The rumors of the incipient revolt also reached the CBC, and on October 19 Peter Mansbridge went to air with The National reporting the party "heading toward a major confrontation … and in the process destroying itself." The exact magnitude of the revolt has never been precisely measured, but it died when Turner refused to allow himself to be pushed out, and the dramatic debate confrontation killed the rebellion in its tracks. "Debate turns into shouting match," the *Gazette* headlined the next morning. "Turner steals show with crisp performance."

The three leaders were back on the hustings the next morning. Mulroney drew large crowds in Sherbrooke and other Quebec towns. Broadbent had his largest rally yet in Toronto and Turner addressed enthusiastic crowds in Cornwall and Ottawa. There, he told admirers that Mulroney would have fallen apart if the debate had gone on any longer. He ridiculed Mulroney's assertion that free trade could be cancelled on six months' notice: "When you're leading a nation, you're playing for keeps. You don't mess around to see how it's going to turn out." As the weekend approached, the public-opinion polls on the debate were painting a bright picture for Turner. He was showing up as the perceived winner in all three major polls, most notably in the Gallup survey where 72 per cent of those who picked a winner chose Turner, to 17 per cent for Mulroney and 11 per cent for Broadbent. Turner went to Halifax in a state of high excitement.

There, he released an economic development plan for the Atlantic provinces entitled the Atlantic Charter, and spoke to a rousing meeting of students at St. Mary's University. "The next time I'm back here I'll be prime minister," he boasted to a television interviewer. Ed Broadbent also went east, but the NDP's internal polls were showing a massive shift to the Liberals. The NDP was no longer a decisive factor in what had become a two-way fight. That weekend the headlines were focusing on a Conservative counter-attack. "Election now a dogfight: Mulroney gets tough" reported the *Gazette*. The first polls after the debate, by Insight Canada for the CTV network, credited the Liberals with an amazing four-point lead over the Conservatives. A Gallup Poll on October 31 showed that while the Tories still led the Liberals 38 per cent to 32, Turner's strong performance had narrowed the Conservative margin from ten points to just six. The NDP, which never recovered from Broadbent's slow start in attacking free trade, had dropped two points to 27 per cent.

By the 1980s, politics in Canada had become as much a matter of advertising and marketing as policy and leadership. The communications strategies of each party were being driven by the polls, and both the Liberals and Conservatives revamped their advertising to deal with the sudden shift caused by the debate. The Liberals' Red Leaf advertising consortium, headed now by David Morton, a marketing veteran from the Quaker Oats Company in Peterborough, Ont., produced the single most devastating commercial of the 1988 election: the "map ad" in which a hand carrying an eraser removes the U.S.-Canadian border. A voice-over intones, "This line here. It's just getting in the way." The 30-second ad, combined with the surprising results of the post-debate polls, shocked the Conservative campaign team. When another Gallup Poll on November 7 cast the Liberals as surging toward a majority – 43 per cent to 31 per cent for the Conservatives – all the resources of the Tories and their allies were directed at smashing the public's new-found confidence in the Liberal leader. The PC inner circle was convinced it was a "rogue poll" – the one time in twenty that a poll's results would be off – but it spurred them to drastic action. In several urgent Tory post-mortems Allan Gregg would famously comment that it was time to "bomb the bridge" in the Liberal campaign structure; the bridge being the gap the Conservatives believed existed between the public's growing fear of free trade, and the personal credibility of John Turner. The election had suddenly become a single-issue campaign, with the prospect that the Liberals might ride free trade to victory.

An avalanche of anti-Turner advertising now hit the airwaves and the public's mailboxes. A response to the map ad, showing the border simply being restored, was quickly put on the air. It led the Liberals, for unexplained reasons, to withdraw what had been their most effective attack piece. The Conservative ad campaign intensified as election day neared, with the biggest push coming in the last ten days of the campaign. Millions of copies of a tabloid entitled "Ten Big Lies" were sent across the country. Full page ads ran in Sunday newspapers across Canada the day before the election, along with 800,000 copies of another pro-free trade brochure. The biggest artillery was fired by a newly-formed business group, the Canadian Alliance for Trade and Job Opportunities. Drawing its main support from companies belonging to the Business Council on National Issues, the Alliance spent several million dollars on advertising, unimpeded by the Election Expenses Act.[5] Perhaps more effectively, many of its 150 member companies ran internal campaigns to promote the agreement. Advocates were brought into employee meetings and letters were sent urging workers to consider the benefits free trade would bring to their companies. Others received letters in their pay packets endorsing the agreement. The all-out assault was reminiscent of two earlier business-led political campaigns: the attack on free trade – or reciprocity, as it was called at the time – in 1911, and the business-led attack on the socialist CCF party in the 1945 federal election.[6]

Opponents of Free Trade, including the nationalist Council of Canadians led by activist Maude Barlowe, had set up their own Pro-Canada Network to oppose the FTA. The Network managed to raise $650,000 to finance the insertion of a brochure in newspapers across the country. A greater limit on the Network's effectiveness was its unilingual English nature and its lack of members in Quebec. Of all the clauses in the Free Trade Agreement, none attracted more controversy than 1807, dealing with unresolved disputes over trade issues such as softwood lumber. Because the Americans would not agree to binding arbitration, each country was left with the right to disregard the FTA and apply sanctions such as trade tariffs. Other controversial clauses called for "national treatment" of each country's companies, meaning that neither could impose restrictions on the other that did not also apply to their own corporations. All of this led critics to interpret the FTA as an open invitation to American companies to assault Canada's treasured public services, especially healthcare. Much of the sting was taken out of this attack when the architect of Canada's national medicare system, former Justice Emmett Hall, absolved the FTA as a threat to public health insurance. "There is nothing in this agreement damaging to medicare in Canada," he told a news conference in Saskatoon. "If I had found there were … I would have opposed the agreement because medicare is perhaps one of the things I hold dearest in life today." The Conservatives also were able to bring out a revered Quebec figure, Claude Castonguay who had introduced medicare in that province in the 1970s. He also gave assurance that free trade would have no effect on healthcare.

Castonguay was not the only Quebec voice in support of free trade. Perhaps because the FTA was seen as opening up trade and contacts that would lessen Quebec's dependence on Canada, it had the backing of both soft nationalists and separatists. Mulroney tied free trade to the Meech Lake accord. On November 9, he told 1,500 workers at the Canadair plant in Montreal that "If Meech Lake and free trade were to disappear, Quebeckers would be the big losers." They were both instruments of Quebec's "dignity and prosperity" and there would be a high price to pay if they were sabotaged. Turner viewed the Tory attacks as "totally false," especially in that he supported Meech Lake despite the reservations of the Trudeau/Chrétien wing of the Liberal party. Another supporter of free trade was Quebec Premier Robert Bourassa, who engineered a resolution in the Liberal-dominated Quebec National Assembly calling the FTA "Quebec and Canada's ultimate insurance policy against any protectionist whim by the government of the United States." As the campaign reached its climax, the Tories struck at Turner on another front. Mulroney's respected finance minister, ex-Bay Streeter Michael Wilson, released an analysis of Turner's campaign promises in which he hung a $37 billion price tag on Liberal commitments. The NDP responded by announcing that their promises would cost only $5.13 billion. The cost of Conservative government commitments was largely ignored; they totaled an estimated $15 billion for projects already under way or announced.

The last weekend of the campaign found John Turner in Vancouver, fresh from enthusiastic rallies in Hamilton and Winnipeg. He suffered excruciating back pain, and as he walked the streets of his Quadra riding and the Granville Island market he was wincing visibly with pain. Sunday night he went to bed in his suite at the Hotel Vancouver satisfied that he had a good chance of winning, but at the very least he'd saved the Liberal party from obliteration. He had played host that night to a relaxing dinner for his media entourage. Across the country, Brian Mulroney, his wife Mila and their children had settled into the guest house at Le Manoir, the regal residence in Baie-Comeau where mill owner Robert McCormick had once put up visitors. He spent the early part of the election night being interviewed by Peter Newman. Ed Broadbent had gone home to Oshawa, after campaigning in the union enclaves of the Niagara peninsula. No one bothered to track the whereabouts of Preston Manning or the prospects of his nascent Reform party, but he was at home in Calgary, sure that the seeds he'd planted among the West's most conservative elements would flourish and flower.

The closing of the polls in Atlantic Canada brought assorted victories for the Conservatives, none more cheering for Mulroney that Ross Reid's defeat of the lone NDP member on the island, Jack Harris in St. John's East. But most of the region was going Liberal, perhaps due more to cutbacks in federal spending than free trade. The Liberal share of the popular vote in the region rose from 35 per cent to 46 per cent, resulting in a 20-to-12 edge in seats. The news comforted John Turner as he received the results a little after five o'clock in Vancouver, but he knew the outcome would be decided in the coming hour as Quebec and Ontario counted their votes. By 8:40 p.m. Eastern time the answer was clear: the networks were proclaiming another Progressive Conservative majority government. Quebec generated stunning results for Mulroney – 63 seats to only 12 Liberals, down from the 17 they held before the election. Ontario was closer: with 38 per cent of the popular vote, the Conservatives won 46 seats, with 43 going to the Liberals (an increase from 14) and 10 to the NDP. The West turned into a battleground between the Conservatives and the NDP; aside from five seats in Manitoba and John Turner's Vancouver Quadra riding, the Liberals were shut out from Winnipeg to Vancouver island. The final Western count was 48 Conservatives and 33 NDP, including 19 of B.C.'s 32 seats. Overall, the Conservatives had withstood a substantial fall-off from their 1984 triumph, but the majority was solid enough – 170 seats to 82 Liberals and 43 NDP – to satisfy Mulroney that he had the mandate to continue with both the free trade and the Meech Lake agreement.

Many of the riding battles had turned into epic personality contests. Frank Stronach, the classic immigrant success story who ran as a Liberal in York-Simcoe was unable to win the seat of disgraced Mulroney cabinet minister Sinclair Stevens. He lost to a new PC candidate, John Cole, by more than 7,000 votes. Joe Clark's wife Maureen McTeer failed to capture the Ottawa suburban riding of Carleton-Gloucester despite the help of top Tory strategists Jodi White and Bill Neville. In Saskatchewan, former justice minister Ray Hnatyshyn was beaten by the NDP's Chris Axworthy by almost 5,000 votes. Hnatyshyn later became Governor General, filling the post with distinction. Alberta held firm for the Conservatives, with key MPs such as Don Mazankowski, Harvie Andre, and Joe Clark all being returned. Of special note was the victory in Wetaskiwin riding of Conservative Willie Littlechild, the first treaty status native to be elected as an MP. Joe Clark's margin of victory over Preston Manning, a comfortable 5,000, represented a sharp drop from the 30,000-vote margin by which Clark had carried the Yellowhead riding in 1984. In British Columbia, newcomer Kim Campbell held Pat Carney's old riding of Vancouver Centre but only a dozen Conservatives withstood the NDP onslaught on the west coast. Not a single Tory was elected on Vancouver island. Among the successful NDP candidates were two former provincial party leaders, Dave

Barrett and Robert Skelly, as well as a former provincial minister of finance.

Mulroney and his party arrived at the Baie-Comeau arena shortly after midnight. In his victory speech, he paid due respect to all the shibboleths of Canadian politics. "This campaign has shown that Canadians agree on what it is that we most cherish in our national life," Mulroney said. "Our sovereignty, the protection of minority rights, our unique social programs, our concern for the environment, our commitment to regional development – these have their source in a Canadian tradition of tolerance and sharing."

"The margin is decisive and the mandate is clear: to implement the Free Trade Agreement, which holds the promise of new opportunities and new prosperity. To ratify the Meech Lake Accord which returns Quebec to the constitutional family on terms that are honourable for all concerned. They constitute a brilliant affirmation of the new spirit of national reconciliation and economic renewal that benefits us all." The speech provided all the headlines the media needed: the next day's Toronto *Star* told it simply: "Mandate clear, PM says – Decisive Tory win gives green light for free trade pact." The *Star's* Val Sears, writing from Vancouver, predicted that the knives would soon be out for John Turner even though his dramatic campaign had turned the party around.

John Turner, having absorbed the results in the quiet of his hotel suite, made his way to a cultural centre where subdued supporters awaited him. He spoke for just a few minutes, recalling that he had campaigned for a strong and sovereign Canada "with all my heart and with all my strength and I have no regret at all." Then he added: "Despite the fact the Conservatives have a larger percentage of the popular vote, Canadians have certainly expressed their wish to keep this country strong, sovereign and independent. They've also chosen to give the Conservative government another mandate. I believe, fundamentally, that the people are always right. I will uphold the confidence you have placed in me. I will honour that trust, and I will continue to hold my country first and foremost." He did not congratulate Mulroney. Nor did he speak of how Jean Chrétien's supporters had worked to undermine him for the past four years.

The Aftermath

Brian Mulroney had won an impressive majority, but the popular vote told a somewhat different story. Fifty-seven per cent of the electorate had voted for opposition party candidates. This fact has allowed opponents of free trade to argue to this day that a true mandate for the FTA never existed. Support for free trade was highest in Alberta, the most Americanized of Canada's provinces. With its prosperity built largely on energy exports, Alberta also shares with the other prairie provinces a long history of resentment over protective tariff policies which until well after World War II kept lower cost American-made farm machinery out of Canada. The other province with significantly strong support for free trade was Quebec, where the traditional alliance of nationalists and Conservatives resulted in electoral success once again. Jacques Parizeau, leader of the Parti Quebecois, hailed the deal as creating the preconditions of a sovereign Quebec. Less than a year after the election the natural home of Quebec conservatives, the *Union Nationale* party, was officially declared dead.

Within six months, both Ed Broadbent and John Turner had submitted their resignations and their parties were preparing for leadership conventions. Turner was disappointed that he'd lost the election, but at the age of sixty he felt he still had time to recoup some of the financial sacrifice he'd made during 25 years in Parliament. Jean Chrétien, defeated Paul Martin at a convention in Calgary on June 23, 1990, one day after the death of the Meech Lake agreement.[7] The refusal of Manitoba and Newfoundland to ratify the agreement within the required one-year deadline set off a rash of fresh constitutional initiatives, most notably a new round of talks leading to an agreement with the premiers in Charlottetown. It was to be voted down by the Canadian public on October 26, 1992. Clearly, Canadians were no longer in any mood to accept either advice or dictation from the political elites. There was one more radical policy shift left to be played out by the Mulroney government: introduction of a consumption tax that would be modeled on the Value Added Tax (VAT) that had become significant revenue-producers for several European countries. Presented to the House of Commons in January, 1990 as a seven per cent Goods and Services Tax (GST), it ran into ferocious opposition – 1.7 million Canadians signed and mailed off protest postcards in a single weekend – but quickly became such a revenue-generator that the Liberals would soon forgot their promise to abolish it. While the GST was a major factor in the growing unpopularity of the Conservative government, the Mulroney government's whole-hearted endorsement of the U.S.-led Gulf War in 1991 also created great unease among Canadian voters. With both the new Liberal leader and the NDP steadfastly opposed to active participation, Canada limited its involvement to a few ships and airplanes; not a single Canadian casualty was recorded. When the five-year Mulroney mandate ran out in 1993, so too did Canadians' patience with his entire record and his party. His successor, Kim Campbell, suffered the most severe repudiation ever handed a governing party when only two Conservative MPs – Jean Charest in Quebec and Elsie Wayne in New Brunswick – survived the election of October 25, 1993.

Provisions of the Free Trade Agreement began to come into effect in 1989 and were soon superceded by an enlarged pact taking in Mexico as well as the United States and Canada. The North American Free Trade Agreement was approved by Parliament on May 27, 1992, by a vote of 140 to 14. It had the support of the Liberal party although Jean Chrétien reserved his right (which he never exercised) to renegotiate the deal following the election. From the beginning, the FTA imposed clear limits on the power of the Canadian government to interfere in commercial activity, although the healthcare system has never been directly challenged. The agreement was instrumental in Canada's reluctant decision to allow U.S. magazines to produce Canadianized editions. Its provisions also ensure there will be no interference in the export of Canadian energy to the United States. But it has not protected Canada from fierce American protectionism over many exports to the U.S., including steel, softwood lumber, dairy products and potatoes. What is indisputable is that the U.S. market has become easier for Canadians to penetrate; exports under free trade are up 169 per cent and the 838,000 new jobs created in Canada since the early-1990s recession is testimony to the durability of the resource and manufacturing sectors. What is less clear is whether the growth is due to free trade, to a lower Canadian dollar and a growing American economy, or a combination of all three. Mulroney and Turner have differing views.

In an interview with the Institute for Research on Public Policy in 1996, Mulroney maintained that Canada would not have been able to overcome its deficit or generate $575 billion a year in exports to the United States without the re-election of his government. "Canada's exports as a percentage of GDP have gone from somewhere in the neighborhood of 23 per cent when we signed the free trade agreement to 41 or 42 per cent today. That indicates the dramatic nature of the transformation of the economy." Turner's view is that the reason Canada's exports rose after free trade is that the dollar declined in value from 87 to 63 cents U.S. "The tariff was only five per cent at the time, and currency levels have always been more important than the tariff in our relationship with the United States. There's not a trade lawyer in Washington who doesn't agree with me that Canada got screwed. If the people had supported me in 1988, that agreement would not have passed."

The 1988 election, by virtue of the results flowing from it, stands as one of the most profound turning points in Canadian history. The Conservative victory came as a result of a convergence of interests of corporate Canada and Quebec nationalists, and was thus reminiscent of earlier Tory victories built on similar alliances. It broke the mold of Canadian economic policy that had been fixed in place since the advent of Confederation. By taking the plunge into free trade Canada moved uncertainly into an expanded continental trading bloc – a likely precursor of even larger economic partnerships that will some day link Europe and North America to the rising powers of the Asia Pacific region.

CHAPTER FIFTEEN

The Quebec Referendum of October 30, 1995

THE ISSUES

The referendum will determine the future of Canada – whether Quebec is to abandon Confederation and in what form or shape post-referendum Canada will enter the 21st century. An emotion-laden campaign driven by the charismatic Lucien Bouchard comes within a few thousand votes of victory. Quebec's narrow rejection of separation shocks Canadians and forces the federal government to adopt new measures to deal with the threat of secession while asserting an independent Canadian voice in the world.

THE QUESTION

"Do you agree that Quebec should become sovereign after having made a formal offer to Canada for a new economic and political partnership within the scope of the bill respecting the future of Quebec and of the agreement signed on June 12, 1995, Yes or No?"

THE PERSONALITIES

YES COMMITTEE
Jacques Parizeau, Premier of Quebec and leader, Parti Québécois
Lucien Bouchard, leader, Bloc Québécois and "chief negotiator"
Mario Dumont, leader, Action Democratique du Quebec

NO COMMITTEE
Daniel Johnson, Leader, Quebec Liberal Party
Jean Chrétien, Prime Minister of Canada and Liberal Party of Canada leader
Jean Charest, leader, Progressive Conservative Party of Canada

THE RESULTS

NO	2,362,648	(50.58%)
YES	2,308,360	(49.42%)
"NO" majority	54,288	(1.16%)
Valid ballots	4,671,008	(98.18%)
Rejected ballots	86,501	(1.82%)
Participation rate	4,757.509	(93.52%)
Registered voters	5,087,009	

Bengamin Ragetlie, 7, Guelph, Ontario sits on his father Norman's shoulder shouting in support of Canadian Unity at the NO rally for the Quebec Referendum in Montreal, 1995.

CANADA AT THE BRINK:
THE CRISIS AND THE FALL-OUT

The Quebec Referendum of 1995

The pre-dawn stillness cloaking the parking lot of the Centerpoint Mall was broken only by the muffled sound of cars bringing volunteers to join the caravan of buses going to Montreal for the big NO rally of the Quebec referendum on sovereignty. It had been called as a hasty response to the emotion-charged campaign that Quebec premier Jacques Parizeau and his "chief negotiator" Lucien Bouchard were waging to win a Yes vote for independence. The rally would demonstrate the fervor of Canadians outside Quebec to keep Canada intact 127 years after Confederation, and would answer the cry of the *oui* side that the people of Quebec could only fulfill their true destiny – and end the humiliation they'd endured at the hands of English Canada – by voting to become a sovereign and independent state.

It was barely four o'clock when Gordon Dowsley and his daughter Martha arrived at the Mall on this Friday of the last weekend before the referendum. As Dowsley welcomed the volunteers who would carry a message for Canadian unity to Quebec, he reflected on the past 24 hours: the call from Jim Peterson, the Liberal MP for Willowdale, asking help in getting buses on the road for Place du Canada in Montreal. It had all been the sudden brainchild of Brian Tobin, the Newfoundland MP and Minister of Oceans and Fisheries. Realizing that the federalist side had been edging into crisis since Bouchard's arrival on the campaign trail, Tobin decided that ordinary Canadians should be given an opportunity to tell Quebecers how much they were wanted in Canada. Dowsley was president of the Willowdale Liberal Association, and he found that buses were harder to come by than volunteers. He had with him a check for four hundred dollars to cover the cost of the two he'd been able to charter.

Contained within Dowsley's one hundred and seventy pound frame was a suppressed fury over the possibility of a verdict on Monday that could change the lives of Canadians, but over which he had no say. Dowsley didn't know whether the rally would influence Monday's vote, but he was sure it would at least answer the separatist claim that English Canada had left Quebecers in isolation, and had little interest in their concerns or cares. The uncertainty of the result matched Dowsley's uncertainty about his own future. Crown Life, the insurance company where he'd worked through the ranks to the position of vice-president, had recently packed up and moved to Saskatchewan. He could have gone with it but he and his wife had chosen not to; their roots were here in Toronto along with their three daughters. Martha was studying biology and archeology at the University of Toronto and was excited to be part of the trip to Montreal.

Promptly at five o'clock, with the sky still dark, the buses left Centerpoint – a nondescript mall on Toronto's northern border that had been bypassed by upscale retail chains that had vaulted to affluent exurbia – and turned south on Yonge street to pick up Highway 401 for the five-hour drive to Montreal. The trip was an emotional one for Gordon and Martha, as it was for the others – citizens who had phoned Peterson's office asking to join the trek, high school students aboard for the experience, and a smattering of members of the local Liberal riding association. With just one stop, at Trenton, Ontario for breakfast, they sang O Canada time and again, and took turns giving little speeches as to why they were on this journey. Especially touching, Dowsley would remember, were the remarks of Robert Burns, a 45-year-old man who had spent a year in hospital after receiving a liver transplant. He would have just a year of life left to him, but was aboard today with his wife Patricia and five-year-old son, Cameron. As the sky lightened and the buses moved through eastern Ontario, early morning radio broadcasts brought crowds out to the overpasses. They waved Canadian flags and cheered the growing caravan of vehicles. Car drivers put No signs in their windows and truck drivers honked their support. At the Quebec border, a lone man stood as a sentinel, holding aloft a Canadian flag on a makeshift pole, saluting every passing vehicle. By the time Dowsley's buses parked in downtown Montreal, others who had arrived by train and by plane from the Maritimes and the West were converging on Place du Canada, the lush green park on Peel street with its bronze statues of Canadian prime ministers Sir Wilfrid Laurier and Sir John A. Macdonald. History had been made here, from the time Jacques Cartier first strode the slopes of Mount Royal, through the era of the fur traders like Alexander Mackenzie of the Northwest Company and the years of the railway barons, Donald Smith and William Van Horne. By the time the rally got underway at noon, close to a hundred thousand people had reached Montreal. It was the greatest movement of people to a single place on a single day in Canadian history.

The speeches at the No rally, as at most large political gatherings, were long on emotion and short on logic, but they provided the colour needed to satisfy those present. It also gave the national media a dramatic finale to what had become the most unpredictable political campaign Canada had ever seen. The crowd of one hundred and fifty thousand, perceiving it inhabited a nation in peril, roared its approval of Jean Chrétien, the Prime Minister, when he declared: "My colleagues and I staunchly believe in our Quebec homeland, but at the same time we have a country, which is called Canada. We say No to those who would strip us of our Canada." Daniel Johnson, the leader of the Quebec Liberal party and the nominal head of the No campaign, thought Place du Canada was a perfect place to ponder why so many people from around the world are so desperate to emigrate to this country. Jean Charest, the leader of the dwindling Progressive Conservative party of Canada, led the crowd in a No No No chant reminiscent of a football cheer, while a huge Canadian flag floated around and above the crowd, held aloft by outstretched arms. One who was not there, Lucien Bouchard – who began his political career as a speechwriter for Pierre Trudeau and would end it as Premier of Quebec – made light of the event. "Blushing suitors who are going to tell us they love us on cheap tickets," he had said of those thronging to the city. While English-language radio and TV went live to cover the rally, French media played it down. CKAC, the leading French-language radio station, stuck to its pre-arranged interview with a PQ cabinet minister but broke in to report that the rally had drawn a crowd of only thirty thousand. That certainly wasn't Gordon Dowsley's impression. "We gave the streets back to the people of Montreal. Before we arrived, the separatists had everyone cowed. Suddenly Montreal was theirs again." For hours afterward, little groups of demonstrators milled around downtown Montreal, carrying flags and signs. Dowsley and Martha wandered along boulevard René Lévesque where, on the steps of the hundred-year old Montreal Cathedral, Marie-Reine-du-Monde, they encountered Claude Ryan, an inconic figure in the public life of Quebec. Ryan was the former editor of *Le Devoir*, a newspaper often considered the conscience of French Canada, and had led the Quebec Liberal party in the early nineteen eighties, commanding the winning No side in the 1980 referendum. Before hurrying off he signed Martha's flag, "With warm thanks." Whether many other French-speaking Montrealers shared that view was hard to say. Jacques Monfette, a doorman at the Queen Elizabeth Hotel, stood in his crisp brown uniform and gold-braided cap watching the rally. "They're here for us. I'm touched. But two days before the vote, it's too late to get me to change my mind. They've shown up at the last minute."[1]

By midnight, Dowsley and most of the others who had journeyed down the 401 were back home. On Monday night, the Willowdale Liberal association invited its members to the All Saints Multicultural Centre where TVs had been set up to view the results. For three hours on that mild autumn evening of October 30, 1995, Canada trembled on the brink of dissolution. With the sovereignist Yes vote at times edging into a narrow lead, the nightmare of separation, the dream of independence – you could take your choice depending on your sentiments – seemed at hand. No one could know what a yes vote might bring. A sudden declaration of unilateral independence was not impossible; it was known that Jacques Parizeau was given to impulsive, unpredictable actions at times of high emotion. At the very least, difficult and disruptive negotiations would lie ahead. Was Canada to be rendered apart by the strife that had beset other countries during the twentieth century – Ireland, Yugoslavia, India – or would it be split by political consensus, as had Sweden and Norway, the Czech Republic and Slovakia? A partial answer might be found in the events that had transpired on another Montreal evening nineteen years earlier, and had made the shocking outcome of this night possible, if not inevitable.

The Night Lévesque Took Quebec

Disheveled and dizzied, René Lévesque found himself hustled into the cavernous Paul Sauvé Arena in Montreal on the evening of November 15, 1976, facing a rapturous crowd of shrieking supporters. It was beyond belief what had happened in the polling booths of Quebec that day. In his coat pocket Lévesque carried three sheets of paper on which he had spent the day scribbling notes. One was headed "defeat" and a second "victory." He'd put down a few thoughts on both. The third sheet titled "miracle" was still a blank. Yet that was the only way to sum up what had happened – a miracle. When Lévesque appeared on stage at ten-thirty, the thousands of supporters crammed into the hall erupted in cheers and chants of "*Le Québec aux Québécois!*" When he was finally able to speak, he began diffidently, "*Je pense que … je pense que …*" After many cheering interruptions Lévesque managed to add, "I must tell you with all my heart that we hoped, but we didn't expect it like that this year." He paused, and went on: "I have never thought that I could be so proud to be a Quebecer this evening!" The victory of the Parti Québécois, a party dedicated to the separation of Quebec from Canada, came with suddenness at twenty minutes to nine that evening when Radio-Canada announced that René Lévesque would command an over-whelming majority in the National Assembly; the PQ in just its third election had gone from a mere six seats to an incalculable sixty-nine (two more were added later on recounts), reducing the Liberals of Robert Bourassa to only twenty-six seats from the one hundred and two they'd held scant weeks before. Before the night was over, drivers were racing up and down the streets of the Anglo bastion of Westmount, honking their horns and shrieking their delight. It was a result dismaying to Canadians, as well as to media around the world. SEPARATISTS WIN IN QUEBEC bannered the New York *Post,* while the London *Evening Standard* screamed SEPARATISTS TAKE QUEBEC. The dollar tumbled by nearly two cents, to just over 97 cents U.S. The PQ victory set off a flight of English-speaking businesses and professionals from Montreal, contributed to a decade of economic decline in what had been Canada's greatest commercial city, and divided a generation of Quebec's rising intellectual class on the single, all-consuming issue of sovereignty for the surviving North American homeland of French language and culture.

René Lévesque emerged from the 1960s – the decisive years of Quebec's political rebirth – committed to interventionist government as a bulwark of social progress and a means of achieving equality of individuals. As Quebec was throwing off its age-old clerical domination and English supremacy in both business and politics, he went one step further than the other notable Quebec figures of the day – Pierre Trudeau, Jean Lesage, Jean Marchand, Claude Ryan – and embraced the *indépendentiste* philosophy of those who argued that Quebec must seize full control of all the levers of the state if it was to realize the historic goal of French Canada: the survival and success of the Quebec people and nation. Lévesque came to that conclusion not from a perspective sheltered by a classical Quebec Catholic upbringing, but from one shaped by experience outside its traditional society and beyond Canada itself. Raised in the largely English-speaking Gaspé village of New Carlisle, the son of a country lawyer, Lévesque attended a local bilingual one-room school before being sent to a proper French boarding school. After the death of his father and his mother's remarriage, young René earned an arts degree at Laval University in Quebec City, enrolled in law, but gave it up after experiencing the thrill of part-time work on local radio stations – and being suspended for smoking in class.

Along with most young French-speaking Quebecers, Lévesque had no desire to be conscripted in World War II. He headed instead to the United States where he joined the American Office of War Information. Assigned to the French-language division of the OWI, Lévesque saw duty in Europe, witnessed the liberation of Dachau, and after the war worked for the international service of the Canadian Broadcasting Corporation. Lévesque began to attract the mythic status that he would carry to his political career by becoming a TV star as host of the Radio-Canada current affairs show, *Point de Mire* (roughly translated as Target or Bull's-Eye). When the producers of Radio-Canada went on strike just after Christmas, 1958, Lévesque became their militant supporter. The strike brought to him the same social awakening that Trudeau and Marchand had found in the great Asbestos workers strike of 1948. With the *ancienne regime* of Union Nationale premier Maurice Duplessis about to expire (hastened by Duplessis' own death in 1959), Lévesque accepted the invitation of Quebec Liberal leader Jean Lesage to stand for election in 1960. Not yet forty, he was elected MNA for Montreal-Laurier and sworn in first as minister of public works, then natural resources, becoming the key figure in the nationalization of the province's electric utilities and the creation of Hydro-Quebec. The Lesage administration gave birth to what would become known as Quebec's "Quiet Revolution," a phenomenon that would accelerate after the return of the UN to power under Daniel Johnson in 1966. Becoming disillusioned with both parties, Lévesque began to rethink his approach to constitutional issues and Quebec's relations with the federal government. Splitting with Lesage's successor, Robert Bourassa, he sat as an independent from 1967 to 1970. He first founded his *Mouvemont souveraineté,* then managed its merger with the rival *Rassemblement pour l'indépendence nationale* (RIN) at the end of 1968, taking the name Parti Québécois. In the 1970 election, the PQ won only seven seats. In 1973, in the wake of the Quebec crisis over the kidnapping of a British diplomat and the murder of a Quebec cabinet minister by members of the extremist *Front de*

Liberation du Québec (FLQ), the PQ did even less well. Lévesque ran and lost both times. By 1976, with the PQ attracting a growing stable of impressive young Quebec technocrats, and amid growing dissatisfaction with Bourassa's Liberals over such scandals as the sale of tainted beef, Quebecers were ready to listen to the PQ.

Lévesque's decisive rejection of violence and his denunciation of separatist extremism, combined with a commitment to hold a referendum before making any move to split from Canada, reassured voters that the PQ offered a "safe" alternative. Lévesque's personality, as described by biographer Graham Fraser, was a combination of the "transparently honest, impulsive, mischievous, modest, outspoken, and provocative."[2] On November 15, 1976, Quebecers demonstrated their confidence and trust in the PQ and its leader in an abundance even Lévesque found hard to accept. They struck down Liberal cabinet ministers and candidates all over the province, giving the PQ forty per cent of the popular vote. One of the sweetest victories was the triumph of poet-journalist Gerard Godin over the now-detested Robert Bourassa in Montreal-Mercier.

Lévesque had gathered around him some of the most brilliant minds of Quebec, including academics and former public servants, as well as the core of a hard-line separatist movement that was now in full flowering. His vice-premier and minister of education, Jacques Morin, had taught in Europe and was a former president of Quebec's Estates General. Labour lawyer Robert Burns, a committed socialist, became parliamentary leader. Lévesque put former civil servants Claude Morin and Jacques Parizeau in senior posts, Morin to intergovernmental affairs and Parizeau to finance. It is said that Parizeau boarded a train to the West for a federal-provincial conference a federalist and got off in Calgary a separatist. Camille Laurin, a psychiatrist, became minister for economic affairs.

All ideological movements – and the Parti Québécois is a primary example – must learn to live with the tensions that arise between its purists and its pragmatists. A movement that fails to accommodate conflict over the ways and means of putting principles into practice can soon be torn apart. In the case of the PQ, the pure separatists have only one goal, full and complete independence, and regard any bending on the road to its achievement as a betrayal of the cause. The pragmatists, as exemplified by Lévesque, understand that the conflicting pressures of a democratic society require accommodation and compromise. This lesson had not been fully learned by the PQ when René Lévesque made his first big speech after the 1976 election, to the Economic Club of New York. Prophetically, it was written largely by Jacques Parizeau, and it contained a blunt warning that the government of Quebec would pursue only one goal: "This government was born of a young political party which had gained strength during the two previous elections, with political sovereignty as its prime objective." The speech, although eloquent, ranked as a disaster in terms of establishing international business credibility for the new government. It served to ease the pressure that the nationalist core of the PQ had been putting on Lévesque to rush to independence, but it also set off warning bells for the business community. The flight from Quebec of English-Canadian businesses and professionals was soon underway. The exodus began in January, 1978 when Thomas Galt, president of the Sun Life Company of Canada announced that after a century in Montreal, it would be moving its head office to Toronto. He blamed the PQ policy to make French the language of work in Quebec; the company would no longer be able to bring in people "with the necessary qualifications and competence in English to transact the daily business of the company." Anglo businesses would eventually learn to live with the francization brought about by the PQ's first piece of legislation, Bill 101. It came at a high price: the replacement by the end of the nineteen eighties of Montreal by Toronto as Canada's foremost commercial city.

From the beginning of the PQ, strains within the party have been heightened by the ethnic and racist tendencies at its separatist core. While Lévesque and others sought to present Quebec as a nation of generous tolerance, an open, pluralist and multiethnic society with equal room for French and English-speaking citizens while offering space to immigrants, a sense of tribalism has always dominated the PQ. Just over eighty per cent of Quebec's population is French-speaking, but as a minority language in North America the position of French has been declining for nearly a century. In Ontario, four out of ten families of French descent no longer speak the language at home. In Quebec, the relative decline of French would have been greater but for the exodus of English-speakers. To the intellectual class, the combination of Quebec's lowest birth rate and the preference of immigrants for the English-language community have left the status of the French language in Quebec – and especially in Montreal – precarious and uncertain.

Language aside, as if that's possible in Quebec, there were other cultural values at work in hastening the growth of separatism. Successive federal governments have sought to build a pan-Canadian national culture in which all provinces have the same rights and responsibilities – all are "equal." This approach implicitly rejects the concept held by Quebec nationalists that Confederation came about as a pact between two founding peoples, English and French, and that Canada is a bi-national or even a multi-national state with Quebec representing a people and a nation within that state. It was this philosophy that gave rise to the view that Quebec is entitled to recognition as a "distinct society"; this is what Quebec, as far as its intellectuals are concerned, really wants. The failure of English Canada to accept this will ultimately, according to this view, seal the fate of the Canadian Confederation. The twin trajectories of two powerful but rival political personalities – René Lévesque and Pierre Trudeau – created a collision of forces as Quebec and Canada began to learn to live with the victory of the PQ in 1976. Aside from a deep personal resentment that existed between the two – Lévesque thought Trudeau an arrogant dilettante – sharply contrasting political philosophies were at work; collectivism vs individualism. Trudeau saw the rights of the individual as paramount and sought to put the state in a subservient role. ("There is no room for the state in the bedrooms of the nation.") Lévesque and even more so the influential intellectual class of French-speaking Quebec supporting him, regarded their duty to protect the collectively of French language and culture as indivisible from their responsibility to the individual citizen.

The 1980 Referendum – First Step to Separation

René Lévesque won the 1976 election by rejecting the insistent pressure of his nationalist core to fight the campaign on independence. He instead focused on unemployment, taxes and the province's mounting debt. The PQ slogan *"on a besoin d'un vrai gouvernement"* (We need a real government) set the tone. As early as 1973, the PQ had promised it would not move toward independence without first gaining the approval of voters in a referendum. Lévesque repeated that commitment in 1976. For a time following Levesqué's New York speech, as the party concentrated on mastering the levers of government power and dealing with the crises that befall governments from day to day, separation receded into the background. One crisis that Lévesque survived admirably was a personal one that arose from his involvement in the road death of a 62-year-old derelict war veteran, Edgar Trottier. Early on the morning of Sunday, February 6, 1977, Levesqué drove over and killed Trottier; the man had been lying on a main thoroughfare, Cotes-des-neiges, apparently drunk, apparently hoping to be picked up and taken either to a hospital or a homeless shelter. Lévesque had spent the evening with his personal secretary and companion (and later wife) Corinne Côté at the home of his good friend, Yves Michaud. A good deal of wine had been consumed. The event shocked Lévesque but the combination of alcohol, a car, a partying premier and a dead body failed to stir the wrath of the public or dull the charismatic glow surrounding him. Five months later, Lévesque paid a twenty-five dollar fine for driving without his glasses.

The strategy of using a referendum as a door opening for independence is generally credited to one of the PQ's originals, Claude Morin. Morin served first as an aide to Liberal Premier

Jean Lesage (writing all his budget speeches), then as deputy minister of federal-provincial affairs under both Lesage and UN Premier Daniel Johnson. Morin advocated moving to sovereignty by stages (*"par étapes"*) although he denies ever having used the precise expression. Nevertheless, Morin, the quiet suburban professor married to a woman from Philadelphia he'd met while studying at Columbia University in New York, became the primary architect of the PQ's cautious approach. It had long been recognized within separatist circles that only a minority of the population – somewhere between one-quarter and one-third – was fully committed to having Quebec pull out of Canada. In a document Morin prepared for the PQ national executive in 1974, he warned: "The achievement of independence cannot be instantaneous, or swift, still less abrupt."[3] At this time, the referendum idea was a hard sell on the PQ's *indépendentistes.* A compromise softened the blow: only if a PQ government was unable to negotiate sovereignty with Ottawa would there be resort to a referendum. That position was watered down further by 1978, when Lévesque began to talk about the idea of sovereignty-association. The concept was spelled out in more detail in a position paper, *D'égal à égal* (Between Equals), adopted formally at a party convention in June, 1979 and brought to full flowering in a white paper tabled in the National Assembly on November 1, 1979. The paper, 118 pages in French and 109 in English, was entitled *La nouvelle entente Québec-Canada* (A New Deal. The Quebec government proposal for a new partnership between equals: sovereignty-association.)

It was in this document that the Quebec independence movement carefully camouflaged its separatist intentions. The paper proposed continued use of the Canadian dollar, a customs union, and free circulation of goods and services. After that, it got more unreal; there would be lots of committees and councils consisting of people in equal numbers from Quebec and Canada. Quebec would be a country with its own seat at the United Nations and would pass its own laws, but wouldn't have its own money or its own fiscal policy. Public opinion polls at the time showed that most looked on sovereignty-association as a mere re-arrangement within Confederation. Nearly half did not think it would mean Quebec becoming a country "distinct from Canada" and nearly three-quarters said they wouldn't want that to happen, anyway. A third thought Quebec would continue to send MPs to Ottawa. It was assumed Canadian old age pensions would still go to Quebecers, and the matter of Quebec having to assume its share of Canada's debt was to be left to future negotiation. It all seemed to support comedian Yvon Deschamp's 1977 joke: "Quebecers want an independent Quebec – in a strong Canada."

Events were moving quickly outside Quebec as well as within. The federal Liberal government of Pierre Trudeau had been defeated in June, 1979, leading Lévesque and the PQ to the conclusion that their time had truly come; a much-feared confrontation between the PQ and Trudeau, who was Quebec's most credible and articulate opponent of separatism, could now be avoided. By the end of the year, however, the miscalculations of the new Conservative Prime Minister, Joe Clark, led to his government's defeat over its first budget. The tumultuous events surrounding the budget debate caused the Liberals to insist that Trudeau reconsider his planned retirement. In a general election on February 18, 1980, the Liberals won a comfortable majority and Pierre Trudeau was back at 24 Sussex street, the home of Prime Ministers, welcoming fellow Canadians "to the nineteen eighties." Quebec's Liberal party began the year with renewed strength, having won three by-elections under its new leader, the revered journalist Claude Ryan who had given up the editorship of *Le Devoir* to take over party leadership from Robert Bourassa. None of these developments deterred Lévesque in his determination to hold the referendum; it would take place during the party's first term in office, and he was convinced it could be won. A two-week debate on the referendum bill occurred in March, and the vote was set for May 20, 1980. The idea of sovereignty-association seemed to be catching on: a poll published by the *Institut Québécois d'Opinion Publique* early in the year found that forty-seven per cent of Quebecers – and fifty-five per cent of francophones – would vote Yes. Strict rules were set up for the referendum campaign, with Yes and No committees to be formally organized. Only the committees would be authorized to raise funds and campaign. The question itself was carefully constructed to gain the broadest possible support:

> "The government of Quebec has made public its proposal to negotiate a new agreement with the rest of Canada based on the equality of nations; This agreement would enable Quebec to acquire the exclusive power to make its own laws, levy its taxes and establish relations abroad – in other words, sovereignty – and, at the same time to maintain with Canada an economic association including a common currency; No change in political status resulting from these negotiations will be effected without approval by the people through another referendum; ON THESE TERMS DO YOU GIVE THE GOVERNMENT OF QUEBEC THE MANDATE TO NEGOTIATE THE PROPOSED AGREEMENT BETWEEN QUEBEC AND CANADA? ____YES___NO.

When one considers that the PQ was a first term government and the party was barely more than a decade old, its referendum campaign was incredibly well organized. As Réne Lévesque recounted in his memoirs, "Committees for the Oui" spread throughout the country "like wildfire." There was at least one in every riding, in addition to ones representing special groups such as economists, lawyers or scientists. Lévesque recruited the prominent businessman, Fernand Paré to chair the "Foundation for the Oui" that would raise more than three and one-half million dollars. Except for a fringe Anglo group, the *comité Anglophone pour la souveraineté-association*, the non-French population was solidly in the *non* camp. Across Canada, pundits and politicians worried about the consequences of Quebec's separation. Toronto economist Abraham Rotstein estimated that one hundred thousand jobs in Ontario were dependent on the Quebec market; figures for other provinces were less dramatic but no less significant. It all led to an overwhelmingly assumption that put to the test, TROC (the rest of Canada) would negotiate the terms of a new association with Quebec. Prime Minister Trudeau was not so sure. In a talk before the Montreal Chamber of Commerce, he ridiculed the logic that a Yes vote would lead to negotiation. It might obligate Quebec to ask for talks, "but can it obligate others," he pondered. "Suppose Cuba, or suppose Haiti would like to make an association, a common market with Canada; it likes Canadian prosperity, likes the Canadian countryside, likes Canadian women, likes the economic level of Canadians, etc. They want to have an economic union with us, a kind of common market, they take a vote. Massively the Cubans or the Haitians say 'YES, we want union with Canada.' In the name of democracy, would we be obligated to form that union?" The audience, as Trudeau knew it would, laughed uproariously. The sarcastic comparison of Quebec with the two impoverished islands also infuriated Réne Lévesque, as it was meant to. Trudeau followed this up with his most important speech at a large No rally on May 14 at the same arena where the PQ had celebrated its 1976 victory. That night, he pledged that "a No will be interpreted as a mandate to change the constitution, to renew federalism. We will start immediately the mechanism of renewing the constitution, and we will not stop until it is done." To Lévesque, this was just so much propaganda, part of the "deluge of threats and blackmail" by the federal government meant to dissuade Quebecers from voting Yes.

In an election or a referendum, little things can have huge consequences. So it was with a chance remark by Lise Payette, Lévesque's minister of state for the status of women. At a PQ regional meeting in Montreal, she read an excerpt from a children's school book in which a little girl, Yvette, is depicted as happily carrying out the traditional domestic role long assigned to girls; while she contentedly sweeps the rug her brother excels in sports and aspires to win lots of trophies. Deploring the sexism of the passage, Payette urged her audience of women not to be afraid like the English, and vote No, but to break out of the bonds of tradition that had been holding them back and vote Yes. Left at this point, the comment would have been little noted. But then Payette added that Claude Ryan, the Liberal chief and leader of the No forces, was the kind of man who wanted a Quebec full of Yvettes, and furthermore, he was married to one. The slander – as it clearly was, for Madelaine Ryan had a distinguished career as a TV talkshow host and as a member of many public bodies, including the Superior Council of Education – reverberated across Quebec. Payette apologized in the National Assembly, saying she had no intention of insulting anyone, especially Ryan's wife. It failed to undo the meanness of the comment. Encouraged by Liberal party activists, thousands of women across the province rallied to form Yvette committees, culminating in a huge rally at the Montreal Forum. No other event of the referendum, including Trudeau's key speech, would give the No side such surging momentum.

In the last two weeks of the campaign, it became evident to Lévesque that support for sovereignty-association was draining away. In rally after rally across the province, he told his French-speaking listeners that only fear of the English establishment and the "infernal propaganda" of the English media stood against Quebec achieving sovereignty. In the campaign's closing days, PQ pollsters concluded that a Yes majority was in doubt even among francophones. Referendum day, May 30, dawned sunny and warm, a beautiful spring day throughout Quebec. The turn-out at the polls was a massive eighty five point six per cent. Within moments of the polls closing at seven o'clock, the outcome was evident. Only twelve ridings, including four strongly nationalist seats in the Saguenay-Lac St-Jean region, withstood the No tide. By a sixty per cent to forty per cent margin, the referendum was lost. At the Paul Sauvé Arena, the five thousand supporters who had gathered to celebrate, instead shed tears as they listened to nationalist songs sung by Pauline Julien. At nine-thirty, Réne Lévesque appeared on stage. For seven minutes, he waited out the adoration of his audience. He spoke but briefly and voice cracking with emotion, led the crowd in the singing of the sovereignist anthem, "*Gen du pays.*" He left the stage after whispering, "*a la prochaine*," until next time.

Lévesque, the Constitution and the Defeat of the PQ

Eleven months later, the PQ would be returned to power with an even stronger majority – eighty seats and forty-nine per cent of the vote, to forty-two seats for the Liberals, with forty-six per cent of the vote. The re-election of the Parti Québécois on April 13, 1981 presented Réne Lévesque with both an opportunity and a dilemma: the opportunity to participate in shaping a new Canadian constitution that might strengthen the powers of Quebec and the other provinces, the dilemma that a successful reshaping of the federation would diminish the rationale for sovereignty.

Two events stand out as seminal in the run-up to the federal government's patriation of the British North America Act and the enactment of a new Constitution Act with Trudeau's cherished Charter of Rights and Freedoms. When the Canadian government sent the British parliament its plan to ignore the provinces and unilaterally patriate the BNA Act, it was turned over to the foreign affairs committee of the UK House of Commons. In a January, 1981, report, the committee challenged Ottawa's position that London should ignore what the provinces might have to say on the matter. It was not willing, as Trudeau had put it, to just "hold their noses and send it back." The opinions of the provinces did count, chairman Sir Anthony Kershaw responded, and the UK should not grant Ottawa's request. Another blow to Trudeau's intentions was dealt, by the Supreme Court of Canada. By a vote of seven to two, the Court found that while Ottawa was under no legal requirement to seek provincial agreement to amend the constitution, to do so without such agreement would defy constitutional convention. At least "substantial" – although not necessarily "unanimous" – agreement of the provinces would be needed. The Supreme Court finding gave Lévesque the rationale for a resolution in the National Assembly asking Ottawa to renounce "its unilateral course of action ... and resume negotiations immediately with full respect for the principles and conventions that must apply to any modification of the federal system." The careful wording left Claude Ryan little option but to support the resolution although nine Liberals, all representing anglophone ridings voted against it. For the rest of his life, Ryan pointed to that vote as evidence that Quebec opposed Trudeau's plan for unilateral patriation. As leader of the Opposition in the Quebec legislature, Ryan had no formal role in the constitutional talks, but the Quebec Liberal party did develop its own plan that Ryan sent to Trudeau. He refused to more than glance at it. "I had gone into politics to save Canada in Quebec, but I never had a chance to discuss our plan seriously with him," Ryan said. "On the whole issue of Quebec nationalism, Trudeau's view was that whatever concession you made to nationalist sentiment would lead to separation."[4]

The ten Premiers met Trudeau in the federal conference center, the old Ottawa railway station, on Monday, November 2, 1981. It was the most important gathering of first ministers in Canadian history, and it created a collision of triangular forces. Trudeau's insistence on quick patriation, accompanied by a seven/fifty formula for future amendments (seven of the provinces having fifty per cent or more of the population) clashed with Lévesque'ss determination to extract added rights for Quebec, even if it meant giving them to other provinces. The English premiers were anxious as always to expand their sphere of influence, but reluctant to grant privileges to Quebec that they would not enjoy themselves. For three days, the three competing forces argued over the Prime Minister's vision for a new con- stitution and a Charter of Rights, deadlocked between Trudeau's take it or leave it version and no fewer than six counter-offers produced at various times by the provinces. Finally, key players in the provincial delegations decided a solution had to be found. Ontario had always been inclined to support Ottawa on federal- provincial issues. Ontario's attorney-general Roy McMurtry, and the Saskatchewan premier, Roy Romanow, met with the federal minister of justice, Jean Chrétien, in a little-used kitchen in the convention center. Their talk has since been credited for bringing about the "kitchen accord" that broke the constitutional deadlock, but it has been equally condemned by Quebec's sovereignists for having set up a "night of the long knives." The understanding the three came away with was finally accepted – over the protests of the Quebec delegation – as the basis for a constitutional agreement. The provinces would be able to opt out of federal programs, but without financial compensation. Trudeau's cherished Charter of Rights would include minority-language education rights, but the provinces would be able to override certain provisions through a "notwithstanding" clause. Trudeau and the nine English Premiers had agreed to a new legal framework for Canada that gave not a single additional power to Quebec. The deal unquestionably met the Supreme Court's requirement for "substantial" agreement, if at the expense of Quebec. Trudeau, speaking particularly to Quebec, viewed the agreement as historic: "*Après 114 ans d'existence, le Canada deviant, au sens technique, au sens legal, enfant, un pays indépendent.*" Lévesque left Ottawa furious with Trudeau, in a rage against the other premiers, and humiliated at having failed to win a single concession for Quebec.

On April 17, 1982, Queen Elizabeth signed the proclamation of the new Constitution of Canada at a ceremony on Parliament Hill. Prime Minister Trudeau had achieved what had eluded all his predecessors, the investing of constitutional rights and powers in the Parliament of Canada. In Quebec, Claude Ryan's reign at the head of the Quebec Liberal party was coming to an end. Liberal MNAs were growing increasingly restive at his autocratic style of leadership, especially when it failed to produce victory at the polls. In one of the most remarkable comebacks in Canadian political history, Robert Bourassa returned to lead the party seven years after having departed in disgrace. By 1985 – a year after Pierre Trudeau's famous "walk in the snow" and the election of a new Progressive Conservative government headed by Brian Mulroney – the time had come for Réne Lévesque to give up the struggle that had consumed almost half his life. He was sixty-two, the polls were bad, he was tired, the referendum had been lost, and the new constitution was being rapidly accepted everywhere in Canada, including Quebec. On June 20, 1985, the final day of the spring session of the National Assembly, after being showered with congratulations on the occasion of the twenty-fifth anniversary of his first election on June 22, 1960, Lévesque resigned. In September, he was succeeded as PQ leader and premier by Pierre Marc Johnson, son of a former Union Nationale premier. Johnson went to the people on December 2, 1985, unsure of the strength of his own sovereignist beliefs, and burdened with an unimpressive record from the government's most recent term in office. There was little surprise when the election brought an end to nine years of Pequiste power, restoring the Liberals to office with ninety-nine seats. The election completed Robert Bourassa's public rehabilitation. Two years later, having written his memoirs and having begun the round of fund-raising dinners and formal conferences that mark the life of a retired premier, Lévesque collapsed and died of a heart attack at dinner. The date was Sunday, November 1, 1987. With Lévesque gone, the PQ led by a man who was about to renounce separatism and a new Liberal government in office, the prospect of Quebec independence seemed more distant than it had for twenty years. In all of Canada, there was one only man who – intentionally or otherwise – could fan the flames of flickering resentment against the new constitution and the iniquitous treatment Quebec was said to have received. He was the Member of Parliament for Manicouagan, Quebec, and he resided at 24 Sussex Street in Ottawa. His name was Brian Mulroney.

Brian Mulroney and the Separatists

The eighteenth prime minister of Canada, Brian Mulroney, son of an electrician from the Quebec paper mill town of Baie Comeau, stormed into office at the head of a new Progressive Conservative government by winning fifty per cent of the popular vote on September 4, 1984. It was enough to give him a record 211 of the 272 House of Commons seats. Mulroney had chosen the law and politics for the access they gave him to power and fame. Without previous parliamentary experience, he ran for the leadership of the Progressive Conservative party in 1973, losing to Joe Clark. In 1983, when Clark put his leadership up for grabs despite having won a sixty-six per cent endorsement in a vote of party members, Mulroney was ready. Friends from the party's back rooms, business allies he'd gained as president of the Iron Ore Company of Canada, and Quebec nationalists he'd cultivated from Union Nationale, PQ and provincial Liberal circles, joined to help him win over the Conservative convention. The substance of Mulroney's politics was difficult to define in his early days in office, but his style – which would ultimately become his undoing – soon became evident. A combination of hubris and overweening ambition would eventually turn him into the country's most detested public figure. Mulroney's willingness to reverse his position on the two great issues of his era – the constitution and free trade – marked him as a pragmatic politician who could break from his party's traditions when it seemed appropriate to do so. His dangerous gambit to undo the newly designed constitution of Canada, on the questionable premise that Quebec had been excluded from its formation, created the opening for a resurgence of sovereignty so powerful that it would come within a few thousand votes of splitting Canada apart.

Before winning the Conservative party leadership in 1973, Mulroney had spoken in support of Trudeau's plan to patriate the British North America Act. Once he became leader and surveyed the wreckage of the Conservative party in Quebec that had been left by Joe Clark, Mulroney understood that he would have to make Quebec's "exclusion" from the constitution the basis of any alliance with Quebec nationalists. Mulroney sought out such well-known separatist supporters as Lucien Bouchard. Parti Québécois organizers campaigned for Conservative candidates, many of whom were avowed separatists who had voted Yes in 1980. Criticized for this, Mulroney responded by asserting that he was drawing in people from all parties and would reconcile them all to a shared Canadian vision. In point of fact, he was comfortable attacking the Trudeau vision of Canada because ever since his days as a Quebec organizer for PC leader Robert Stanfield, he had been a supporter of the newly-adopted Tory *"deux nations"* policy. Seen as a way to break the Liberal grip on Quebec, *deux nations* was based on the concept of Canada as a partnership of two founding peoples, the English and French. Its effect was to treat Quebec and the rest of Canada as two equal entities, exactly the goal of Quebec separatists. They eagerly embraced the Conservative strategy, knowing they could never achieve such accommodation with the Liberal party, especially after the advent of Pierre Trudeau. Ironically, the results Mulroney achieved from his alliance with Quebec nationalists differed considerably from those of previous Conservative Prime Ministers. Robert Borden had won a majority in Quebec but didn't need his nationalist supporters to govern, and didn't use them; Joe Clark needed them but didn't have them; only Brian Mulroney had them, didn't need them, but allowed himself to be used by them.

Mulroney's most prominent separatist recruit in 1984, although he did not run for Parliament then, was Lucien Bouchard. As a speechwriter and an advisor on Quebec strategy, Bouchard crafted Mulroney's fateful August 6, 1984 speech at Sept-Isles. It promised Quebec a new constitutional deal. It would be a deal, Mulroney assured listeners, to which the Quebec National Assembly could "give its consent with honour and enthusiasm." Premier Lévesque responded warmly and hinted broadly that Quebecers should vote Conservative. The soon-to-be Prime Minister was, in fact, committing Canada to dismantle its constitutional framework and meet the demands of Lévesque and his successors by permitting the legislature of Quebec, rather than Quebec's MPs (seventy of seventy-five of whom had voted for the 1981 constitution) to speak for the people of Quebec on constitutional issues. Claude Ryan remembered that Mulroney "was not a very scrupulous man intellectually; he could shift from one position to another according to the needs of the operation." The approach worked well, enabling the Conservatives to win fifty-eight of Quebec's seventy-five seats. Once in office, Mulroney condemned the constitution as "not worth the paper it was written on." Later he would deliver a series of ultimatums to English Canada warning that Quebec would become a distinct society either under the terms that he was offering, or it would leave and become one "outside Canada." Support for sovereignty in Quebec, negligible at the time he took office, rose to almost two-thirds of the population by the end of the twin disasters of Mulroney statecraft – the Meech Lake and Charlottetown accords. Mulroney, who could never be accused of being a supporter of separatism himself, had legitimized separatist complaints against English Canada and had raised expectations in Quebec that could not be fulfilled. It was the Prime Minister's policies, more than the strength of sovereignist advocacy, which led to the inevitable anti-federalist backlash that brought Canada to the brink of disruption in 1995.

The Meech Lake Accord, named after the lake that is the site of a government conference center near Ottawa, was hailed by the Prime Minister as a "historic accomplishment" when he presented it to Parliament on May 1, 1987. Treating Quebec almost as if it were already outside the Canadian legal framework, Mulroney said the Accord would "allow Quebec to rejoin the Canadian constitutional family." The agreement, in fact, represented the almost-complete fulfillment of Quebec's constitutional agenda, "superimposed on a blank canvas provided by Mulroney."[5] Its essence was to meet five conditions set out by Quebec, most notably to give it a recognition granted to none other, that of a "distinct society," as well as restoring its veto over most constitutional amendments. A number of other changes were proposed to strengthen provincial powers at the expense of the federal government, in effect setting a course for the "Swissification" of Canada – giving provinces the kinds of powers enjoyed by the small, historically autonomous regions of Switzerland, known as cantons.

The fatal flaw in Meech Lake was the three-year time frame allowed for public hearings and ratification by the provinces. By early 1990, New Brunswick and Newfoundland had elected new governments with premiers opposed to many aspects of the deal. The idea of one province, Quebec, having rights not possessed by the others had never been accepted in Canada and the trials of Meech Lake demonstrated how opposed English Canada remained to that principle. Only in Quebec did polls show a majority in support of the accord. Meech Lake died on a pleasant week in June, 1990, interred at the hands of two unlikely pallbearers. In Manitoba, Elijah Harper, a native MLA disturbed at the possible consequences for Canada's aboriginal population, laid an eagle feather on his desk in the legislature as he stood alone to deny an extension to the debate on ratification. In Newfoundland, the newly-elected premier, Clyde Wells, rejected a last-minute maneuvre by the federal government to extend the three-year deadline for ratification. He adjourned the Newfoundland House without a vote. Meech was buried, but it was actually killed by hostile public opinion across Canada. Ironically, opposition to Meech was brought to a fever pitch by Mulroney's own boasting of how he had bested the premiers. His assertion in a *Globe and Mail* interview that he had "rolled the dice" and won in a test of wills with the premiers caused a sensation. Polls showed that only 25 per cent of voters approved of his actions. Desertions from Mulroney's Quebec caucus, disgruntled over concessions and delay, began to mount. The cruelest blow was delivered by Lucien Bouchard, by now Mulroney's minister of the environment. Weeks before the expiry of Meech, Bouchard resigned from the cabinet and the Conservative party, convinced that Quebec's demands would never be met. He foreshadowed his leave-taking by sending a congratulatory message to the Parti Québécois on the tenth anniversary of the 1980 referendum. "This country does not work anymore," he wrote. Joined by a handful of defecting Conservatives and Liberals, Bouchard soon became leader of the first federal party committed to sovereignty, the Bloc Québécois. It was made up initially of five separatist-leaning Conservative MPs that Mulroney had helped bring into the party: Francois Gerin, Gilbert Chartrand, Louis Plamandon, Benoit Tremblay and Nic Leblanc.

The defeat of Meech set crisis bells ringing in Ottawa, Quebec City, and provincial capitals across the country. Following the re-election of the Mulroney government in the free trade election of 1988, a flurry of special inquiries and public commissions, some set up by Mulroney and others by Quebec, pondered Canada's constitutional future. Quebec premier Robert Bourassa, who had been re-elected in 1989, insisted he would no longer take part in federal-provincial talks. The boom of the nineteen-eighties was petering out, federal debt was doubling under Mulroney's free-spending ways, and new taxes such as the GST were being imposed in a desperate attempt to head off a budget crisis. Amidst this, the government's focus was on the constitution, with former prime minister Joe Clark given the task of finding a formula to satisfy Quebec. He faced an urgent deadline: the Liberal-dominated Quebec National Assembly had voted to hold a referendum no later than the fall of 1992. Its purpose would be either to ratify a new offer from Canada, or if none were forthcoming, to measure public opinion on an alternative, i.e., independence. Clark's solution was to rebundle the principles of Meech, broadened by concessions to Canada's native population, now styled as First Nations, and to the smaller provinces, offering them more seats in the Senate. This all became known as the Charlottetown Accord, the label attached to the set of proposals that were finally agreed on at a meeting of first ministers in the island capital in August, 1992. October 26 was set as the date for both the Quebec and federal referendums.

Because Charlottetown retained the "distinct society" clause, Premier Bourassa accepted it as a "starting point" but Quebec's sovereignists (a term popularized by the Toronto *Globe and Mail* as a more respectful way of referring to separatists) saw it as more betrayal. Prime Minister Mulroney, overstating the case as was his habit, hailed Charlottetown as "the result of the most far-reaching and thorough process of consultation and discussion ever held by a Canadian government, and perhaps by any government in a modern industrialized world." None of this impressed Lucien Bouchard. He laconically told the House, "the Prime Minister has been extolling the so-called virtues of the accord, rallying to his cause the leader of the official opposition, his new friend, and dead sovereignists. I would like to give the Prime Minister an opportunity to confront a real live sovereignist. I ask him to accept the challenge of meeting me in public debate in Quebec, anywhere and at any time during the referendum campaign." It never happened, but a fierce public debate did ensue. In Toronto, Prime Minister Mulroney told the Empire Club, a bastion of the Ontario establishment, that "the choice is simple: Quebec will either be a distinct society within Canada, or it will develop as a distinct society outside Canada." In Montreal, the former prime minister, Pierre Trudeau, denounced Charlottetown as "a big mess." He used the setting of a Chinese restaurant, The Egg Roll, to deliver a stinging indictment that seemed to capture public apprehension about further tinkering with the constitution. Trudeau wrote critiques for *Maclean's* and *l'Actualité* magazines in which he described Quebec nationalists as "master blackmailers" feeding on an insatiable appetite for power. The criticism drove Mulroney to distraction. Rejection of the agreement, he thundered, would mean "the beginning of the process of dismantling Canada."

The defeat of the Charlottetown proposals in the referendum of October 26, 1992, delighted separatists, satisfied many federalists outside the Mulroney government, and put the Quebec sovereignty movement in a stronger position than at any time since 1980. The agreement was decisively repudiated by voters in six of the ten provinces, including Quebec, all the western provinces, and Nova Scotia. The margin of support in Ontario was razor-thin; across the country, fifty-four per cent voted against Charlottetown. A year later, Mulroney and the Conservatives were out of office, his chosen successor Kim Campbell humiliated in the greatest rejection ever dealt an outgoing government. Only two Tories, including Jean Charest in Sherbrooke, survived the Liberal sweep engineered by Jean Chrétien. Bouchard and the Bloc Québécois, capitalizing on the humiliation of Meech and Charlottetown, carried fifty-four of Quebec's federal seats. The party dedicated to the break-up of

Canada was now the Official Opposition in Parliament. The next year, 1994, found the Parti Québécois back in power, led by the rock-hard separatist Jacques Parizeau, vowing to talk about sovereignty "before, during and after elections." The PQ took seventy-seven seats that year, against forty-seven for the Liberals, and Parizeau intended to put Quebecers to the test at the first opportunity. As the date of the 1995 Quebec referendum approached, Brian Mulroney's prophecy was edging ever closer to fulfillment. He had failed to gain for Quebec the status of the distinct society he had promised. Quebec's sovereignists were now determined to do everything in their power to win that ranking on their own terms.

The Campaign and the Cause

Jacques Parizeau, who had risen to prominence as minister of finance in the Lévesque years, found comfort in his role at the heart of the separatist hard core of the party. The PQ had always chafed under their founder's more moderate approach, but now, taking a hard line stance, Parizeau even resurrected the dread word 'separation,' intending to run the referendum campaign on a clear commitment to independence. The party's polls showed that while it could win a majority if the referendum question linked sovereignty with economic association with Canada, a question on independence alone would fail among even francophone voters. Other polls produced a tantalizing variety of results: younger, better educated francophones living outside Montreal were more likely to support sovereignty; fifty-three per cent of those supporting sovereignty thought it did not mean separating from Canada and seventy-eight per cent hoped to "remain Canadians in a sovereign Quebec."[6] The polls forced Parizeau to listen to more moderate voices, especially that of Lucien Bouchard. The Bloc leader was calling for a formal economic association between Canada and a newly-sovereign Quebec. It was just one of many instances that saw the two at loggerheads. Parizeau, the arrogant, insistent autocrat who sprinkled his gallic witticisms with anglicisms ("by Jove") picked up from his London school days; Bouchard, the more emotional but shrewder schemer, with the pragmatist's ability to select what might look like a detour in the road to an independent Quebec, but one that would keep the separatist bus filled with gas while its driver searched for another route.

The fateful year of 1995 opened with Premier Parizeau off to Paris, where he received the assurances of President Jacques Chirac that France would quickly recognize a sovereign Quebec. Public hearings on the future of Quebec launched in February were boycotted by federalists, and found only lukewarm support from even traditional friends of sovereignty. Then, as often happens, a small incident, the closing by Ottawa of the *Collège Militaire Royale* in St Jean-sur-Richelieu, seemed to reinforce the idea that the federal government was somehow abandoning Quebec. It was time to gather sovereignist forces for the final push. "Parizeau was sure that if he rushed into the referendum the chances were greater of winning," says Claude Ryan. "He was impatient to become the first president of the Republic." On June 12, Parizeau brought together Bouchard and the former Liberal party youth leader, Mario Dumont of the fledgling *Action Démocratique du Québec*, to sign an agreement with the PQ on Quebec's future. It set out the terms by which a sovereign Quebec, following a Yes vote, would offer Canada "a formal treaty of economic and political partnership." It was breath-takingly presumptuous. There would be a council of ministers with equal representation from Quebec and Canada, each side having a veto. There would also be a joint parliament with little real power, and a tribunal to settle disagreements. The inevitable photo opportunity posed Parizeau in a double-handed handshake with his two partners, as if to signal who was the real boss. Within days, however, sovereignists were to be embarrassed by Parizeau. He off-handedly told a meeting of foreign ambassadors in Ottawa that after a Yes vote, Quebecers would be "trapped like lobsters thrown into boiling water." Throughout the summer, Parizeau went on the offensive, accusing Ottawa of "ganging up" with the

English premiers against Quebec. Busloads of PQ and BQ members toured nationalist strongholds in Quebec. On September 1, Bill 1, outlining Quebec's plans to establish sovereignty, was tabled in the National Assembly. The official decree launching the referendum was issued on October 1, and voting was set for October 30. Quebecers would be asked:

> "Do you agree that Quebec should become sovereign, after having made a formal offer to Canada for a new Economic and Political Partnership, within the scope of the Bill respecting the Future of Quebec and of the agreement signed on June 12, 1995. Yes or No?"

As the referendum campaign got underway, PQ strategists hoped to benefit from lingering dissatisfaction over the constitutional impasse and the continuing concern about Canada's troubled economic circumstances. The loss of seven hundred thousand English since 1976 no longer mattered and in fact was welcomed by many; most of the million and a half immigrants who had arrived since were integrating smoothly into French society. Still one of North America's most vibrant cities, Montreal was suffering from high unemployment, just as Canada was undergoing a crunching adjustment from the triple blows of recession, the introduction of free trade, and the new GST. Quebec's francophone intellectual class wields a powerful influence on public opinion. In 1995 it was almost unanimously pro-sovereignty; academics, artists, writers, radio and TV producers and other artisans viewed the dream of an independent Quebec as an idea whose time had come. For years, political leadership on both sides of the sovereignist argument had promoted Quebec as a nation and its population as a people. Even before the PQ, the provincial legislature had become the National Assembly and the traditional speech from the throne had been replaced with an inaugural address. Now signs outside Quebec City welcome drivers to the national capital, where the Quebec Museum has become the Quebec National Museum of Fine Arts.

Police are trained at the National Police School and firefighters at the National Firefighters School. There is a National Patriots Day that commemorates those who died in Lower Canada during the rebellions of 1837-38.

For these intellectuals the dream of a sovereign Quebec also envisioned a kinder, more cooperative society than the one that was emerging from the slash-and-burn deficit reduction tactics of Liberal finance minister Paul Martin in Ottawa, or Mike Harris' newly-launched Common Sense Revolution in Ontario. While the Quebec government struggled to contain its own spending, Parizeau ordered a freeze on all reductions until after the referendum. The collectivist bent of the PQ made it inevitable that the sovereignist movement would collide not only with the Trudeauesque philosophy about the supremacy of individual rights, but with the downsizing of government being pushed by free market advocates everywhere in North America.

Despite these circumstances, early polls indicted that the Yes side was failing to pick up the crucial "soft" nationalist vote needed for a majority. Then, a week after the calling of the referendum, the campaign changed suddenly and dramatically, exploding into a fierce emotional contest pitting the honour of a "humiliated" Quebec against the monolithic forces of a federal government intent on denying the people of Quebec their destiny. Premier Parizeau, recognizing he had failed to mount the momentum needed for a Yes victory, turned to Quebec's most popular politician, Lucien Bouchard, to rekindle sovereignist fire. Virtually surrendering control of the campaign, Parizeau named Bouchard the "chief negotiator" for Quebec in the discussions that would take place after a sovereignist victory. At a rally on October 7 at the Université de Montréal, Parizeau set off a fevered chant of "Lucien, Lucien, Lucien" when he asked, "Who will defend our interests? Who will represent us with honesty and efficiency? Who will keep his word?" There was no doubt that Bouchard's enormous personal popularity – reinforced by the sympathy he'd gained in losing a leg to flesh-eating disease – would radically change the tenor of the campaign.

The relationship between the campaign twins, for all that they both celebrated the goal of Quebec independence, was filled with friction and tension. The two often took contradictory stands. Bouchard briefly agreed with Parizeau's assertion that Quebec could proclaim sovereignty "within weeks or months" after the referendum, then hastily reversed himself, conceding that Quebec would have a "political, moral and even legal obligation" to work out a partnership with Canada. Bouchard shunned arguments on the economic merits of sovereignty; Parizeau went before the Montreal Junior Board of Trade to present a dizzying array of statistics on what he called "the costs of non-sovereignty." More appealing was Bouchard's bland assurance that a Yes vote – a *'baton magique'* – would solve all of Quebec's problems: "A Yes has magical meaning, because with a wave of a wand it will change the whole situation." Bouchard appealed to the deep emotional attachment of Québécois to their homeland and the symbols of nationhood, such as a distinctive passport. "The Quebec passport will be a beautiful thing. It will be a symbol of what we are, the symbol of our people, the symbol of our state, the symbol of our identity, and we'll be well-received everywhere with a Québécois passport."[7] Within days, the polls were showing the sovereignists had moved into the lead. The news cut another cent from the Canadian dollar and sent the Toronto Stock Exchange on its biggest drop in six years. There was much speculation about border posts being set up on the highways leading into Quebec.

Bouchard's intervention completely upset the federalist strategy, which had been built on a complacent belief that most Quebeckers were federalists at heart and would again vote to reject sovereignty. Under Quebec's referendum legislation, the No campaign was officially under the management of Daniel Johnson, the new leader of the Quebec Liberal party. His critics, of which there were many, thought Johnson lacked both imagination and sparkle. Prime Minister Jean Chrétien, who polls showed to be unpopular in Quebec, made himself virtually invisible. He assigned referendum responsibility to his new labour minister, the not especially effective Lucienne Robillard. Pierre Trudeau, aging and out of the public eye, was intentionally ignored. According to the view from Ottawa, the referendum was not to be seen as a threat, nor was there any serious possibility of a Yes victory. A more powerful reason for Ottawa's failure to intervene effectively and early was the success that separatists/sovereignists enjoyed in painting federalists as barely respectable *"vendus"* if not actual traitors to the cause of the Quebec people and nation.

It was only as evidence mounted of the escalating strength of the Yes side that worried federalists began to react. "It was realized two weeks before the referendum," recalls Claude Ryan, "that if nothing spectacular were done, we might well lose." Ottawa drew down large sums from its national unity reserve, a fund set up by Prime Minister Mulroney in 1992, to finance advertising, polling and field work for the federalist cause. In a near-panic, Daniel Johnson called Jean Chrétien to plead for some new federal commitment that would bring voters back from the Yes camp. The Prime Minister's response was to promise that the federal government would recognize the distinct status of Quebec. Chrétien made two interventions in as many days – a speech at the Verdun arena followed the next night by a TV address to all of Canada. Ryan believes these two talks may have drawn fifty thousand voters back to the federalist cause. In Verdun, seven thousand determined federalists jammed the arena while another six thousand filled the rain-soaked parking lot to watch the PM on video screens. They heard Chrétien warn that the referendum was about separatism, not about a renewal of Confederation. "For (Bouchard and Parizeau) there is no question of renewing federalism or obtaining recognition of Quebec as a distinct society," he said. "What they want is a separate country. The country they are planning is not an improved Canada, it is a separate Quebec. Think it through before you vote." The next night, Chrétien carried a stark message to Canadians: "What is at stake is our country. What is at stake is our heritage. To break up Canada or build Canada. To remain Canadian or no longer be Canadian. To stay or to leave. This is the issue of the referendum."

Chrétien was addressing the country, but he was speaking mainly to Quebec. He was trying to overcome sovereignist soft-pedaling of the consequences of a Yes vote, especially among the ten to fifteen percent who were thought to be ready to cast a "strategic" Yes ballot in the belief it would help Quebec win more power from Ottawa. "A Yes vote means the destruction of the political and economic union we already enjoy, nothing more." Chrétien said. "Are you ready to tell the world that people of different languages, different cultures and different backgrounds cannot live together in harmony? Have you found one good reason to destroy Canada? Do you really think it is worth abandoning the country we have built, and which our ancestors left us?" Chrétien was summoning up memories of the generations of French Canadian *habitants* who had built a homeland amidst the harsh terrain of this new world colony. He was appealing to their sense of history and family. He also was promising to support Quebec as a distinct society and to ensure that nothing would be done to affect the powers of Quebec without the consent of Quebecers.

The referendum split families and friends as it had never done in 1980. It split the federal cabinet; several ministers worried that Chrétien, as a Quebec MP, would be forced to resign if the federal government had to negotiate independence. "Who could speak for Canada?", Brian Tobin, the fisheries minister, wondered. The referendum also set off arguments over the territorial integrity of the province. Yes supporters insisted Quebec's territory was inviolable. When it separated, all of it would go. Anglo voters and First Nations residents held a different view. If Canada was divisible, they thought, so was Quebec. In northern Quebec, the home of twelve thousand Cree Indians and seventy-five hundred native Inuit, mini-referendums were organized with a simple and direct question: "Do you agree that Quebec will become sovereign? Yes or No?" In both cases, voting went ninety-six per cent against sovereignty. Quebec's first inhabitants were signaling that they would not be bound by the outcome of the referendum.

Among the big francophone majority, Bouchard's campaign was unfolding brilliantly. Its success emboldened Premier

Parizeau to assert that Anglophones had come to realize "sovereignty is part of the bargain" of living in Quebec. "They've known it for ten or fifteen years. " In a visit to a neighborhood packed with Haitian and other black immigrants, Parizeau confidently told them they had nothing to fear, that they'd get a Quebec passport and citizenship just like everyone else. There were, nevertheless, bumps along the road. Bouchard misspoke when he lamented the low birth rate among old-stock Quebecers, hinting that immigrants (non-white) could eventually become a majority. From the U.S. came quiet signals that Quebecers should resist the temptation to leave Canada. President Clinton put it into the careful language of international diplomacy: it's up to Canadians to decide their future but he couldn't understand why Canada, "a model to the world," would want to break up. The Quebec government bought up hundreds of millions of Canadian dollars in an effort to shore up the currency. The U.S. Secretary of State, Warren Christopher, weighed in with a warning that an independent Quebec couldn't take close ties with the U.S. for granted. All this drove the PQ strategists to distraction. In a clumsy attempt at damage control, the deputy premier, Bernard Landry, fired off a crusty letter to Christopher. "If the Yes side wins, as is now probable," he wrote, "Quebec voters and the historians will remember that the sovereignty of Quebec was achieved despite or even against the American will. If victory eludes the Yes side by a slim margin, as is plausible, those who did vote Yes – a clear majority of francophone Quebecers – will be tempted to assign responsibility to the United States for part of their profound disappointment. I do not know how many decades it will take to dispel that feeling." Canada's deputy prime minister, Sheila Copps, seized on these and other examples of PQ truculence to declare "they've spit on the federal government, they've spit on Canada and now they're spitting on the Americans with whom we do ninety per cent of our trade."[8] None of it seemed likely to change very many votes.

What could turn the tide, insiders at the Prime Minister's Office in Ottawa hoped, would be the giant rally they'd orchestrated for Friday before the vote. The rally seemed a success, but no one in the crowd spilling over the lawns of Place du Canada could be sure it would have much effect. Some No strategists even feared a backlash among Quebecers; how sincere were these demonstrators from elsewhere; why hadn't they come sooner, who were they to tell us what we must do?

October 30, 1995, was a brisk fall day throughout Quebec. Some light showers fell and maple leaves – the emblem of Canada – lay scattered on the ground. At many polling stations, voters are in line at the opening hour. The procession keeps up all day, slacking only at mid-afternoon. There is a frenzied rush as voters line up through the dinner hour. Scrutineers for both sides check and re-check the voter's list. Workers for the Yes side are especially vigilant at challenging non-francophone voters; there is a report that sovereignist-appointed polling officials have orders to "get three or four more votes per poll." When the count gets underway, any excuse that can be found to challenge a No vote – where the X is placed or even how it is shaped – is used to argue that the ballot has been spoiled. In the end, it will be revealed, almost five million Quebecers – an incredible ninety-three and one-half per cent of eligible voters, have cast ballots.

While Lucien Bouchard had been carrying the Yes campaign across Quebec, Jacques Parizeau had been using the machinery of the Premier's office to develop plans for prompt action in the event of a Yes victory. A unilateral declaration of independence was not out of the question; Parizeau had been assured of strong support by France in whatever course he might pursue. Letters had gone to Quebec officers in the Canadian Forces to urge them to not act against their homeland in the event of a military response. In Ottawa, cabinet ministers such as Transport Minister David Collenette pondered having to use Canadian Forces stationed in Quebec to secure federal installations in event of a lurch to independence.[9] The Department of Finance asked the International Monetary Fund to be ready to take action to forestall an anticipated crash of the Canadian dollars. Millions of dollars of federal reserves left Montreal by Brinks trucks, to be taken to safety in Ottawa. For Parizeau, the referendum was like the third period of a hockey game. The separatists had won the first two periods, the election of fifty-four Bloc Québécois MPs in 1993 and the victory of the PQ in the provincial election in 1994. The referendum would fire the game-winning puck into the federalist net.

As the referendum results begin to come in after eight o'clock, the worst fears seem about to be realized. The Yes side takes an early lead as votes from outlying ridings reached the TV and radio studios in Quebec City and Montreal. The Prime Minister paces the floor at 24 Sussex Street, unable to contain his nervousness. He takes a phone call from Pierre Elliott Trudeau, and spends some moments trying to reassure him. At the CBC's headquarters in Montreal, a panel of political veterans including the former Liberal leader, Claude Ryan, and the one-time chief of staff to Réne Lévesque, Jean-Roche Boivin, waits out the results. Within moments of the first votes being reported, and Ryan already feeling discouraged, Boivin turns to him and says, "You ought not to be pessimistic, there will be reversals as we move west, this is far from finished." Boivin, according to Ryan, then adds: "This will be a 51-49 game and I pity the side that wins; I don't think I'd like to be on the winning side." For millions of Canadians, that night is excruciatingly long, with the lead shifting from one camp to another until finally, three hours after the closing of the polls, results from all the Montreal ridings give the No side their slight edge. Boivin's forecast had been prescient: the final result, 50.6 per cent voting against sovereignty and 49.4 per cent in favour, left Canadians exhausted, confused and only a little relieved that they'd escaped a full-blown crisis.

In Ottawa, Prime Minister Chrétien told the country at midnight that the time had come to "put aside what divides us, to turn a new page. The population of Quebec wants us to work together, to walk along the avenue of change together." To add to the drama, Parizeau ended the evening with an incredible adieu to the disappointed crowd that had gathered at Yes headquarters in the Montreal Convention Centre. His departing speech, one of the most graceless in Canadian history, exposed again the usually hidden racist side of sovereignty. Parizeau blamed the loss of the referendum on "money and the ethnic vote," clearly aiming his remarks at Montreal's still considerable Jewish population. The comments shocked supporters and critics alike. The next day, Bernard Landry phoned Parizeau to demand his resignation, according to biographer Pierre Duchesne. It was quickly forthcoming. All the PQ's high hopes were gone, including the plan to stage a huge independence rally at Olympic Stadium and then ask for admission to the United Nations as a sovereign state. Even Preston Manning, the Reform leader, would have had a role to play in the drive to independence; after the Yes victory he could have been expected to demand Jean Chrétien's resignation, according to Duchesne.[10] Bouchard, meanwhile, appealed to Quebecers to accept the result in calm and good grace. "Let us recognize that democracy has spoken," he said. "As we all did in 1980, we must bow to the will expressed by the majority, however minimal, of our fellow citizens." Newspaper headlines the next day reflected the drama of the moment: CANADA SURVIVES, shouted the Montreal *Gazette* while in Quebec City *Le Soleil*, perhaps interpreting the close result as evidence that sovereignty was moving forward, declared *ON RECOMMENCE* (We begin again). The Toronto *Star* headline asked the question most Canadians had on their minds the day after the referendum, WHAT NOW?

The Aftermath

Canada's narrow escape from the disaster of a pro-separation vote in Quebec left the federal government of Jean Chrétien adrift in a sea of indecision. The dangerously close outcome brought the "little guy from Shawinigan" to the nadir of his career, roundly condemned by critics as diverse as Preston Manning of the new western-based Reform party (calling for a "Plan B" to deal with an anticipated Quebec split), and central Canadian editorialists who lamented Ottawa's apparent inability to match the sovereignist vision of Bouchard and Parizeau. The country was exhausted by its constitutional wars, yet Chrétien felt compelled to fulfill his commitment given at Verdun to gain special status for Quebec. Backed by a strong Liberal majority in Parliament, Chrétien put through legislation recognizing Quebec as a distinct society with a veto on future constitutional change. The veto was made palatable to the rest of the country by offering a like privilege to Ontario, the Atlantic provinces and the West. Even this tactic stumbled on the pride of British Columbians who demanded they be treated as a separate region. This was quickly agreed to, but in Quebec the changes were seen as little more than cosmetic and face-saving, falling far short of real change. With Parizeau gone from the Quebec government, Lucien Bouchard was unanimously chosen leader of the Parti Québécois and became Premier on January 18, 1996.

The ever-boiling stew of separatism and sovereignty had to be taken off the stove of the Canadian federation. Prime Minister Chrétien, embarrassed at home, was mortified by international reaction to the near loss of Quebec. The Secretary-General of the United Nations, Boutros Boutros Ghali was said to have warned Chrétien that if Canada allowed Quebec to leave, "we will have five hundred new states and the world will be impossible to govern."[11] It was also clear that eventually, if enough referendums were held, and the question was fuzzy enough to satisfy "soft nationalists" that they could vote Yes and still keep their links with Canada, Quebec would vote for sovereignty. The Montreal *Gazette* coined the term "neverendum" to describe this nightmare scenario. New thinking was needed in Ottawa, and Jean Chrétien found it in the person of Stéphane Dion, a forty-year-old professor of political science at the Université de Montreal. He became Minister of Intergovernmental Affairs on January 25, 1996, and took his seat in the House of Commons after winning a by-election in Saint-Laurent-Cartierville. Dion, who some regard as an unsung hero of the referendum, appeared on the French language TV network Radio Canada almost nightly during the campaign to argue the federalist side. He clearly had no doubts about how to deal with Quebec separation. After joining Chrétien's cabinet, he set out to articulate his views in a series of remarkable open letters to Quebec politicians, journalists, and public figures across Canada. The idea of a Canadian politician waging his arguments via public correspondence was a novel one; it harkened back to an earlier age when principles, not polls, set the agenda of public discourse.

On August 11, 1997, Dion wrote to Premier Bouchard to challenge his assertion that a referendum result of "fifty per cent plus one" would be sufficient for separation. Such a thin margin, Dion argued, would never justify an irreversible change that would "deeply affect not only our own lives but also those of future generations." On November 19, he waded into the argument over whether an independent Quebec could be partitioned to keep English and native enclaves within Canada. He sent a blunt warning to Quebec's minister of intergovernmental affairs, Jacques Brassard: "Your government is mistaken in claiming that the law protects Quebec's territory but not Canada's and commits a moral error when it proposes to force populations to renounce Canada against their will."

The argument over Quebec separation was shifting; now the sovereignists were being challenged to prove the logic of their case. While Dion was spreading his ideas via fax and email, a series of private lawsuits in Quebec was testing the legality of the very concept of separation. Finally, the federal government joined the process by asking the Supreme Court of Canada to rule on three questions: Does Quebec have the constitutional right to secede unilaterally from Canada, does international law give Quebec the right to do so, and in the event of a conflict between Canadian law and international law, which would take precedence? On August 20, 1998, the Supreme Court gave its answers: No to the right of unilateral secession under both Canadian law and international law, there being no conflict between the two. The Court went further, however. First it ruled that secession could not be achieved "without principled negotiation with other participants in Confederation within the existing constitutional framework."

Because Quebec "does not meet the threshold of a colonial people or an oppressed people," it has no right in international law to secede from Canada unilaterally. Then the Court made this crucial point: "A clear majority vote in Quebec on a clear question in favour of secession would confer democratic legitimacy on the secession initiative which all of the other participants in Confederation would have to recognize."

Premier Bouchard seized on the obligation the Court was imposing on the other players in Confederation to negotiate with Quebec in the event of a vote favouring sovereignty. He thought this smoothed the path to independence. Stéphane Dion thought otherwise. On August 25, he wrote to Bouchard to set out Ottawa's position: "The Government of Canada could never undertake negotiations on secession based on a question addressing such vague concepts as 'sovereignty-association' or 'sovereignty with an offer of political and economic partnership.' The risk of misinterpreting the vote would be too great, as many polls demonstrate. Requiring that Quebecers be asked a clear question does not insult their intelligence. A clear question is an essential condition of a valid referendum in a democracy, in Quebec as elsewhere."[12] Here was the genesis of the federal government's insistence that a clear question must lead to a clear majority before there could be negotiations on leaving Canada. That insistence was spelled out in the federal government's legislative response to the Supreme Court, the Clarity Act, which became law on June 29, 2000. By spelling out the conditions governing the secession of a Canadian province, Ottawa for the first time was giving Confederation the sanctity of protective law. It was putting an end to two decades of attempts to achieve separatism by stealth.

The Clarity Act had its English opponents, including Joe Clark. He warned it would bring down the wrath of the Quebec population (it didn't). The act gives Parliament thirty days (to be extended to seventy days if necessary) to determine whether a referendum question is a clear one. The test of a clear question, according to the act, is whether it would result "in a clear expression of the will of the population of a province on whether the province should cease to be part of Canada and become an independent state." None of this partnership or association hocus-pocus. Questions of that ilk, the act makes clear, wouldn't stand a chance of qualifying. There would have to be a straight-out question, Do you want to be independent of Canada? There'd be no negotiations if the question wasn't clear. Even if it was clear, Parliament would still have to consider the size of the majority, the percentage of eligible voters taking part, and "other matters or circumstances it considers to be relevant" in determining whether negotiations are warranted. Passage of the Clarity Act brought dire warnings from Clark, Bouchard and others that the people of Quebec would rise in opposition. This was not to be. The Parti Québécois government, having won re-election under Bouchard in November, 1998, tried to mount a crusade against the new law. Its campaign sputtered and soon died. When Jean Chrétien went early to the polls to seek his third mandate on November 27, 2000, Quebec showed its increasing disinterest in sovereignty by reducing the Bloc Québécois from fifty-four to thirty-eight seats. The BQ lost its Official Opposition status to the Reform party, winners of sixty-six seats in the West. Chrétien's Liberals were back with another majority, one hundred and seventy-two seats. It was strengthened by the nearly dozen and a half seats the Liberals picked off from the BQ.

The Clarity Act has not been tested, so it is impossible to measure its effectiveness in making it more difficult for sover-eignists to win a referendum. Certainly, it was a factor in Lucien Bouchard's conclusion that during his time in office, the necessary "winning conditions" for a successful referendum did not exist. Claude Ryan maintained that while the Clarity Act (which he opposed) makes it more difficult in principle for the Yes side, "in practice we do not know. Let's suppose we had a referendum with a majority of 52 per cent in favour of the question asked by the government. If the question was not judged satisfactory by the federal Parliament, what kind of a messy situation would we find ourselves in? It (the Act) resolves nothing; everything will depend on the circumstances in which a referendum will have taken place, and the prevailing political situation in Quebec and in the rest of Canada."

If Jacques Parizeau's analogy of Quebec politics being akin to a hockey game is apt, it could now be said that the sovereignists lost all three periods: the defeat of the referendum in 1995; the setbacks suffered by the Bloc Québécois in 1997 and 2000 and perhaps most important, the loss of the 2003 Quebec provincial election by the Parti Québécois under Bouchard's successor, Bernard Landry. Even the charismatic Bouchard had been unable to arouse Quebecers to espouse the break-up of Canada. On January 11, 2003, he resigned as Premier. It came after a difficult struggle to balance the budget and preserve a high level of healthcare spending. What bothered Bouchard even more, and may have given him the final push over the edge, were remarks by the popular PQ veteran and old Lévesque colleague, Yves Michaud that were deeply offensive to the Jewish community. Bouchard's wife Audrey came from a mixed Jewish family that had lost relatives in the holocaust. In stepping down, Bouchard said only that "I accept my share of the blame for failing to rekindle the flame and to impress upon our fellow citizens the gravity of the situation. I recognize that my efforts to revive the debate (over sovereignty) were in vain."

The provincial election of April 14, 2003 gave Jean Charest a second opportunity to connect with Quebec's francophone majority, something he'd failed to do in the 1998 election. The campaign was a difficult one for Bernard Landry who had to defend the PQ's sovereignist principles at a time when voters clearly had lost interest in independence. Landry conceded that a referendum might not be in the works if the PQ was re-elected, and suggested instead that Quebec would set out to build what he called a "confederal union" with the rest of Canada. It seemed all too similar to the present set-up of Confederation. The election results effectively reversed the 1998 outcome, giving the Liberals seventy-six seats, the same number the PQ had won five years previously. "The threat of separatism has disappeared," Jean

Chrétien pronounced on hearing the results. It sounded alarmingly like Pierre Trudeau's declaration of two decades ago: "Separatism is dead." Newly inducted as Premier, Jean Charest contented himself to promising that he would work with Ottawa and the premiers to protect Quebec and build a stronger Canada. Scant weeks later, the Bloc Québécois had lost two more seats in by-elections.

In the wake of the referendum, Canada regained a sense of itself. The country's narrow escape from constitutional crisis made it clear how ineffective the federal government had been in its ad hoc defense of federalism. For the first time, there would be a clear set of rules to defend Confederation. The new approach also made it clear that the decades-old debate between Quebec and the rest of Canada would be no longer conducted by Quebec's rules; it was a province like the others and would enjoy all of the rights and privileges of the others, including control of language and education, but nothing more. Having established that principle, the federal government was obliged to recognize the realm of provincial rights in any new national initiatives. In one example, Ottawa's Millennium Fellowship – a federal program celebrating the twenty-first century – had to be individually negotiated with the provinces in recognition of provincial control of education. With little public fanfare, amicable arrangements were worked out between Quebec's PQ government and Ottawa. Steps were also taken to aggressively raise the federal presence in Quebec through government exhibits, flag displays and sponsorships of cultural and sporting events; some $250 million later the Chrétien administration would hand over a damaging scandal about these sponsorships to the new government of Paul Martin.

Montreal's economic vibrancy has grown steadily since the No victory. By the early 2000s real estate values had rebounded, with house prices rising 85 per cent. By 2004, homeowners outnumbered renters for the first time in the city's history. Smart new shops and boutique hotels contributed to Montreal having regained its glamour. Stéphane Dion was no longer in the cabinet, a sad loss to the nation. There has been no more astute observer of the Canadian condition than Ryan, whose forty years in national public life carried him from the tumult of the FLQ crisis to the quiet harbour of early twenty-first century national reconciliation. Shortly before his death, he put it this way: "A strong nation must first count on itself, and have enough pride in what it represents to cultivate it and grow it. This applies both to Canada in its relations with the United States, and to Quebec in its relations within Canada." In the 1995 Quebec referendum Canada endured the painful turning point that finally enabled the nation to resolve the issue of English-French duality that has dominated our life on this continent since 1759. The unified Canada foreseen by John A. Macdonald and dreamt of by Wilfrid Laurier and Henri Bourassa, transmuted into the "one Canada" of John Diefenbaker and the bilingual, multicultural society of Pierre Trudeau, was now a seamless whole, not without tensions or even occasional tears to its national fabric, but a model for the world.

Moving West:
Fulfilling the Canadian Dream
in Big Sky Country

Before the 2004 election Paul Martin, as Prime Minister, vowed that he would regard his time in office as a failure if he did not overcome Western Canadian alienation. He renewed that commitment in his election night statement. Stephen Harper also swore his undying fealty to achieving a greater role for the West, pledging to press on with the struggle to ensure that "the voice of the West is some day heard and accepted in the corridors of power."

It is conventional wisdom that the roots of Western alienation lie in economic and trade policies that have favoured Central Canada (often to the disadvantage of the Atlantic region as well as the West). Because these grievances were seen as less threatening to national unity than Quebec separatism, they received less attention under Prime Ministers from Pearson to Chrétien. Some of the nostrums directed at overcoming sovereignty in Quebec – notably increased provincial autonomy and opting out of federal programs without penalty – have brought benefits to the West. Other strategies (especially bilingualism) have generated resistance and resentment. Regional development programs have failed to deliver their promised economic benefits. Agencies such as the Canadian Wheat Board are blamed for denying a billion dollars a year of earnings to prairie farmers. Fundamental changes that would devolve power more equally to the regions, such as equality of Senate representation, are locked in a constitutional freeze.

Drawing on resources, technology and international trade – especially with the vast Asia Pacific economy – Western Canada has become the most dynamic economic region in the country. Alberta has joined Ontario as one of Canada's only two "have" provinces that that do not receive equalization payments from the federal government. Five of the six fastest growing metropolitan economies in Canada, according to the Conference Board of Canada's 2004 Spring report, are located in the West: Calgary, Regina, Winnipeg, Edmonton and Vancouver. All were all set to post real gross domestic product (GDP) growth above three per cent for the year. More than just a "big sky country," the West has matured economically, socially and culturally, but has never secured the political means that would allow it to equalize the role of the old Canada in shaping our destiny in the twenty-first century.

The next great step in Canadian nation-building now awaits us: the shifting of power out of Ottawa and into the West by designating a Western city as a co-capital of Canada, equal to the old capital in responsibility and authority. Some will see this as an audacious proposal and will dismiss it without trying to understand it. Others, in time a majority, will see it as the solution to democratic equality in a vast and magnificent country; a historic transformation that will change the relationship between the West and the federal government, address Western alienation, strengthen Canada's federal unity, and bring a dynamic new spirit of optimism and Western "can do" attitude to tackling Canada's opportunities and problems.

The West has said it wants in. That aspiration will be met when a Western city becomes a co-capital of Canada along with Ottawa, *equal but not separate*, sharing the mechanisms of national government in the legislative, executive and judicial spheres. Any one of a number of Western cities would make a suitable co-capital, preferably either Vancouver, Calgary, or Saskatoon. (I have left the four Western provincial capitals off this list on the theory they have enough government already). My choice would be Calgary, a sufficiently large, dynamic city with the infrastructure to absorb the addition of federal offices and facilities. Calgary is also approximately in the geographic centre of the West.

Creation of a Western co-capital should not be a partisan issue, and will require neither constitutional change nor a fundamental revision of government procedures. It will be achieved by Parliament passing an act to designate Calgary (for example) as a co-capital of Canada along with Ottawa. Passage will breathe new life into Confederation, signaling recognition that the future of Canada will be built as much in the New Canada of the West as in the Old Canada east of the Manitoba border.

The House and the Senate will sit for part of each year in the Western co-capital. Several federal departments, notably Energy, Agriculture, Indian and Northern Affairs or possibly Citizenship and Immigration – each with national, pan-Canadian responsibilities, could be permanently located there. The Governor General would need a residence, along with offices for the Prime Minister and a new Parliament Building. Most of this could be organized by a new National Capital Commission-West (modeled on the existing National Capital Commission covering the present-day Ottawa and Hull capital region). There would be no need to burden the taxpayer with capital costs, as the new Parliament Building and other offices could be built as private investments, to be leased back by the government. All types of federal agencies now bound to Ottawa, ranging from the Canadian Polar Commission to the National Literacy Secretariat and the Western Economic Development commission could as effectively discharge their responsibilities in Calgary as in Ottawa. Moving a chunk of the Ottawa civil service to the West and exposing MPs from all parts of Canada to a Western environment will bring two great benefits. It will give non-Westerners a first-hand experience of Western life and attitudes. It will move Western concerns to the top rung, giving Westerners a fully justified sense of being in a position for the first time of exercising a level of influence that is equal to their contribution to Canada. The building of a new federal capital, in or around Calgary or at another location, is an investment that will repay itself many times over in jobs, enterprise and tax revenue.

Just as a Western capital will not be a constitutional issue, neither should it be a cost issue. The principle of transferring a portion of federal operations from Ottawa to other centres has already been established, as in the case of the GST processing centre which was set up in Prince Edward Island. The operation of Parliament, costing under $500 million a year, represents one of the smaller items in the $180 billion federal budget. More has been lost in government boondoggles, or squandered in sponsorship and the gun registry, than the entire cost of creating and operating a co-capital in the West. Even if the cost of sharing Parliament with a second capital increased its operating cost by fifty per cent, it would be a bargain. Nor would Canada be leaping into something not already pioneered by other countries. Tiny Holland shares its capital between Amsterdam and The Hague and South Africa has *three* capitals – Capetown for its legislature, Pretoria for its civil service, and Bloemfontein for its judiciary. In the United States, President Dwight Eisenhower maintained an informal "Western White House" in Denver, Colorado. In Canada itself, the twin capitals of Kingston and Montreal met the needs of 19th century Upper and Lower Canada.

The designation of a Western city as a co-capital will powerfully strengthen the east-west connection, counteract the north-south pull and strengthen Canada as a whole. It will demonstrate the practicality of bilingualism by giving civil servants whose first language is French exposure to a more English-speaking environment than Ottawa offers. It will expose Westerners to native French speakers who are adept at English, something that might surprise a few people. It will give all MPs and public servants a better understanding of the West while delivering a fairer share of federal spending.

Assume we all agree to put on cowboy chaps and 10-gallon hats and ride off, metaphorically speaking, to Calgary. Will it really change anything? The answer is yes, indisputably. Never would a Canadian prime minister dare stand in a Parliament in session in Calgary and explain that he has given a contract to a Quebec company over a more qualified, and less costly, Western competitor. Marshall McLuhan's dictum that the medium is the message, meaning that content is shaped by its form, applies with equal effectiveness to government: power flows to the centre. In Canada, the result has been an overcentralized, remote bureaucracy obsessed with maintaining control, generally without the full awareness or knowledge of its political masters. The alternative advocated by provincial politicians, that of transferring more authority to the provinces, merely leads to a set of new problems – the balkanization of Canada and a loss of common national goals and purpose, putting Confederation further at risk.

Regardless of which political party is in power federally, what is needed is a more effective means of exercising federal powers on behalf of all Canadians. No less prominent a Liberal than Anne McLellan, the deputy prime minister under Paul Martin, has said that "People have to see manifestations of their government where they live. If you never see any meaningful presence of the government of Canada where you live, I think it's not unreasonable to say 'What have you done for me lately?'" The dispersal of federal authority out across the country, a process that has already begun in a minor way, needs to be accelerated. People who are naturally skeptical and cynical about normal things – like most Canadians – are admittedly going to be skeptical and cynical about a proposal as radical as putting a Western Canadian city on a par with Ottawa. Perhaps it is worth recalling that Canadians once were asked to make a "leap of faith" about free trade; now it is time for a similar leap of faith about how and from where we are to govern ourselves.

Rating the Campaigns

All the campaigns scrutinized in this book have brought important changes to Canada. Their results have deeply affected the personal lives of Canadians who at various times have been sent to war, given land grants in the West, forced to pay high taxes, and have enjoyed the benefits of the health and education systems built on their efforts. By measuring the overall effect of each campaign on the fundamental direction of the country, each can be assigned to one of three broad categories: those that had an immense impact on the country's destiny, those resulting in a significant measurable effect, or those leading to important but more regional consequences.

Four federal elections stand out for the immense, long-term impact they had on Canada, both economically and socially. The issues in two of them, the elections of 1878 and 1988, were rooted in the country's commercial policies and our relations with the United States, and both were won – although on the strength of diametrically opposed policies – by the Conservative party. The other two pivotal elections, in 1896 and 1945, were fought over issues that shaped the broader Canadian social fabric that would be stitched together in the twentieth century, patterned on the twin values of English-French tolerance (later extended to all ethnic and cultural groups) and the social welfare safety net, both championed by the Liberal party. While John A. Macdonald in 1878 and Brian Mulroney in 1988 were a century apart in the attitudes and problems of their eras, the careers of Mackenzie King and Wilfrid Laurier overlapped, giving them a commonality of experience and understanding from which both benefited.

Just as these four campaigns dominate the roster of Canada's turning points, so can four Prime Ministers be recognized for their pre-eminent positioning among the 21 that have served the office since 1867. The greatest Prime Minister, and also the most controversial, did not participate in any of the four front-rank campaigns but Pierre Elliott Trudeau nonetheless warrants the title for the profound influence he had on the formation of the New Canada that emerged late in the twentieth century. In many respects, he shaped the soul of the new Canadian society by force of his intellect and ideas, his personality, and his universalist concepts of human rights, personal dignity and individuality. The Charter of Rights and Freedoms and the Canadian Constitution are Pierre Trudeau's most memorable achievements but his notion of a just society and his commitment to the principle of equality in immigration policy are equally important aspects of his legacy.

Next to Trudeau, one must rank Wilfrid Laurier, Mackenzie King and John A. Macdonald among the greatest Prime Ministers; Laurier for successfully imparting a vision of how French and English could work together peaceably in building a great new land, Mackenzie King for his adroit acceptance of the mid-century pressures to construct a Canadian welfare state, and John A. Macdonald for having been there in the beginning.

Of the 11 other campaigns we have covered, the one with the most significant measurable effect was clearly the 1995 Quebec referendum, where the near-victory by the separatist movement caused a fundamental re-evaluation of how to deal with secession. Whether the Clarity Act will stand as the firewall that it is meant to provide, will only be fully determined when Canada faces its next sovereignist thrust. The other provincial campaigns described in this book, the Newfoundland referendums of 1948 and the British Columbia election of 1952, had important regional consequences that qualify them as turning points, while the only Pre-Confederation campaign, the 1866 New Brunswick election, made all the other turning points possible.

The great lesson of these turning points is that there is still much unfinished work in the building of the Canadian democracy. While Canada has a scrappy parliamentary system, it also harbours serious impediments to democratic self-government. Fortunately, there are ways to deal with these without changing the constitution, which no one wants to do. The Prime Minister's near-dictatorial control of Parliament and the public service must be reduced. The public should be allowed a choice in the selection of not just Senators, but also the Governor General. A fixed date for federal elections and a system of proportional representation in choosing MPs would further democratize Canada. The dispersal of federal decision-making more broadly throughout the country also would complete Canada's transition from an elitist state to a popular democracy, as well as leading to greater public involvement and more open and better public policy.

If you were asked to name a country where one person appoints the stand-in for the head of state, selects the members of the governing cabinet, and names the jurists who will sit on its supreme court, you'd be forgiven if you picked a third world oligarchy or some other dysfunctional democracy. The correct answer, of course, is Canada, where we combine a parliamentary democracy with a constitutional monarchy and end up placing virtually untrammeled power in the hands of a single individual, the Prime Minister. A small measure of this power is demonstrated in the fact that the Prime Minister has the power to personally decide who is to fill no fewer than 2,350 federal appointments. These include all the senior non-elective positions in the Canadian establishment, from the Governor General to members of the Senate, the Supreme Court, and such quasi judicial bodies as the Canadian Radio and Television Commission, the Refugee Appeal Board, and the Canadian Citizenship Court.

An internal study conducted for the government made the case forcefully: "While the House (of Commons) abounds in representation, it has little power." The real power is with the cabinet that "retains a virtual monopoly on the use of democratic authority." Canadians are left with the feeling, the reports adds, that Ottawa is "remote, self-serving, inaccessible, non-responsive, occasionally inept, excessively adversarial and increasingly irrelevant."

Canadians are determined to change this. The confidence of voters in future elections will flow to the party that most effectively connects responsive leadership to responsible citizenship. There will be found the turning points of tomorrow.

The End

Source Notes

Preface

1   *The Calgary Herald*, Aug. 29, 1911.
2   F.A. McGregor, *The Rise and Fall of Mackenzie King; 1911-1919*, Toronto, Macmillan Company of Canada Limited, 1962, p37.
3   Peter Newman, *Renegade in Power*, Toronto, McClelland and Stewart Limited, 1963, p54.

Chapter One

1   Warren Kinsella, a former aide to Prime Minister Chrétien, maintains that the Martin team spurned Chrétien's offer to stay on long enough to absorb the shock of the Auditor General's report. He told the author that Chrétien would have handled it the same way he did the first three reports of sponsorship mismanagement: stay calm, answer every question, call in the RCMP, and hand the file to Ralph Goodale, then minister of public works.
2   The richest plum in Canadian advertising, the federal government's advertising program – worth some $30 million a year in agency fees – went to Media IDA Vision, then a little-known Quebec agency, in 1997. The company was partly owned by Groupe Everest, whose president, Claude Boulay, was Paul Martin's communications director in the 1990 leadership campaign. Partly on the strength of the government AOR assignment, Media IDA Vision was sold to Draft International, a unit of the global advertising conglomerate, Interpublic.
3   *The National*, CBC-TV, May 12, 2004.
4   The *Globe and Mail*, June 10, 2004
5   *Globe and Mail* Online, June 25, 2004
6   Paul Wells, *Maclean's*, July 12, 2004.
7   The *Hill Times*, Ottawa, July 5, 2004.

Chapter Two

1   This incident was reported in the Saint John Morning Freeman of June 14 and June 16, 1866, based in part on reprints from the Saint John Journal. (Throughout, I have used the current form, Saint John, rather than the 19th century spelling, St. John).
2   For a fuller description of the strategy to circumvent public opposition to Confederation, see William Menzies Whitelaw, *The Maritimes and Canada Before Confederation, Toronto*, Oxford University Press, 1966 (first published, 1934), pp 263-265.

3 Newspaper advertisements of the time advanced bold claims for such products. See also Chauncey D. Leake, and Charles C. Thomas, *An Historical Account of Pharmacology to the 20th Century*, Springfield, Ill., 1975.

4 James Hannay, *The Makers of Canada*, v. XVII, 1910. See also Hannay, *The Life and Times of Sir Leonard Tilley, Being a Political History of New Brunswick for the Past Seventy Years*, Saint John, 1897.

5 Public Archives of Canada, Galt Papers, Tilley to Galt, November 11, 1864.

6 A. G. Bailey, The Basis and Persistence of Opposition to Confederation in New Brunswick, Canadian Historical Review, v. XXI, no. 4, December, 1940, pp. 367-383.

7 PAC, New Brunswick Despatches, Gordon to Cardwell, September 12, 1864, cited in Wilson, George E. Wilson, New Brunswick's Entrance into Confederation, CHP, March, 1928. This is perhaps the most convincing account of the conspiratorial nature of the pressures applied in New Brunswick to bring about Confederation.

8 Ibid., Tilley to Gordon, January 30, 1865.

9 Fredericton Head Quarters, February 1, 1865.

10 Hannay, *History of New Brunswick*, Saint John, John A. Bowes, 1909, p. 232.

11 Ibid., p. 233.

12 PAC, New Brunswick Despatches, Gordon to Cardwell, March 6, 1865.

13 George E. Wilson opp. cit., p. 11.

14 Carl Wallace, *Albert Smith, Confederation, and Reaction in New Brunswick: 1852-1882*, CHR, v. XLIV, 1963, p. 290.

15 A.C. Bailey, op. cit.

16 PAC, Macdonald Papers, Tilley to Macdonald, September 13, l865.

17 PAC, New Brunswick Despatches, Gordon to Cardwell, December 4, 1865.

18 PAC, Macdonald Papers, Tilley to Macdonald, April 14, 1866.

19 Ibid., April 20, 1866.

20 "It has been asserted, with good show of proof, that ... money from the Secret Service Fund of Canada changed from mysterious hand to mysterious hand ..."— A.P.H. Lower, Colony to Nation, Toronto, Longmans Canada Limited, 1964.

22 Cited in the *Morning Freeman*, June 2, 1866.

23 Government of New Brunswick web site, www.gov.nb.ca/elections

24 Eugene Forsey, *Freedom and Order*, Toronto, McClelland and Stewart Limited, 1974, p. 22. Forsey describes Dominion as an old French word which has disappeared from that language but retained in English.

Chapter Three

1 *Toronto Mail*, Aug. 28, 1878.

2 Joseph Pape, *Memoirs of the Rt. Hon. John Alexander Macdonald*, London, 1894, Vol. 2, p202.

3 Macdonald Papers, Public Archives of Canada, Macdonald to D.L. MacPherson, cited in John R. Williams, The Conservative Party of Canada, 1920-1949, 1956, p18.

4   Historical Statistics of Canada, M.C. Urquhart, ed., Toronto, Macmillan Company of Canada Limited, 1966.

5   Statements of Mackenzie are from accounts in the Toronto Globe from June to September, 1878.

6   The *Toronto Mail*, August 28, 1878.

7   Letter to Hon. James Young, September 26, 1878, in The Hon. Alexander Mackenzie: His Life and Times, Wm. Buckingham and G.W. Ross, Toronto, Rose Publishing Co., 1892, p. 523.

8   Benefits of the National Policy were lauded in the Dominion Annual Register, 1880-81, cited in *Pendulum of Power*, J.M. Beck, Prentice-Hall of Canada, Ltd., Toronto, 1968, p 38.

Chapter Four

1   Laurier LaPierre, *Sir Wilfrid Laurier and the Romance of Canada*, Toronto 1996, Stoddart Publishing Co. Ltd., p90.

2   *Toronto Globe*, February 21, 1896.

3   Joseph Schull, *Laurier: The First Canadian*, Toronto, Macmillan of Canada Ltd. 1965, p304.

4   Hansard, March 27, 1894.

5   Lapierre, Ibid., p197.

6   *Toronto Daily Mail and Empire*, May 21, 1896

7   What Laurier actually said in his address of Jan. 18, 1904 to the Canadian Club of Ottawa was "I think we can claim that it is Canada that will fill the twentieth century." Addresses Before the Canadian Club of Ottawa: 1903-1909 (1910).

Chapter Five

1   The description of the "assemblée contradictoire" is based on accounts in the *Ottawa Citizen*, *Ottawa Free Press*, *Toronto Globe* and *Montreal Gazette* of Aug. 14, 1911.

2   Addresses Delivered Before the Canadian Club of Toronto, 1907.

3   *Montreal Herald*, Jan. 27, 1911

4   Public Archives of Canada, Laurier Papers, Laurier to Lash, Gen. 15, 1911

5   For further on the Toronto Eighteen, see Robert D. Cuff, *The Toronto Eighteen and the Election of 1911, Ontario History*, v.57, no.4, Dec., 1965.

6   PAC, Willison Papers, Vol. 105, Undated Memorandum.

7   PAC, Laurier Papers, Laurier to Clarke, Aug. 1, 1911.

8   PAC, George Graham Papers, W.S. Fielding to Graham, May 24 and May 30, 1911.

9   *Toronto Mail and Empire*, Aug. 15, 1911.

10   PAC, Laurier Papers, Lemaire to Brown, Sept. 8, 1911.

11   Ibid., McAlpine to Laurier, Sept. 8, 1911; reply, Sept. 12, 1911.

12   Ibid., MacKenzie King Papers, King to Violet Markham, Dec. 15, 1911.

13   Ibid., Borden Papers, O.C.27A, Reid to Borden, June 17, 1911.

14   Ibid., Laurier Papers, Laurier to New York World, Jan. 31, 1911.

15   Ibid., Desroches to Laurier, Sept. 22, 1911.

16 R.H. Coats, *The Rise in Prices and the Cost of Living in Canada, 1900-1914*, Department of Labour, Ottawa, 1915.

Chapter Six

1 *Calgary Herald*, Dec. 18, 1917. (Fort William is now part of Thunder Bay, Ont.)
2 *'Terrifying and Beautiful,' The Beaver*, Vol. 7-22, April-May 1992.
3 *Robert Laird Borden: His Memoirs, Henry Borden*, ed., McClelland and Stewart Limited, Toronto, 1969.
4 A lawyer, Newton would successfully argue the Persons case before the Supreme Court of Canada in 1929, winning for Nellie McClung and other females the recognition of women as "persons" and thus eligible to serve in the Senate. In 1940, Rowell authored the Rowell-Sirois Royal Commission report on federal-provincial relations which set out the framework for fiscal arrangements between Ottawa and the provinces after World War II. His grandson, Henry Newton Rowell Jackman, made a fortune in the trust business. A prominent Conservative, he served as Lieutenant Governor of Ontario in the 1980s.
5 *Vancouver World*, November 3, 1917.
6 Canadian Party Platforms, "Campaign of 1917."
7 *Vancouver World*, November 17, 1917
8 *Calgary Herald*, December 13, 1917
9 *Winnipeg Free Press*, November 22, 1917.
10 Elizabeth Armstrong, *The Crisis of Quebec, 1914-1918*, Columbia University Press, New York

Chapter Seven

1 Attributed by Bruce Hutchison in Mr. Prime Minister, Longmans Canada Ltd., Toronto, 1964.
2 Mackenzie King's Diary is posted at http://king.archives.ca
3 Crerar later joined King's administration and served in the World War II cabinet, making him the only politician to serve in two wartime cabinets.
4 Winnipeg Tribune, September 2, 1926.
5 Eugene Forsey, *A Life on the Fringe*, Oxford University Press, Toronto, 1990.

Chapter Eight

1 Doris French Shackleton, *Tommy Douglas*, McClelland and Stewart Ltd., Toronto, 1975.
2 Ibid
3 As late as 1953, the Western Producer, a weekly farm paper published in Saskatoon, was telling farm families how to have their house wired for electricity. "Even a bare light bulb hung from the ceiling and operated by a pull chain seems wonderful. But that is only the beginning and even if you decide that is enough for the upstairs bedrooms, it won't be long before you wish you had a convenient wall switch from which you can turn on the

lights as you enter a room and eliminate groping in the dark for a pull chain."

4   Doris Shackleton, op. cit.

Chapter Nine

1   Mackenzie King Diary, Public Archives of Canada, MG26, J13, 1945.
2   Canadian Institute of Public Opinion, Sept. 30. 1943.
3   Forsey, *Freedom and Order*, McClelland and Stewart Limited, Toronto, 1974, p310.
4   J.M. Beck, *Pendulum of Power*, Scarborough, Ont., Prentice-Hall Of Canada ltd., 1968, p224.
5   J.L. Granatstein, *The Politics of Survival, the Conservative Party of Canada, 1939-1945*, Toronto, University of Toronto Press, 1967, p95.
6   House of Commons Debates, Jan. 22, 1942, p2.
7   Gerald L. Caplan, *The Dilemma of Canadian Socialism*, Toronto, McClelland and Stewart Limited, 1973, p94.
8   J.W. Pickersgill, *The Liberal Party*, Toronto, McClelland and Stewart Limited, 1962, pp33-34.
9   Bruce Hutchison, *The Unknown Country*, Toronto, McClelland and Stewart Limited,
10   Reginald Whittaker, *The Government Party*, Toronto, University of Toronto Press, 1977, p157.
11   Granatstein, op. cit., p191.

Chapter Ten

1   Terrible living conditions didn't stop the Newfoundland Regiment from exhibiting incredible heroism in World War I, losing all its officers and most of its men on the opening day of the Battle of the Somme in France, July 1, 1916. Of the 801 who left their trenches that morning, only 69 returned to answer the roll-call.
2   These figures were cited by Joey Smallwood in a speech to the Empire Club of Toronto on November 17, 1983. At the time of joining Canada, Smallwood said, "Newfoundlanders had no productive meadows, almost no local or any other roads, precious few substantial houses and no standard of material prosperity anywhere near that known in any other part of North America."
3   See Chapter 2, *The Confederation Conspiracy*. There was similar collusion between Canada and London in achieving popular acceptance for Confederation in the election of New Brunswick of 1866.
4   Smallwood recounts this incident in his memoir, *I Chose Canada*, Macmillan of Canada, Toronto, 1973. A similar version appears in Wayne Johnson's fictional biography of Smallwood, *The Colony of Unrequited Dreams*, Alfred A. Knopf Canada, Toronto, 1998. Richard Gwyn also deals with the matter in his definitive biography, *Smallwood: The Unlikely Revolutionary*, McClelland & Stewart, Toronto, 1972.
5   Smallwood, *I Chose Canada*.

6   This political-religious antagonism lasted for years. The Archbishop refused to give an audience to Prime Minister St. Laurent, himself a Catholic, when he visited St. John's. The denominational school system continued until 1995, when another referendum organized by Premier Brian Tobin approved amending the terms of union to allow "a single school system where all children, regardless of their religious affiliation, attend the same schools."

Chapter Eleven

1   Margaret A. Ormsby, *British Columbia: A History, Vancouver,* 1958, p439.
2   David J. Mitchell, *W.A.C. Bennett and the Rise of British Columbia* (Douglas & McIntyre Ltd., Vancouver, 1983) p. 124. Mitchell's account of the advent of Social Credit in B.C. offers by far the best analysis of Bennett's career.
3   Canada's softwood lumber dispute with the U.S. that broke out anew around 2000 centered largely on B.C.'s low stumpage fees; Americans regard these as illegal subsidies under international trade rules.
4   *Vancouver Sun,* May 29, 1952
5   Shelford won the riding and I served in the press gallery of the B.C. Legislature when he arrived in Victoria to take up his seat. It didn't take long for the gallery to make him the butt of jokes over his country ways. Tall, sunburned, uncomfortable in a suit and tie, Shelford fit the stereotype of the rural "redneck" but his dedication to his constituents' needs and his loyalty to Social Credit won him Bennett's constant support during the years he sat as an MLA.
6   David J. Elkins, *Politics Makes Strange Bedfellows: The B.C. Party System in the 1952 and 1953 Provincial Elections,* B.C. Studies, No. 30, Summer 1975.
7   "The greatest thing we did was the Two Rivers policy," Bennett told an interviewer (www.sunnyokanagan.com) in 1976. "They never thought I was going to build the Peace."
8   Ibid

Chapter Twelve

1   Peter Newman, *Renegade in Power,* McClelland and Stewart Ltd., Toronto, 1963.
2   John Diefenbaker, *One Canada: The Crusading Years 1895 to 1956,* Macmillan of Canada, Toronto, 1975.
3   Ibid
4   Denis Smith, *Rogue Tory: The Life and Campaigns of John George Diefenbaker,* Macfarlane Walter & Ross, Toronto, 1995.
5   Ibid.
6   John Meisel, *The Canadian General Election of 1957,* University of Toronto Press, Toronto, 1962.
7   Dick Spencer, *Trumpets and Drums: John Diefenbaker on the Campaign Trail,* Douglas & McIntyre, Toronto, 1994.

8   Dale C. Thomson, *Louis St. Laurent Canadian*, Macmillan of Canada, Toronto, 1967.

9   John Meisel, *A Study of One Constituency in the Canadian Federal Election of 1957*, Canadian Journal of Economics and Political Science, May 1958. (Meisel did not identify either the riding or the candidates.)

10   John English, *The Worldly Years, the Life of Lester Pearson 1949-1972*, Alfred A. Knopf Canada, Toronto, 1992.

11   Dennis Smith, *Gentle Patriot: A Political Biography of Walter Gordon*, Hurtig, Edmonton, 1973.

Chapter Thirteen

1   Pierre Elliott Trudeau in his "Epilogue", p329, *La Gréve de l'amiante, Editions Cité Libre, Montreal*, 1956.

2   George Radwanski, *Trudeau*, Macmillan Company of Canada Limited, Toronto, 1978, p119.

3   Ibid

4   *London Evening Standard* dispatch by Jeremy Campbell, March 13, 1968.

5   Winters declined to run in the 1968 election and returned to the world of business where he served on the boards of several large companies. He died in 1969 while travelling overseas.

6   Peter Stursberg, *Lester Pearson and the Dream of Unity*, Doubleday Canada Ltd., Toronto, 1978.

7   Donald Peacock, *Journey to Power*, Ryerson Press, Toronto, 1968, p316.

8   Christina McCall-Newman, *Grits*, Macmillan of Can ada, Toronto, 1982, p118.

9   J.M. Beck, *Pendulum of Power*, Prentice-Hall of Canada, Toronto, 1968, p401.

10   George Radwanski, p282.

11   For a fuller description of this episode, see Chapter 15, *Canada at the Brink: The Crisis and the Fall-out*.

12   Toronto *Globe and Mail*, January 15, 2004.

13   Stephen Clarkson and Christina McCall, *Trudeau and Our Times: Vol. 1*, McClelland and Stewart Inc., Toronto, 1990.

Chapter Fourteen

1   Graham Fraser, *Playing for Keeps*, McClelland & Stewart Inc., Toronto, 1989, p293.

2   John Sawatsky, *Mulroney The Politics of Ambition*, Macfarlane Walter & Ross, Toronto, 1991, p51.

3   Greg Weston, *Reign of Error*, McGraw-Hill Ryerson, Toronto, 1988, p109.

4   This comment and the account of the lunch with U.S. Senators is from the author's interview with John Turner, March 18, 2004.

5   It was not until 2000 that the Act was amended to put a limit of $150,000 on third-party spending. It was challenged before the Supreme Court in 2004. Nick Fillmore estimated in *This Magazine* that $56 million may have been spent promoting free trade in 1988.

6   See Chapters 5 and 9, respectively, for details of the 1911 and 1945 elections.

7   Meech Lake and other constitutional initiatives of the Mulroney government are more fully analyzed in Chapter 15, *Canada at the Brink: The Crisis and the Fall-out.*

Chapter Fifteen

1   Montreal *Gazette*, October 28, 1995.
2   Graham Fraser, *René Levesqué and the Parti Québécois in Power*, McGill-Queen's University Press, 1984.
3   Morin in 1992 was revealed in a Radio-Canada investigative documentary to have been on the payroll of the RCMP while a PQ cabinet minister. The disclosure shocked the sovereignty movement and is said to have caused René Lévesque a mild heart attack.
4   Claude Ryan's views on constitutional negotiations and the 1995 referendum were expressed to the author in an extensive interview on June 6, 2003, eight months before Ryan's death.
5   Jeffrey Simpson, *Faultlines: Struggles for a Canadian Vision*, HarperCollins, Toronto, 1992.
6   l'Actualité survey, March 15, 1995.
7   *Canadian Annual Review*, 1995.
8   Montreal *Gazette*, October 27, 1995.
9   Lawrence Martin, *Iron Man: The Defiant Reign of Jean Chrétien*, Viking Canada, Toronto, 2003.
10 Pierre Duchesne, *Le Régent, Editions Québec Amérique*, Montreal, 2004.
11 Michael Vastel, *Chrétien; Un Canadien Pure Laine*, Montreal, 2003.
12 Many of Stéphane Dion's letters were posted to the Government of Canada web site www.pco-bcp.gc.ca.

Index
Main Characters and Events

Parizeau, Jacques 425, 429, 431,
434, 438-9, 457-62, 464-5,
468, 472
Parrish, Carolyn 24
Patterson, William 126, 150
Patterson, Wm. A. 209, 212,
220-21, 227-8
Payette, Lise 445-6
Pearson, Lester B. 323, 327,
341, 345, 347, 350, 353, 355,
357-9, 363-4, 366, 370-3,
377, 379, 387, 412, 475
Pelletier, Gérard 359, 364-5,
371, 379, 387
Pelletier, Jean 7
Peterson, Jim 431-2
Pettigrew, Pierre 34
Pickersgill, Jack 241, 249-50,
257, 292, 346
Pharmacies in 19th century 50
Power, C. G. 252
Pratt, David 33
Proportional representation,
481

Q

Quebec Conference 49, 274

R

Ralston, Col. J. L. 252
Ralston, Tilly Jean 297, 300,
304, 313, 320
Raymond, Maxime 237, 266
Reciprocity 55, 79, 82, 98, 124-
131, 133-135, 139, 141, 143,
145-49
Reid, Scott 10, 27, 35, 38
Reynolds, John 21, 36
Riel, Louis 75, 78, 96
Robinson, Michael 10
Robinson, Svend 11
Roblin, Duff 377, 388
Rocheleau, Yves 22
Rowell, Newton W. 155, 167-9,
175
Ryan, Claude 375, 387, 392,
434, 436, 443, 448-9, 452,

458, 466, 471, 473
Ryan, Madelaine 446

S

St. Laurent, Louis xii, 240, 265,
269, 294
and 1957 federal election
323, 326-8, 334, 340-2,
345-6, 348
Sawatsky, John 409
Sharp, Mitchell 293, 371-2, 375
Scherrer, Héléne 33
Sifton, Clifford 117, 129, 131-3,
155, 165, 168
Sinclair, James 259, 267, 348
Smallwood, Joseph R. 271-3,
277-296, 375
Smith, Albert J. 43-66, 84-86
Smith, Dr. Sydney 349
Smith, Sen. David 11
Sommers, Robert 300, 321
Sorbara, Greg 22
Speller, Bob 33
Stanbury, Robert 357, 372
Stanfield, Robert 357, 377-80,
382, 384, 386-7, 389, 392,
394, 452
Stevens, Harry H. 181, 191-2,
204
Stirling, Geoffrey W. 271, 287
Stronach, Belinda 16, 35
Strong, Maurice 9
Supreme Court of Canada 78,
396, 447, 469, 482

T

Tarte, J. Israel 84, 91, 100, 105,
108, 112-13
Thompson, John 99
Thompson, Myron 36
Tilley, Samuel Leonard 43, 50-
55, 57-60, 62-66
Tobin, Brian 431, 463
Trestrail, Burdick A. 251, 260,
264
Trudeau, Margaret 369, 371
Trudeau, Pierre Elliott xi, 7, 9,
38, 40, 259, 354-5, 403-4,

In keeping with White Knight's mandate to support new Canadian authors who bring books of social and historical value to our readers, I must admit to being thrilled to work with Ray Argyle, a highly experienced journalist and writer (and friend of long standing) in the publication of his first literary work.

In the past we often met during political campaigns in which I was also involved so I have first hand knowledge of his skillful output as a political observer and insider player. His book, more than ten years in the writing, is a significant contribution derived from his thirty-five-year involvement and will be a welcomed addition to private book collections, and school and library shelves across Canada.

Turning Points will help to fill the gap that exists from lack of Canadian-written books in our cross-Canada educational programs that are so badly in need of well-researched, interestingly-written, factual narratives with a Canadian point of view.

I am indeed fortunate as a Canadian publisher (and nationalist) to have been closely involved with Ray Agyle's first major book and to be able to look keenly forward to his contributions to Canada's literary future.

If you share our concern about the future of our great nation, pass this book along to young people to study so they will understand where we came from and why we are who we are today and not northern Yankees.

Bill Belfontaine

Genres of White Knight Publications

Biography
The Life and Times of
Nancy Ford-Inman
– Nancy Erb Kee

Gay Adoption
A Swim Against The Tide
– David R.I. McKinstry

Inspiration – Self Help
Conscious Women –
Conscious Lives
– Darlene Montgomery
Sharing MS (Multiple Sclerosis) –
Linda Ironside
Sue Kenney's My Camino
– Sue Kenney

Personal Finances
Don't Borrow Money
Until You Read This Book
– Paul Counter

Poetry
Two Voices – A Circle of Love
– Serena Williamson Andrew

Politics
Turning Points – Ray Argyle

Self-help
Books by Dr. K. Sohail
– *Love, Sex and Marriage*
– *The Art of Living*
   in Your Green Zone
– *The Art of Loving*
   in Your Green Zone
– *The Art of Working*
   in Your Green Zone

True Crime – Police
"10-45" Spells Death
– Kathy McCormack Carter
Life on Homicide
– Former Toronto Police Chief
Bill McCormack
The Myth of The Chosen One
– Dr. K. Sohail

Recommended reading from
other publishers

History
An Amicable Friendship
– Jan Th. J. Krijff

Religion
From Islam to Secular Humanism
   – Dr. K. Sohail
Gabriel's Dragon
   – Arch Priest Fr. Antony
   Gabriel
Pro Deo
   – Prof Ronald M Smith